D1130759

BF
311
.H334
v.2

Handbook of learning and cognitive process /
edited by W. K. Estes. -- Hillsdale, N. J. :
Lawrence Erlbaum Associates ; New York :
distributed by the Halsted Press Division
of Wiley, 1975-
    v. : ill. ; 24 cm.
Includes bibliographies and indexes.
Each vol. has also a distinctive title:
v.1. Introduction to concepts and issues.
v.2. Conditioning and behavior theory.
v.3. Approaches to human learning and
    motivation.   (continued next card)
                    5/24/79

Handbook
of Learning and
Cognitive Processes

Volume 2

Conditioning
and Behavior Theory

Handbook
of Learning and
Cognitive Processes

Volume 2
Conditioning
and Behavior Theory

EDITED BY

W. K. ESTES

Rockefeller University

 LAWRENCE ERLBAUM ASSOCIATES, PUBLISHERS

1975   Hillsdale, New Jersey

DISTRIBUTED BY THE HALSTED PRESS DIVISION OF

John Wiley & Sons

New York   Toronto   London   Sydney

Lawrence Erlbaum Associates, Inc., Publishers
62 Maria Drive
Hillsdale, New Jersey 07642

Distributed solely by Halsted Press Division
John Wiley & Sons, Inc., New York

Library of Congress Cataloging in Publication Data

Handbook of learning and cognitive processes.

   Includes bibliographical references and indexes.
   CONTENTS: V. 1. Introduction to concepts and issues.
   v. 2. Conditioning and behavior theory.
1. Cognition.   2. Learning, Psychology of.
I. Estes, William Kaye.   [DNLM: 1. Cognition.
2. Learning.   LB1051 H236 (P)]
B311.H33   153   75-20113
ISBN 0-470-24586-7

Printed in the United States of America

Contents

Foreword

This volume is the second in a series planned to organize and present a picture of the current state of the psychology of learning and cognitive processes which will be fairly up to date with regard to theoretical and even technical developments and yet readable for anyone with a reasonable scientific background, regardless of his acquaintance with the technical jargon of particular specialties. Working within this constraint, our first emphasis has been to present the major concepts, theories, and methods with which one should be familiar in order to understand or to participate in research in any of the various facets of cognitive psychology. Secondly, each of the authors has taken on the assignment of giving explicit attention to the orienting attitudes and long-term goals that tend to shape the overall course of research in his field and to bring out both actual and potential influences and implications with respect to other aspects of the discipline.

In Volume 1 of this Handbook, we attempted to present an overview of the field and to introduce the principal theoretical and methodological issues that persistently recur in the expanded treatments of specific research areas that comprise the later volumes. Areas traditionally associated with learning theory are treated in the present volume (conditioning, discrimination, and behavior theory) and in Volume 3 (human learning and motivation). The last three volumes range over the many presently active lines of research identified with human cognitive processes: Volume 4, attention, memory storage and retrieval; Volumes 5 and 6, information processing, reading, semantic memory, problem solving, and artificial intelligence. The organization by volumes is of necessity somewhat arbitrary, but as far as possible the lines of demarcation have been drawn with respect to theory rather than to method. Thus, for example, developmental approaches are represented by chapters in several volumes rather than being collected as a unit.

The philosophy and overall plan of the Handbook have been presented more fully in the Foreword and Introduction to Volume 1.

W. K. Estes

Introduction to Volume 2

W. K. Estes

This volume deals with concepts and theories growing principally out of laboratory studies of conditioning and learning. Our intention is to treat mechanisms, processes, and principles of some generality—applicable at least to all vertebrates. It is becoming well understood that detailed interpretations of particular behaviors require us to take account of the way general principles operate in the context of species-specific behavioral organizations and developmental histories; but detailed consideration of just how these interpretations are accomplished for different animal forms is another enterprise. Here we limit our task to abstracting from the enormous literature facts and ideas which seem general enough to be of interest and perhaps utility to investigators in other disciplines.

Among the latter, we are concerned most importantly with human cognitive psychology. Why, one may ask, should we expect principles of animal learning to help understand human mental functioning? We know that human cognitive activity is inextricably tied up with functions of language and that the presence versus absence of language is perhaps the greatest difference between man and other animals. It is because of this fact, rather than in spite of it, that the direct analysis of human learning and memory must be supplemented by a comparative approach. In the normal human being we have no way of turning language off so as to determine how various aspects of learning are modified or controlled by linguistic processes. We can, however, discover how learning occurs in the vertebrate brain in the absence of language by studying animals. The idea is not to make direct comparisons between human and animal learning in the manner of Donders' subtraction method, but rather to use the animal laboratory as a source of hypotheses and models to be employed as research tools in the analysis of human learning.

Investigators of human learning who wish to extend their findings beyond the confines of the laboratory have always been frustrated by the inordinate difficulty of relating the learning they observe in their experiments to important motivational systems of their subjects. There is no great problem in motivating human subjects to perform in a laboratory situation, but the motives involved are far from those that govern people's activities in their ordinary affairs. Here again we have a problem that defies direct attack on any significant scale. Still, we may hope for some elucidation from research on animals where we have methods of controlling and observing relationships between learning and major motivational systems.

In line with these purposes we have, in organizing this volume, largely avoided the review of bodies of research which are highly specific to particular experimental situations and especially those aimed more at the shaping of behavior than the abstraction of laws and principles. Our main objective has been to include thorough presentations of all of the basic concepts of conditioning and learning, with most emphasis on those that have proved to be extendable, with or without modification, to human learning.

It is of some interest to compare the organization that emerges with the organization laid down by Hilgard and Marquis (1940) and Hilgard (1948), which structured the field of conditioning and learning for many decades. Most conspicuously, perhaps, the tendency to treat theories of learning as a special topic revolving around the systems or schools identified with particular individuals has become progressively less widespread and is missing entirely from our chapter organization. This change in surface structure does not signify, of course, that the ideas of the major theorists of the 1940s have vanished without a trace. Many of Hull's concepts are well represented in the present chapter by Rudy and Wagner, many of Skinner's in the chapters of Staddon and Hearst, many of Tolman's in the chapter by Shimp, and those of Thorndike continue to be pervasively influential. An interesting change of emphasis with regard to individual theorists is the rediscovery of Pavlov, curiously missing from the lineup in Hilgard's treatise, but well represented in the present chapters by Rescorla, Kimmel and Burns, and Gormezano and Kehoe.

With regard to Hilgard and Marquis' organization of conditioning and learning, it is certainly the case that there has been little change in the identification of the concepts conceived to be basic to all forms of conditioning and learning, in particular, excitation, inhibition, reinforcement, and generalization. The dichotomization of classical and instrumental conditioning, first given major visibility by Hilgard and Marquis, has continued to polarize much research in this entire area, and we find substantial attention given to the issue in this volume 35 years later. If anything like a consensus is developing, it is perhaps that at the level of operational definitions, clarity in distinguishing classical and instrumental procedures is essential (Gormezano & Kehoe, Chapter 4) but that at the conceptual level it has not proved useful to think in terms of two distinct forms of learning (Hearst, Chapter 5).

The concept of reinforcement has receded somewhat from its position as the central organizing concept of Hilgard and Marquis' volume, being replaced by greatly increased emphasis on selectivity of association (Rudy & Wagner, Chapter 7), generalization (Heinemann & Chase, Chapter 8) and choice (Staddon, Chapter 2; Shimp, Chapter 6). The increasingly influential role of concepts having to do with selective attention and selective association was foreshadowed in Mackintosh's treatment of the relationships between conditioning and discrimination (this Handbook Volume 1, Chapter 5) and extends into Medin's treatment of theories of discrimination and learning set in both animal and children's learning (Volume 3, Chapter 4). Thus, on the whole, major trends in organization have been from persons toward ideas and from paradigms toward processes. In our more sanguine moments we might take these trends to represent necessary, if not sufficient, conditions for progress toward more general theory.

In order to identify the events responsible for the major shifts in emphasis, it is necessary to look back at the circumstances under which reinforcement theory rose to its position of dominance from about 1940 to 1960. The two theorists most conspicuously associated with this development played quite different roles. Hull (1937), seeking a way to bring the ideas of Pavlov and of Thorndike together under one theoretical roof, found a solution in a redefinition of reinforcement (originally simply the unconditioned stimulus in Pavlov's conception), broadened to include changes in the organism's motivational system produced by the reinforcing stimulus. Hull noted, for example, that presenting food as an unconditioned stimulus not only evokes reflexes such as salivation, but also reduces hunger. The onset of a shock not only elicits reflexes such as withdrawal but also activates a drive whose reduction is rewarding. Thus, the idea that the common element in all instances of reinforcement is the ultimate occurrence of a reduction in a drive or need provided a possible route to the unification of learning theory. Skinner (1938), in contrast, took almost exactly the opposite orientation. Noting that reinforcement in the sense of response-contingent reward is conspicuous in some situations and not in others, Skinner was satisfied to label the former class as a special category, operant behavior, and elevate this class to become the major concern of "the experimental analysis of behavior."

Followers of each path went through a period of ebullient prosperity followed by some more trying times. In the first case, the primary issues surrounding the nature of reinforcement instigated much work directed at testing the monistic conception of reinforcement versus both pluralistic stimulus–response interpretations and more cognitive theories. This path eventuated in fruitful bodies of research and theory on such topics as secondary motivation (Miller, 1959), incentive motivation (Logan & Wagner, 1965; Spence, 1960), and latent learning (MacCorquodale & Meehl, 1954; Tolman, 1948). However, the theoretical issues proved refractory to any lasting resolution and the time was ripe in the early 1950s for the appearance of a new approach, which held promise of shortcutting the way to solution of the problems of reinforcement by allowing the investigator to insert electrodes into an animal's midbrain and turn the underlying mechanisms on and off at will (Olds & Milner, 1954). Students of learning in the tradition of reinforcement theory lost interest in the T maze and learned instead to implant stereotaxic instruments. But after a decade of intense activity, the route to solution of theoretical problems of behavior theory by way of probing the midbrain also began to seem long and tortuous. The electrophysiological studies of motivation and reward have proved to be of much intrinsic interest in their own right, but it is unclear whether these methods are helping to elucidate the mechanisms whereby the intact animal learns in its ordinary environment, or whether they are simply creating a new research situation with its own problems (Ball, 1972; Hilgard & Bower, 1966).

Research on operant behavior in the "experimental analysis" tradition took a quite different path, depending heavily for its momentum on practical results, both actual (as for example, those with animals which have proved the mainstay of psychopharmacology in the drug industry) and projected (as for example, the revolutionary effects on education that were hoped for upon the promulgation of teaching machines). The direct and tangible outcome of a vast amount of research in this tradition has been the generation of a body of theory bearing largely on the way in which the intricate scheduling of reward contingencies leads to the shaping and reshaping of an animal's behavior in highly restricted learning situations. The investigation of operant conditioning has become a technically well-developed and highly respected, but somewhat compartmentalized, specialty. One harvest of this work is a collection of methods and empirical generalizations which simply must be mastered by every investigator of animal learning, whether his interests are behavioral or physiological, and which have proven extendable to the training of low-level mental defectives (Bijou, 1966) and even the management of intellectually normal human beings in such institutional settings as prisons.

However, because of the strong preference for keeping theoretical generalizations very close to experimental operations and for the avoidance of abstraction, the experimental analysis of operant conditioning has not led to concepts and theories of the type that investigators of human learning and cognition, whether in theoretical or educational contexts, are likely to turn to. In consequence, during the rapid acceleration of research in cognitive psychology during the 1960s, there was an increasing disposition on the part of investigators in this area to regard the theories and methods of animal learning and conditioning as constituting, if not a dead horse, at least a horse too slow afoot and too narrow in vision to be of much help in carrying psychologists toward the solution of human problems.

Nonetheless, there are some indications that the extreme segregation of research on human and animal learning may not represent an irreversible trend. At a theoretical level, some investigators have begun to move toward decompartmentalizing the study of operant conditioning by relating its concepts to broader conceptions of biological and evolutionary thought. Others are seeking the same end by exploring the possibility that conceptions of memory and attention growing out of human cognitive psychology can be fruitfully applied to the study of animal behavior. The first of these trends is represented in the chapter by Staddon and the latter in the chapters by Shrimp and by Heinemann and Chase in this volume.

Also, there have been new ferments in the animal learning laboratories, generating in some instances novel findings sufficiently at variance with classical ideas to interest psychologists of all persuasions. Among these are the discovery of instances of conditioning at extremely long temporal intervals by Garcia and others (Revusky & Garcia, 1970); findings concerning the "blocking of conditioning" and stimulus selection in associative learning by Kamin (1969) and Wagner (1969); and the overlearning-reversal effect, which has led to a burgeoning of research on both animals and children dealing with dimensional shifts, selective attention, and the role of mediators in discrimination learning (Estes, 1970; Kendler & Kendler, this Handbook, Volume 1; Medin, this Handbook, Volume 3).

These findings bring home the fact that there is still much about the learning of animals as well as man that we do not understand. The information-processing activities of subhuman organisms look simple and mechanical only when viewed from afar through foggy, anthropocentric spectacles. When we look more closely, we are struck by a recurring trend: again and again aspects of learning formerly assumed to be reserved for the higher positions on the scale of intellect turn out to be demonstrable at progressively lower levels. Thus, Mackintosh (this Handbook, Volume 1) argues cogently that selectivity of attention and association, attributes commonly conceived to fall into the special province of control processes used by human beings to deal with complex discrimination and concept learning tasks, actually characterize even the presumably simple processes of classical conditioning. In a similar vein, Wagner and his associates (Wagner, Rudy, & Whitlow, 1973) have presented a case for rehearsal-like processes in animal learning; and Premack's laboratory produces phenomena which mimic ever more closely syntactical properties of language in the communicative behavior of chimpanzees (Premack, 1973). From these observations, the thought arises that the processes and mechanisms of human cognition represent specializations and elaborations of processes and mechanisms which can advantageously be studied in animals that learn as well as in machines that think.

REFERENCES

Ball, G. Self-stimulation in the ventromedial hypothalamus. *Science,* 1972, **178,** 72–73.

Bijou, S. W. A functional analysis of retarded development. In N. R. Ellis (Ed.), *International Review of Research in Mental Retardation,* 1966, **1,** 1–19.

Estes, W. K. *Learning theory and mental development.* New York: Academic Press, 1970.

Hilgard, E. R. *Theories of learning.* New York: Appleton-Century-Crofts, 1948.

Hilgard, E. R., & Bower, G. H. *Theories of learning.* (3rd ed.) New York: Appleton-Century-Crofts, 1966.

Hilgard, E. R., & Marquis, D. G. *Conditioning and learning.* New York: Appleton-Century-Crofts, 1940.

Hull, C. L. Mind, mechanism, and adaptive behavior. *Psychological Review,* 1937, **44,** 1–32.

Kamin, L. J. Selective association and conditioning. In N. J. Mackintosh & W. K. Honig (Eds.), *Fundamental issues in associative learning.* Halifax, N.S.: Dalhousie University Press, 1969. Pp. 42–64.

Logan, F. A., & Wagner, A. R. *Reward and punishment.* Boston: Allyn & Bacon, 1965.

MacCorquodale, K., & Meehl, P. E. Edward C. Tolman. In W. K. Estes, S. Koch, K. MacCorquodale, P. E. Meehl, C. G. Mueller, Jr., W. N. Schoenfeld, & W. S. Verplanck, *Modern learning theory.* New York: Appleton-Century-Crofts, 1954. Pp. 177–266.

Miller, N. E. Liberalization of basic S–R concepts: Extensions to conflict behavior, motivation, and social learning. In S. Koch (Ed.), *Psychology: A study of a science.* Vol. 2. New York: McGraw-Hill, 1959. Pp. 196–292.

Olds, J., & Milner, P. Positive reinforcement produced by electrical stimulation of septal area and other regions of rat brain *Journal of Comparative and Physiological Psychology,* 1954, **47,** 419–427.

Premack, D. Cognitive principles? In F. J. McGuigan & D. B. Lumsden (Eds.), *Contemporary approaches to conditioning and learning.* Washington, D.C.: Winston, 1973. Pp. 287–309.

Revusky, S., & Garcia, J. Learned associations over long delays. In G. H. Bower (Ed.), *The psychology of learning and motivation.* New York: Academic Press, 1970. Pp. 1–84.

Skinner, B. F. *Behavior of organisms.* New York: Appleton-Century-Crofts, 1938.

Spence, K. W. *Behavior theory and learning: Selected papers.* Englewood Cliffs, New Jersey: Prentice Hall, 1960.

Tolman, E. C. Cognitive maps in rats and men. *Psychological Review,* 1948, **55,** 189–208.

Wagner, A. R. Stimulus validity and stimulus selection in associative learning. In N. J. Mackintosh & W. K. Honig (Eds.), *Fundamental issues in associative learning.* Halifax, N.S.: Dalhousie University Press, 1969. Pp. 90–122.

Wagner, A. R., Rudy, J. W., & Whitlow, J. W., Jr. Rehearsal in animal conditioning. *Journal of Experimental Psychology,* 1973, **97,** 407–426. (Monograph)

1

Pavlovian Excitatory and Inhibitory Conditioning

Robert A. Rescorla

Yale University

I. INTRODUCTION

All organisms face a world composed of multiple events bearing various relations to each other. Most of those events are outside of the control of the organism, and they vary widely in biological significance. But any adaptive organism must show a sensitivity to at least some of these events and the relationships among them. It is clearly advantageous to change as a result of exposure to different relations among events in the environment, to learn about what Tolman and Brunswik (1935) called the "casual texture" of the world. The problem of interest for the psychologist is that of conceptualizing how the organism learns these relations and what relations he learns.

One way to view Pavlovian conditioning is an example of this kind of learning about environmental events over which the organism has little or no control. Thus, the historically prominent salivary experiments of Pavlov (1927) can be viewed as simply the most familiar examples of the laboratory study of interevent learning. Those experiments employed particular kinds of events and a rather narrow range of relations among them, but they nevertheless represent a beginning to the general problem. It is to be hoped that the principles derived from such experiments may be generalizable well beyond the particular events and relations studied.

This is a somewhat liberal way of describing Pavlovian conditioning but it has the advantage of placing such studies in perspective within the general field of learning. It shifts attention away from many of the situationally specific issues with which conditioning has often concerned itself to the

7

more general problem of studying the learning of relations. Consequently, this chapter ignores many of the issues historically associated with conditioning and concentrates instead on learning relations.

Two major conceptual tools have emerged in an attempt to understand how the organism organizes his learning about events in his environment, conditioned excitation and conditioned inhibition. Speaking casually, conditioned excitation has to do with the learning that two events are not independent but instead tend to cooccur in the environment; conversely, conditioned inhibition has to do with the learning that events tend to occur apart from each other. Most approaches to conditioning attempt to use just these two kinds of learning constructs to describe all of the information about relations among events which an organism retains. Consequently, attention here centers upon these two notions.

Historically, the notion of conditioned excitation has been considered primary. Indeed, for many psychologists excitatory conditioning is still synonomous with the general term "conditioning." Normally, psychologists infer the presence of conditioned excitation whenever proximal presentation of two events results in a change in the behavior of the organism. In the classic case, presentation of a neutral conditioned stimulus (CS) contiguously with a food unconditioned stimulus (US) enables that CS to subsequently evoke a salivary response. It is the observation that behavior during the CS changes as a result of its temporal relation to the US that forms the basis for the inference of conditioned excitation. This description turns out to be unduly restrictive with regard to both the interevent relation and to the behavior from which excitation is inferred, but it will serve for the present.

Equally important to Pavlov, but slighted by many students of conditioning is learned inhibition. Historically, the conceptualization and specification of conditioned inhibition has been derivative of that of excitation. This subordinate role fits with an aspect of the intuitive meaning of inhibition—it acts not to generate its own effects but rather to modulate the effects of other processes. Thus, the common, although often inexplicit, procedure has been for theorists to begin by defining excitation in terms of operations and outcomes and only later to search out stimuli that might attenuate the action of excitation. Those stimuli are identified as inhibitors, and one may then raise the empirical question of what particular past experiences are necessary to endow stimuli with such inhibitory power.

The present usage of the terms "excitation" and "inhibition" will become clearer in subsequent sections, but two points should be made explicit here. First, those terms are used in many different ways by psychologists. This chapter by no means attempts to discuss all of those usages or even all of those usages within the framework of a conditioning experiment. Rather, since concern is with modification by experience, the discussion is confined to those examples of excitation and inhibition that involve learning, that is, are conditioned. Second, the current use of these terms is theoretical in character; inhibition and excitation are conceptual terms inferred from operations and outcomes, within the context of some more or less explicit theoretical structure. They are not, for instance, uniquely identified with a particular behavioral outcome, such as increase or decrease in the probability of some response. Indeed, little attention is paid here to the nature of the response changes from which excitation and inhibition are inferred. Instead this chapter emphasizes the nature of the relations learned and remains liberal in accepting a wide range of changes in behavior as indicating modification by exposure to a relation.

II. EXCITATORY CONDITIONING

Excitatory conditioning has been casually identified as the learning that two events are positively related in the environment. Further empirical and theoretical specification necessarily centers on two intertwined questions. First, what specific environmental relations are necessary and sufficient for generating such excitatory conditioning? Second, what is the nature of the learning so generated? How do we conceptualize the way in which experience with relations modifies the organism?

A.   What Relation Produces Learning?

In addressing the first question, virtually all students of conditioning have agreed that contiguity in time is the primary condition for the establishment of excitation. Organisms learn that a CS and US go together when they occur contiguously in time. Such diverse theorists as Pavlov (1927), Tolman (1932), Hull (1943), Guthrie (1959), Spence (1956), and Konorski (1967) have been unanimous on this point. Furthermore, there is now a vast store of empirical information supporting the proposition that, as the contiguity between a CS and US is destroyed, the CS becomes a less adequate conditioned excitor. Studies of the so-called CS–US interval have been a popular activity of American psychologists and virtually all response systems studied thus far have supported this gross conclusion (see, for example, Black & Prokasy, 1972).

An important, and historically often troubling, limitation on that conclusion should be mentioned. Apparently, strict simultaneity in time does not maximize excitatory conditioning; rather, the CS should slightly precede the US. Although there are several results that suggest that conditioning can be obtained with CSs that follow USs, there can be little question that the sequence of events, as well as their proximity in time, dramatically affects conditioning.

It turns out, however, that in evaluating positive relations among events the organism is considerably more sophisticated than this initial, historically popular, description suggests. Although contiguity among events is important, in many conditioning situations the animal does much more than simply tabulate coincident occurrences of CS and US. Speaking casually, the organism seems to demand not only that the CS and US be contiguous but also that a CS provide "information" about the occurrence of the US in order to condition excitation to that CS.

Two examples will illustrate this point. Both examples come from fear-conditioning situations in which aversive foot shock is the US paired with neutral CSs in rat subjects. With such pairing, CSs typically come to elicit suppression of the ongoing behavior of the organism, indicating the development of excitatory fear conditioning. In the first example, Rescorla (1968) explored the effect of intermingling "intertrial" shocks among tone–shock pairings. He found that if such USs were presented with sufficient frequency in the absence of a CS, they severely disrupted the ability of CS–US contiguities to condition excitation to that CS. Notice that such "extra" USs left intact the CS–US contiguity but occurred with sufficient frequency to make the CS useless as a predictor of the US. Further parametric investigation suggested that the organism is sensitive to the relative rates of occurrence of the US in the presence and absence of the CS. The amount of excitatory fear conditioning to the CS was well predicted by the degree to which shock was more probable during the CS than in its absence; conditioning was poorly predicted by the simple number of USs during the CS. Such findings led to the suggestion that CS–US contingencies (or correlations), not simply contiguities, govern excitatory conditioning (Rescorla, 1967). The same contiguities apparently have quite different effects depending upon the context in which they occur.

In a related experiment, Kamin (1968, 1969) first paired a noise CS with a shock US in rat subjects. He then added a (redundant) light to the noise and continued the pairing with shock. Under those circumstances, the light acquired little conditioning despite its repeated contiguity with shock. Apparently, because the light provided no new information, conditioning did not occur. Again, this situation has been explored in great parametric detail and yields a data pattern generally consistent with the informational notion. Other examples of such findings are reviewed elsewhere (Rescorla, 1972a). Together, they suggest that animals demand a higher quality of evidence than simple coincidence to conclude that events are positively related and thus show excitatory conditioning.

There are now available several descriptions of excitatory conditioning which try to capture this sophistication without abandoning the primacy of temporal contiguity. These descriptions have been given in different languages and in different levels of specificity, but all share one assumption: the effectiveness of a US depends not simply upon its own physical properties but also upon the current status of excitatory conditioning. Put informally, they assume that conditioning is dependent upon the discrepancy between the US received and that anticipated; unanticipated, surprising USs are especially effective, whereas anticipated ones (ones derived when a substantial CR occurs) are reduced in effectiveness.

One specific version of such a theory, suggested by Rescorla and Wagner (1972), is described below. Conditioned excitation is specified in terms of the changes in associative strengths of stimuli, as a result of a contiguity with the US. Thus, if a single stimulus A is followed by a US, the change in its strength is specified by the equation

$$\Delta V_A = \alpha_A \beta (\lambda - V_A).$$

In this expression α and β are rate parameters acknowledging the individual features of the CS and US; λ is the asymptote of conditioning supportable by the US employed. The important feature is that increases in excitation (ΔV) depend upon the discrepancy between the asymptote (λ) and the current level of conditioning of the CS (V_A). For such a simple case, this formulation is simply an adaptation of the notions of Bush and Mosteller (1955) and of Hull (1943) and consequently predicts a variety of elementary findings, such as negatively accelerated acquisition curves.

The distinction between this formulation and those earlier ones becomes most apparent when a compound CS, AX, is followed by a US. In that case, the separate associative strengths of the elements A and X are changed according to the following equations:

$$\Delta V_A = \alpha_A \beta (\lambda - V_{AX}),$$
$$\Delta V_X = \alpha_X \beta (\lambda - V_{AX}).$$

The feature of interest is that the current strength of the total AX compound is relevant to the increment in strength which each stimulus receives. Since V_{AX} is assumed to equal the sum of V_A and V_X, this means that the current strengths of all stimuli present at a US occurrence modulate its effectiveness for conditioning each individual stimulus. It is this feature that enables such formulations to account for the "informational" character of conditioning.

The two examples mentioned above provide convenient examples of the power of such theories. Consider first the Kamin blocking experiment. In that experiment, A is first presented singly and paired with shock until it is asymptotic at $V_A \rightarrow \lambda$. Then the redundant X is added and the AX compound reinforced. Notice that the quantity ($\lambda - V_{AX}$) determines the conditioning to X on such compound trials. Since V_{AX} is assumed to equal $V_A + V_X$, which in turn is close to λ, that quantity is close to zero, and so V_X receives little increment. Speaking casually, because the US was expected on the basis of A (i.e., V_A is high), it is ineffective in conditioning X. Thus, conditioning to X is blocked despite its presentation in contiguity with a physically potent US. A similar description can be given of Rescorla's data. In that case, the role of A is played by situational cues and X by the experimenter's stimulus. If the background stimulus is conceptualized as divisible into temporal units in the presence of which shocks may or may not occur, then the organism is exposed to two kinds of trials: A alone and AX (background plus CS). The distribution of shocks to A alone establishes some level of background conditioning; that level in turn blocks conditioning to X on the AX trials. Because the organism generally anticipates shock in the situation, the CS provides no special information, and so it receives no excitatory conditioning.

There are already available in the literature detailed discussions applying theories of this sort to a broad range of conditioning data (e.g., Wagner & Rescorla, 1972; Rescorla, 1972a). Such theories turn out to do a remarkably good job of integrating a wide variety of data which otherwise seem to demand sophisticated computational abilities on the part of the organism. They do so by providing an account not only of asymptotic performance but also of the trial by trial events which generate that performance. Furthermore, such theories have served the important role of generating new and often counterintuitive findings, many of which are not easily generated by earlier theories or even by a casual informational intuition.

Instead of rehearsing this range of findings here, only one is mentioned for purposes of illustration. According to this theory, the separate associative strengths controlled by the elements of a compound determine the consequences of reinforcing that compound. Thus, if AX is followed by a US, there may result increases, decreases, or no change in the strengths of A and X, depending upon their total strength prior to that reinforced occasion. If V_A and V_X are weak, then one anticipates the usual observation that they will be augmented when AX is reinforced. But if V_A and V_X each have been previously highly trained toward the asymptote of λ, then $V_{AX} = V_A + V_X$ will be greater than λ. When AX is then reinforced, the quantity which determines ΔV_A and ΔV_X, $(\lambda - V_{AX})$, may be negative, and consequently V_A and V_X may decrease. That is, reinforcement in compound of two previously well-trained CSs should lead to their individual decrements. Similarly, careful titration of the level of previous individual element conditioning might yield a composite very close to λ and thus prevent reinforced AX trials from changing either stimulus. Both of these results have been observed in fear conditioning experiments (e.g., Wagner & Rescorla, 1972). This is the sort of observation which supports the notion that the same CS–US contiguity does not always produce the same outcome but rather generates quite different changes, depending upon the CS strength at the time of that contiguity.

Despite the success of such theories, the present goal is not to urge their correctness, but rather to make two more general points. First, such theories and outcomes illustrate that the empirical relations responsible for the generation of conditioned excitation are complex ones; simple contiguity fails to capture the sophistication of the organism. Yet, second, one need not attribute to the organism the ability to learn a whole range of complicated interevent relations. Rather, there is available a class of models in which the relation responsible for excitatory conditioning is only contiguity but in which the organism is nevertheless allowed to behave in this sophisticated manner. This is an important observation if one would like to generate complex representation of the environment on the basis of only a few learned relations.

B. What Is Learned?

The above discussion provides a convenient summary which incorporates many of the interevent relations governing excitatory conditioning: excitation occurs when there is a discrepancy between the expected and actual US. But it leaves virtually untouched the question of the nature of excitatory conditioning. What is learned when excitation is conditioned?

The most frequent answer has been given in terms of "associations." Normally, psychologists have assumed a kind of ismorphism between the events of the world and the way in which the organism stores information about those events. Because Pavlovian conditioning involves the contiguous occurrence of two independently manipulable events, it has seemed natural to impute to the animal some association between multiple events. Most frequently, this notion of association has received relatively little analysis itself; rather it is intended as a primitive in terms of which more complex processes can be understood. In most usages it has little content beyond the assumption that presentation of one member of an association can sometimes activate the other member.

Dispute over the issue of what is learned in Pavlovian conditioning has centered more on the items associated than on the nature of association itself. Most would agree that conditioning involves an association, one member of which is the CS. As discussed elsewhere, there is disagreement both about how particular aspects of a CS are chosen over others and about the mechanisms accomplishing that selection, but there are few dissenters to the notion that in conditioning CSs become associated with something. Disputes arise over the nature of that something. Only two experimental attacks on the issue are discussed here: one the most popular historically, which seems to have shed little light on the question, and another more recently explored possibility, which perhaps holds more promise.

Historically, this issue of what is learned has received two solutions, "stimulus" and "response." Psychologists have been struck by the observation that conditioning normally involves pairing a CS with a reinforcer that is both a salient stimulus and also regularly evokes a response. Consequently, it has been natural to offer those two aspects of the reinforcing event as candidates for what is associated with the CS. Most attempts to resolve this issue have taken the form of investigating manipulations that influence the acquisition of excitation. The approach is based on the assumption that contiguity of events is a primary relation responsible for the formation of associations. If so, then conditioning should be best when the entities to be associated are most nearly contiguous; therefore, if one aspect of the reinforcing event is manipulated so as to vary its proximity to the CS, then its importance in the association will be mirrored by variation in the level of conditioning.

In the most dramatic examples of this approach attempts have been made to eliminate entirely one aspect of the reinforcer. This logic has been applied in two interrelated literatures to the elimination of the response elicited by the reinforcer. In the sensory preconditioning experiment (see Thompson, 1972), the experimenter selects as his US an event that evokes no regularly observable response. For instance, a neutral light might be used following a tone. Evidence that the two have become associated, despite the inability of light to evoke a response, comes from two subsequent stages of the experiment. There, the light is paired with some potent reinforcer until it evokes response, and then the tone is tested. The observation of interest is that often the tone will then evoke a response; furthermore, its ability to do so depends upon its prior contiguity with the light. This dependence is taken to mean that an excitatory association must have been formed during the light–tone pairings. Since the "reinforcing" light was deliberately selected to have no response, it is argued the association cannot be stimulus–response and therefore must be stimulus–stimulus in character.

In a second literature aimed at eliminating responses, the experimenter selects a reinforcer that would normally provoke a response, but then prevents the occurrence of that response by one physiological intervention or another. For instance, the application of curare (a peripheral paralytic agent) or the crushing of the motor nerves at the spinal level can be used to prevent an electric shock from evoking skeletal reactions. One can demonstrate that, if conditioning is carried out during such states, then upon removal of the physiological block the CS nevertheless evokes a conditioned response (e.g., Solomon & Turner, 1962). Consequently, the inference may be drawn that excitatory conditioning occurs without responding and so must not intimately involve the response.

Conversely, one may apply the same logic in an attempt to select stimulus-free reinforcers. Here the major technique has been the application of electric current directly to the motor cortex, thus directly evoking a response without the normal sensory input. Again, recent experiments have suggested that this event is capable of serving as a reinforcer, although some have questioned the Pavlovian nature of this learning (Wagner, Thomas, & Norton, 1967).

A third example of such logic stems from the realization that reinforcers vary in the latency between stimulus onset and the unconditioned response. By judicious selection of reinforcers, therefore, one might hope to separately vary the contiguities of the CS with the stimulus and response aspects of the reinforcer. White and Schlosberg (1952), for instance, argued that the similarity in optimum CS–US interval across USs differing in unconditioned response (UR) latencies was evidence against the participation of the UR in learning. On the other hand, Jones and her collaborators, (e.g., Jones, 1962) have made the opposite claim that the optimum interval depends upon the UR latency.

In one sense, experiments of this kind, manipulating acquisition, have been quite successful; they have identified as unnecessary certain features of various reinforcers for the production of conditioned excitation. However, this approach has had relatively little lasting impact for several reasons. The first reason is experimental in nature. The investigations have been designed as demonstrations, intended to show that one or another feature of the reinforcer is or is not needed. And the outcomes are of the form that, despite some degradation of the reinforcer, some conditioning still occurs. What is lacking, however, is any systematic assessment of the relative contributions of those reinforcer features. One would like to know, for instance, not only whether conditioning occurs under conditions that depress responding, but also the ways in which that conditioning is different in form and amount from that obtained without the intervention.

A more important reason for the relative lack of impact of these studies has to do with their theoretical interpretation. It turns out that investigators are not entirely clear on the meaning of the alternatives, "stimulus" and "response." It is obvious that those terms do not refer to external world events; surely, no one believes that associations exist among external events. Rather associations must take place among internal representations of those events. For some psychologists, therefore, those internal representations have taken on physiological connotations, referring to portions of the central nervous system. But increasingly, psychologists have come to use them to refer to constructs within a particular theory. Furthermore, when faced with difficult data, theorists have been willing to invent purely conceptual "stimuli" and "responses" whose function is primarily to preserve the unitary stimulus–response of stimulus–stimulus position. As a consequence, the stimulus–response dichotomy has not seemed a particularly promising dimension along which to partition reinforcers.

Finally, it should be pointed out that the logic of such experiments depends heavily upon the presumption of isomorphism between the events of the world and the way in which information is stored. The need for a particular aspect of the reinforcer to be contiguous with the CS does not imply that that aspect of the reinforcer is represented in the learning. Something may be a condition of learning without being itself involved in that learning. We need to distinguish between learning because of a relation between events and learning about that relation.

A second, perhaps more promising, way of experimentally investigating the participants of an excitatory association was originally suggested by Rozeboom (1958) and has recently been investigated in my laboratory. The idea behind this approach is to identify the items involved in an association by attempting to modify the representation of those items *after* conditioning. If we entertain the notion that event representations are themselves subject to learning, then we might hope to identify which aspects of an event participate in an association by seeing which affect the exhibition of excitation when they are subsequently modified. Such a strategy would not be confined to distinguishing between "stimulus" and "response" aspects of a reinforcer but would permit assessment of any of its properties.

One example of such an approach is a recent series of experiments attempting to manipulate the value of the US following conditioning (e.g., Holland & Rescorla, 1975; Rescorla, 1973). Those experiments established emotional conditioning to a CS with either a shock or food US; in the former case, conditioning was measured by suppression, whereas in the latter conditioning was measured by the general activity which the anticipation of food produces. After the completion of conditioning, various manipulations designed to modify the organism's evaluation of the reinforcer were carried out: habituation of the US, exposure to USs of the same modality but of higher intensity, satiation, and use of that US as a signal for an oppositely signed second US. All of these procedures are known to modify the effectiveness of the reinforcer if applied prior to conditioning. The finding of interest is that all of these procedures also retroactively induced changes in the conditioned responding controlled by the CS. Results like this suggest that the reinforcer value somehow mediates the production of the conditioned response and that its value continues to be important even after conditioning is completed. This is the kind of evidence that directly encourages the notion that conditioning involves an association with an internal representation of the reinforcer itself. Furthermore, such experiments open the possibility of detailed study of those aspects involved in conditioning by analytic studies manipulating various aspects of the reinforcer representation following conditioning.

It is also worth noting that parallel experiments with second-order conditioning have yielded quite different patterns of results. In such experiments, one stimulus (S_1) is first paired with an effective US until conditioned excitation results; then another neutral stimulus (S_2) is followed by S_1 but without the reinforcer. There is now substantial empirical evidence that second-order conditioned excitation of considerable magnitude may be attached to S_2 in several emotional conditioning paradigms. More interestingly, postconditioning manipulation of individual events provides some insight into the structure of that learning. If, after second-order conditioning, we manipulate the value of either S_1 or of the original US itself, that manipulation has little retroactive consequences for second order excitation. Such value changes have been induced by procedures like those described above for first-order conditioning and additionally by extinction or further excitatory conditioning of S_1. Those results suggest that neither S_1 nor the original reinforcer continue to importantly participate in second order conditioned excitation (Rescorla, 1973).

There are two asides worth making about experiments of this sort. First, they suggest that perhaps second-order conditioning is not just a weaker form of first-order conditioning. Indeed, these results indicate that second-order conditioning displays a remarkable lack of sensitivity to manipulations that might normally be expected to modify conditioned responding and do affect first-order excitation. The independence of its origins displayed by second-order conditioning is reminiscent of the problem of "functional autonomy." Many of the troublesome instances described by Allport (1937) in which the values of acts and objects become independent of their original goals and motivations may find explanation in higher-order conditioning. Second, these experiments may speak to a distinction which runs through the history of (at least emotional) conditioning. A question frequently asked, but often considered meaningless, is whether CSs simply serve as a signal for reinforcers or whether the value of the CS itself changes (see Gleitman, 1974). After pairing with shock, does the organism come to dislike the CS for its own sake or does he only dislike it because it heralds the coming of shock? The sensitivity of the first-order CR to modifications in the US suggests that a first-order CS at least partly plays the role of a signal. The reaction of the organism to this CS depends upon the maintenance of the status of the event it signals. In contrast, the second-order results may point to a situation in which the actual value of the CS is changed so as to become more independent of the event it signals.

Although these specific outcomes of the postconditioning reinforcer modifications are of interest, the point made here is somewhat more general. Such experiments may provide a general approach to the investigation of the participants in learning. It is possible, of course, to force the results into a stimulus versus response framework, but this has been explicitly avoided because it does not seem particularly profitable. Rather the value of this kind of experiment is that it may permit exploration of the detailed features of event representation along multiple dimensions. Furthermore, this approach is consonant with a notion which has become increasingly favored among general psychologists, if not among investigators of Pavlovian conditioning: that participants in associations may not be static structural features of the organism. Rather they may be event representations built up from experience and which are consequently themselves modifiable. Indeed, the learning of those representations may be an important "nonassociative" process which normally occurs but has been largely unstudied in Pavlovian experiments.

C. A Comment on the Domain of "Excitatory Conditioning"

Before leaving this brief discussion of excitatory conditioning, it is worth pointing out just how restricted is the domain to which students of learning have applied that phrase. Throughout, excitatory conditioning has casually been described as a process inferred when a change in behavior is produced by regular presentation of events in a positive relation to each other. But in practice investigations have been severely limited in three important respects: the range of relations studied, the events among which relations are arranged, and the behavioral changes used to index excitation. If one takes the general view that interest in conditioning experiments lies in the learning of relations, these restrictions seem odd.

For instance, excitation might in principle be indexed by *any* behavior change attributable to exposure to a relation between events. On purely logical grounds, we should be glad for any behavioral index we can get. Yet not all behaviors have been viewed as equally acceptable for inferring excitation. For instance, many discussions of conditioning appear to demand that the conditioned response be similar to the unconditioned response. Even though this requirement is sometimes denied, investigators do not search randomly in the animal's behavior for evidence of conditioned excitation; rather, they examine behaviors like those the US evokes. It may be noted that this constraint is encouraged by historical theories, since both the stimulus–stimulus and stimulus–response interpretations of conditioning anticipate similarity between the CR and UR. Similarly, we do not search randomly in time for behavioral evidence of excitation. Instead we normally ask whether experience produces changed behavior during some specific time interval initiated by the CS. Again, this constraint is encouraged by traditional thinking about conditioning in which the CS, through its association, activates behavior. Moreover, we normally ask of the CS only whether it produces a response, not a host of other questions, such as whether it serves to reinforce other stimuli. The important point is that these decisions as to acceptable behaviors from which to infer excitation are all based upon theoretical conceptions of the conditioning process. It is essential to be aware that these theoretical conceptions sharply limit the data collected, and so have a way of preventing the accumulation of disruptive evidence simply by circumscribing the behaviors examined.

Equally restricted are the items that we normally choose to play the roles of CS and US. Many investigators select CSs for their inability to provoke responses and USs for their ability to regularly do so. This has considerable advantage if we use as our index of learning the observation that the CS comes to provoke new behavior. But that advantage should not become so sacrosanct that we do not attempt to study learning of relations among events that do not meet those criteria.

Perhaps of most importance is the limited range of interevent relations that have been explored under the rubric of excitatory conditioning. For instance, although contiguity has been treated here in a general way, Pavlovian investigations are almost exclusively ones of *temporal* contiguity. Yet it seems plausible that organisms are also sensitive to spatial relations; surely they can learn that two external events are spatially contiguous even if they are not temporally correlated. Rescorla and Holland (1975), argue further for the investigation within a Pavlovian framework of nonarbitrary relations inherent in the structure of the organism and the world, relations such as similarity.

The point is that temporal contiguity is only one example of how two events might bear some positive relations to each other. The previous discussion points to ways in which somewhat more subtle informational relations can be understood in terms of a more sophisticated version of contiguity. But if Pavlovian conditioning is to have any success as a general model for the learning of relations, we must explore the applicability of such principles to a much broader range of relations. And we must explore more widely the events related as well as the range of behavior indicating conditioning.

III. INHIBITORY CONDITIONING

Previous paragraphs indicate the kinds of relations between CSs and reinforcers that are known to establish conditioned excitation. But recent evidence strongly suggests that other relations among these events may be learned and result in conditioned inhibition. Inhibition is used here in the specific sense of attenuating the effects which conditioned excitation would normally produce. Thus, a conditioned inhibitory stimulus is one that has become capable, through experience, of interfering with the production of a response by an excitor.

The determination that a stimulus indeed controls conditioned inhibition can involve some additional complications. The difficulty is that identification of a stimulus as an inhibitor requires the presence of something to inhibit. In the absence of some excitation, one would not necessarily expect an inhibitor to have an effect identifiably different from that of an untrained, neutral stimulus. Indeed, one might argue that the failure to have any effect in the absence of excitation has been an implicit defining characteristic of inhibitors; the presence of such an effect would encourage the alternative that a stimulus is not an inhibitor at all but rather an elicitor of alternative excitation. In any case, this lack of separate consequence has often made psychologists skeptical about the notion of inhibition; it is often argued that inhibition could be replaced in theorizing by the simple absence of excitation.

Fortunately, several assessment techniques have been developed that permit identification of an inhibitor as distinct from the absence of excitation. The first is a summation procedure, in which a stimulus known to control conditioned excitation is selected; then one can assess whether another stimulus is an inhibitor by presenting it in conjunction with that excitor. If the response to the combination is less than that to the excitor alone, one may infer that the added stimulus is an inhibitor. The second technique is highly related. If a stimulus is an inhibitor, then it should be especially retarded in developing excitation when subsequently exposed to an excitatory treatment. The preexisting inhibition should attenuate the display of the new excitation. To most clearly identify a stimulus as an inhibitor, it is best, of course, to examine the results of both techniques. Such multiple assessments aid in eliminating alternative interpretations (Rescorla, 1969). Successful outcomes with these two techniques permit the conclusion that a stimulus is an inhibitor, but they do not identify it as a *conditioned* inhibitor. For the conclusion that the inhibitor is learned, we need the further demonstration that its inhibitory power depends upon specific past experiences of the organism, as discussed below.

A. What Produces Conditioned Inhibition?

With these assessment techniques in hand, one may then ask what relations among events seem to establish conditioned inhibition. I mention here a number of examples of such relations (see Rescorla, 1969, for a fuller account) and then turn to a statement attempting to summarize them. A recently popular procedure has been to arrange a negative temporal correlation between CS and US, such that although the US is occasionally unpredictably presented in the absence of the CS, it never occurs in its presence. More generally, one can arrange for the probability of the US to be reduced during the CS, compared with that in its absence. In several preparations (e.g., Wagner & Rescorla, 1972) this treatment endows CSs with inhibitory power. This result parallels the finding, mentioned earlier, that positive correlations produce excitation. A more traditional procedure was explored in detail by Pavlov, a procedure he termed "conditioned inhibition." This consists of employing two kinds of trials: A, followed by the US, and AX compound trials, after which no US is presented. Under these circumstances, A becomes excitatory because of its positive correlation with the US, whereas X becomes inhibitory owing to its negative correlation. The simplest evidence for the latter conclusion is that A evokes a strong response, whereas the AX compound evokes a considerably weaker response. A special case of this procedure omits A altogether on the nonreinforced trials. This discriminative procedure has also been found to generate conditioned inhibition.

The above procedures make a stimulus inhibitory by virtue of its nonreinforcement. Therefore, it is of interest to ask about two simpler cases of nonreinforcement. The first is extinction, in which a previously reinforced stimulus, now presented without the US, declines in ability to produce a response. This case is discussed in more detail below, but it should be noted here that present evidence does not suggest that an extinguished stimulus becomes inhibitory. It loses its power to provoke excitation, but it does not gain power to inhibit (see Rescorla, 1969). The second case is repeated nonreinforced presentation of a neutral stimulus prior to any presentation of the US. Although it will be seen below that such a treatment modifies the neutral stimulus, it does not appear to convert it into an inhibitor. These two examples illustrate the important point that all occurrences of a nonreinforcement are not equivalent in producing inhibition. They suggest that the context in which the stimulus is nonreinforced is critical for the establishment of inhibition.

One historically important theory which captures that contextual dependence was suggested by Konorski (1948). He argued that excitatory conditioning consists of establishing associations between a CS and a US center; the latter was also viewed as activated by the reinforcer itself. The condition for establishing excitation was described as the presentation of the CS at a time of increase in the activity of the US center. Conversely, stimuli present during a decrease in that activation were thought to become inhibitors. For instance, on compound AX trials of an $A+/AX-$ procedure, A activates the US representation, but the omission of reinforcement dictates that the compound will be followed by a decrease in that activity. Consequently, X acquires inhibition. On those $AX-$ trials, A also acquires inhibition, but the intermingled $A+$ trials serve to keep it primarily excitatory. Similar accounts may be given of other successful inhibitory procedures. In contrast, simple presentation of a neutral stimulus involves no activation of the US center and so produces no conditioning, either excitatory or inhibitory. Furthermore, decrements during extinction cease when the US center is no longer activated, and so extinction stops short of establishing a net inhibitor.

Put into casual language, the Konorski view captures an intuition about inhibition similar to that we described for excitation: only stimuli that are informative about nonreinforcement generate inhibition. A more formal way of capturing that intuition can be accomplished by an application of the Rescorla–Wagner model. To describe inhibition one may employ the same equations as those used for excitation, except that nonreinforcement is treated as the minimum reinforcement, supporting an asymptote of zero and having a different rate parameter. Thus, the change in strength on an $AX-$ trial may be described by

$$\Delta V_A = \alpha_A \beta_2 (0 - V_{AX}),$$
$$\Delta V_X = \alpha_X \beta_2 (0 - V_{AX}).$$

In this framework, decrements will result from reinforcement whenever V_{AX} is positive and net conditioned inhibitors are represented as having negative associative strength.

Consider the $A+/AX-$ paradigm. The associative strength of A will rise toward λ on $A+$ trials since those trials apply a discrepancy of $(\lambda - V_A)$, but the strength of AX will be forced down toward zero on the $AX-$ trials. Since V_A will remain high and V_{AX} $(= V_A + V_X)$ will approach zero, V_X will necessarily become negative, that is, X will become a conditioned inhibitor. That is, X becomes an inhibitor because it is present when an excitatory A is nonreinforced. Thus, the classic conditioned inhibition paradigm is easily understood in terms of this model.

The case of negative correlation is accommodated by considerations similar to those for positive correlation. In the case of perfect negative correlation, presenting the US in the absence of the CS means presenting it during the background alone. If one describes that background as A and the CS trials as adding X to A, one can view negative correlations as an example of the $A+/AX-$ paradigm. Wagner and Rescorla (1972) display in detail such an interpretation and document its successful account of negative correlations, as well as those of the other inhibitory paradigms mentioned above. Finally, notice that this description also correctly predicts the outcome of several related but noninhibitory paradigms. For instance, the simple nonreinforcement either of a neutral stimulus (associative strength of zero) or of a previously reinforced stimulus, should drive its value toward zero but should not make it inhibitory.

It is of interest to note that this particular theory suggests that there is no special tie between the development of inhibition and nonreinforcement. As noted earlier, decrements in associative strength are expected whenever expectations exceed outcomes, even if those outcomes involve some level of reinforcement. If, for instance, A were followed by a powerful US but AX by one of lesser magnitude, then V_A might approach an asymptote greater than that approached by V_{AX}. That is, even though followed by reinforcement the X would still be predictive of a lesser event and develop conditioned inhibition. Wagner and Rescorla (1972) present some evidence for this prediction, but considerably more investigation of this proposition is needed. This is one example of the kind of novel prediction that theories of this sort are capable of making.

In any case, such theories provide a convenient summary for the conditions producing inhibition, a summary which parallels that given earlier for excitation. Inhibition and excitation are conditioned whenever there is a discrepancy between the associative strength present and the strength the subsequent reinforcer will support. Excitation occurs when that discrepancy is positive (the US is "underexpected") whereas inhibition occurs when it is negative (the US is "overexpected").

One final feature of this description should be noted. We earlier casually described conditioned inhibition as the learning that two events occur only apart from each other. At first blush such learning seriously undermines the primary role which American psychology has accorded temporal contiguity, for it is learning because of the absence of contiguity. However, the present description displays how events which are widely separated in time nevertheless generate learning based on contiguity. It is the contiguity of CSs with discrepancy that produces conditioning.

B. What Is Learned in Inhibitory Conditioning?

Having summarized many of the conditions which produce learned inhibition, the nature of that learning is still left relatively unconstrained. What does a subject learn when he develops conditioned inhibition? The preceding paragraphs have developed the view that such learning results from a relation among events in the environment, a view which suggests an associative interpretation of inhibition. But before turning to various associative alternatives mention should be made of an historically prominent nonassociative possibility.

Pavlov (1927) argued that in the cases of extinction, discrimination, and various other decremental procedures, the inhibition that developed was a feature of the CS representation. He maintained that the reason that the CS lost its power to provoke conditioned responses (CRs) had little to do with the integrity of its associations but rather involved a modification of the CS itself. Roughly speaking, the CS representation, simply as a result of its repeated presentation, became fatigued; consequently, as a stimulus it was less effective altogether. In Pavlov's view, this degeneration of the CS occurred as an invariant feature of its presentation, whatever the consequent events; the ability of the CS to produce a CR during acquisition resulted from the greater rate of growth of excitation outdistancing that degeneration. Hull (1943) offered a similar proposition for his response-based reactive inhibition.

There is some modern evidence that a process of the sort envisioned by Pavlov does take place and does interact with conditioning. For instance, if a stimulus is simply repeatedly presented without consequence, then it is subsequently very difficult to train when subjected to a conditioning procedure (see Lubow, 1973). This phenomenon, which has come to be termed "latent inhibition," is very powerful, often doubling or tripling the number of conditioning trials required to reach asymptote. However, this is apparently an example of learning about a stimulus itself, not of learning about its relation to particular other events. Such a preexposed stimulus is reduced in effectiveness in just about *any* subsequent associative learning situation we employ. It is as though the salience or attention-getting value of the stimulus were reduced, making it correspondingly difficult to learn about it as an event.

As suggested by the previous discussion, however, the "latent inhibition" induced by simple preexposure is not the same as the conditioned inhibition described here. First, some of the paradigms in which such a stimulus is resistant to training are ones that generate conditioned inhibition. That is, a preexposed stimulus shows not only slower development of excitation but also slower development of conditioned inhibition in say an $A+/AX-$ paradigm. Such negative transfer would not be expected if the processes were the same. Second, stimuli preexposed in this way show no evidence of inhibition in summation test procedures; they do not interfere with the excitation controlled by other stimuli.

Furthermore, although seemingly consistent with results from extinction, no view of conditioned inhibition in terms of a stimulus becoming ineffective can accommodate the range of available findings. For instance, many situations from which inhibition is inferred involve more than simple failure to produce behavior. In a summation test a conditioned inhibitor must be highly effective if it is to counteract the strong excitor; simple ineffectiveness would not produce interference. Moreover, Asyratyan (1972) reviews a number of experiments indicating that following various kinds of inhibitory operations the CS remains very effective in evoking alternative behaviors. Thus, although some procedures do seem to make CSs less effective and thus have powerful effects upon behavior, simple reduced CS potency does not seem to account for the range of conditioned inhibitory findings.

We turn then to a discussion of conditioned inhibition as an associative phenomenon. Within that position, two broad alternatives are presented. One possibility is that inhibition involves a new kind of association which binds together the same items as does conditioned excitation. On this view the same events are related but the organism learns a different relation among them. Alternatively, one might eschew the need to postulate a new kind of association and instead argue that "inhibition" involves the same kind of association but that different interfering items are associated. On this view, a so-called inhibitor simply involves competition among associations of the same type.

To examine the first of these alternatives in more detail, consider the conditioned inhibition paradigm which intermixes $A+$ and $AX-$ trials. Over trials, X develops the ability to interfere with the response which A alone would otherwise have produced. There are various possibilities for the building up of inhibitory associations, possibilities which differ mainly in the nature of the events involved in that association. An obvious candidate is the reinforcer itself. An analogy with conditioned excitation in which CS–US associations are formed would lead naturally to the suggestion that inhibition also involves CS–US associations, but that the nature of the associations differs. This view is encouraged by the casual description of inhibition as learning that two events occur apart from each other. A particular version of this view has been suggested by Konorski (1948) and more recently by Rescorla (1974). They argue that inhibitors have the power to raise the threshold for activation of the US representation, but are otherwise without effect. So one possibility is that the CS develops an inhibitory association with the US.

Another plausible alternative is that an inhibitory association forms between A and $X,$ such that X interferes with the ability of A to provoke a response. This alternative is encouraged by the observation that in this paradigm the function of X is to countermand the information given by A. Yet another view might suggest that the conditioned response itself participates. Conditioned inhibition might involve learned inhibitory associations between X and the response normally evoked by A, thereby making difficult the display of that response on an AX trial. Finally, one might take a more hierarchic view of the inhibitory connection and argue that its action is not on individual events at all but rather upon the excitatory association itself. The X might specifically depress the association between, say, A and the US without direct action on either of the individual event representations.

These alternatives are by no means exhaustive, but they are illustrative of some of the specific forms which an inhibitory association view might take. It turns out that various transfer tests, carried out after the establishment of conditioned inhibition, permit some assessment of these alternatives. Three particular tests of X are mentioned for illustration.

One test involves the transfer to another CS (B) which has been followed by the same reinforcer as was A, but which did not participate in creating the inhibitory power of X. If inhibition involves an association between X and either the reinforcer or the CR, then we might expect the inhibitory effect of X to transfer readily to a B, which evokes the same CR as a result of pairing with the same reinforcer. On the other hand, if X either acts upon the excitatory A with which it was trained or is specific to the entire excitatory association of A, then we would anticipate minimal transfer. Early findings by Pavlov and Konorski (1948) as well as recent ones by Marchant, Mis, and Moore (1972) and from our laboratory find substantial transfer of inhibition across excitatory CSs based on the same reinforcer. Furthermore, that transfer persists to B even if A first undergoes extinction of its excitation; that finding indicates that generalization of excitation from A to B does not mediate the transfer. It is also worth pointing out in passing that such transfer results belie accounts of summation tests in terms of the AX compound forming a special stimulus that the animal simply discriminates from A. Instead, X appears to retain a sufficient portion of its integrity in the AX compound to acquire an inhibition that it is capable of evoking in a wider range of settings.

Another transfer test is the converse: will the ability of X to interfere with the response to A persist even if the response to A is modified by its pairing with a new reinforcer? If the inhibitory association is between X and A such transfer should occur, whereas none of the other alternatives predict it. Here the evidence is less clear but favors the lack of transfer. Pavlov found transfer of the inhibitory power of X when A was originally paired with food but subsequently converted into a signal for acid; but Konorski (1967) severely criticizes that report. In my own laboratory I have recently used an $A+/AX-$ paradigm with a shock US to set up conditioned inhibition of fear. When A was then paired with food, X showed no ability to modulate the food-based excitation to A. Similarly, we have found no transfer of inhibition when the roles of food and shock are reversed. After $A+/AX-$ training with a food US, X inhibits the ability of A to produce increases in activity, but does not affect the ability of A to elicit fear when it is subsequently paired with shock. These results suggest that conditioned inhibition does not involve learning of an inhibitory association between A and X.

Finally, the standard assessment procedure based on retardation of acquisition constitutes a third relevant transfer paradigm. Here the issue is whether a pretreated X is slower than control stimuli in acquiring conditioned excitation. The successful use of this procedure in detecting inhibitors for stimuli given a variety of pretreatments (see Rescorla, 1969) seems most consistent with either the X–US or X–CR alternatives. It is not clear why learning either an inhibitory connection between X and A

or one between X and the excitatory association of A should interfere with forming excitatory connections to an independently presented X. Indeed, the very acceptance of the retardation procedure indicates a strong theoretical bias in favor of the former alternatives.

The previous paragraphs are intended more to illustrate how one might make empirically meaningful assessments of these alternatives than to select among the alternatives themselves. Although many situations seem to yield results consistent with the view that inhibitors involve an association of X with the US or with the CR, it seems possible that conditioning preparations will differ in this regard. With such a range of possibilities, nature may very well have solved the problem with different mechanisms in different places.

The historically popular alternative to the postulation of a separate inhibitory association has been to view conditioned inhibition as involving competition between associations of the same sort. Typically, this hypothesis has taken the particular form of a competing response notion, in which "inhibition" is envisioned as an excitatory association which evokes a response competitive with the one the experimenter terms "excitatory." More generally, one could consider the view that excitation and inhibition involve the same type of association among items, whether viewed as responses, neurological centers, or simply as internal representations, which are not simultaneously elicitable (see Konorski, 1967). This alternative appears to have the advantage of parsimony. We know that different reinforcers can establish behaviors which interfere with each other. Could one not view inhibition in that way with nonreinforcement and nonreinforcement as the two USs?

In the absence of more specific theories, it may seem gratuitous to distinguish between competing associations with the same item and similar associations among competing items. The distinction becomes particularly artificial when one examines historical attempts to specify the nature and origin of the competing item. Often, competing responses are of indefinite form and are specified only in terms of their ability to compete with the original response. They may even be described baldfacedly as the "not response." Similarly, if the language is that of US centers, one may find inhibition described as an excitatory association with the "no-US" center. Furthermore, in order to account for the differential effects of various occurrences of the "no-US" (see the above description of contextual effects), theorists sometimes have adopted views of that competing center which give it little role other than that of inhibiting the US.

Nevertheless, at least the most frequent version of this view, the competing response notion, does suggest some empirical issues. All of these issues center around the question of whether an inhibitor should be expected to have consequences in the absence of excitation or whether it should only function to attenuate excitation. The competing response position seems to anticipate independent action of an inhibitor parallel to that seen with excitors.

One empirical issue concerns the details of performance. Consider a competing response account of the $A+/AX-$ paradigm. According to that view, A evokes an excitatory response that fails to appear in the presence of X because X evokes a competing response. The strength of that competing response is assumed to be substantial enough to prevent display of the strong excitation by A. It then seems plausible to expect that X, if presented alone, would display that strong competing response. Yet, a problem which has continually plagued the study of inhibition is precisely that separately presented inhibitors have little observable consequence. It is that problem which necessitated the development of special summation and retardation procedures for the measurement of inhibition and which has led many to question the very existence of inhibition. Those who hold the special inhibitory-association notions described above, in which the action of an inhibitor is only to fight excitation, are not surprised by difficulties in measuring inhibition in the absence of an excitor. But if one takes seriously the claim for parsimony of the competing response position, that inhibition is only an example of excitation, but to another response, then why is that response so reluctant to occur separately? One could, of course, give those competing responses special properties, but that is to sacrifice the parsimony and blur the uniqueness of the position.

A second empirical issue centers around the rules describing the acquisition and elimination of inhibition and excitation. If the same kind of association is involved in both, it is reasonable to anticipate that the laws of their change could receive common description. To a large extent this expectation has won experimental support in recent years. For example, the Rescorla–Wagner model seems to provide a very good general description for the acquisition of both kinds of learning with only parameter values changing from one to the other. More empirically, many of the detailed features of the acquisition of excitation, such as blocking and overshadowing, seem to appear in the acquisition of inhibition. Furthermore, both inhibitory and excitatory stimuli seem to modulate the conditioning effects of reinforcers and nonreinforcers in parallel ways. In contrast, some recent evidence suggests lack of parallels in the extinction of these two processes. For instance, Zimmer-Hart and Rescorla (1974) found that repeated separate presentation of an inhibitor did not extinguish its power. This is of interest not only because it disputes the detail of the particular Rescorla–Wagner model (see Rescorla, 1974, for a discussion of this issue) but also because it suggests a lack of parallel with excitation. Although separate nonreinforced presentation is capable of establishing neither excitation nor inhibition, it apparently eliminates excitation, but leaves inhibition intact. Whether this finding can be incorporated into a competing response theory remains to be seen. However, if a stimulus controls a competing response, even if that response is unseen, one might expect its nonreinforced presentation to lead to extinction.

Finally, mention should be made of the power of an inhibitor or excitor to serve as a reinforcer. As noted above, a conditioned excitor is capable of establishing considerable higher-order conditioning to stimuli that precede it. If a conditioned inhibitor elicits a process like that of an excitor, then one might expect that it too could transfer its power to antecedent neutral stimuli. In contrast, if inhibitors are relatively ineffective when presented alone, they should not serve as reinforcers. In my laboratory, I have repeatedly produced substantial second-order conditioning of excitation but have only seen moderate evidence of second-order conditioning of inhibition. Although this may be simply a parametric difference in magnitude, there is also the possibility that a fundamental difference is at work.

These research strategies have not yielded a complete answer to the nature of conditioned inhibition. But the raising of the question of the parallel between excitation and inhibition has led to new and interesting data. Furthermore, it has centered attention on questions of the details of the nature of conditioned inhibition where considerably more exploration is needed.

C. A Comment on Extinction

This discussion of inhibitory conditioning is not complete without some consideration of extinction. Before the modern interest in stimuli which are explicitly trained to be purely inhibitory in character, most of the evidence emphasizing a role for inhibition in conditioning came from extinction experiments. A major interpretation of the decrement that ensued when a stimulus ceased to be reinforced was that some inhibitory process developed and overlaid the previously established excitatory conditioning. Extinction decrement was then viewed as the result of counterbalancing of inhibitory and excitatory processes.

However, direct tests of extinguished stimuli do not reveal them to be net inhibitors; therefore, evidence for an inhibitory interpretation must be sought elsewhere. The primary historical evidence for such a position came from experiments indicating an absence of independence of path in conditioning. A number of phenomena have indicated that the low level of responding produced by the sequence of training followed by extinction is not due to the same underlying processes as the low level of responding produced by failing to train. The key results are those of spontaneous recovery, disinhibition, and the very rapid reacquisition of an extinguished stimulus. Although experiments seldom have explicitly compared an extinguished stimulus with a neutral stimulus, it has been widely assumed that these phenomena distinguish between them. Since a major competitor to an inhibitory account of extinction has been that nonreinforcement removes the excitation established in acquisition, these phenomena have seemed to support the notion that extinction leaves excitation intact and superimposes inhibition.

Those results certainly do indicate that extinction does not simply restore a stimulus to its earlier state. But the logic which concludes that inhibition must therefore be involved is less than compelling. First, there are both associative and nonassociative alternative interpretations. For instance, despite some claims to the contrary, a simple competing response theory can do reasonably well in accounting for such data (see Estes, 1955). Furthermore, an animal that has been trained and extinguished has had many kinds of experience which differentiate it from a naive one; it has had exposure to the individual conditioning events to the situation, etc. In the absence of more analytic experiments it would be very difficult to attribute the observed differences to specific features of the learned associative relationships. So the attempt to demonstrate inhibition by default is not convincing.

Second, the argument in favor of inhibition from these features of extinction demands the attribution of special features to inhibition. Historically, thinkers have readily followed Pavlov in describing inhibition as fragile, fading in time, and generally less stable than excitation. Indeed, those properties seem to have been postulated precisely to deal with aspects of extinction such as disinhibition and spontaneous recovery. However, aside from extinction, we have little evidence that learned inhibition displays those properties. The evidence is rather that an explicitly trained pure inhibitor is as stable over time as is learned excitation.

Third, there is a flaw in thinking of which some have been guilty. Because they have been willing to conclude that inhibition is involved in extinction, some have seemingly concluded that it can account entirely for that decrement. The inference of an inhibitory process overlaying the excitation has sometimes been expanded to the further conclusion that therefore the excitation must remain *fully* intact after extinction. Of course this conclusion does not follow at all; indeed, we do not even have experiments that are properly designed to evaluate the extent to which the excitation might remain intact. All of the experiments have been directed toward showing that something is left rather than evaluating its extent. So even if extinction does involve inhibition, it may involve much more.

Perhaps the strongest argument for the participation of inhibition in extinction lies not with such historically important phenomena but rather in modern thinking about the nature of inhibition. It is clear that the extinction situation involves procedures related both logically and theoretically to those known to establish net inhibitors. When a previously trained stimulus, A, is nonreinforced, theories such as those discussed above anticipate decrements in net associative strength. One interpretation of those theories is that the decrement is a consequence of the building up of a special inhibitory process; but the fact that decrements cease when the net value of the stimulus approaches zero makes it impossible to reveal the underlying inhibition by simple examination of the net value of the stimulus.

Those theories do suggest, however, an analytic strategy which might reveal that inhibition. If a neutral stimulus X were added to A during its nonreinforcement, then X should acquire associative meaning similar to that acquired by A. But since X is uncomplicated by prior training, it should reveal more purely the nature of the change occurring during extinction. That is, these theories suggest that if following $A+$ training, we carry out $AX-$ extinction, then subsequent evaluation of X should reveal it to be an inhibitor. That outcome seems particularly plausible since this paradigm is identical to the $A+/AX-$ paradigm used to establish conditioned inhibition, with the exception that the A and AX trials are presented in sequence rather than intermixed. Furthermore, experiments by Kamin (1968) and others indicate that this difference is not crucial; even with sequential presentation, X becomes inhibitory. So, apparently, we must conclude that inhibition occurs during extinction if we are to account for the changes in X. But then it seems a small step to believe that the same process accounts in part for decrements in the strength of the simultaneously present A. Indeed, if this reasoning is accepted, one might use such an X as an evaluative tool to investigate in more pure form the associative changes taking place during extinction.

The point of these comments is that although historically the early arguments for inhibition came from extinction, those are perhaps not the strongest current arguments. Rather, while we have ample evidence for inhibitory processes, we remain less certain about their role in extinction. Instead, we may wish to use our knowledge about inhibition from more current sources to return to the investigation of extinction, for there are still available only a few theories of extinction and relatively few studies intended to elucidate the associative changes which take place in extinction. Our energies appear to have been diverted instead to the study of the intriguing partial reinforcement effect; but most accounts of that effect say little about associative changes.

IV. CONCLUSION

This chapter began with the proposition that Pavlovian conditioning might provide insights into the way in which organisms learn a broad range of relations among events. Two kinds of learning that have been prominent in theories of conditioning have been discussed. But there remains the question of how likely it is that one could construct the organism's representation of the world simply in terms of those two elementary relations being learned.

The preceding paragraphs were partly intended to indicate that on a gross level the use of those two elementary kinds of learning provides a fairly comprehensive description of the results of Pavlovian experiments. The learning of apparently complex interevent relations spanning long time intervals was described in terms of these two relations, both learned under conditions reducible to contiguity of events. However, a somewhat subtle change in the nature of the elements that entered into learned relations has crept into the analysis. The preservation of the role of contiguity and the primitiveness of the relations learned was accomplished at the cost of increased complexity of the events associated. Thus, the contiguity that emerged was not one between two unanalyzed events but rather one between a CS and a reinforcer that received rather thorough separate evaluation by the organism.

Inevitably, any extension of a set of such simple principles to more complex relations will force the introduction of complexity either into the relations learned or into the conceptualization of the events about which they are learned. In Pavlovian conditioning by far the most frequent theoretical route has been to permit complex description of events while preserving the simplicity of relations learned. The Rescorla–Wagner theory may be viewed as one example that permits complication of the reinforcer. But there are abundant parallel examples for the case of CS. For instance, recent years have shown a rejuvenation of interest in "configural" conditioning in which an organism emits one response to a simultaneously presented set of stimuli and another, incompatible, response to each of the stimuli when presented separately (e.g., Rescorla, 1972b). Most theoretical responses to such findings have eschewed the introduction of complex relations and instead have searched for ways of analyzing the stimulus events themselves in such a way as to permit explanation in terms of standard associations among elaborated events. Attempts to account for the molecular aspects of conditioning when temporal variations are made present a similar option. If a long time intervenes between the onset of a CS and the occurrence of the US, then over trials the CR often becomes confined to the later part of the CS–US interval. One account of this phenomenon of "inhibition of delay" would permit the organism a complex relational knowledge: but the account most frequently given instead conceptualizes the CS as divisible into temporally distinct stimuli, each of which controls some mixture of inhibition and excitation (for example, Wagner & Rescorla, 1972).

The success of these accounts, of course, encourages a theoretical route preserving a small set of relations among increasingly complicated events.

However, as we pointed out above, the kinds of data with which we have been faced have also been severely limited in scope. It seems almost inevitable that this field, which has so recently admitted the operation of a second, inhibitory relation, will eventually be forced to acknowledge the learning of yet more complex relations.

One final point should be made in closing. Throughout I have emphasized Pavlovian conditioning as a model for general learning of relations. This is only one of the important contributions which it can hope to make to psychology. This is a contribution to intellectual function. But Pavlovian conditioning makes an equally important contribution to emotional functioning. Although I have not discussed in any detail the paradigms currently in use for the study of conditioning, many concern themselves with the learning about emotionally significant stimuli, such as electric shock and food. The use of such procedures is not an accident. One of the important roles which Pavlovian conditioning plays is to govern much of the emotional and motivational life of the organism. It is this role that makes it of particular interest to the psychologist who would understand not only what the animal knows but what motivates him.

ACKNOWLEDGMENTS

The writing of this chapter was facilitated by grants from the National Science Foundation. The author has benefited greatly from discussions with Peter Holland and Donald Heth.

REFERENCES

Allport, G. W. *Personality: A psychological interpretation.* New York: Holt, Rinehart & Winston, 1937.

Asyratyan, E. A. Genesis and localization of conditioned inhibition. In R. A. Boakes & M. S. Halliday (Eds.), *Inhibition and learning.* New York: Academic Press, 1972.

Black, A. H., & Prokasy, W. F. (Eds.), *Classical conditioning II: Current Theory and research.* New York: Appleton-Century-Crofts, 1972.

Bush, R. R., & Mosteller, F. *Stochastic models for learning.* New York: Wiley, 1955.

Estes, W. K. Statistical theory of spontaneous recovery and repression. *Psychological Review,* 1955, **62,** 145–154.

Gleitman, H. Getting animals to understand the experimenter's instructions. *Animal Learning and Behavior,* 1974, **2,** 1–5.

Guthrie, E. R. Association by contiguity. In S. Koch (Ed.), *Psychology: A study of a science.* Vol. 2. New York: McGraw-Hill, 1959.

Holland, P. C., & Rescorla, R. A. Second-order conditioning with food unconditioned stimulus. *Journal of Comparative and Physiological Psychology,* 1975, **88,** 459–467.

Hull, C. L. *Principles of behavior.* New York: Appleton-Century-Crofts, 1943.

Jones, J. E. Contiguity and relation to CS–UCS intervals in classical aversive conditioning, *Psychological Review,* 1962, **69,** 176–186.

Kamin, L. J. Attention-like processes in classical conditioning. In Jones, M. R. (Ed.), *Miami symposium on the prediction of behavior: Aversive stimulation.* Miami, Florida: University of Miami Press, 1968.

Kamin, L. J. Predictability, surprise, attention, and conditioning. In R. M. Church & B. A. Campbell (Eds.), *Punishment and aversive behavior.* New York: Appleton-Century-Crofts, 1969.

Konorski, J. *Conditioned reflexes and neuron organization.* Cambridge, England: Cambridge University Press, 1948.

Konorski, J. *Integrative activity of the brain.* Chicago: University of Chicago Press, 1967.

Lubow, R. E. Latent inhibition. *Phychological Bulletin,* 1973, **79,** 398–407.

Marchant, H. G., Mis, S. W., & Moore, J. W. Conditioned inhibition of the rabbit's nictitating membrane response. *Journal of Experimental Psychology,* 1972, **95,** 408–411.

Pavlov, I. P. *Conditioned reflexes.* London and New York: Oxford University Press, 1927.

Rescorla, R. A. Pavlovian conditioning and its proper control procedures. *Psychological Review,* 1967, **74,** 71–80.

Rescorla, R. A. Probability of shock in the presence of CS in fear conditioning. *Journal of Comparative and Physiological Psychology,* 1968, **56,** 1–5.

Rescorla, R. A. Pavlovian conditioned inhibition. *Psychological Bulletin,* 1969, **72,** 77–94.

Rescorla, R. A. Information variables in Pavlovian conditioning. In G. Bower (Ed.), *The psychology of learning and motivation.* Vol. 6. New York: Academic Press, 1972. (a)

Rescorla, R. A. "Configural" conditioning in discrete-trial bar pressing. *Journal of Comparative and Physiological Psychology,* 1972, **79,** 307–317. (b)

Rescorla, R. A. Second-order conditioning: Implications for theories of learning. In F. J. McGuigan & D. B. Lumsden (Eds.), *Contemporary approaches to conditioning and learning.* Washington, D.C.: Winston, 1973.

Rescorla, R. A. A model of Pavlovian conditioning. In V. S. Rusinov (Ed.), *Mechanisms of formation and inhibition of conditional reflex.* Moscow: Academy of Sciences of the U.S.S.R., 1974.

Rescorla, R. A., & Holland, P. C. Some behavioral approaches to the study of learning. In M. R. Rosenzweig & E. L. Bennett (Eds.), *Neural mechanisms of learning and memory.* Cambridge, Massachusetts: MIT Press, 1975.

Rescorla, R. A., & Wagner, A. R. A theory of Pavlovian conditioning: variations in the effectiveness of reinforcement and nonreinforcement. In A. H. Black & W. A. Prokasy (Eds.), *Classical conditioning II: Current theory and research.* New York: Appleton-Century-Crofts, 1972.

Rozeboom, W. W. "What is learned?" An empirical enigma. *Psychological Review,* 1958, **65,** 22–33.

Solomon, R. L., & Turner, L. H. Discriminative classical conditioning in dogs paralyzed by curarei can later control discriminative avoidance responses in their normal state. *Pscychological Review,* 1962, **69,** 202–219.

Spence, K. W. *Behavior theory and conditioning.* New Haven, Connecticut: Yale University Press, 1956.

Thompson, R. F. Sensory preconditioning. In R. F. Thompson & J. F. Voss (Eds.), *Topics in learning and performance.* New York: Academic Press, 1972.

Tolman, E. C. *Purposive behavior in animals and men.* New York: Appleton-Century-Crofts, 1932.

Tolman, E. C., & Brunswik, E. The organism and the causal texture of the environment. *Psychological Review,* 1935, **42,** 43–47.

Wagner, A. R., & Rescorla, R. A. Inhibition in Pavlovian conditioning: Application of a theory. In R. A. Boakes & M. S. Halliday (Eds.), *Inhibition and learning.* New York: Academic Press, 1972.

Wagner, A. R., Thomas, E., & Norton, T. Conditioning with electrical stimulation of motor cortex: evidence of a possible source of motivation. *Journal of Comparative and Physiological Psychology,* 1967, **64,** 191–199.

White, C. T., & Schlosberg, H. Degree of conditioning of the GSR as a function of the period of delay. *Journal of Experimental Psychology,* 1952, **43,** 357–362.

Zimmer-Hart, C. L., & Rescorla, R. A. Extinction of Pavlovian conditioned inhibition. *Journal of Comparative and Physiological Psychology,* 1974, **86,** 837–845.

2

Learning as Adaptation

J. E. R. Staddon

Duke University

I. INTRODUCTION

There is still little agreement on the processes responsible for learning in man and animals. As these volumes show, work with people has tended to foster an active, information-processing view of learning, whereas research on instrumental and classical conditioning in animals is dominated by simpler theories. The usual view of classical conditioning is that it represents a cumulative process that moves progressively toward one or other asymptote of performance with each reinforcement or nonreinforcement (see Rescorla, Chapter 1 of this volume). There is less consensus about the processes responsible for instrumental (operant) conditioning.

Clark Hull's theories (1943, 1952) have for years provided the reference point. Hard nosed and physicalistic, this approach attempted exhaustively and mathematically to describe the changes wrought by reward, nonreward, and punishment on each link in the chain from physical stimulus through sensory receptor and central nervous system to motor response. Little survives of the specifics of Hull's proposals, but his intellectual descendants continue in the spirit of this approach. Equally hard nosed, but less specific, is the competing approach of B. F. Skinner (1938, 1961). With Hull, Skinner agrees that the processes of operant conditioning must be automatic and relatively simple, but his focus is on the immediate "stamping in" effect of reward (reinforcement).

The theoretical views of both men derive from the methods they used. Hull and his students typically looked at hungry rats learning to run down straight alleys or to solve simple mazes, for food reward (the *acquisition* of behavior). He measured the number of trials taken by groups of animals to learn these tasks under various conditions (or the proportion of animals reaching some criterion of performance, or the average latency of response in classical conditioning situations). Skinner, in contrast, was more interested in the steady-state pattern of behavior produced in individual animals (usually pigeons) by schedules of reinforcement, that is, with the *maintenance* of behavior rather than its acquisition. His theoretical views on the automatic, trial-by-trial action of reinforcement are derived from a very different situation, however: the "shaping" of behavior by rewarding successive approximations to the final form, in a manner familiar from circus training. Unfortunately, this interesting process has received little direct study, either from Skinner or others.

It is conventional to contrast with these two schools the cognitive approach of E. C. Tolman (for example, 1932), but in truth Tolman's impact depended more on his personal influence and ingenuity than on a body of theory or methodology. The influence of Hull and Skinner was closely tied to their methodology, to which is added the technology of the Skinner box and reinforcement schedules in Skinner's case. The Tolmanian cognitive, "information-processing" approach reappears from time to time in various guises (for example, Bolles, 1972, Chapter 7, Volume 1 of this *Handbook;* Shimp, Chapter 6 of this volume), and is undergoing a resurgence at present, but it lacks the coherence and historical continuity of the other two and is not yet as influential.

In this chapter I describe an approach to animal learning that is not in the direct line of descent from any of these, although it owes a substantial debt to Skinner's methods and ideas. Rather than being hypothetico-deductive (like Hull), or analytic (like Skinner), or cognitive (like Tolman), it begins with an analogy. Darwin (1859, 1875) showed that new species can be created by a process of selective retention of unpredictably generated variants. New adaptations result from the joint action of two opposed processes: *selection* and *variation*. More recently, several people have pointed out the many similarities between learning, either of the trial-and-error or "insight" varieties, and the process of evolution (for example, Campbell, 1960; Pringle, 1951; Russell, 1962; Skinner, 1969; Staddon & Simmelhag, 1971). Each of these theorists has applied the evolutionary analogy to learning in a different way, yet all agree that: (*a*) all adaptation, either of a species to its ecological niche or of an individual animal to a particular learning situation, involves transmission of information from environment to organism; and (*b*) that this transmission occurs via *selection* by the environment from among a pool of phenotypic or behavioral variants. In what follows I try to show how the concepts of selection, variation, and adaptation can be applied to behavioral data in a way that both integrates existing experimental results and suggests experimental tests.

II. THE CONCEPT OF REINFORCEMENT

Animals persist in behavior that is rewarded and give up punished behavior. This observation is the basis for the first empirical principle of learning, E. L. Thorndike's "Law of Effect" (1911):

> Of several responses made to the same situation, those which are accompanied or closely followed by satisfaction to the animal will, other things being equal, be more firmly connected with the situation ... those which are accompanied or closely followed by discomfort to the animal will, other things being equal, have their connections with that situation weakened [p. 244].

In modern terms a "satisfier" is a *reinforcer,* its opposite is a *punisher,* and collectively both classes may be termed *hedonic* (the opposite of neutral) stimuli. The presentation of such stimuli constitutes the operation of *reinforcement* (or *punishment*). Thorndike's idea that reinforcers must "accompany or closely follow" behavior to have an effect has turned out to be too restrictive. Reinforcers may be related to behavior in many ways, direct and indirect, reliable and intermittent. The study of these relations and their effects constitutes the topic of *schedules of reinforcement,* which is the main experimental focus of this chapter. The way in which behavior becomes "connected with the situation" is the topic of *stimulus control.* These two topics are closely related.

Most learning textbooks begin with definitions of *learning* and *reinforcement,* usually in connection with a discussion of the difference between operant (instrumental) and respondent (classical, Pavlovian) conditioning. However, the distinction between operant and respondent conditioning is not as clear as it once appeared (see Hearst, Chapter 5 of this volume); it is not obvious that a definition of learning is helpful in the absence of an understanding of the processes responsible; and the more precisely reinforcement is defined, the more problems the definition raises. So I begin descriptively, with some examples of the action of reinforcers.

Imagine a hungry, naive rat placed in a Skinner box that delivers a food pellet following each lever press. At first the animal may "freeze" in the novel environment. Later it will begin to explore—sniff and paw at salient objects, rear, look around, and so on. After a while, it may inadvertently press the lever and release a pellet. The noise of the mechanism may induce freezing once again, but after a while the rat will look around and find and eat the pellet. This, in turn, will probably be followed by further vigorous exploration until the lever is depressed again and a second pellet is delivered. This time the pellet will probably be eaten at once and the rat may immediately begin to press the lever again. Figure 1 is an example

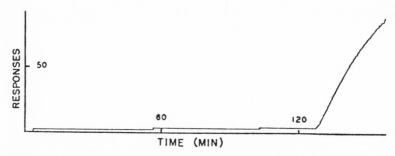

FIGURE 1. A cumulative record of level pressing by an experimentally naive, hungry rat. Each response on the lever was reinforced by the delivery of a food pellet. (From B. F. Skinner, *The behavior of organisms*, p. 67. © 1938 renewed 1965. Reprinted by permission of Prentice-Hall, Inc. Englewood Cliffs, New Jersey.)

of a cumulative record of lever pressing that illustrates this process of *acquisition:* the first few reinforcements produced no obvious effect on lever pressing, and when the animal "caught on," it did so apparently at once.

This example illustrates four characteristics of instrumental learning situations: (*a*) the animal's behavior in a new situation is at first variable; (*b*) the first reinforcement generally *increases* variability (there are some exceptions to this, to be discussed later);(*c*) if the task is simple, learning may be rapid; (*d*) the behavior that eventually predominates is the one on which the reinforcer is dependent (technically: *contingent*); by this time behavioral variability is much reduced.

Each of these four characteristics has a place in the following account. The initial variability of behavior provides a range of *behavioral phenotypes,* so called because these different overt performances may or may not correspond to different generating processes (behavioral *genotypes*). Skinner considered this initial repertoire of "spontaneous" behavior to be "emitted" in an unpredictable way by the animal. However, I argue later (Section IV) that there are rules describing the origin of at least some of it. The *reinforcement contingency* selects a certain class of behavior from this pool. The way in which this happens, and the proper way to describe the steady-state relation between the contingencies of reinforcement and the resulting behavior, is discussed in a moment. At a common-sense level, if a particular response is required for food (say), that response will tend to predominate; and if the response is only effective at a certain time (as on a fixed-interval (FI) schedule, for example),[1] the response will tend to occur more at that time than at other times.

[1] For a simple account of the procedures and nomenclature of reinforcement schedules, see Rachlin (1970) and Reynolds (1968). For the classical, but not very well organized account, see Ferster and Skinner (1957). Nevin (1973) and Zeiler (1976) provide more advanced treatments.

III. CONTINGENCIES OF REINFORCEMENT

Hedonic stimuli can be presented to an animal independently of its behavior (classical or Pavlovian conditioning procedures) or contingent on some aspect of behavior (instrumental or operant conditioning procedures). Neutral (*conditioned* or *discriminative*) stimuli may occur, signaling the presence or absence of reinforcers. There will always be certain kinds of regularity or predictability associated with the series of reinforcer presentations. Six common procedures, three Pavlovian and three operant, that illustrate these regularities are shown in Figure 2.

Temporal conditioning, also called a *fixed-time* schedule (FT) is the simplest procedure. The only regularity here is temporal: the occurrence of an unconditioned stimulus (US, for example, food) depends on time since a *time marker* (in this case, the preceding US presentation). This is a *temporal contingency*. The second panel shows the standard Pavlovian conditioning procedure, in which a stimulus (the *conditioned* or *conditional* stimulus, CS) signals the imminent occurrence of the US. The US reliably follows the CS; the CS therefore *predicts* the occurrence of the US. This is a *stimulus contingency*. The third panel, trace conditioning, illustrates both temporal and stimulus contingencies. The time marker is a "neutral"

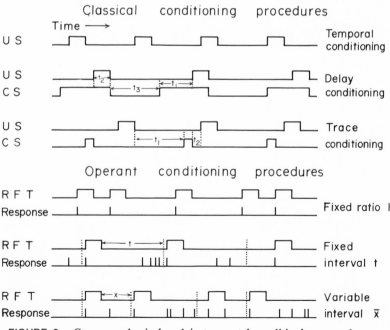

FIGURE 2.   Common classical and instrumental conditioning procedures.

stimulus (rather than the US), but the fixed temporal relation between the trace stimulus and the US is otherwise similar to temporal conditioning.

The trace-conditioning example shows that the "strength" and sign of a contingency depend critically on quantitative factors. In Figure 2, t_1 is much greater than t_2, so that the CS is a good predictor of US occurrence. If t_2 had been much greater than t_1, the CS would have been a much poorer predictor of the US, perhaps poor enough for the contingency to shift from positive to negative. The best predictor of US *non*occurrence, of course, is the US itself, so that the time just after the US is generally associated with a negative contingency on these procedures. In the delay-conditioning case, it is obvious that the degree to which the CS predicts the US depends on temporal factors: the shorter t_1 relative to t_3 (the *intertrial interval,* ITI), the more positive the contingency. As Rescorla has shown (see Chapter 1 of this volume), the strength of the contingency also depends on the relative frequency of cooccurrence of CS and US: the conditional probability of the US, given that the CS occurs, $p(US|CS)$, relative to the probability of the US in the absence of the CS, $p(US|\overline{CS})$.

There is no consensus as yet on how best to describe these temporal and stimulus contingencies in a formal way (see Gibbon, Berryman, & Thompson, 1974), largely because the best description is the one that relates most naturally to the behavior produced. When we know the laws of adaptive behavior, we will know how best to describe contingencies. A qualitative summary, the *relative proximity principle,* is given later (Section IV.A) when I consider the effects of contingencies on behavior.

The bottom three panels of Figure 2 show common operant conditioning procedures. The first is fixed ratio 1 (FR 1, sometimes called continuous reinforcement, CRF). Here the occurrence of a response is the best predictor of the occurrence of a reinforcer; this is a *response contingency.* If responses occur in other than a random fashion, there may also be a temporal contingency, as in the next example: the fixed-interval (FI) schedule. Here there are both response and temporal contingencies, since responding generally occurs at a high enough rate that reinforcers are delivered quite soon after they become available (the "reinforcer available" time is indicated by the dashed lines in the figure: the first response after the line produces the reinforcer)—and thus occur at more or less fixed time intervals. On typical fixed intervals of 1 or 2 min, pigeons may peck a key scores of times; in practice, therefore, reinforcer delivery is much better predicted by time than by the occurrence of a response. The bottom panel shows the variable-interval (VI) schedule, which is similar to fixed interval, except that the minimum interreinforcer interval, x, is variable (with mean $\bar{x}$), rather than fixed. If the actual (that is, *obtained*) distribution of reinforcers in time is random, then there may be no temporal contingency in the strict sense, since the occurrence of a reinforcer does not depend on time. However, the overall *rate* (reinforcers/time) of reinforcement[2] may enter into stimulus contingencies. For example, on a *multiple* variable-interval variable-interval schedule, two stimuli, each associated with a different VI, alternate. The overall rate of reinforcement in one stimulus relative to the other defines the stimulus contingency. Such contingencies have strong effects on behavior (see the discussion of *behavioral contrast,* Section V.C.1).

IV. THE EFFECT OF REINFORCEMENT CONTINGENCIES

Contingencies of reinforcement bear the same relation to the behavior of an individual animal that an ecological niche bears to the biota in a habitat. A niche has no real existence unless a species fills it, and a contingency can hardly be said to exist if no aspect of behavior is sensitive to it. In this section I discuss the effects of some simple contingencies on behavior. This leads to a discussion of interactions among contingencies in operant conditioning situations, and to the statement of four summary principles that are used later to explain a range of experimental results. The section ends with an analysis of the acquisition of operant behavior.

Figure 3 shows the temporal pattern of behavior induced in a hungry pigeon by prolonged exposure to periodic food presentation (temporal conditioning). In panel (a) is shown the relative frequency with which the indicated behaviors occurred in each of the 12 sec between successive food presentations. Another way of looking at this behavior is shown in panel (b). Its data are taken from a series of studies by Killeen (1975) with a similar procedure; the figure shows the pigeon's rate of locomotion (general activity) as a function of postfood time. The inverted-U shaped functions are typical of results with temporal conditioning procedures. The steepness of the function depends on absolute reinforcement rate, how hungry[3] the pigeon is, and perhaps on other factors that affect the stimulus contingency associated with the situation as a whole (for example, the rate of reinforcement in the situation relative to the rate of reinforcement at other times, when the animal is not in the Skinner box): the hungrier the pigeon, or the more frequent the food, the steeper is the function. At short (less than 20 sec) interfood intervals, pigeons, in particular, show vigorous

---

[2] The term *reinforcement* is used throughout in the sense of "hedonic stimulus occurrence," not in the strict Skinnerian sense of "presentation of a reinforcer contingent on a response." Thus, the term can be used to refer to both classical (Pavlovian) and instrumental procedures. Similarly, the terms *conditioned stimulus* and *discriminative stimulus* are used interchangeably to refer to any "neutral" stimulus that has a signal function.

[3] As measured, for example, by hours of food deprivation, or body weight.

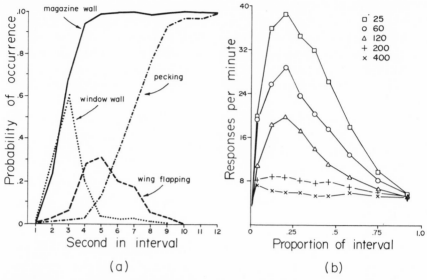

FIGURE 3.   (a) The relative frequency of various behaviors induced in a hungry
pigeon by food delivery every 12 sec. (From Staddon & Simmelhag, 1971, p. 8.)
(b) The rate at which a hungry pigeon activated six floor panels as a function of
time since food delivery, for five different interfood intervals from 25 to 400 sec.
(Adapted from Killeen, 1975, Fig. 1.)

and strikingly stereotyped induced behaviors. These were first observed
by Skinner (1948) and termed "superstitious" behavior. I return to
Skinner's analysis later (Section IV.C).

The pattern of behavior is sensitive to, or "controlled by," the temporal
contingency in the sense that the temporal pattern is adapted to the interfood interval. If the interval is lengthened, for example, the peak of the
function moves to the right, and the onset of the *terminal response* (the
activity that increases in rate until food delivery—"pecking" in Figure 3;
see Staddon & Simmelhag, 1971) is delayed, so that it continues to occupy
an almost fixed proportion of the interval duration (Killeen, 1975;
Schneider, 1969).

The U-shaped functions on the right in Figure 3 show the pigeon's rate
of change of location (locomotion) as a function of postfood time. This
measure does not correspond to the vigor of behavior, since observational
data, such as those in Figure 3a, show that if anything the most vigorous
activities tend to occur at the beginning or the end of the interfood interval.
Both the terminal response and common interim activities (those that occur
early in the interval) tend to be vigorous and stereotyped. At short interval
durations, for example (20 sec or less), pigeons tend to show pecking as
a terminal response; attack, in pigeons, or excessive drinking, in rats, are
typical interim activities. All these are stereotyped "consummatory" or

"unconditioned" responses (see Staddon, 1976, for a review). A better interpretation is that the U-shaped functions in Figure 3 are an indication of behavioral *variability*. This inference is supported by the observational data, which show that more different activities can occur at a given point in the middle of the interval than at points at either end.

The temporal contingency on a fixed-time schedule is strongly positive toward the end of the interval (long postfood times predict food), strongly negative at the beginning of the interval (short postfood times predict no food) and neutral in the middle. These and other observations suggest the following RANGE OF VARIATION HYPOTHESIS:

> *The range of behavioral variation is inversely related to the "strength" of a contingency, without regard to its sign.*

This hypothesis implies that at times, or in the presence of stimuli, that strongly signal either the presence or the absence of a reinforcer, the range of activities (repertoire) of the animal will tend to be restricted.

The common observation that the variability of behavior decreases with training suggests that the range of behavioral variation is also inversely related to time spent under a fixed set of contingencies. The relative importance of practice versus contingency strength is not precisely known. However, it is probable that contingency strength sets a limit on the restriction of variability, and practice allows behavior to approach this asymptote more or less closely.

There are often limitations on the type, as well as the range, of behavior that occurs under strong contingencies. For example, Brown and Jenkins (1968) trained hungry pigeons on a variant of the delayed conditioning procedure shown in Figure 2. At variable intervals averaging 1 min in length, in the presence of a dark response key, the birds were presented with a brief (8-sec) stimulus on the key, ending with food delivery. Naive pigeons reliably pecked the key within 50–100 trials on this "autoshaping" procedure. The form of the key peck is related to the type of reinforcer presented, food or water; and the pecking in this situation behaves in many ways like salivation in Pavlov's dogs (see Schwartz & Gamzu, 1976, for a review of autoshaping and related effects). The strong positive contingency associated with the 8-sec CS suggests that behavior during that time will be stereotyped. The range of variation hypothesis does not require that *pecking* (rather than some other stereotyped activity) occur, however. This restriction on the type, as well as the range, of behavior reflects constraints peculiar to pigeons. I return to this topic later (see Section IV.D.2).

The restriction implied by the range of variation hypothesis might be entirely caused by restriction of the type of behavior. For example, Pavlov

(1927) proposed a "stimulus substitution" hypothesis to account for the similarity of conditioned and unconditioned responses; a more general "object substitution" view has been proposed recently to account for auto-shaping data: animals treat as food stimuli that strongly predict food (Jenkins & Moore, 1973). The restriction on variation is probably the more fundamental effect, however. There is some evidence that particular behaviors induced by procedures like delayed and temporal conditioning can be modified (for example, Hursh, Navarick, & Fantino, 1974), and the type of behavior induced by these situations often depends critically on "supporting" environmental stimuli (for example, Bindra, 1972; Morse & Kelleher, 1970). However, restriction of variation under strong contingencies seems to be universal.

A. Contingency Strength

As mentioned earlier, there is no generally agreed upon measure of the strength of a reinforcement contingency. Relative frequency of reinforcement, information (in the communication theory sense) and probability measures of various sorts have all been proposed (Bloomfield, 1972; Herrnstein, 1970; Rescorla, 1967). All these are *relative* measures. It is convenient to summarize this aspect of the matter in the form of the following RELATIVE PROXIMITY PRINCIPLE (Staddon, 1972):

> *The strength of a contingency is determined by relative*
> *proximity to reinforcement (temporal contingencies)*
> *and relative frequency of reinforcement (stimulus*
> *contingencies).*

This means, for example, that the strength of a temporal contingency at some point depends not just on time until the next reinforcement, but on that time relative to the maximum possible time. On a fixed-interval schedule, that is the time between reinforcements; in general, it is the time between the time marker and reinforcement. Similarly, the strength of a contingency in the presence of a stimulus depends not just on the rate of reinforcement associated with it, but also on the rate of reinforcement associated with other stimuli, especially those in the same situation or those to which the animal has been exposed in the recent past. The relative duration of stimuli also has an effect. For example, in the delay-conditioning situation, the tendency for pigeons to peck the CS is inversely related to its duration (t_1 in Figure 2), and directly related to the duration of the intertrial interval (t_3).

This kind of relativity is common in adaptive systems. The strength of phenotypic selection, natural or artificial, depends on the relative reproductive successes of different genotypes, not their absolute reproductive rates. In visual perception, the apparent lightness of a surface depends on the amount of light it reflects relative to the light reflected by other surfaces. Edwin Land's retinex model of color perception has properties very similar to those of the contingency measures discussed here (Land & McCann, 1971). In this model, perceived color is predicted from a three-coordinate system in which each coordinate depends on the rank-order brightness of the object, as viewed through one of three colored filters. In a similar way, the strength of the contingency associated with a given stimulus may be predicted from its *rank-order reinforcement rate,* relative to other stimuli in the situation. Stimuli high in the ordering are strongly positive, those low in the ordering are strongly negative, and those in the middle are relatively neutral.

B.   Induced Behavior and Stimulus Control

1.   Positive and Negative Stimulus Contingencies

Strongly positive contingencies induce stereotyped behavior (the terminal response) that is closely related to the reinforcer. For example, pigeons peck a CS that signals food, raccoons "wash," and pigs root, a token that can be exchanged for food (see Staddon & Simmelhag, 1971; Schwartz & Gamzu, 1976, for reviews and other examples). Strong negative contingencies induce *interim* activities that are also often stereotyped, and related to motivational systems antagonistic to that associated with the terminal reinforcer. For example, hungry rats on a periodic food schedule drink copious quantities of water just after each food delivery or indeed in the presence of almost any stimulus that signals the absence of food; food schedules induce aggressive behavior in pigeons in a similar way (see Staddon, 1976, for a review); and strong interim and terminal behaviors are induced by schedules of periodic electric shock (Hutchinson, Renfrew, & Young, 1971).

Induced behaviors come under the control of stimuli involved in reinforcement contingencies: pecking that occurred initially because the CS predicted food, soon comes under the control of the CS and continues to occur (for a while), even in extinction, when the CS no longer predicts food.

2.   Generalization Decrement

Control of behavior by a stimulus can be demonstrated in two ways: by omitting the stimulus and observing that the behavior does not occur, or by varying the properties of the stimulus (its color, intensity, etc.) and seeing a change in the strength of the behavior, for example, a drop in the rate of pecking (see Rudy & Wagner, Chapter 7, and Heinemann & Chase, Chapter 8, of this volume). The latter effect can be formalized as the empirical PRINCIPLE OF GENERALIZATION DECREMENT:

> *When the properties of a stimulus are varied, the*
> *dominant behavior that occurred in the presence of the*
> *stimulus is likely to decrease in strength relative to*
> *other behaviors.*

This means that behavior that occurs at a high rate in the presence of a given stimulus is likely to decrease in strength when the stimulus is varied (excitatory stimulus control), but because behaviors in schedule situations are usually reciprocally inhibitory (Staddon, 1976), behavior that occurs at a low rate is likely to increase (inhibitory stimulus control). The decrease in the first case is generally sharper than the increase in the second, because the dominant behavior is the main one to lose strength by generalization decrement, but compensation for this decrease is shared among several subdominant behaviors, each of which must therefore increase in strength by a smaller amount. Consequently, inhibitory (incremental) generalization gradients are usually shallower than excitatory (decremental) ones (Heinemann & Chase, Chapter 8). If stimulus variation increases the total range of behavior (which seems to occur often), this difference between excitatory and inhibitory gradients is likely to be further exaggerated.

A study by Catania, Silverman, and Stubbs (1974) illustrates these effects. Hungry pigeons obtained food for pecking each of two concurrently available keys. The schedule on each key was a variable interval of 1 min. The stimulus on one key was three vertical lines; on the other key, it was a color. After some discrimination training to assure that the birds attended to line orientation, the orientation of the lines was varied in a generalization test. The colored key remained lit. In the test, the birds pecked more slowly on line stimuli differing in orientation from the training stimulus, but at the same time pecked more rapidly on the concurrently available colored key: the gradient was excitatory, for pecks on the line key, but inhibitory, and shallower, for pecks on the other, colored, key. Pecking the colored key is clearly a subdominant behavior when the pigeon is attending to the line key. Its increase in strength concomitant with a decrease in the strength of pecking on the line key is therefore a good illustration of the generalization decrement principle.

It is possible to distinguish two types of stimulus control simply on a procedural basis—although it is unlikely that completely separate mechanisms are involved. *Temporal control* refers to control of behavior by an antecedent event, for example, the CS in a trace conditioning procedure, or reinforcement in temporal conditioning. *Synchronous control* refers to control of a behavior by a stimulus that is simultaneously present. Temporal control is the usual result of a temporal contingency, a synchronous control of a stimulus contingency.

Later in Section V.E I discuss important differences between temporal and synchronous control. First, however, it is necessary to deal with the detection of response contingencies and the interaction among stimulus, temporal and response contingencies during the acquisition of operant behavior.

C. Response Contingencies and the Problem of "Superstitious" Behavior

1. Detection of Contingencies

To detect a response contingency the animal must first make the response, and then vary its properties—force, distribution in time, etc.—so as to separate real from accidental contingencies. Again the process has a perceptual analogy. Many three-dimensional objects are compatible with a given two-dimensional retinal image. Animals are able to identify the correct object by varying the image, by head movement and by having two eyes, so as to separate real correlations from those that are an accidental consequence of a fixed viewpoint.

As a behavioral example, suppose that animals typically engage in a more or less fixed sequence of activities in the few seconds after eating. Such an animal, if exposed to a short fixed-time food schedule would fill the time between food deliveries with a reliable sequence of behaviors: (food) *A, B, C, D,* (food), etc. This stereotyped pattern establishes an accidental correlation between behavior *D* and the delivery of food. Given that response contingencies act to select behavior, this might tend to "fix" behavior *D* in this situation just as if the behavior were necessary to the production of food. Indeed, this is the line of argument adopted by Skinner (1948) in a classic paper describing the behavior of pigeons exposed to fixed-time schedules. His argument was even stronger, since he assumed that temporal contiguity was the necessary and sufficient condition for a response to be strengthened by reinforcement. This makes perfect stereotypy unnecessary, since one or two pairings of a behavior with reinforcement are assumed to be sufficient to "fix" it in the situation.

It is obvious that the kind of reinforcement mechanism proposed by Skinner must often lead to maladaptive behavior. If a response can be fixed after only one or two pairings with reinforcement, animals will often "jump to conclusions" and acquire unnecessary or inefficient behaviors. Yet so-called "superstitious" behaviors are actually quite rare. More commonly, the instrumental response drifts in the direction of the most economical form. This cannot be due to some general "law of least effort," because strong stimulus and temporal contingencies by themselves are sufficient to induce vigorous activity: animals behave even when their behavior cannot affect the delivery of reinforcers. Since there are obvious benefits to rapid learning, and it can often be demonstrated, it is clear that means must exist for reconciling the need for quick learning with the dangers of settling too soon on a response.

2. Response-Reinforcer Correlation and Behavior Variation

Animals have several protections against Skinner's "adventitious" reinforcement:

1. Pairing of a response with a reinforcement does not have an invariable "stamping in" effect; animals are sensitive to indirect and partial correlations between their behavior and its consequences (Baum, 1973). For example, on interval and ratio schedules, reinforcement never occurs without being preceded by an instrumental response. If occasional response-independent (free) reinforcers are delivered, a response is no longer as good a predictor of reinforcement: the response contingency is weakened. Animals often show that they are sensitive to this change by responding more *slowly* when free reinforcements are added, even though the added reinforcements strengthen the stimulus contingency (Rachlin & Baum, 1972). Exactly how the change is detected is not known. The problem can be looked at from the point of view of the time period over which response-reinforcer relations have an effect (for example, are one or two pairings sufficient, or are pairings and nonpairings averaged over some time period?) or in terms of the reversibility of effects. A single response-reinforcer pairing may have little effect, or the "strengthening" effects of pairing may be partially undone by the occurrence of a reinforcement not preceded by a response. In most situations animals are sensitive not just to moment-by-moment pairings and nonpairings, but rather to the overall relative proximity of responses to reinforcement.

2. In novel situations, or following a change, animals typically show variable behavior. This means that the kind of regularity postulated in the fixed-time schedule example is rarely found. As in the perceptual analogy, this variability serves an indispensable adaptive function: it allows the animal to separate real contingencies from those that are accidental consequences of behavioral stereotypy. If the behavior of the animal on first exposure to a schedule is variable from interval to interval, and food is delivered independently of behavior, then there will be no correlation between any particular behavior and the delivery of food. Eventually, some stereotyped pattern of behavior will develop, owing to the effect of stimulus

and temporal contingencies in limiting behavioral variation. But the type of behavior will not be the result of an accidental "stamping in" process, but of the animal's past history, the strength of the contingencies, and biological considerations related to type of reinforcer. I discuss later (Section V.G) the severely maladaptive effects of procedures that minimize the variable response to change.

3. Novelty-Induced Change

Variable behavior in a novel situation often appears "exploratory" or "curious," and applied to higher primates and some other animals this kind of empathic description may not seriously mislead. However, the pattern is so reliable, and sometimes appears so irrational, that this label may give the wrong impression. Pavlov (1927) wrote of the "orienting reflex," a general response to novelty which suppresses any conditioned response that might otherwise occur. In the instrumental-learning literature the "generalization decrement" that affects the dominant response when stimulus conditions are changed is a related effect. Observation of unrestrained animals shows that these effects are usually associated with the induction of incompatible "competing" activities, such as looking about, sniffing, manipulating and walking around.

This general "exploratory pattern" may be elicited repeatedly by changes that are important to the animal, even in a highly familiar situation. For example, Kello (1973) studied the behavior of rats running to a food reward in a bare straight alley. He found that essentially the same exploratory pattern occurred during initial acquisition, following a decrease in reward size, and after the introduction of a novel stimulus—even though the latter changes occurred after many trials in the apparatus. This apparently irrational behavior makes sense, given the vital function of behavioral variability in protecting the animal against "superstition."

The nature of the direct effect of the response contingency on response acquisition is problematic. For the reasons already discussed, a direct "stamping in" effect (connecting the response to situational cues) is unlikely. Yet, as Figure 1 illustrates, response-contingent reinforcement often appears to have immediate guiding effects. This is even more compelling in the process of "shaping" behavior by reinforcing successive approximations to the final form. At issue, therefore, is the permanence of the effect, and its strength relative to other factors such as stimulus control due to past training, and inducing factors due to stimulus and temporal contingencies.

4. Linkage Hypothesis

Once behavior in a situation has stabilized, it is often difficult to demonstrate much effect of response contingencies. Behavior becomes increasingly "ballistic" and controlled in reflexive fashion by external stimuli, rather than guided by immediate consequences. Many authors, from William James on, have provided illustrations of the "blindness of habit." Other examples, such as the persistance of behavior when reinforcements are maintained in the absence of a response contingency (for example, Uhl, 1974), and the persistence of induced behavior in the face of negative response contingencies, suggest that the direct effects of a response contingency may be transient and relatively weak, especially when stimulus factors (either inducing, or due to past training) are strong.

A reasonable hypothesis is that response contingencies affect behavior mainly indirectly, through their effect on stimulus and temporal contingencies, and that their direct effect, if any, is limited to the guiding of behavior over the short term (over periods of less than 1 min, for example).:

> The "fixing" of behavior in a situation, that is, the development of stimulus control, may depend on two other factors: (a) practice: i.e., how long the animal has made the response in the situation, and (b) the strength of stimulus and temporal contingencies: the stronger the contingencies, the more rapidly a response will be fixed.

This will be termed the LINKAGE HYPOTHESIS.

D. Acquisition of Operant Behavior

1. Autoshaping and the Action of Stimulus Contingencies

The autoshaping situation is a convenient one for illustrating the application of these principles to the acquisition of operant behavior. The procedure is similar to delay conditioning, with the additional provision that an instrumental response (for example, a key peck) in the presence of the CS (a lighted key) immediately produces food; if no response occurs, food is delivered at the end of the CS. On first exposure to this procedure, pigeons typically show quite variable behavior, but after a few trials the stimulus contingency begins to constrain behavior. If the CS is localized on the response key, the birds begin to look at and move toward it when it comes on, spending more and more time in front of the stimulus. During the intertrial interval, however, they are likely to move away from the key and walk about. Within a few trials, most pigeons peck the lighted key; thereafter they are likely to peck the CS as soon as it occurs.

The development of this behavior is illustrated in Figure 4. The circles on the left represent the set of behaviors induced by the situation (CS). The circles are large at first, indicating the initial variability of behavior;

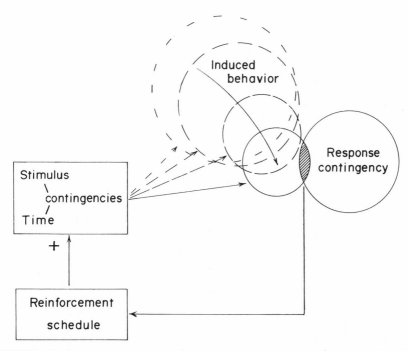

FIGURE 4. Interactions among stimulus, temporal, and response contingencies during operant conditioning.

they decrease in size with exposure to the situation, indicating the effect of stimulus and temporal reinforcement contingencies in restricting the variability of behavior. The types, as well as the range, of behavior also change under the influence of stimulus and temporal contingencies. This is illustrated by the progressive displacement of the circles representing induced behavior. Eventually, "pecking the key" is one of the induced behaviors, and this response is one that falls in the shaded area where the two lower circles intersect, that is, it is a response that enters into the response contingency defined by the reinforcement schedule. Key pecking is a response that affects the delivery of food. The response contingency has two kinds of effect: (a) it may strengthen (or at least, not weaken) the tendency to make responses in the shaded area and, more important (b) it strengthens the stimulus contingency because the duration of the CS is reduced if food is produced by a key peck; this is indicated by the "plus" arrow connecting the two boxes. These two effects act jointly to move the set of induced behaviors until it lies almost completely within the set of effective behaviors. The response contingency weakens ineffective behaviors, and the stimulus contingency restricts the range of behavior that occurs in the presence of the CS. Eventually, most of the behavior in the

CS is instrumental in procuring food; the pigeon appears to behave efficiently and "rationally."

The inducing process is symmetrical. At the same time that "terminal" responses are induced in the CS, antagonistic "interim" behaviors appear in the intertrial interval, the stimulus associated with a negative contingency (Rachlin, 1973; Staddon & Simmelhag, 1971). The stronger the positive and negative contingencies, the more restricted is the range of induced behaviors in each stimulus, and the less is the overlap between them.

The set of induced behaviors depicted in Figure 4 may be termed a "state" or "mood." It corresponds to a set of internal changes, a behavioral genotype, that is closely related to the observed behavior (the behavioral phenotype), but not identical to it. For example, a tone may induce a state in a rat because it has in the past predicted food delivery contingent on pressing a lever, but if the lever is absent the animal cannot make the response. Yet it would be absurd to imagine that the tone on this occasion had no effect, or an effect greatly different from the one it had when the lever was present. In many cases the distinction between behavioral phenotypes and genotypes can be ignored; however, there are instances (for example, "learned helplessness," see Section V.G.3) in which it is important.

2. The Omission Procedure

In this example, the response contingency was positive: it strengthened both the instrumental response and the stimulus contingency associated with it. A negative response contingency provides a more interesting illustration of the operation of these processes, however, and shows that the apparent efficiency of the pigeons' adaptation to the autoshaping situation is the result of a fortuitous conjunction between the requirements of the response contingency and pigeons' tendency to peck at stimuli that signal food.

The autoshaping procedure is easily modified so that a response to the CS, rather than producing food, turns off the stimulus and prevents food delivery on that trial (negative automaintenance or *omission training:* Williams & Williams, 1969). Nevertheless, pigeons come to peck the key on as many as 50% of trials. This outcome can be understood as a compromise between two antagonistic effects. The CS contingency tends to induce directed pecking. However, because the link between response and reinforcement is negative (rather than positive, as in Figure 4), pecks here impair the stimulus contingency by preventing food delivery on some trials. This allows the variability of behavior to increase (the set of behaviors moves in a direction opposite to the arrow in Figure 4). Thus, fewer key pecks occur, the stimulus contingency increases in strength, more pecks begin to occur, and so on. The result is a compromise in which key pecks

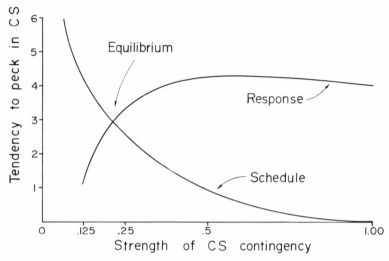

FIGURE 5. Curves illustrating the dependence of pecking on the CS contingency (response function), and the dependence of the CS contingency on pecking (schedule function) for the omission training procedure. The response function is a smooth curve drawn through data from Gonzalez (1974, bird 406). The units of the ordinate are key pecks per second, of the abscissa, $p(US|CS)$. The schedule function is an estimate.

occur on a certain fraction of trials. In this situation restriction of the range of variation, together with the restriction of behavioral type labeled *sign tracking* by Hearst and Jenkins (see Hearst, Chapter 5 of this volume), leads the pigeon to behave in an inefficient and apparently irrational way.

3. Response and Schedule Functions

This process is illustrated in Figure 5 in a way familiar from the supply and demand curves of economics. The plot shows two functions:

1. The strength of induced pecking (measured as, for example, rate of pecking in the CS) as a function of the strength of the CS contingency (which depends on both the duration of the CS and the probability of food in its presence). This relation, the *response function,* reflects a property of the pigeon: how its tendency to peck is affected by the strength of a stimulus contingency.

2. The strength of the contingency as a function of the pigeon's tendency to peck in the CS. This relation, the *schedule function,* reflects the properties of the reinforcement schedule, which here prevents food delivery if the animal pecks in the CS.[4]

[4] The empirically derived response and schedule functions described here are closely related to Baum's (1973) concepts of *O rules* (input–output properties of the organism) and *E rules* (input–output properties of the environment).

The point where these two curves cross represents an equilibrium in which the strength of the contingency sustains a rate of pecking that produces the same contingency strength.

The exact form of the schedule function in Figure 5 is not known because it depends on the distribution of responses in time as well as on the overall rate of responding. Indeed, the figure is simplified in another way because contingency strength depends on both CS duration and $p(US|CS)$. A more realistic representation would show the tendency of the animal to peck as a function of both of these variables, that is, as a surface. Equilibrium would then be represented by points on the line defined by the intersection of this "response surface" with the corresponding "schedule surface" defining the relation between responding and the time and probability variables.[5]

4. Is There a Direct Effect of Response Contingency?

The model illustrated in Figure 5 assumes that stimulus contingencies alone account for the equilibrium tendency to peck. It emphasizes stimulus and temporal contingencies partly because of their neglect in previous accounts (for example, Skinner, 1948), but also because in the case of autoshaping (and of many other operant conditioning effects) the evidence appears to justify it. The persistence of pecking in the omission training procedure strongly argues against much direct effect of the response contingency on the maintenance of key pecking, and a response contingency obviously cannot affect the origin of a response. However, the constraint that leads pigeons to peck during omission training is not absolute. For example, Hursh et al. (1974) were able to eliminate pecking by most birds by making CS offset contingent on a brief period of not pecking: the stimulus remained on until at least 2 sec elapsed without a response. They interpreted this result as showing the reinforcing effect of stimulus offset, that is, as owing to a response contingency with respect to a new reinforcer (see Herrnstein & Loveland, 1972). However, their procedure also resulted in a worsening of the stimulus–food contingency, because of a lengthening of the CS. Since Schwartz (1972) has obtained substantial pecking of the CS under a modified omission training procedure in which pecks do not turn off the CS, it is likely that the worsening of the CS contingency, rather than elimination of "stimulus-offset reinforcement," is the reason for the elimination of CS pecking reported by Hursh and his colleagues. This conclusion is supported by a yoked-control experiment recently reported by Myerson, Myerson, and Parker (1974).

[5] This approach can be further extended to n-dimensional representations, so as to include cases in which the US can occur at times other than during the CS, $p(US)|CS) \neq 0$, as well as comparable measures of response contingency.

The negative response contingency may have some effect apart from its effect on stimulus contingencies. In their original experiment Williams and Williams (1969) showed that pigeons prefer to peck a CS not associated with the negative response contingency to pecking one that is, even if the stimulus contingencies are the same. Furthermore, Schwartz and Williams (1972), using a within-animals yoked procedure, showed that pigeons are more likely to peck, and prefer, a stimulus not associated with a negative response contingency to one that is, even when both stimuli are associated with identical stimulus contingencies. Moreover, when stimulus and temporal contingencies are weak (on long variable-interval schedules, for example), pigeons will not learn to peck in the absence of a strong response contingency. Even when stimulus and temporal contingencies are strong, responses such as lever pressing by rats usually will not be maintained in the absence of a response contingency.

These results are usually interpreted as direct effects of a response contingency. However, they are also consistent with the linkage hypothesis—the idea that differences in response contingencies in two stimuli lead to rate differences that are fixed by the stimulus (and temporal) contingencies prevailing. Moreover, if, in the Williams and Williams two-key situation, the pigeon attends to one or the other of the two keys, but not to both, on most trials, then the *perceived* stimulus contingency associated with the neutral key is better than that associated with the omission-training key. This difference might also tend to concentrate pecking on the key where it has no negative consequences. Whatever the mechanism, the final behavior depends on both stimulus and response contingencies, and the contribution of each depends on their relative strength, the type of behavior, and the species of animal in ways that are still imperfectly worked out (Schwartz & Gamzu, 1976; Seligman & Hager, 1972; Shettleworth, 1972; Staddon & Simmelhag, 1971).

5. Initial Repertoire and Principles of Variation

The way in which a reinforcement schedule affects behavior depends, sometimes critically, on the animal's initial repertoire of behavior (the location and size of the large circle in the representation of Figure 4). For example, pigeons pretrained to peck for food somewhere other than on the response key (for example, to one side of the key) are likely to be much more resistant to the effects of the omission training procedure than naive pigeons. The stimulus contingency is likely to induce off-key pecking that does not enter into the negative response contingency, leaving the inducing factors unaffected. What factors determine this initial repertoire?

The most important factor is *transfer*. To the extent that the new situation is similar to something in the past experience of the animal, similar behavior may occur. To the extent that it is different, other behavior (the exploratory pattern referred to earlier) will tend to occur. "Similarity" is, of course, not an absolute, but depends on the animal's constitution and past experience in complicated ways (see Rudy & Wagner, Chapter 7; Heinemann & Chase, Chapter 8). Hedonic stimuli play an important role in defining "similarity." I return to this later (see Sections V.F and G).

Several past experiences may combine to affect behavior in a new situation. Some of the rules of combination are studied under the heading of *memory,* for example, those describing how experiences prior or subsequent to a given experience may interfere with its effect on later behavior (proactive and retroactive interference). More constructive kinds of "subjective organization" (Tulving & Donaldson, 1972) of past experience are possible. For example, past experiences may combine productively rather than interfering, as in "insight" experiments. Köhler (1925), in a classic account, describes how a chimpanzee "saw" how to fit together two sticks to pull in a banana that was out of reach. Later work has shown that this "insight" depends on past experience with sticks and bananas and that the insight consists in ordering these elements in a new way. This is an instance of what might be termed *compositional transfer.* The rich combinatorial flexibility of human language provides daily examples of this kind of transfer.

I have referred elsewhere to the rules that describe the origin of behavior as *principles of behavioral variation* (Staddon & Simmelhag, 1971). It is important to emphasize that although these principles are most clearly evident on the animal's first exposure to a new situation (thereafter, attention tends to focus on reinforcement contingencies as determiners of behavior), they continue to operate afterward—a "new" situation may appear more familiar as the animal gains experience with it, for example. These principles represent the *rules of operation* of the behaving organism, and thus they underly not only its behavior in new situations, but all of its behavior, including adaptations to contingencies of reinforcement (Staddon, 1973). Nevertheless, even though the effects of contingencies are indirect, it is often convenient to treat them directly, without worrying about "underlying mechanisms." However, we have already seen examples of how the effects of contingencies depend on species, particular responses, and past history, and so the dependency of "control" of behavior by reinforcement schedules on the adaptive mechanisms of the animal can never be entirely neglected.

6. Summary

In this section on the effect of reinforcement contingencies, I have dealt with explanations at two levels:

1. A molar or "teleonomic" level[6] concerned with the nature of the equilibrium relation between contingencies and behavior, that is, the steady-state relation between behavior and stimulus, temporal, and response contingencies once behavior has adapted to a reinforcement schedule. The range of variation hypothesis and the relative proximity principle are accounts at this molar level.

2. At the level of the mechanisms (functional, not necessarily physiological) that allow the molar principles to work—presumably the relative proximity principle, for example, depends on processes that measure times, compute rates, and allow comparisons in the same way that, for example, Boyle's Law depends on molecular kinetics.

Much less is known here and the present account is certainly incomplete and perhaps mistaken in some respects. The principle of generalization decrement, the linkage hypothesis, and the brief discussion of memory and compositional transfer are attempts at this level of explanation. Some of these hypotheses are less widely accepted than others. The range of variation hypothesis and the linkage hypothesis, in particular, are novel proposals, and the form in which the generalization decrement hypothesis has been expressed is also novel, although less controversial than the other two. The justification for these propositions is that they seem to be the minimum necessary for a coherent and comprehensive account of the by now substantial body of data describing the effects of hedonic stimuli on behavior. The applications of this scheme to some key phenomena are illustrated in the next section.

V. APPLICATIONS TO REINFORCEMENT SCHEDULE EFFECTS

A. Interval and Ratio Schedules

1. Fixed-Interval Schedules

Figure 6a is an illustration of some cumulative records of stable performances on a number of fixed-interval food reinforcement schedules. The records differ in their details, but common to all is the pattern of a pause

---

[6] *Teleonomic* is a useful word, coined by G. C. Simpson, to refer to the kind of functional argument common in discussions of adaptation, in which some characteristic is explained by its outcome: the form of the weaver-bird nest by its rain-proof qualities, the speed of the gazelle by its lion-proof qualities, and so on. Explanations like this are not teleological because they can in principle be reduced to causal explanations by reference to evolutionary mechanisms. Equilibrium principles such as the matching law have a similar status: they explain behavior by referring to some outcome, but tacitly assume that in principle a causal analysis is possible, even though the details are not clear as yet.

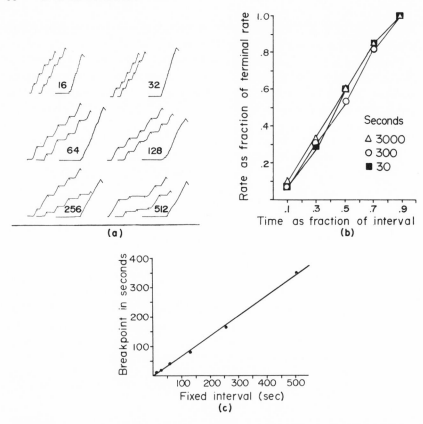

FIGURE 6.   (a) Cumulative response records of typical food-reinforced fixed-interval performances by a pigeon. The duration of the fixed interval, in seconds, is given by each set of records, and one interval is presented on a larger scale. Diagonal blips indicate food delivery. (From Schneider, 1969, p. 679). (b) Response rate as a function of proportion of the fixed interval, for three different interval values: Rates in each segment are plotted as a fraction of rate in the last segment. (Adapted from Dews, 1970, p. 48.) (c) Breakpoint as a function of fixed-interval duration (average of six pigeons) (Adapted from Schneider, 1969, p. 683. Copyright 1969 by the Society for the Experimental Analysis of Behavior, Inc.)

in the instrumental response after food, followed by responding at an accelerating rate until the next food delivery. In Figure 6b and c are fixed-interval performances averaged over several intervals. Figure 6b gives response rate in successive fifths of the interval as a fraction of the rate in the last fifth, for several different interval durations. Figure 6c gives the postfood time of the "break point" (the point in the interval at which rate changes sharply, a measure closely related to pause) as a function of interval duration. These data show that the pattern of responding is very similar at all interval values. Not everyone agrees in finding such perfect independence of absolute interval duration (for example, Catania & Reynolds,

1968), but all find that postfood pause is approximately proportional to interval duration over a considerable range.

Data from fixed-interval schedules show that when reinforcement is response contingent, the rate of the instrumental response depends on relative proximity to the next reinforcement opportunity. A more complicated example (Catania & Reynolds, 1968) is shown in Figure 7. The curves show the effect on the pattern of responding of providing an occasional extra

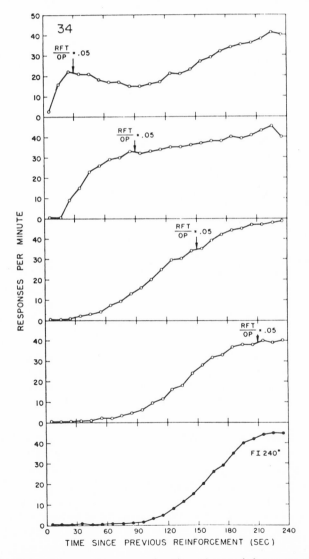

FIGURE 7. Rate of key pecking as a function of postreinforcement time on five interval schedules. (From Catania & Reynolds, 1968, p. 360. Copyright 1968 by the Society for the Experimental Analysis of Behavior, Inc.)

opportunity for reinforcement at different times after food on a fixed-interval 240-sec schedule (mixed fixed interval x, fixed interval 240 sec). The point in the interval when the pigeon could sometimes receive food is shown by an arrow. Even though the food opportunity marked by the arrow paid off in only one interval in 20, it produced a substantial change in behavior. This is most obvious in the top panel, where the animal shows a spurt in the rate of pecking in the vicinity of the 30-sec postfood reinforcement opportunity. The rate declines afterward and then increases as the time for the 240-sec reinforcement approaches.

These temporal patterns are all examples of temporal control of behavior. The time marker here is food delivery, and the main causes of the differences in pattern between a simple fixed interval and the mixed schedule are differences in temporal contingency. Although variation in the details of performance from animal to animal, and from one exposure to another, make quantitative modeling of the schedule–behavior relation difficult, the sensitivity of behavior to the distribution of reinforcement opportunities in time is obvious.

Interval schedules entail a second kind of temporal contingency. Because reinforcement opportunity depends on time, a reinforcement is more likely to follow a long wait between responses (a long *interresponse time*, IRT) than a short one. Ratio schedules lack this contingency; because reinforcement depends only on response number, it is independent of time since the preceding response (except for indirect contingencies resulting from regularities in the animal's temporal distribution of responses). Ratio and interval schedules also differ in the form of the feedback relation between overall response and reinforcement rates.

2. Ratio Schedules

This feedback relation (schedule function) is positive on ratio schedules: the faster (or slower) the animal responds, the more (or less) frequently it receives reinforcement. However, on interval schedules, providing the animal's initial response rate is high relative to the maximum reinforcement rate allowed by the schedule (which is usually the case), further increases in response rate have a negligible effect on the rate of reinforcement, that is, there is essentially no feedback. If response rate falls to a very low value, however, the probability that a given response will be followed by reinforcement increases; when responses are very infrequent, response and reinforcement rates are positively related (positive feedback).

Although animals generally respond at a high rate on ratio schedules (as long as they respond at all), their rate is usually stable. Hence, factors must exist that limit the effect of the positive feedback schedule function. These must be reflected in the form of the response function, that is, the

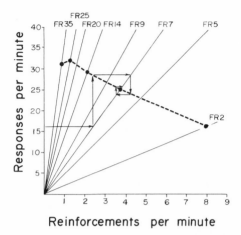

Reinforcements per minute

FIGURE 8. Fixed-ratio schedule functions, and the response function for steady-state responding by rats on various fixed-ratio schedules. (Data adapted from Boren, 1953.)

relation between reinforcement and response rates owing to the animal. Figure 8 shows data from Boren (1953) on the rate of lever pressing by rats as a function of fixed-ratio size. The data have been replotted to derive the response function, which is shown as the dashed curve. The key to stable behavior on these schedules is the form of this function, which shows an *inverse* (rather than a direct) relation between response and reinforcement rates over most of its range. Only at very low reinforcement rates does the function show signs of tipping over into a direct relation—and at the high ratio values associated with these rates, responding may show ratio "strain" (long pauses) or even cease altogether.

The stabilizing property of the function shown in Figure 8 is illustrated by the lines with arrows around the fixed ratio 7 schedule function. The lines show the direction of change of behavior given a starting response rate less than the equilibrium value. A response rate that is too low produces a rate of reinforcement that can sustain a higher response rate, and so response rate increases. This increased response rate may produce a reinforcement rate insufficient to maintain it, so that rate decreases again (but by a smaller amount). As this process is repeated, response rate gets closer and closer to the equilibrium value. A similar convergence occurs if the initial response rate is too high.

Over much of its range, the ratio response function is approximately linear with negative slope. This turns out to be true for several species and response-reinforcer combinations. The general form of the relation is $r + k\rho = C$, where r is the amount (measured in any linear unit) of the required response and ρ is the amount of the reinforcer in an

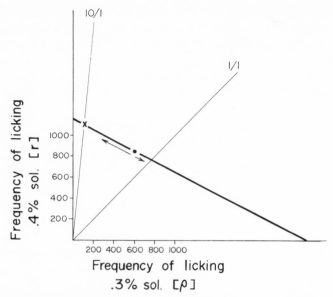

Frequency of licking
.3% sol. [ρ]

FIGURE 9. Conservation model. Illustrated by data from an experiment in which licking .3% saccharine solution was contingent on licking .4% saccharine solution (Data from Allison & Timberlake, 1974.)

experimental session of fixed duration. The term k is a weighting constant specific to the situation, and C represents the total weighted amount of r and ρ when opportunities for each (for example, both lever pressing and eating, in the situations just discussed) are freely available. Allison (1974) has termed this relation the *conservation model* and used it to explain a range of data. The model is especially useful for predicting the outcome in situations where the reinforcement is an opportunity to engage in an activity such as running that might actually be less frequent, under free conditions, than the activity (for example, licking) on which it is contingent. This is illustrated in Figure 9 for the two activities, licking .4% saccharine solution (r) and licking .3% saccharine solution (ρ) by rats. The filled circle shows the amounts of these two activities when both are freely available. The cross shows the equilibrium when licking .3% saccharine solution is made contingent on licking a .4% solution, according to a fixed-ratio 10 schedule. The diagonal line with negative slope is the inferred form of the response function (conservation relation) in this experiment. The 10/1 fixed-ratio contingency leads to an increase in the frequency of the contingent response (upward arrow). However, it is easy to see that on a fixed ratio 1 schedule, the conservation model would predict a decrease in the contingent response. [It is, of course, necessary for this result that the animal be required to engage in the amount of activity ρ made available by activity r (see Dunham, 1976; Terhune & Premack, 1974, for a discussion of this problem).] This schedule was not imposed in this particular experiment, but comparable predictions are supported by other data cited by Allison.

This general approach to understanding the effect of making access to one activity contingent on the performance of another is obviously not restricted to the linear response function prescribed by the conservation model. Once the form of the response function is known, the effect of any ratio contingency on the rates of the two activities is given. Although the linear assumption appears to have some generality, it is not universally true; indeed a linear relation between r and ρ is to be expected when there is no *selective* effect of ρ on r, although the converse is not true.

There are no data on fixed-ratio responding in pigeons directly comparable to Boren's (1953) rat data. Brandauer (1958) has reported data on random ratio schedules with pigeons that show a response function very different from that in Figure 8. However, there is some reason to doubt the stability of his data, and unfortunately there are no comparable rat data.

3. Variable-Interval Schedules

The response function for interval schedules is very different from that for fixed-ratio schedules. An example from variable-interval experiments with pigeons pecking for food reinforcement is given in Figure 10. The response function increases monotonically and is negatively accelerated, with large changes in reinforcement rate producing little change in response

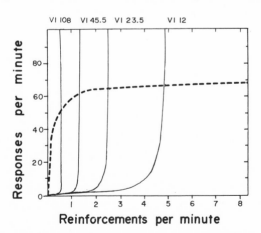

FIGURE 10. Schedule and response functions for variable-interval schedules. (Pigeon data from Catania & Reynolds, 1968, fit by Herrnstein's model, 1970, p. 255, bird 279; schedule functions are redrawn from Baum, 1973.)

rate over much of the range. The schedule function involves a proportional relation between response and reinforcement rates when response rate is very low, and essentially no relation when response rate is high relative to the maximum scheduled reinforcement rate. This arrangement is highly stable, since the two sets of curves intersect even at very low reinforcement rates. There is always a nonzero equilibrium, and responding does not extinguish.

Despite these response function differences, there are several similarities between performance on interval and ratio schedules. Behavior on both fixed-interval and fixed-ratio schedules shows a pause followed by responding, and for both the duration of the pause is determined by the minimum obtained interreinforcement interval (for example, Killeen, 1969). (However, the fixed-ratio pattern tends more toward "break and run" than the smooth "scallop" characteristic of at least long fixed-interval schedules.) Variable-interval and variable-ratio schedules with similar distributions of interreinforcement intervals show similar patterns of responding, for example, a fairly steady rate if the distribution of reinforcements is random. Thus, temporal contingencies exert similar effects on both interval and ratio schedules.

This analysis would have been more satisfying if it had revealed the same response function underlying both interval and ratio schedules. Unfortunately, data that would permit a point-by-point comparison, in the same species under similar conditions, are lacking: the best ratio data are from rats, and the best interval data are from pigeons. The largest discrepancy between the two functions seems to be at low to moderate reinforcement rates, in the region of .5 to 3 reinforcements per minute.

B. Spaced-Responding Schedules

1. Response and Schedule Functions

On spaced-responding (or differential reinforcement of low rate, DRL) schedules, the animal is required to wait t sec between successive responses for the second response to be reinforced. If the interresponse time is too short, the response just restarts the waiting time. When the required pause time, t, is relatively short (less than about 60 sec for rats, or 30 sec for pigeons) animals adapt quite well to this procedure and most interresponse times are close to the required value. At longer t values, however, performance is not as good: response rate is higher than the required rate, the interresponse-time distribution becomes more "random," and reinforcement rate in consequence is considerably lower than the maximum possible. Most animals on this schedule show some tendency to respond in "bursts,"

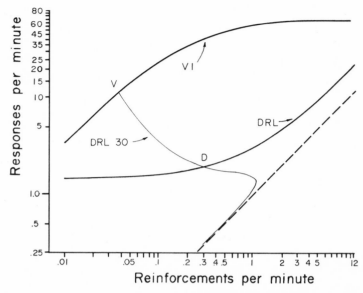

Reinforcements per minute

FIGURE 11. Response function for spaced-responding (DRL) schedules, and estimated schedule function for DRL 30 sec. The variable-interval response function is derived from that shown in Figure 10 (see Footnote 7).

that is, groups of closely spaced responses. In pigeons this tendency decreases with practice and is more pronounced at long t values (Catania, 1970; Staddon, 1965).

These characteristics are shown in a quantitative way in Figure 11. The dashed line on the right of the figure is the locus of equal response and reinforcement rates, and "perfect" responding at a given t value is defined by the intersection of this line with the vertical line through the abscissa point $1/t$. The curve labeled DRL 30 is an estimate of the schedule function for DRL 30 sec. This curve is approximate, because its exact form depends on the form of the interresponse time distribution. These details do not affect the general properties of the DRL schedule function, which are as follows: (a) the rate of response which yields the highest reinforcement rate is close to, but slightly less than, $1/t$; (b) this maximum reinforcement rate is slightly lower than the maximum possible $(1/t)$; (c) reinforcement rate falls off at response rates either above or below the optimum; and (d) as response rate decreases below the optimum, reinforcement rate approaches response rate.

In Figure 11, the DRL response function (labeled DRL) is almost proportional $(p = kr,$ 45° slope in these log–log coordinates) at high reinforcement rates (short t values), but flattens out at longer t values.[7] This suggests a dependence of DRL performance on absolute time that is greater than on other temporal schedules: on fixed intervals, for example, postreinforcement pause is proportional to interval duration over a wide range (see Figure 6).

2. Response and Species Constraints

Spaced responding schedules require animals to respond more slowly than their "natural" rate. Figure 11 makes this intuitive statement more precise and also suggests a possible explanation for the poor performance of pigeons and other animals at long t values. The figure shows the response function for variable-interval schedules (extrapolated from the data shown in Figure 10; see Footnote 7), plotted in the same coordinates as the DRL response function. Variable-interval and DRL schedules are similar in many respects: the distribution of reinforcements in time is irregular in both, the response contingency is the same for both, and for both reinforcement becomes more likely as time goes by without a response. Yet as the comparison in Figure 11 shows, their response functions are very different: Over most of the range, response rate on variable interval is much higher than on DRL.

Figure 11 shows that the variable-interval and DRL response functions deviate most strikingly in the middle range of reinforcement rates, from about .4 to 1 per minute. Pigeons average about one reinforcement per

---

[7] No published study gives this response function directly. However, the data of Staddon (1965) show that at t values less than about 25 sec, stable responding by pigeons on DRL schedules is approximated by the equation, $P = 1/t + C$, where P is response rate and C may be quite small. The same study also showed that the relation between reinforcement rate and t over the same range is approximately $R = (k_1/t) - k_2$, where k_1 and k_2 are constants. These relations simplify to $P = (R/k_1) + (k_2/k_1)$. The DRL response function in Figure 11 is this relation with $k_1 = .60$ and $k_2 = .87$ (estimated from Staddon, 1965, bird 420). Richardson and Loughead (1974) have studied DRL schedules with t values from 1 to 45 min. They propose a relation of the form 1 $P = kt^n$, where n is close to unity and k ranges from .18 to .27. However, it is not possible to obtain a simple estimate of the relation between P and R from their data. The variable-interval response function shown in Figure 11 is also not obtainable (for the whole range of R) directly from published data. It is derived from Herrnstein's model: $P = kR/(R + R_0)$, with $k = .69$ and $R_0 = .192$ (parameters fitted to variable-interval data for bird 279 and corrected for the present units of response rate, see Herrnstein, 1970, Figure 1). These curves are plotted in log–log coordinates both to accommodate the large range of reinforcement rates, and because it seems reasonable to compare response rates in terms of proportionate, rather than absolute, changes. It is in some sense easier for an animal to shift its response rate from 60 to 50 per minute as compared to shifting from 20 to 10; it seems more reasonable to assume that a change from 20 to 10 is comparable to a change from 60 to 30, and on a logarithmic scale these two are equal. The proper scaling of response measures is still a matter of contention, however, and the present assumption is provisional.

minute at t values of 20-25 seconds; and these are at the limit of t values for which they show good temporal discrimination (most interresponse times in the vicinity of t). Thus, the DRL performance of pigeons begins to break down at t values corresponding to the maximum separation between variable-interval and DRL response functions. Even though the response function may not be an invariant property, DRL and variable-interval schedules are so similar that wide deviations from the unconstrained (variable-interval) form may be difficult to maintain, and this may account for the difficulty pigeons encounter in adjusting optimally to this range of DRL values. Moreover, as the value of t increases beyond 22 sec or so, and performance begins to deteriorate, reinforcement rate drops so that opportunities for the animal to learn about the interresponse-time contingency (the only thing which differentiates the schedule from the variable interval) necessarily become less and less frequent. The schedule must therefore more and more appear to resemble a variable-interval schedule. This may account for the frequent observation that at t values greater than 22 sec or so, performance often deviates markedly from the smooth response function shown in the figure. Instead of settling down at an equilibrium on the DRL response function (for example, point D), a new equilibrium may be established close to the point at which the DRL schedule function and the variable interval response function intersect (for example, point V). At this point the interresponse-time distributions shows little evidence of temporal discrimination (an interresponse-time peak close to t), and performance is more like that typical of variable-interval schedules.

This account is consistent with the observations of "burst" responding, and with its dependence on t value: bursts of closely spaced responses allow the animal to approximate its natural (variable-interval) rate with minimal effect on reinforcement rate. Provision of a second, ineffective response key for "overflow" response has a similar effect and also aids DRL performance (Schwartz & Williams, 1971).

This analysis suggests that DRL performance should show more than usual dependence on factors such as type and amount of reinforcer, type of response, and species. For example, although complete parametric data are not available, it is clear that pigeons press a treadle for food much more slowly than they peck a key. Hence, the discrepancy between the variable-interval response function and optimal DRL performance should be much less for this response than for pecking, and performance should therefore be better (in terms of rate of reinforcement), especially at long t values. This seems to be the case, provided that the birds do not peck at the treadle (Hemmes, 1970). Rats also press levers for food more slowly than pigeons peck keys for food; hence, it is not surprising that their DRL performance is better (see Richardson & Loughead, 1974). The DRL performance is also better with smaller amounts of food reinforcement (Beer

& Trumble, 1965). All these species and response differences affect performance over a rather modest range, however. There seem to be no data showing that any animal can readily develop optimal DRL performance with t values on the order of minutes rather than seconds. This constraint may reflect limitations imposed by memory mechanisms, as is discussed later (see Section V.E).

C. Classical/Instrumental Interactions and Behavioral Contrast

1. Behavioral Contrast

Behavior on reinforcement schedules is the joint product of response, stimulus, and temporal contingencies. Stimulus and temporal contingencies particularly, shift continuously as the behavior of the animal interacts with the schedule requirement. The end result, stable schedule performance, is therefore the product of a complex dynamic history. Since strong stimulus and temporal contingencies have powerful effects on both the type and range of behavior, it would be surprising if the final performance always conformed to the intuitive optimum. Animals sometimes behave in ways that are apparently maladaptive, or variable from species to species or individual to individual. Autoshaping and negative automaintenance provide one kind of example of the often overriding effect of stimulus contingencies. The phenomena to be discussed in this section are another.

In 1961 Reynolds showed that pigeons pecking for food on a variable-interval schedule would peck faster if the schedule were alternated with periods of extinction signalled by a separate stimulus (positive behavioral contrast). Conversely, pecking slowed if the schedule was alternated with one providing more frequent food (negative contrast). Contrast effects can be analyzed in terms of a general contingency principle such as the *matching law* (a quantitative version of the relative proximity principle, see de Villiers, 1976; Shimp, Chapter 6 of this volume), or in more molecular terms. Herrnstein, Davison, Shimp, and others have pursued the former approach; Rachlin (1973) has explored the latter (see also Schwartz & Gamzu, 1976; Staddon, 1972).

The operations that produce large positive and negative contrast effects are changes in the stimulus contingency associated with the fixed component: shifts in the rate of reinforcement associated with the variable component affect the relative reinforcement rate associated with the fixed component. By the range of variation hypothesis, an increase in the strength of a stimulus contingency should lead to an increase in behavioral stereotypy. The effect on the instrumental response thus depends on whether this increase in stereotypy is also associated with a change in the type of behavior. There are two possibilities:

2. Compatibility of Induced and Instrumental Behavior

1. The induced behavior is compatible with the instrumental response. Strong position contingencies often induce rather specific terminal responses: pigeons peck a CS light that signals food, as in autoshaping, for example. Moreover, the CS need not be a signal for invariable food. A stimulus in the presence of which the pigeon receives food intermittently (variable-time schedule) will induce pecking, provided that it is alternated with an extinction stimulus (Schwartz & Gamzu, 1976). If the instrumental response is sufficiently similar to that which would be induced by the stimulus contingencies alone, then an increase in the strength of those contingencies leads to facilitation of the instrumental response (positive contrast). Conversely, suppression (negative contrast) is likely if the stimulus contingency is worsened. This interpretation accounts easily for contrast effects with pigeons pecking for food.

2. The induced response is incompatible with the instrumental response. An unlocalized-tone CS is less effective in inducing pecking by pigeons than a CS such as a lighted key. Induced pecking is generally directed at the CS, so that even a visual CS will not facilitate the instrumental response unless it appears on the response key. Strong positive-stimulus contingencies usually do not induce lever pressing by rats or treadle pressing by pigeons. Thus, contrast effects are unlikely with tone stimuli, stimuli off the instrumental key, or a treadle-press response in pigeons, or with lever pressing by rats. The data generally confirm this analysis. In these cases, a response rate change in the same, rather than the opposite, direction in both fixed and variable components is usually observed.[8] This is what would be expected if the behavior induced by an increase in the stimulus contingency interferes with the instrumental response.

Few experiments with multiple schedules have measured induced behavior. One exception is an experiment by Jacquet (1972), who studied the behavior of rats on multiple variable-interval schedules of food reinforcement. She found that, if reinforcement rate in one component was reduced, the lever-press rate in the other component sometimes decreased, but the rate of induced water licking increased or remained constant. At short absolute interval durations (high food rates), when lever pressing

---

[8] Skinner's term *induction* is sometimes used for this effect, but this usage has nothing to do with the concept of "induced behavior" used in this chapter.

and induced drinking together may take up almost all of the available time (see Staddon, 1976), the greater sensitivity of licking to relative (food) reinforcement rate means that, instead of contrast, induction (in Skinner's sense) might be observed in terms of lever pressing, along with contrast in terms of licking. In rats, therefore, there is some direct evidence that the behavior induced by strong positive food contingencies can interfere with lever pressing.

3.   Effect of a Positive Conditioned Stimulus
Superimposed on an Instrumental Base Line

This kind of analysis can also be applied to procedures in which a CS is superimposed on responding maintained by response-contingent food. The base-line schedule is usually variable-interval (or sometimes DRL) and typically a relatively large quantity of food (for example, 5 food pellets versus the normal 1, 10-sec access to food versus the normal 4) is delivered at the end of each CS presentation. The critical variables are the strength of the stimulus contingency (the relative reinforcement rate in the CS, and its duration relative to the non-CS period), type of instrumental response, and the species of animal. If the stimulus contingency is strong, the effect on the instrumental response depends on whether the behavior induced is compatible or incompatible with it.

Thus, pecking for food generally is facilitated by a superimposed CS, provided that the CS is located on the response key. Pecking may not be facilitated by a tone CS, however, and lever pressing is generally depressed in both rats and squirrel monkeys, especially at short CS durations (see LoLordo, McMillan, & Riley, 1974; Schwartz & Gamzu, 1976; Staddon, 1972, for reviews).

There are some exceptions to this simple picture. Some people find contrast effects in lever-pressing situations with rats (Pear & Wilkie, 1971); others report contrast in pigeons with auditory stimuli not localized on the response key (Westbrook, 1973). At long (>30-sec) CS durations, lever pressing by rats and squirrel monkeys may be facilitated. Such apparent exceptions do not necessarily invalidate this general analysis, but they do point to the difficulty in predicting the type of behavior induced by a CS. The range of variation hypothesis suggests that prediction should be easier when the CS contingency is strong (which usually means a short CS). This seems to be true, since expectations based on the induction of reinforcer-related terminal responses in the CS are generally borne out. At long CS durations, however, the range of possible induced behaviors may or may not include the instrumental response.

There are data to show that the type of base-line schedule may be important. For example, Kelly (1973) has shown that a CS facilitates lever pressing by monkeys on a DRL base line, but suppresses responding on a nose key maintained by a random-ratio schedule; Smith (1974) has shown facilitation of high and low base-line key peck rates by a 5-sec CS, but suppression of high rates by long CSs. Animals with an extensive history of responding for food on a lever, say, may be more inclined to show facilitation in a food-signal CS than animals with less training with that response. Some of these effects may be related to the "linkage" effects discussed later (see Section V.D). Full understanding of these complex situations awaits more parametric data and detailed analysis of particular cases.

All of these effects involve base-line responding maintained by positive (usually food) reinforcement and a food CS. A similar, and historically prior, set of procedures involves negative reinforcement (for example, avoidance of electric shock on a shock-postponement schedule; see Sidman, 1966) and a CS signaling response-independent shock. A similar analysis (with similar gaps in the available data) appears to hold for such negatively reinforced behavior (see Blackman, 1976, for a review). Combinations of the two (for example, a food base line and a shock CS, an avoidance base line and a food CS) have also been extensively explored. Detailed consideration of these negative and mixed procedures is omitted here for reasons of space (but see Rescorla, Chapter 1, and Hearst, Chapter 5, of this volume).

D. "Linkage" and "Superstition" Effects

1. "Sensory Superstition"

Some years ago Morse and Skinner (1957) showed that if a stimulus is presented infrequently to a pigeon responding for food on a variable-interval schedule, the animal pecks faster (or slower) after a while in the presence of the occasional stimulus. They called this a "sensory superstition" and explained it as a sort of sampling error. Even though the base-line schedule is in effect all the time, on first exposure to the occasional stimulus reinforcement rate in the stimulus is bound to be either higher or lower than the overall rate. This local difference, in turn, produces either an increase or a decrease in rate of responding. If response rate decreases, some reinforcements available in the stimulus will not be collected, further depressing the rate, and conversely, if rate in the occasional stimulus increases. This interpretation suggests that the magnitude of the effect should depend on the duration of the added stimulus, relative to the interstimulus period and to the mean interreinforcement interval on the variable interval. It should also be possible to relate the direction of change in response rate to the local rate of reinforcement in the first one or two stimulus presentations. Unfortunately, Morse and Skinner (1957) presented no detailed data of this sort to back up their ingenious account.

Subsequently, other experiments have shown similar effects. For example, Kieffer (1965) and Lander (1968) both have shown reliable and persistent rate differences in alternating stimuli associated with the same reinforcement schedule. However, in both cases the two components were of equal duration, and in the Lander experiment no reinforcement was delivered in either. These results cannot easily be given a sampling error interpretation.

In all these cases animals respond initially at different rates in the presence of two stimuli, and these differences persist although the stimuli are associated with the same conditions of reinforcement. The direction of the rate differences is idiosyncratic, and they are probably *metastable,* that is, they persist as long as conditions remain the same, but are not recoverable following a change. Such effects usually disappear when conditions are repeated, as in the common *ABAB* comparison. The effects are of interest not because they contaminate within-animal comparisons, but for the light they shed on general conditioning principles. What causes the initial rate difference, and why does it persist?

Morse and Skinner show cumulative records for two pigeons. The one with the higher base-line response rate shows a depressed rate in the added stimulus; the one with the lower rate shows an enhanced rate in the added stimulus. These two results suggest a simple generalization decrement explanation for the initial effect of the added stimulus (see Section IV.B): If the base-line response rate is high, a novel stimulus will depress response rate; if the base-line response rate is low, responding will be enhanced. This interpretation may not be general, since Morse and Skinner (1957) report changes in the direction of the difference in response rates over time. A generalization decrement interpretation also cannot be applied easily to the two other experiments mentioned, in which the animals were exposed to the two stimuli from the outset. Although there is no reason to suppose that principles other than transfer are necessary to account for the initial direction of these effects, analysis in particular cases is obviously difficult. It is more profitable to inquire into the reasons for their persistence.

2. Effects of an "Eccentric" Stimulus

In Figure 12 are data from an experiment in which large and reliable effects similar to "sensory superstition" were produced (Kello, Innis, & Staddon, 1975). The base-line schedule was a multiple fixed interval 60 sec, fixed interval 180 sec; the components were alternated, and each was 12 min long (12 60-sec intervals and 4 180-sec intervals). The two components were signaled by red and green key lights. Figure 12 shows

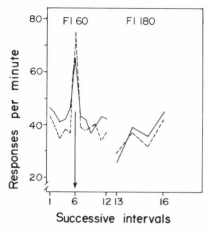

Successive intervals

FIGURE 12. Response rate in successive intervals of a multiple fixed-interval schedule in which a novel ("eccentric") stimulus occurred in one interval (arrowed). The figure shows average responding during one cycle, which comprised 12 60-sec intervals followed by 4 180-sec intervals. (From Kello, Innis, & Staddon, 1975, Fig. 2.)

the results from two conditions in which a novel ("eccentric") stimulus was presented throughout the sixth 60-sec interval (arrowed) in each cycle. Although the eccentric stimulus had exactly the same significance as the stimulus during the other 11 60-sec intervals, it reliably produced a large and persistent elevation in response rate (and a corresponding decrease in postfood pause). Test conditions showed that the effect does not depend on the particular interval in which the eccentric stimulus appears, although it may depend on the relative infrequency of the stimulus.

The two factors that appear to be essential for the effect are (a) that the eccentric stimulus produce an initial increase in response rate, and (b) that the stimulus appear in a component associated with a strong stimulus and/or temporal contingency. The first condition is met if the eccentric stimulus is novel, since such a stimulus will generally elevate ("disinhibit") responding on a fixed-interval schedule. A "familiar" eccentric stimulus did not produce the rate elevation shown in Figure 12. The second condition is met if the component in which the eccentric stimulus is presented is alternated with a less favorable one. The effect seen in the figure was abolished when the schedule was changed from multiple fixed interval 60, fixed interval 180 sec to simple fixed interval 60 sec, and it was not obtained either when the eccentric stimulus occurred in one of the 180-sec intervals, or in one of the 60-sec intervals on a multiple fixed-interval 20 sec, fixed-interval 60 sec schedule, that is, in a component that was not relatively favorable.

3. Linkage Hypothesis
and the Maintenance of Normally Transient Effects

These two factors correspond to those earlier implicated in stimulus control by the linkage hypothesis (Section IV.C). The first factor, the normally transient disinhibitory effect of a novel stimulus on a fixed interval, contributes a certain amount of *practice,* whereas the second factor, the relatively favorable reinforcement rate associated with one of two fixed-interval components, provides the second, *contingency strength.* By the hypothesis, the development of stimulus control ("conditioning" or the "fixing" of a behavior in a situation) depends jointly on these two. In response-contingent procedures, the guiding effect of the response contingency provides as much practice as is needed, so that behavior can become fixed even if the stimulus contingencies are weak (compare the previous discussion of feedback relations on interval schedules, Section V.A.3). On response-independent procedures, however, everything hinges on the strength of the stimulus contingency, and the initial variability of behavior. If initial variability is low, and the stimulus contingency is strong, the behavior that happens to occur during the first few stimulus presentations may become permanently linked to the situation and will persist as long as conditions remain the same—even if, as with disinhibition, the effect is transient under normal conditions.

A given behavior may be considered to have two sources of "strength" that is, two classes of controlling stimuli: (*a*) the behavior itself—once begun most activities have a certain "momentum" and will persist for a while in the absence of further stimulation, and (*b*) external stimulus factors. In the case of a pattern such as "disinhibition," the first factor is the only one, and its effects decrease with time as the disinhibited response habituates. By the present hypothesis, however, the second factor, control by stimuli present as the behavior occurs, grows with time at a rate determined by the strength of the stimulus contingency.

These interactions are illustrated in a highly schematic way in Figure 13, which shows how these two components of response strength might change in the presence of a CS associated with a strong (CS2) or a weak (CS1) contingency. The monotonically declining function represents the strength of the behavior in the absence of other factors (Point *a,* above), that is, the fact that it is normally transient. The two monotonically increasing functions represent the growing contribution to response strength of conditioning to the CS. Since CS2 is associated with a stronger contingency than CS1, its function grows more rapidly to reach a higher asymptote. The dashed lines show the resultant response strength in CS1 and CS2. The curves show that conditioning in CS2 is sufficiently rapid to counterbalance the initial decline in the strength of the behavior, so that it persists

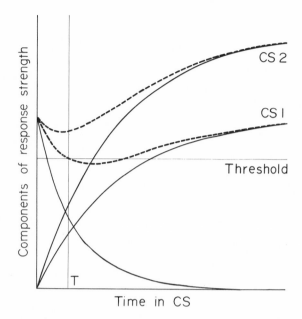

FIGURE 13. Rate of extinction versus rate of conditioning in a conditioned stimulus.

indefinitely. However, the slower conditioning in CS1 means that the behavior falls below threshold; hence, it ceases to occur and cannot be conditioned further.

In this diagram is also a suggestion why short stimuli may be especially effective in producing "sensory superstition" and similar phenomena. Disinhibition and other transient effects are subject to spontaneous recovery, especially if the time between stimulus presentations is long. If the duration of CS1 were to be limited to time T, so that the behavior continued to occur throughout the first CS1 presentation, then subsequent brief presentations might allow further increments until the strength of conditioning to CS1 rises above threshold.

This analysis can account for rate-dependent effects of a food CS superimposed on a food-reinforcement base line. Thus, Kelly (1973) reports that a stimulus previously paired with food suppresses lever pressing by rhesus monkeys on a high-rate (random-ratio) base line, but enhances responding on a low-rate (DRL) base line. Both effects are what would be expected from generalization decrement; their persistence may reflect fixing of the initial effect of the CS on the instrumental behavior by the strong positive CS contingency. In general, the linkage interpretation may be relevant when the superimposed CS has no specific inducing effect, a case not considered in the previous section.

It is clear that the effects discussed in this and the preceding Section
V.C are often complex; present data are sometimes incomplete and hard
to interpret; and interpretation must often hinge on hard-to-determine
quantitative properties of hypothetical processes. Much more remains to
be done. My intent is to propose an account of these effects that does
not have the "self-fulfilling prophecy" character of the adventitious reinforcement view, and is not open to the same adaptive and empirical
objections.

E. Temporal and Synchronous Control
and the Special Properties of Hedonic Stimuli

Periodic reinforcement schedules reliably produce periodic behavior. If reinforcement is response contingent, the instrumental response typically increases in frequency as the time for reinforcement approaches, and the
response may not begin until half or more of the interval has elapsed. A
considerable body of research has shown that this temporal periodicity reflects temporal control by reinforcement and events associated with it.

Temporal control by reinforcement can be demonstrated in several ways.
The most obvious is to omit reinforcement at the end of an interval. If
a stimulus is presented in its place, the behavior in the ensuing interval
depends on the similarity between stimulus and omitted reinforcer: the
more similar, the longer is the poststimulus pause and the lower the rate
of the instrumental response. This is an example of inhibitory temporal
control because the generalization gradient is incremental. Conversely, on
a synthetic schedule that produces the highest rate of instrumental responding just after reinforcement, reinforcement omission tests produce a
decremental (excitatory) gradient: the more similar the stimulus to reinforcement, the higher is the ensuing response rate.

In many respects, therefore, temporal or "trace" control by a stimulus
is similar to synchronous control, when the stimulus is present at the time
the response is made. There are substantial quantitative differences, however, connected with the greater dependence of temporal control on
processes related to *memory*. For example, it is easy to show good synchronous control by a dimension such as line orientation, even though in
the same situation no temporal control by that dimension may be apparent.
Temporal control by a brief "neutral" stimulus such as a key light can
be abolished by intermixing it in time (intercalating) with another neutral
stimulus, whose temporal significance (in terms of time to reinforcement)
is different. In contrast, intermixing a synchronous stimulus with another,
whose reinforcement significance is different, is a classic way of sharpening
stimulus control (discrimination).

Space precludes detailed discussion of these effects (see Staddon, 1974, for review). For present purposes it suffices to point out that (*a*) temporal control is especially dependent on memory processes and is therefore more susceptible to interference than synchronous control; (*b*) the memorability of stimuli is closely related to their *hedonic value,* so that reinforcers and punishers are particularly effective; and (*c*) because of the involvement of memory, instrumental responding may come under the control not just of the immediately preceding time marker, but also of earlier ones. Since reinforcers are much more effective than other time markers, this means that instrumental responding under conditions of intermittent reinforcement is influenced by the whole preceding temporal *reinforcement context* (for example, Capaldi, 1966; Neely & Wagner, 1974). This is important to an understanding of extinction, to which I now turn.

F. Extinction and the Partial-Reinforcement Effect

1. Persistence of Behavior in Extinction

Operant behavior is, by definition, affected by its consequences. Yet the emphasis in this chapter has been on the relatively weak direct effect of response contingencies. Studies of operant extinction—the omission of reinforcement, or its presentation independently of behavior—provide perhaps the strongest evidence that if response contingencies act directly at all, it is only during the acquisition of behavior. They affect maintained behavior only indirectly, via stimulus and temporal contingencies.

For example, extinction that involves the complete omission of food reinforcement is much more effective in eliminating instrumental behavior than the replacement of response-contingent food by "free" food that maintains the same stimulus and temporal contingencies. Rats eventually cease to lever press, but pigeons may continue to key peck indefinitely, especially if the rate of food delivery is high (Herrnstein, 1966; Rescorla & Skucy, 1969; Staddon & Frank, 1975; Zeiler, 1968). Even if food is delivered only infrequently, pigeons continue indefinitely to make a few key pecks during most interfood intervals.

The traditional explanation for the persistence of behavior when food delivery is maintained has been adventitious reinforcement of occasional instrumental responses owing to accidental response–food contiguities. However, the evidence against this is very strong: rats extinguish more slowly when food delivery is maintained, even if a delay is imposed between occurrences of the instrumental response and the delivery of food (omission training: Rescorla & Skucy, 1969). On fixed-time (response-independent) food reinforcement schedules, following fixed-interval (response-dependent) training, instrumental responding is often restricted to the middle of the interfood interval, so that very few response–food contiguities occur (Shull, 1970; Staddon & Frank, 1975). It is sometimes hard to show any effect of response contingencies. For example, Uhl (1974) compared rapidity of extinction for groups of rats trained under two kinds of omission procedure, with yoked control groups that received the same distribution of food deliveries independently of behavior. He found no difference in the rate at which the yoked and experimental groups ceased to lever press. This result is similar to that of Myerson *et al.* (1974), mentioned earlier, who found no difference in maintained behavior between pigeons exposed to the omission-training variant of the autoshaping procedure and their yoked control birds who received food in the CS with the same probability.

All these results suggest that habitual behavior is "reflexive" in the sense that it is controlled almost entirely by situational stimuli. Such hedonic stimuli as food and electric shock are evidently very effective in this respect, but with this addition the well-known discrimination hypothesis (Kimble, 1961)—that resistance to extinction depends on the *similarity* of extinction and training situations—appears to fit most of the facts just mentioned. This view is too simple, however, although the contrary evidence is rather scattered. The alternative is that habits are maintained not just by stimuli, but by stimulus (and temporal) *contingencies*. This view is just an application of the linkage hypothesis to extinction: If the acquisition and maintenance of operant behavior depends on stimulus contingencies, its abolition should depend on their elimination.

2. Linkage Hypothesis and Extinction

There are several lines of evidence in favor of the linkage hypothesis of extinction:

1. Zeiler (1972) trained pigeons to respond for food on fixed-interval percentage-reinforcement schedules in which as few as 7% of intervals ended with food (the other 93% ended with a brief neutral stimulus). After extensive training, performance on this procedure was very similar to normal fixed-interval performance. The pigeons paused and "scalloped" after both food and the neutral stimulus. Nevertheless, when food was eliminated (100% of intervals ended with the neutral stimulus), responding rapidly ceased. The *pattern* of behavior was maintained as long as the birds responded at all, and so it is hard to argue that stimulus control was directly affected by the elimination of food. Both stimulus and temporal contingencies were abolished, however.

2. Even after months of training on very intermittent variable-interval schedules, pigeons cease to respond within two or three extinction sessions.

Food exerts no temporal control on variable-interval schedules, so that its role as a stimulus is problematic.

3. The eccentric stimulus effects discussed earlier were abolished by a change in stimulus contingencies, even though stimulus factors remained constant.

These are all cases in which factors involved in stimulus control are unchanged, but behavior is abolished by elimination of stimulus and temporal contingencies. Most extinction procedures (for example, the elimination of reinforcement on simple fixed-interval or fixed-ratio schedules) involve a change in both stimulus factors (leading to generalization decrement) and contingency factors, so that the instrumental response loses strength rapidly. Extinction after variable-interval training involves little change in stimulus-control factors (as indicated by the small initial effect of extinction on response rate), and only a reduction in the strength of the stimulus contingency. Hence, extinction is slow. Zeiler's (1972) percentage reinforcement procedure is intermediate, since there is no change in stimulus factors in extinction, but both temporal and stimulus contingencies are affected by the omission of food.

3. Range of Variation and Contingency Strength

Why does the instrumental response extinguish at all, as long as stimulus and temporal contingencies are maintained? The most obvious answer is that the range of behavioral variation depends on the strength of these contingencies. If they are strong, or if the animal has had much practice, the range may not include behavior other than the instrumental response, so that it will persist indefinitely. This is often the case when food is delivered frequently, and it also seems to be true on procedures involving electric shock over a wide range of shock intensities and frequencies (see later discussion, Section V.G). If stimulus contingencies are not strong, or if training has not been prolonged, the range of behavioral variation may allow activities other than the instrumental response, and behavior may drift away from that during training. Presumably such drifts also occur during training, when the response contingency is in effect. Then, however, they result in a drop in reinforcement rate, which will usually be followed by some increase in behavioral variability. This variability is likely to result in a few occurrences of the instrumental response, some of which may be reinforced. This strengthens the stimulus contingencies, restricting the range of behavior and maintaining the response. Even a relatively weak guiding effect of this sort should be sufficient to correct slow drifts in behavior, especially on interval schedules, where the schedule function ensures that the temporal correlation between food and the instrumental response increases as the rate of the response decreases.

4. Partial Reinforcement Effect

Intermittent reinforcement often leads to behavior which is almost as strong as under continuous reinforcement but is much more persistent when reinforcement is eliminated. This is the partial-reinforcement effect (PRE). It depends on a number of factors: size of reinforcement, spacing of trials (in trial-by-trial situations) and whether the spacing in extinction is the same as the spacing during training, type of response, type of reinforcer, whether the response is instrumentally or classically conditioned, type of intermittent schedule, and species of animal (see D'Amato, 1970; Kimble, 1961; Mackintosh, 1974, for reviews). The interactions among all these factors are not yet fully worked out, even though the partial-reinforcement effect has attracted a great deal of experimental attention.

The approach that has been elaborated in this chapter suggests a simple way of relating many of these factors. It rests on the following assumptions:

1. The strength of habitual behavior depends almost entirely on stimulus and temporal contingencies.

2. Resistance to extinction depends entirely on the strength of the instrumental response at the beginning of extinction.

3. The contribution of reinforcer delivery (as a stimulus) to response strength is directly proportional to frequency of reinforcement in training, and directly related (by some other function) to reinforcer magnitude.

Thus, the strength of the response at the beginning of extinction is equal to its asymptotic strength at the end of training, minus the contribution due to reinforcer delivery as a stimulus (that is, minus the effect of generalization decrement).

The evidence in favor of the first assumption has just been reviewed. The second assumption is quite general and seems implicit in any notion of response strength. The third assumption is also relatively noncontroversial. Whatever role reinforcement plays as a stimulus, it seems reasonable that the effect of its elimination should be proportional to its frequency during training. The effect of reinforcer magnitude on stimulus control is less obvious. In experiments explicitly designed to study the effects of reinforcer delivery as a stimulus it is usually only possible to show substantial effects of reinforcer magnitude when different magnitudes are intermixed within each experimental session (see Staddon, 1974, for a review). When different groups of animals receive different magnitudes of reinforcement, there is much less effect. It seems likely, therefore, that variation in reinforcer magnitude will have more effect on response strength than on the effect of reinforcer delivery as a stimulus. I will discuss this in a moment.

Figure 14 shows how these assumptions can be applied to deduce resistance to extinction following different frequencies of variable-interval

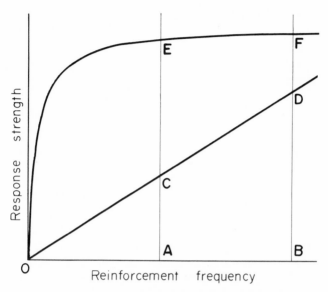

FIGURE 14. Prediction of the effects of intermittent reinforcement on resistance to extinction.

reinforcement. Curve *OEF* is the familiar variable-interval response function that describes the relation between response strength (here measured as response rate) and frequency of reinforcer delivery (compare Figure 10). This function corresponds to Assumption 1 above. Line *OCD* corresponds to Assumption 3; it shows the fraction of response strength at each rate of reinforcement associated with reinforcer delivery as a stimulus. It can be labeled the *decrement function*. It is linear because of the assumption that the degree of control exerted by reinforcer delivery as a stimulus is proportional to its frequency. It is easy to see that because the variable-interval response function is negatively accelerated and the decrement function is linear, the residual response strength left when reinforcer deliveries are eliminated (representing stimulus control by cues other than reinforcer delivery) is considerably less following training at the higher rate of reinforcement *B*, than after training at the lower rate, *A*. *DF* is less than *CE*. Hence, by Assumption 2, resistance to extinction following training at rate *B* should be less than following training at rate *A*. This is the partial-reinforcement effect: less frequent reinforcement leads to greater resistance to extinction.

The critical feature of this analysis is that it attributes the partial-reinforcement effect to the joint effect of two functions: the response function and the decrement function. Relatively small changes in either function, or comparisons between extreme points, might not yield the usual partial-reinforcement effect. For example, a comparison between resistance to extinction following training at a very low reinforcement rate versus rate B might fail to yield a partial-reinforcement effect because of the greatly reduced training response strength at such a low reinforcement rate. Most tests of the partial-reinforcement effect involve comparisons between some intermittent schedule and continuous reinforcement (fixed ratio 1). In both runway and free-operant situations, response rate (or running speed) is less under continuous reinforcement than under many intermittent schedules (for example, Macdonald & de Toledo, 1974; Mackintosh, 1974), a paradoxical result that corresponds to a downturn in the response function at very high reinforcement rates. This does not conflict with the

Macdonald and de Toledo (1974) reported a failure to find the partial-reinforcement effect), but the effect may be an artifact due to time spent eating or in other postreinforcement activities, or to interference from consummatory activities induced by high food rates. The more general comparison, which is the one considered here, is the function relating resistance to extinction to reinforcement frequency during training.

Macdonald and de Toledo (1974) reported a failure to find the partial-reinforcement effect with water, rather than food, as reinforcer. There is evidence that water delivery is much less effective as a stimulus than food delivery. Levy and Seward (1969) failed to find a "frustration" effect when water reward was omitted in a double-runway apparatus. This effect is an increase in running speed in the second runway when reward is omitted in the first goal box. I have argued (Staddon, 1970) that it is probably related to the function of reward as an inhibitory temporal stimulus. Lack of a "frustration" effect with water reward suggests that water is less effective as a discriminative temporal stimulus than food. Hence, the slope of the decrement function, Line OD in Figure 14, should be less for water than for food. Macdonald and de Toledo (1974) also show data suggesting that the downturn in the response function for water at the continuous-reinforcement point is less than for food. Both of these differences tend to reduce the difference between the residual strength of responding following intermittent reinforcement (CE) compared to strength after continuous reinforcement (DF), leading to a smaller, or even reversed, partial-reinforcement effect.

5. Effects of Reward Amount

This approach can also account for the fact that the partial-reinforcement effect is larger with large rewards than small rewards. It is only necessary to assume that an increase in reinforcer magnitude causes the response function to reach asymptote at a lower reinforcement rate. There seem to be no parametric data on this for responding on variable-interval schedules, but it follows directly from Herrnstein's matching-law model (1970),

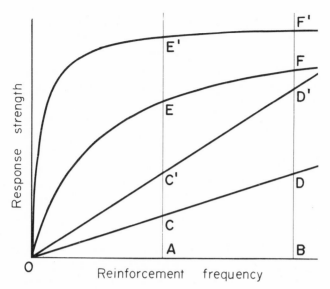

FIGURE 15. The effect of reinforcement magnitude on the partial-reinforcement effect.

which predicts that as the scheduled reinforcement for the measured response approaches 100% of all available reinforcement (as reinforcer magnitude increases), the response function approaches asymptote at lower reinforcement rates. These relations are illustrated in Figure 15. The straight line OCD is the decrement function for small reward; $OC'D'$ is the decrement function for a large reward. Similarly, the response function OEF is for small and $OE'F'$ for large reward. It is clear that the partial-reinforcement effect for small reward ($CE–DF$) is generally smaller than for large reward ($C'E'–D'F'$). However, resistance to extinction following small reward training at high reward frequency (DF) is greater than that following training with large reward ($D'F'$), as Hulse (1958) and others have found. This result, of course, should be reversed following training with intermittent reward ($CE < C'E'$).

The partial-reinforcement effect has been found in some experiments with classically conditioned responses and not in others (see Sutherland & Mackintosh, 1971; Kimble, 1961, for reviews). The important factor seems to be the nature of the conditioned response, rather than the classical-conditioning procedure itself. (It would be surprising if the procedure made much difference since one of the main points of this chapter is that stimulus contingencies, that is, the relations involved in classical conditioning, underlie response strength on instrumental procedures.) Thus, Pavlov found that partial reinforcement seriously impairs the salivary conditioned response, whereas Gonzalez (1974) shows that key pecking in the delayed-conditioning (automaintenance) situation bears the familiar negatively accelerated relation to probability of food delivery.

6. Elasticity of the Response Function

Responses can be classified as more or less *elastic* with respect to a given reinforcer.[9] Pecking by pigeons is generally inelastic with respect to food, since its rate is insensitive to the rate of food delivery over a wide range. Food-reinforced lever pressing and running in an alley or a running wheel for food by rats also appear to be inelastic. Salivation (and perhaps all autonomic responses) appears to be elastic, since its strength is very sensitive to rate and probability of food reinforcement. Responses such as treadle pressing by pigeons for food, or running by rats for water, may also be elastic. Other things being equal, the more inelastic the response function, the more likely that there will be a partial-reinforcement effect. In Figure 16 it is shown that a relatively elastic response function yields greater residual response strength following high (DF) compared to low (CE) frequency of reinforcement, that is, a reverse partial-reinforcement effect. This result has been reported for autonomic responses such as heart-rate and salivation, and for skeletal responses such as swimming in goldfish and mouth breeders and activity in pigeons. The common feature in all these cases may be the elasticity of the response function. The finding of Gonzalez and Bitterman (1967) that some failures to find the partial-reinforcement effect in fish can be reversed by using larger rewards are consistent with this interpretation, since increasing reward size increases the inelasticity of the response function (Figure 15).

In addition to the elasticity of the response function, the partial reinforcement effect also depends on the slope of the decrement function: the steeper the slope, the greater the difference in residual response strength between partially and continuously rewarded groups. In discrete-trial experiments, intertrial interval is an obvious variable that might be expected to affect the slope of the decrement function. Reward delivery is likely to make up a larger fraction of the effective stimulus complex when trials are frequent (so that reward from the preceding trial is temporally close to the succeeding trial) than when they are spaced far apart. Hence the slope of the decrement function should be inversely related to trial spacing.

[9] The term *elasticity* is borrowed from classical economics (for example, Marshall, 1925, p. 102). It is defined for two points on a response (or demand) function, as follows: elasticity coefficient equals the percentage change in response rate divided by the percentage change in reinforcement rate. Strictly speaking, therefore, most response functions are inelastic, since they have no region where the elasticity coefficient is greater than one. However, the terms "elastic" and "inelastic" are used here entirely in a relative sense.

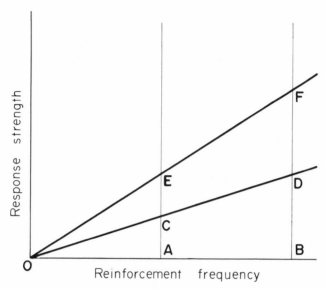

FIGURE 16. The effect of elasticity of the response function on the partial-reinforcement effect.

The partial reinforcement effect is in fact enhanced by short intertrial intervals, as this argument leads one to expect.

7. Multiple and Concurrent Schedules

In superficial discussions of the effects of intermittent reinforcement, the persistence of responding so maintained is often contrasted with the commonsense view that an infrequently rewarded response should be more readily given up. The present account shows that in most cases common sense actually has the edge, since the single-response laboratory situation is rarely met with in the natural world. The natural situation usually involves *choice,* in which alternative responses compete for expression. In the parallel laboratory situation, a concurrent schedule, the response function for one response, with the reinforcement rate for the others held constant, is much more elastic than the comparable single-response function. Hence, partial-reinforcement effect is much less likely under these conditions (or in a comparable multiple schedule), as most people would expect.

It is important to emphasize that the form of the response function is not fixed for a given response, or even for a given response-reinforcer combination. It can be changed by introducing the element of choice, but also, in all probability, by practice, age of the animal, effortfulness of the response, and numerous other variables. All of these variables are likely to have an effect on resistance to extinction and on the partial-reinforcement effect.

In summary, it seems likely that the persistence of an instrumental response when reinforcement is omitted depends on the difference between two functions: the response function, which relates the strength of the response to the frequency of reinforcement, and the decrement function, which describes the contribution to response strength of reinforcer delivery as a stimulus. This analysis is easiest to describe by using the independent and dependent variables of free-operant research: reinforcement and response rates. The approach is quite general, however, and variables such as reinforcement probability and response latency (or running rate) can also be used. De Villiers (1976) has pointed out that models of asymptotic response-reinforcer relations such as Herrnstein's (1970) matching law apply just as well to data from discrete-trial runway experiments as to the familiar operant results. If the response function is measured as the relation between running rate and reward probability, this analysis can be applied directly. Running by rats for food reward appears to be inelastic (over the usual range of reinforcement probability), like pecking for food, and this is the major warrant for applying this approach to the very extensive runway data on the partial-reinforcement effect.

I have suggested that a normally inelastic response can be converted to an elastic one by considering only one component of a concurrent schedule. Here the increase in elasticity comes about because a second, competing source of control, the alternative choice, has been introduced. This suggests that responses which are elastic under all conditions may be controlled by internal factors that compete with the external reinforcement. This is obviously true of autonomic responses such as heartrate and salivation. It will be interesting to see if it is true of all such responses.

G. Maladaptive Behavior in Procedures Involving Electric Shock

1. Set

Strong reinforcement contingencies restrict behavioral variation. This is usually adaptive since such situations are associated with something of great importance to the animal, where it cannot afford to take a chance and abandon a winning combination. However, behavioral sterotypy—"set" in an older terminology—is risky because the animal may fail to detect that the world has changed. For example, in the classic Luchins problem-solving experiments (for example, Luchins & Luchins, 1959), students well trained on a particular rule were induced to apply it to a new problem for which there was a much simpler solution that was obvious to untrained people. Their failure was a failure to consider alternatives, to sample their environment.

There are two kinds of protection against the bad effects of behavioral stereotypy. First, the stronger the contingencies and the longer the practice, the narrower is the range of stimuli that are attended to. Hence the smaller the stimulus change necessary to induce behavioral variation (generalization decrement). There is risk here too, of course, since many environmental aspects cease to be attended to at all: an experienced typist will not notice if her typewriter keys are mislabeled, providing their positions are not changed; a hungry, but overtrained, rat may run right past food strewn in the runway, although it shows great agitation when the food cup in the goal box is moved a few centimeters. Second, as we have already seen, habitual behavior is maintained by stimulus and temporal contingencies. Consequently, elimination of the relevant hedonic stimulus soon results in elimination of the behavior, no matter how "reflexive" it has become.

2. Electric Shock

Situations involving electric shock, an extremely aversive hedonic stimulus, provide interesting illustrations of how these safeguards can misfire. The linkage hypothesis refers only to the strength of contingencies, not to the affective type of the hedonic stimuli involved. It appears to make little difference whether the hedonic stimuli are pleasant or unpleasant: behavior that occurs in situations in which there are periodic strong aversive stimuli is just as likely to become fixed as if the stimuli were pleasant. This is not to say that schedules of food and shock have the same effect on naive animals. Both the eliciting and inducing effects of these two stimuli are very different. Food usually produces variable, active behavior at first, whereas shock tends to produce "freezing" and stereotyped escape or attack reactions. The induced behaviors are similar to the elicited ones, although less variable; the difficulty in training animals to remain immobile, as an instrumental response for food, is an illustration of the food-induced bias toward activity. Conversely, so-called "passive avoidance" (refraining from making a punished response) is a very easy task (see Bolles, 1970). Presumably these differences in elicited activities are critical in allowing animals to learn to obtain food but to avoid shock (although the latter task notoriously requires more carefully engineered pretraining than the former).

3. Learned Helplessness

If dogs are placed in a harness and given several severe electric shocks, their ability to learn a simple barrier-crossing escape—avoidance response 24 hr later is impaired, often irreversibly. The catchy but inexact term "learned helplessness" has been coined for this effect (see Seligman, Maier,

& Solomon, 1971, for a review). It can be understood in light of the present scheme in the following way. The initial shock experience induces passive behavior that transfers (if the intervening time is not too long) to the shuttle-box situation. The basis for the transfer is the presence of shock in both situations. In the shuttle box the dog fails to jump the barrier and gets shocked. The shock, as a stimulus, produces passive behavior, which prevents avoidance, which means more shocks, hence more passive behavior, and so on in a vicious circle. The longer the animal behaves passively, the more likely it is that the behavior will become fixed in the situation. The process is the same kind of horse race as that depicted in Figure 13.

Animals can be "inoculated" against the helplessness effect by pretraining them to avoid or escape shock. In this case, the behavior linked to shock is not passive. Even if the animal is subsequently exposed to response-independent shocks, the same nonpassive "mood" or "behavioral genotype" is induced, rather than a different "passive" mood. Consequently, when the animal again is exposed to a situation where escape or avoidance is possible, he retains the necessary behavioral variability and is much more likely to make, and learn, the avoidance response.

Reduction of behavioral variation is critical to the production of helplessness. Thus, if more than 24 hr intervene between training with response-independent shock and shuttle-box training, transfer may be incomplete and the dog may show enough behavioral variability (or recover quickly enough from the enervating effects of the initial shocks) to enable it to learn. Rats in a shuttle box do not show helplessness as readily as dogs (Maier, Albin, & Testa, 1973), because they shuttle from the start.

Some "helpless" dogs make a few barrier crossings in the shuttle box, but nevertheless fail to learn to avoid. This behavior may represent escape to a relatively safe *place,* rather than genuine avoidance. It fails to persist because, in the shuttle box, there is no safe place. In the hierarchy of behaviors induced by shock, escape to a safe place stands quite high, whereas an arbitrary barrier-crossing response, although topographically similar, is much less probable. The restriction in variation produced by helplessness training might well eliminate the latter but not the former. This distinction between phenotypically similar but genotypically different behaviors emphasizes that the overt activities induced by reinforcement contingencies are sometimes an imperfect guide to the underlying behavioral genotype: "what is learned" is not just what is observed.

4. Response-Produced Shock

Even more striking effects of electric shock have been demonstrated by Morse, Kelleher, and their associates (for example, Morse & Kelleher, 1970, 1976). Squirrel or macaque monkeys or cats are first trained to respond either for food reinforcement or on a shock-avoidance schedule. Then response-independent shocks are gradually introduced so that the animals gain experience responding in a situation in which periodic shocks occur. The apparatus is expressly designed to limit the opportunities for behavioral variation. Under these conditions, electric shock may by itself elicit the instrumental response:

> The restraining chair used in most of the studies ... had smooth walls, except for a response key protruding from the front panel. When a monkey ... received an electric shock, the monkey usually bit or grasped the response key. Thus the explicit shaping of a response that terminates electric shock may not be necessary when the apparatus itself has been appropriately shaped [Morse & Kelleher, 1970, p. 182].

After this training, the food or avoidance schedule is faded out, and the instrumental response is arranged to *produce* the shock, according to some intermittent schedule. Even though the animals are now responding to produce very painful shocks, they persist indefinitely and high rates of responding can be maintained in this way for many months.

This behavior cannot be explained in hedonistic terms. The animals do not "like" the shock. They show aversion to the situation in which they receive shock; yet once in the apparatus, they continue to produce shocks.

The key to this "self-punitive" behavior appears to be (*a*) the strong stimulus and temporal contingencies maintained by the shock, and (*b*) the restriction of behavioral variation by means of the apparatus and progressive training procedures, so that the animal continues to respond even though it is shocked. The result is that the instrumental response becomes linked to the shock situation.

An intermittent shock schedule appears to be necessary so that behavior elicited by the shock is compatible with the instrumental response. If shock is delivered for every response, for example, the effects of successive shocks summate, animals "freeze," instrumental responding is suppressed and such a schedule will not maintain lever pressing.

As with food reinforcement, elimination of the shock eliminates responding, even if the other stimuli controlling behavior remain (McKearney, 1969). The behavior appears to be maintained by stimulus and temporal contingencies, and, as with food, the response contingency has little direct effect: given the proper apparatus and/or training history, lever pressing can be maintained indefinitely by periodic response-independent shock (for example, Hutchinson & Emley, 1972).

VI. CONCLUSION

Research on operant behavior has gone through a boom in recent years. As a consequence, the clarity of the original findings, and the theories based

on them, has become increasingly obscured by masses of new, often conflicting, facts. The "simplifiers" are on the wane, the "complicators" are
in the ascendant, and there are a flock of exceptions to almost any
generalization.

Bucking the trend, the present chapter is an attempt to provide a coherent account of the interactions between hedonic stimuli and behavior,
that is, of operant (instrumental) conditioning and related processes. I
have been especially influenced by two kinds of exception to older views.
(a) findings showing that response-reinforcer contiguity is much less important than was once believed, and temporal and stimulus contingencies
(correlations between the temporal pattern of hedonic stimuli and other
signals) are much more important, especially to the maintenance of behavior as opposed to its acquisition; (b) findings with both familiar and
novel species showing "constraints on learning"—animals adapt differently
to apparently similar conditions of reinforcement, reinforcers affect different responses differently, and so on. These results make clear empirically
what was always obvious logically, that a true psychology of learning must
also be a comparative psychology. Learning principles must allow for the
differences, as well as the similarities, among species.

In the present scheme, the principles of generalization, range of variation, linkage, and relative proximity are assumed to be quite general. However, species differ in the type of behavior induced by stimulus and
temporal contingencies and in the elasticity of the response function relating particular responses and reinforcers.

The concepts of elasticity and induced behavior can be related to
Skinner's well-known distinction between *operant* and *respondent* behavior.
Operant behavior is inelastic over a wide range, and not usually induced
by strong stimulus contingencies. It is also susceptible to the "guiding" effect
of response-reinforcer continguities and can therefore be "shaped." Perhaps this property is the objective concomitant of the subjective label "voluntary." The dwindling importance of response-reinforcer contiguity with
practice corresponds to the "involuntariness" of habit. As William James
pointed out, this involuntariness has the obvious adaptive function of
freeing attention to deal with new situations—with the shaping of new responses, in modern terms. Respondent behavior is generally elastic, induced by strong stimulus contingencies, insensitive to the direct effects of
response-reinforcer contiguity, and involuntary.

The operant–respondent distinction has come under fire recently, both
on general epistemological grounds (Staddon, 1973), and because of its
failure to follow exactly the "natural lines of fracture along which behavior
and environment actually break." The most striking anomaly was the
demonstration that pecking by pigeons, the prototypical operant response,
behaves in many ways like a respondent: in the present terms it is inelastic

(fine), guided by peck-reinforcer continguities (fine), but also induced by strong stimulus-food contingencies (!). The concepts of elasticity and behavioral induction are not open to this kind of objection, and allow for both the similarities and differences between the effects of instrumental and classical procedures.

This emphasis on the importance of behavioral variation follows directly from the analogy with evolution by natural selection. It suggests an approach to the classical problem of *set,* which has received little attention in this field in recent years, and brings a number of apparently maladaptive behaviors—"superstition," "learned helplessness," and self-punitive behavior—within the range of general behavior theory.

This approach suggests testable hypotheses, but it also raises problems for which there are not even hypothetical solutions. What is "linkage?" The simple occurrence of behavior in a situation associated with strong contingencies appears to be sufficient for "conditioning" to occur. Why? Behavior is apparently sometimes guided by response-reinforcer contiguity and sometimes not. What makes the difference, and why? Granted that stimulus contingencies restrict behavioral variation, how does this come about? What determines the type of behavior induced by such contingencies? Partial answers to some of these questions have been suggested, but we are still a long way from the kind of mechanism that modern genetics provides for the theory of evolution.

ACKNOWLEDGMENTS

This research was supported by a grant from the National Science Foundation to Duke University. I thank James Allison, Janice Frank, Steven Forgey, James Kalat and Susan Roth for comments on the manuscript.

REFERENCES

Allison, J. A conservation model for the facilitation and suppression of responding by controlled-time contingencies. Paper presented at a meeting of the Psychonomic Society, Boston, 1974.

Allison, J., & Timberlake, W. Instrumental and contingent saccharin licking in rats: Response deprivation and reinforcement. *Learning & Motivation,* 1974, **5,** 231–247.

Baum, W. M. The correlation-based law of effect. *Journal of the Experimental Analysis of Behavior,* 1973, **20,** 137–153.

Beer, B., & Trumble, G. Timing behavior as a function of amount of reinforcement. *Psychonomic Science,* 1965, **2,** 71–72.

Bindra, D. A unified account of classical conditioning and operant training. In A. H. Black & W. F. Prokasy (Eds.), *Classical conditioning II: Current research and theory*. New York: Appleton-Century-Crofts, 1972.

Blackman, D. E. Conditioned suppression and the effects of classical conditioning procedures on operant behavior. In W. K. Honig & J. E. R. Staddon (Eds.), *Handbook of operant behavior*. Englewood Cliffs, New Jersey: Prentice-Hall, 1976 (In press).

Bloomfield, T. M. Reinforcement schedules: Contingency or contiguity? In R. M. Gilbert & J. R. Millenson (Eds.), *Reinforcement: Behavioral analyses*. New York: Academic Press, 1972. Pp. 165–208.

Bolles, R. C. Species-specific defense reactions and avoidance learning. *Psychological Review*, 1970, **77**, 32–48.

Bolles, R. C. Reinforcement, expectancy, and learning. *Psychological Review*, 1972, **79**, 394–409.

Boren, J. J. Response rate and resistance to extinction as functions of the fixed ratio. Unpublished doctoral dissertation, Columbia University, 1953.

Brandauer, C. M. The effects of uniform probabilities of reinforcement upon the response rate of the pigeon. Unpublished doctoral dissertation, Columbia University, 1958.

Brown, P. L., & Jenkins, H. M. Auto-shaping of the pigeon's key-peck. *Journal of the Experimental Analysis of Behavior*, 1968, **11**, 1–8.

Campbell, D. T. Blind variation and selective retention in creative thought as in other knowledge processes. *Psychological Review*, 1960, **67**, 380–400.

Capaldi, E. J. Partial reinforcement: A hypothesis of sequential effects. *Psychological Review*, 1966, **73**, 459–487.

Catania, A. C. Reinforcement schedules and psychophysical judgments: A study of some temporal properties of behavior. In W. N. Schoenfeld (Ed.), *The theory of reinforcement schedules*. New York: Appleton-Century-Crofts, 1970.

Catania, A. C., & Reynolds, G. S. A quantitative analysis of the responding maintained by interval schedules of reinforcement. *Journal of the Experimental Analysis of Behavior*, 1968, **11**, 327–383.

Catania, A. C., Silverman, P. J., & Stubbs, D. A. Concurrent performances: Stimulus–control gradients during schedules of signalled and unsignalled concurrent reinforcement. *Journal of the Experimental Analysis of Behavior*, 1974, **21**, 99–107.

D'Amato, M. R. *Experimental psychology: Methodology, psychophysics, and learning*. New York: McGraw-Hill, 1970.

Darwin, C. *The origin of species*. London: John Murray, 1859.

Darwin, C. *The variation of animals and plants under domestication*. London: John Murray, 1875. 2 vols.

de Villiers, P. A. Choice in concurrent schedules and a quantitative formulation of the law of effect. In W. K. Honig & J. E. R. Staddon (Eds.), *Handbook of operant behavior*. Englewood Cliffs, New Jersey: Prentice-Hall, 1976. (In press)

Dews, P. B. The theory of fixed-interval responding. In W. N. Schoenfeld (Ed.), *The theory of reinforcement schedules*. New York: Appleton-Century-Crofts, 1970.

Dunham, P. J. The nature of reinforcing stimuli. In W. K. Honig & J. E. R. Staddon (Eds.), *Handbook of operant behavior*. Englewood Cliffs, New Jersey: Prentice-Hall, 1976. (In press)

Ferster, C. B., & Skinner, B. F. *Schedules of reinforcement*. New York: Appleton-Century-Crofts, 1957.

Gibbon, J., Berryman, R., & Thompson, R. L. Contingency spaces and measures in classical and instrumental conditioning. *Journal of the Experimental Analysis of Behavior*, 1974, **21**, 585–605.

Gonzalez, F. A. Effects of varying the percentage of key illumination paired with food in a positive automaintenance procedure. *Journal of the Experimental Analysis of Behavior*, 1974, **22**, 483–489.

Gonzalez, R. C., & Bitterman, M. E. Partial reinforcement effect in the goldfish as a function of amount of reward. *Journal of Comparative and Physiological Psychology*, 1967, **64**, 163–167.

Hemmes, N. S. DRL efficiency depends upon the operant. Paper presented at the Psychonomic Society Meeting, San Antonio, 1970.

Herrnstein, R. J. Superstition: A corollary of the principles of operant conditioning. In W. K. Honig (Ed.), *Operant behavior: Areas of research and application*. New York: Appleton-Century-Crofts, 1966. Pp. 33–51.

Herrnstein, R. J. On the law of effect. *Journal of the Experimental Analysis of Behavior*, 1970, **13**, 243–266.

Herrnstein, R. J., & Loveland, D. H. Food-avoidance in hungry pigeons, and other perplexities. *Journal of the Experimental Analysis of Behavior*, 1972, **18**, 369–383.

Hull, C. L. *Principles of behavior*. New York: Appleton-Century-Crofts, 1943.

Hull, C. L. *A behavior system: An introduction to behavior theory concerning the individual organism*. New Haven: Yale University Press, 1952.

Hulse, S. H. Amount and percentage of reinforcement and duration of goal confinement in conditioning and extinction. *Journal of Experimental Psychology*, 1958, **56**, 48–57.

Hursh, S. R., Navarick, D. J., & Fantino, E. "Automaintenance": The role of reinforcement. *Journal of the Experimental Analysis of Behavior*, 1974, **21**, 117–124.

Hutchinson, R. R., & Emley, G. S. Schedule-independent factors contributing to schedule-induced phenomena. In R. M. Gilbert & J. D. Keehn (Eds.), *Schedule effects: Drugs, drinking and aggression*. Toronto: University of Toronto Press, 1972. Pp. 174–202.

Hutchinson, R. R., Renfrew, J. W., & Young, G. A. Effects of long-term shock and associated stimuli on aggressive and manual responses. *Journal of the Experimental Analysis of Behavior*, 1971, **15**, 141–166.

Jacquet, Y. F. Schedule-induced licking during multiple schedules. *Journal of the Experimental Analysis of Behavior*, 1972, **17**, 413–423.

Jenkins, H. M., & Moore, B. R. The form of the auto-shaped response with food or water reinforcers. *Journal of the Experimental Analysis of Behavior*, 1973, **20**, 163–181.

Kello, J. E. Observation of the behavior of rats running to reward and nonreward in an alleyway. Unpublished doctoral dissertation, Duke University, 1973.

Kello, J. E., Innis, N. K., & Staddon, J. E. R. Eccentric stimuli on multiple fixed-interval schedules. *Journal of the Experimental Analysis of Behavior*, 1975, **23**, 233–240.

Kelly, D. D. Suppression of random-ratio and acceleration of temporally spaced responding by the same prereward stimulus in monkeys. *Journal of the Experimental Analysis of Behavior*, 1973, **20**, 363–373.

Kieffer, J. D. Differential response rates correlated with the presence of "neutral" stimuli. *Journal of the Experimental Analysis of Behavior*, 1965, **8**, 227–229.

Killeen, P. Reinforcement frequency and contingency as factors in fixed-ratio behavior. *Journal of the Experimental Analysis of Behavior*, 1969, **12**, 391–395.

Killeen, P. On the temporal control of behavior. *Psychological Review*, 1975, **82**, 89–115.

Kimble, G. A. *Hilgard and Marquis' conditioning and learning*. New York: Appleton-Century-Crofts, 1961.

Köhler, W. *The mentality of apes.* (Translated by E. Winter) New York: Harcourt, Brace & World, 1925.

Land, E. H., & McCann, J. J. Lightness and retinex theory. *Journal of the Optical Society of America,* 1971, **61,** 1–11.

Lander, D. G. Stimulus bias in the absence of food reinforcement. *Journal of the Experimental Analysis of Behavior,* 1968, **11,** 711–714.

Levy, N., & Seward, J. P. Frustration and homogeneity of rewards in the double runway. *Journal of Experimental Psychology,* 1969, **81,** 460–463.

LoLordo, V. M., McMillan, J. C., & Riley, A. L. The effects upon food-reinforced pecking and treadle-pressing of auditory and visual signals for response-independent food. *Learning & Motivation,* 1974, **5,** 24–41.

Luchins, A. S., & Luchins, E. H. *Rigidity of behavior.* Portland, Oregon: University of Oregon Press, 1959.

Macdonald, G. E., & de Toledo, L. Partial reinforcement effects and type of reward. *Learning & Motivation,* 1974, **5,** 288–298.

Mackintosh, N. J. *The psychology of animal learning.* London and New York: Academic Press, 1974.

Maier, S. F., Albin, R. W., & Testa, T. J. Failure to learn to escape in rats previously exposed to inescapable shock depends on nature of escape response. *Journal of Comparative and Physiological Psychology,* 1973, **85,** 581–592.

Marshall, A. *Principles of economics.* London: Macmillan, 1925.

McKearney, J. W. Fixed-interval schedules of electric shock presentation: Extinction and recovery of performance under different shock intensities and fixed-interval durations. *Journal of the Experimental Analysis of Behavior,* 1969, **12,** 301–313.

Morse, W. H., & Kelleher, R. T. Schedules as fundamental determinants of behavior. In W. N. Schoenfeld (Ed.), *The theory of reinforcement schedules.* New York: Appleton-Century-Crofts, 1970. Pp. 139–185.

Morse, W. H., & Kelleher, R. T. Determinants of reinforcement and punishment. In W. K. Honig & J. E. R. Staddon (Eds.), *Handbook of operant behavior.* Englewood Cliffs, New Jersey: Prentice-Hall, 1976. (In press)

Morse, W. H., & Skinner, B. F. A second type of superstition in the pigeon. *American Journal of Psychology,* 1957, **70,** 308–311.

Myerson, J., Myerson, W. A., & Parker, K. Acquisition and maintenance of a keypeck response that postpones both reinforcement and stimulus change. Paper presented at a meeting of the Psychonomic Society, Boston, 1974.

Neely, J. H., & Wagner, A. R. Attenuation of blocking with shifts in reward: The involvement of schedule-generated contextual cues. *Journal of Experimental Psychology,* 1974, **102,** 751–763.

Nevin, J. A. The maintenance of behavior. In J. A Nevin (Ed.), *The study of behavior.* Glenview: Scott, Foresman, 1973.

Pavlov, I. P. *Conditioned reflexes.* London and New York: Oxford University press, 1927.

Pear, J. J., & Wilkie, D. M. Contrast and induction in rats on multiple schedules. *Journal of the Experimental Analysis of Behavior,* 1971, **15,** 289–296.

Pringle, J. W. S. On the parallel between learning and evolution. *Behaviour,* 1951, **3,** 174–215.

Rachlin, H. *Introduction to modern behaviorism.* San Francisco: Freeman, 1970.

Rachlin, H. Contrast and matching. *Psychological Review,* 1973, **80,** 217–234.

Rachlin, H., & Baum, W. M. Effects of alternative reinforcement: Does the source matter? *Journal of the Experimental Analysis of Behavior,* 1972, **18,** 231–241.

Rescorla, R. A. Pavlovian conditioning and its proper control procedures. *Psychological Review,* 1967, **74,** 71–80.

Rescorla, R. A., & Skucy, J. C. Effect of response-independent reinforcers during extinction. *Journal of Comparative & Physiological Psychology,* 1969, **67,** 381–389.

Reynolds, G. S. Behavioral contrast. *Journal of the Experimental Analysis of Behavior,* 1961, **4,** 57–71.

Reynolds, G. S. *A primer of operant conditioning.* Glenview: Scott, Foresman, 1968.

Richardson, W. K., & Loughead, T. E. Behavior under large values of the differential-reinforcement-of-low-rate schedule. *Journal of the Experimental Analysis of Behavior,* 1974, **22,** 121–129.

Russell, W. M. S. Evolutionary concepts in behavioral science: IV. The analogy between organic and individual behavioral evolution, and the evolution of intelligence. *General Systems,* 1962, **7,** 157–193.

Schneider, B. A. A two-state analysis of fixed-interval responding in the pigeon. *Journal of the Experimental Analysis of Behavior,* 1969, **12,** 677–687.

Schwartz, B. The role of positive conditioned reinforcement in the maintenance of keypecking which prevents delivery of primary reinforcement. *Psychonomic Science,* 1972, **28,** 277–278.

Schwartz, B., & Gamzu, E. Pavlovian control of operant behavior: An analysis of autoshaping and its implications for operant behavior. In W. K. Honig & J. E. R. Staddon (Eds.), *Handbook of operant behavior.* Englewood Cliffs, New Jersey: Prentice-Hall, 1976. (In press)

Schwartz, B., & Williams, D. R. Discrete-trials spaced responding in the pigeon: The dependence of efficient performance on the availability of a stimulus for collateral pecking. *Journal of the Experimental Analysis of Behavior,* 1971, **16,** 155–160.

Schwartz, B., & Williams, D. R. The role of the response-reinforcer contingency in negative automaintenance. *Journal of the Experimental Analysis of Behavior,* 1972, **17,** 351–357.

Seligman, M. E. P., & Hager, J. L. (Eds.) *Biological boundaries of learning.* New York: Appleton-Century-Crofts, 1972.

Seligman, M. E. P., Maier, S. F., & Solomon, R. L. Unpredictable and uncontrollable aversive events. In F. R. Brush (Ed.), *Aversive conditioning and learning.* New York: Academic Press, 1971. Pp. 347–400.

Shettleworth, S. Constraints on learning. In D. S. Lehrman, R. A. Hinde, & E. Shaw (Eds.), *Advances in the study of behavior.* Vol. IV. New York: Academic Press 1972.

Shull, R. L. The response-reinforcement dependency in fixed-interval schedules of reinforcement. *Journal of the Experimental Analysis of Behavior,* 1970, **14,** 55–60.

Sidman, M. Avoidance behavior. In W. K. Honig (Ed.), *Operant behavior: Areas of research and application.* New York: Appleton-Century-Crofts, 1966.

Skinner, B. F. *The behavior of organisms.* New York: Appleton-Century, 1938.

Skinner, B. F. "Superstition" in the pigeon. *Journal of Experimental Psychology,* 1948, **38,** 168–172.

Skinner, B. F. *Cumulative record.* New York: Appleton-Century-Crofts, 1961.

Skinner, B. F. *Contingencies of reinforcement.* New York: Appleton-Century-Crofts, 1969.

Smith, J. B. Effects of response rate, reinforcement frequency, and the duration of a stimulus preceding response-independent food. *Journal of the Experimental Analysis of Behavior,* 1974, **21,** 215–221.

Staddon, J. E. R. Some properties of spaced responding in pigeons. *Journal of the Experimental Analysis of Behavior,* 1965, **8,** 19–27.

Staddon, J. E. R. Temporal effects of reinforcement: A negative "frustration" effect. *Learning and Motivation,* 1970, **1,** 227–247.

Staddon, J. E. R. Temporal control and the theory of reinforcement schedules. In R. M. Gilbert & J. R. Millenson (Eds.), *Reinforcement: Behavioral analyses.* New York: Academic Press, 1972. Pp. 209–262.

Staddon, J. E. R. On the notion of cause, with applications to behaviorism. *Behaviorism,* 1973, **1,** 25–63.

Staddon, J. E. R. Temporal control, attention, and memory. *Psychological Review,* 1974, **81,** 375–391.

Staddon, J. E. R. Schedule-induced behavior. In W. K. Honig & J. E. R. Staddon (Eds.), *Handbook of operant behavior.* Englewood Cliffs, New Jersey: Prentice-Hall, 1976. (In press)

Staddon, J. E. R., & Frank, J. A. The role of the peck–food contingency on fixed-interval schedules. *Journal of the Experimental Analysis of Behavior,* 1975, **23,** 17–23.

Staddon, J. E. R., & Simmelhag, V. L. The "superstition" experiment: A reexamination of its implications for the principles of adaptive behavior. *Psychological Review,* 1971, **78,** 3–43.

Sutherland, N. S., & Mackintosh, N. J. *Mechanisms of animal discrimination learning.* New York: Academic Press, 1971.

Terhune, J. G., & Premack, D. Comparison of reinforcement and punishment functions produced by the same contingent event in the same subjects. *Learning and Motivation,* 1974, **5,** 221–230.

Thorndike, E. L. *Animal intelligence.* New York: Macmillan, 1911.

Tolman, E. C. *Purposive behavior in animals and man.* New York: Appleton-Century-Crofts, 1932.

Tulving, E., & Donaldson, W. (Eds.) *Organization of memory.* New York: Academic Press, 1972.

Uhl, C. N. Response elimination in rats with schedules of omission training, including yoked and response-independent reinforcement comparisons. *Learning and Motivation,* 1974, **5,** 511–531.

Westbrook, R. F. Failure to obtain positive contrast when pigeons press a bar. *Journal of the Experimental Analysis of Behavior,* 1973, **20,** 499–510.

Williams, D. R., & Williams, H. Auto-maintenance in the pigeon: Sustained pecking despite contingent non-reinforcement. *Journal of the Experimental Analysis of Behavior,* 1969, **12,** 511–520.

Zeiler, M. D. Fixed and variable schedules of response-independent reinforcement. *Journal of the Experimental Analysis of Behavior,* 1968, **11,** 405–414.

Zeiler, M. D. Fixed-interval behavior: Effects of percentage reinforcement. *Journal of the Experimental Analysis of Behavior,* 1972, **17,** 177–189.

Zeiler, M. D. Schedules of reinforcement. In W. K. Honig & J. E. R. Staddon (Eds.), *Handbook of operant behavior.* Englewood Cliffs, New Jersey: Prentice-Hall, 1976. (In press)

3

Adaptational Aspects of Conditioning

H. D. Kimmel
R. A. Burns

University of South Florida

From the very earliest days of Pavlov's investigations of classical conditioning, it has been known that the conditioning process involves considerably more than the basic finding that a previously indifferent conditioned stimulus (CS) becomes an effective elicitor of learned responses following some number of appropriately paired presentations with an originally effective unconditioned stimulus (US). Notwithstanding the enormous biological significance of the initial conditioned association, in Pavlov's view it was only the opening movement in a subtle and dynamic interplay of excitatory and inhibitory mechanisms by means of which, "... a continuous and most exact adaptation of the organism to its environment is effected" (Pavlov, 1927, p. 106).

Admittedly greatly influenced by Sechenov, whose *Reflexes of the brain* (1863) established the validity of the objective method for the study of what later came to be called "higher nervous activity," Pavlov readily accepted Sechenov's idea that inhibitory processes serve a regulatory function in modulating behavior mediated by the central nervous system. Sechenov had emphasized effects such as the cessation of cardiac muscle activity resulting from stimulation of the vagus nerve, in presenting what might be called his "operational definition" of unlearned inhibition. Analogously, Pavlov defined learned inhibition operationally by emphasizing the observed reduction, delay, or other temporal modulation of conditioned responses (CRs) by CSs. For both Pavlov and Sechenov, "inhibition" referred to regulation of responses, whether the responses were originally unlearned or learned.

Following this tradition, in this chapter we mean nothing more by the term "inhibition" than the response modulation (for example, reduced strength or frequency, delayed onset, delayed maximal strength, trial-by-trial movement of CR onset or CR peak) that can be demonstrated experimentally to be under the control of the CS following the initial appearance of the CR. Although growth in response strength during CR acquisition might also properly be labeled "modulation," only brief comment on it is made. And, because CSs may sometimes be shown to have either response eliciting (excitatory) or regulating (inhibitory) effects that are not a consequence of experimental pairing of CSs and USs, adjectives such as "conditioned" or "learned" are used to modify the term "inhibition" only when experimental controls are such as to support the assumption of an associative mechanism. The main focus of our attention is those apparently inhibitory effects that occur during or are consequences of paired conditioning trials, as distinguished from inhibitory effects, which result from explicitly inhibitory (involving nonreinforcement) experimental procedures, such as those used in experimental extinction or differential conditioning. We have chosen the term "adaptational" to refer to these aspects of conditioning in order to emphasize their continuously changing nature and because they so often appear to result in increasingly precise environmental adjustment. Nothing more teleological is implied by this usage of "adaptational" than is meant when the term is used in discussions of biological evolution.

As has been noted above, several different alleged manifestations of adaptational regulation, or inhibition during conditioning have been studied in conditioning laboratories. And, as is discussed later, a variety of competing explanations of these effects have been offered. Our plan in this chapter is to review sequentially the principal experimental results on the topics of *inhibition of delay, inhibition with reinforcement, response shaping, diminution of the unconditioned response* (UR), and *postacquisition consequences* of these allegedly inhibitory phenomena, for example, immediate postacquisition elevation of CR strength, reduced resistance to extinction. Explanatory proposals are discussed at appropriate points in our presentation, both to facilitate comprehension of experimental strategies and to highlight differences among conflicting viewpoints. Our own theoretical position, based in part upon recent suggestions by Anokhin (1974), assumes a two-stage model of conditioning, the first stage reflecting a "preadaptive" chemical coupling of sequential repeated events and the second stage serving to consolidate these preadaptive couplings if they may be utilized adaptively. In the absence of the possibility of adaptive utilization in the second stage, the couplings of the first stage tend to vanish. Although we present evidence in support of our theoretical position, a generally eclectic stance prevails, because of both the tentativeness of our own views and the empirically unresolved disparity among the various approaches.

I. INHIBITION OF DELAY

Pavlov used the term "inhibition of delay" to refer to at least two different features of the total reaction to the CS in delayed conditioning: (*a*) the fact that the long-delayed CR does not begin until some time *after* the beginning of the CS which elicits it; and (*b*) the fact that the point of maximal CR strength systematically shifts toward the time of delivery of the US ["Finally, if a regular interval of sufficient duration is established between the commencement of a conditioned stimulus and its reinforcement by the unconditioned stimulus, the former becomes ineffective during the first part of its isolated action; during the second part of its action a positive excitatory effect appears, and this increases progressively in intensity as the moment approaches when the unconditioned stimulus has customarily been applied" (Pavlov, 1927, p. 106)].

Pavlov found that when an initially brief (5-sec) CS–US interval was lengthened gradually over several trials to a much longer one (for example, 2 min), the onset of the CR moved away from the beginning of the CS in the direction of US onset, stabilizing finally at a temporal point about midway between the two stimuli. The total absence of conditioned salivation during the early portion of the CS was taken as evidence of inhibition under the control of the CS. This means simply that the CS controls both *whether* and *when* the CR occurs. If the transition from a short to a much longer CS–US interval was sudden, the CR at first disappeared entirely for several trials. When the CR eventually reappeared, it was found to begin very near the point of US delivery. Additional trials at the longer interval resulted in some movement of the CR *toward the CS* and ultimate stabilization of CR onset somewhere in the middle of the CS–US interval. The eventual finding was that, whether the shift was abrupt or gradual, turning on the CS elicited a long period of nonresponse followed by a CR in the latter portion of the CS–US interval.

Gormezano (1972) and Gormezano and Moore (1969) have argued that a systematic increase over trials in the latency of the onset of the CR depends on a gradual lengthening of the CS–US interval. Their argument is based upon studies of the rabbit's nictitating membrane, which consistently show gradual *shortening* of CR onset latency concurrent with gradual lengthening of the latency of the peak of CR amplitude (for example, Smith, 1966), under conditions of constant CS–US intervals. Increases in CR onset latency with constant CS–US intervals do not occur in this preparation. The human GSR also shows shortening of CR onset latency, followed, however, by gradual *lengthening* of CR onset latency, plus continuous *lengthening* of latency of the peak CR amplitude. Figure 1 shows Kimmel's (1965) CR onset latency results using a constant 7.5-sec. CS–US interval during galvanic skin response (GSR) conditioning of 50 human

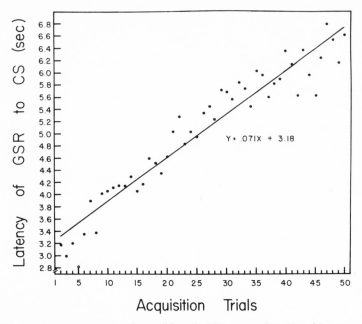

FIGURE 1. Average latency of conditioned GSR onset for 50 subjects receiving a 7.5-sec tone paired with 0.1-sec shock. Nonresponse trials were scored as 9.0 sec. (From Kimmel, 1965.)

subjects. Of interest in these data is the fact that CR onset latency first decreased, attaining its smallest value on Trial 5, and subsequently began to increase systematically. In other words, *both* shortening and lengthening of CR onset latency may be found under conditions of constant CS–US intervals, with shortening occurring first. Lengthening of the latency of *peak* CR amplitude, however, appears to occur quite regularly in salivary, nictitating membrane, human eye blink, and electrodermal preparations even with unchanging CS–US intervals, and without an early phase of shortening. Although Gormezano (1972) has suggested that the inclusion of the progressive increase in latency of the peak of the CR amplitude curve under the label "inhibition of delay" is a misguided expansion of the original Pavlovian concept, attributing this "error" to Ellison (1964), Pavlov quite explicitly included both delayed CR onset and shift in peak CR amplitude in his description and theorizing regarding "inhibition of delay" (see quotation above, Pavlov, 1927, p. 106). Indeed, it was because of the fact that both the onset and peak amplitude of the CR had asymptotic latencies proportional to the CS–US interval that Pavlov felt that inhibitory regulation of the response was involved in both.

Coleman and Gormezano (1971) have reported rabbit nictitating membrane results that shed additional light on the question of changes in CR

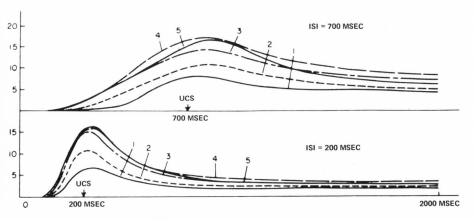

FIGURE 2. Average amplitude curves for the conditioned nictitating membrane response of rabbits run with CS–US intervals of 700 or 200 msec. The numbers in the graph indicate successive daily sessions. (From Coleman & Gormezano, 1971.)

onset latency during conditioning. Using a constant CS–US interval of either 200 or 700 msec and infraorbital shock as the US, they observed that CR onset latency decreased during the first four days of conditioning and was unchanged on the fifth day. Conditioned-response peak latency increased over all five days of training. Of particular importance was their finding that CR amplitude followed a course that was negatively correlated across days with CR onset latency. They constructed average CR amplitude curves by summing momentary CR amplitudes at 20-msec points during four nonreinforced test trials on each day of acquisition. Figure 2 shows these average amplitude curves for rabbits conditioned with either the 200- or the 700-msec interval.

As can be seen in Figure 2, CR amplitude grows over the first four days of training and stabilizes on the fifth day. Latency of CR onset reduces for the first four days and also stabilizes on the fifth day; and the peak of the CR amplitude curve moves gradually away from the time of CS onset, indeed, to a point well beyond the time of US delivery. These effects are understandably more noticeable in the 700-msec CS–US interval condition.

The data in Figure 2 and the results of other studies showing that CR onset latency reduces at the same time that CR amplitude grows, whereas latency of the peak amplitude of the CR increases systematically, suggest that two different types of change in the CR may be occurring, perhaps simultaneously. One type of change involves increases in the amplitude of the CR and correlated reductions in CR onset latency. The second type of change, which is partly masked by and partly masks the first, involves

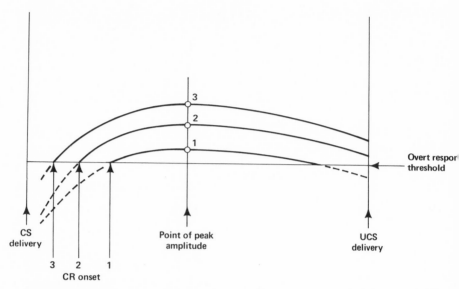

FIGURE 3. Hypothetical curve of CR amplitude for CRs at three stages of acquisition. In this figure the point-of-peak amplitude remains constant, to illustrate negative correlation between CR amplitude and CR onset latency.

movement of the peak amplitude of the CR toward the time of onset of the US.

Figure 3 shows a hypothetical version of the way the first type of change might occur separately. As conditioning progresses and greater and greater numbers of neurons are recruited in the elicitation of a CR, two correlated changes in the observed CR are seen: the strength of the CR grows and the latency of CR onset reduces. Both changes are indicative of CR recruitment. It is significant to note that on the fifth day of training in Coleman and Gormezano's (1971) study (see Figure 2), when CR amplitude was no different from that on the fourth day, CR onset latency also stopped reducing. In fact, some depression in the early portion of the CR amplitude curve can be seen on the fifth day when compared with the curve of the fourth day, as the latency of the CR peak continued to move away from CS onset on the fifth day. In Figure 3 the peak amplitude of the hypothetical CR arbitrarily was made to occur at the same time in all three CRs, in order to illustrate changes in CR onset latency and CR strength uncomplicated by temporal shifting of the CR peak.

Figure 4 shows hypothetically how movement of the CR peak may combine with CR changes resulting from recruitment to produce results similar to those found by Coleman and Gormezano (1971). Even though the latency of the CR peak moves systematically away from the onset of the

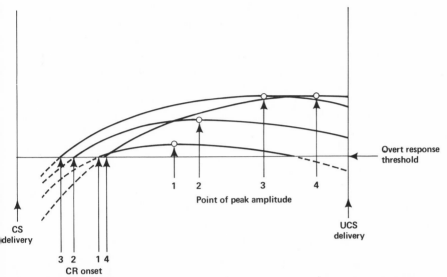

FIGURE 4.   Hypothetical curve of CR amplitude for CRs at four stages of acquisition. In this figure the point of peak amplitude shifts away from CS delivery. The CR amplitude increases over the first three stages, accompanied by corresponding decreases in CR onset latency. With no further increase in CR amplitude between the third and fourth stages, shift in peak amplitude is accompanied by a corresponding *increase* in CR onset latency.

CS in Figure 4, CR recruitment is still manifest in reduced CR onset latencies for the first three hypothetical test trials shown. On the fourth hypothetical test trial, when CR amplitude remains at the same level as it was on the previous trial, CR onset latency begins to increase, a trend similar to that reported by Kimmel (1965) and summarized in Figure 1. At this point, with both onset and CR peak latencies increasing, it would not be inappropriate to say that the entire "response" is shifting toward the US. We take up this suggestion again when the topic of response shaping is discussed.

Although admittedly ad hoc, the notion that two separate factors are responsible for the changes in CR topography reported in the literature— the first reflecting increased strength of conditioning via CR recruitment and the second manifest in gradual movement of the peak CR away from the onset of the CS—appears to have considerable descriptive as well as potential heuristic value. Descriptively, it accounts for the negative correlation between trial-by-trial changes in CR amplitude and CR onset latency, as shown in investigations of the rabbit's nictitating membrane. This notion is also in accord with the fact that CR onset latency ceases to reduce when CR amplitude attains asymptotic strength. Its heuristic possibilities are also considerable. It predicts that continued increases in latency of the CR peak, *after* the CR amplitude has reached asymptote, should be accompanied by increases in CR onset latency. Kimmel and Greene (1964) reported that CR onset latency did begin to increase on the sixth acquisition trial (following reduction for the first five trials), when the largest CR occurred at approximately the same stage in acquisition of GSR conditioning.[1]

As will be elaborated upon in connection with the hypothesis that changes in CR topography may reflect a process of *response shaping,* our suggestion that observed reductions in CR onset latency are a concomitant of CR recruitment and simply may mask the appearance of delayed CR onset is in substantial agreement with the position of Martin and Levey (1969) in their analysis of human eyelid conditioning. These authors point out: "As the amplitude of the response increases, however, latency must decrease in order to accommodate that increase, preserving fairly narrow limits observed for rate of rise" (Martin & Levey, 1969, p. 84). Without commitment to any particular theoretical explanation of the facts of response topography change, it seems fair to conclude that observations of reduction in CR onset latency in one response system or another do not, in and of themselves, justify dismissal of the possibility that inhibition of delay, in the form of increased CR onset latencies, may be a general consequence of CS–US pairings after maximal CR strength is attained. Furthermore, once it is recognized that movement of the CR peak away from CS onset is as much a part of the regulatory pattern of inhibition of delay as is the more often mentioned delayed CR onset (and, indeed, may be the more significant), both types of change may become amenable to more comprehensive analysis.

When the phenomenon of inhibition of delay is conceptualized as one in which the CR peak moves away from the onset of the CS toward, and even beyond, the onset of the US, as suggested by the data of Coleman and Gormezano (1971) and depicted schematically in the hypothetical curves shown in Figure 4, it becomes possible also to characterize a hypothetical mechanism for *disinhibition* of "inhibition of delay" in related terms. If, as Pavlov thought, disinhibition is the result of "external inhibition" of the internal inhibition of delay, we may assume that "external inhibition" in this case means the same as what would currently be labeled "elicitation of an orienting reflex" (OR). Indeed, Pavlov related the degree of disinhibition produced by a novel stimulus to the extent to which the stimulus elicited investigatory behavior. Elicitation of the OR may be expected to result in temporarily lowered thresholds, both within and outside of the sense modality of the novel stimulus itself (Sokolov, 1963;

---

[1] Kimmel and Greene (1964) actually showed CR magnitude data for subjects tested only on the second or tenth acquisition trials, indicating that the peak in CR size occurred somewhere between these two trials.

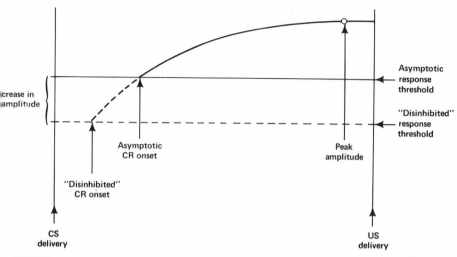

FIGURE 5.   Hypothetical curve of CR amplitude illustrating the manner in which lowering of the CR threshold via "disinhibition" is manifested in increased apparent CR amplitude and decreased apparent CR onset latency.

Yaremko, 1969). The extent to which elicitation of the orienting reflex is reflected in lowered thresholds depends upon the number of prior presentations of a repeated, nonnovel stimulus (Grings, 1960). This may explain the fact that Kimmel and Greene (1964) found increasing amounts of disinhibition with increases in the number of conditioning trials prior to a disinhibition test.

As is shown schematically in Figure 5, lowering of the threshold for eliciting the CR should have the effect of increasing CR amplitude and reducing CR onset latency. This implies, interestingly, that CR amplitude should be greater when disinhibited than it was prior to "inhibition of delay," a ubiquitous empirical finding that has never seemed to sit well with the assumption that disinhibition merely "removes inhibition" and thus permits the CR to be restored in strength. The schematic, hypothetical representation of the effect of disinhibition in terms of an orienting reflex-generated lowering of response threshold predicts elevated CR amplitude when a novel disinhibitor is presented. Furthermore, since the effect is not assumed to influence the temporal "placement" of the CR, other than to make it appear to begin earlier via a lowered threshold, the latency of the CR *peak* should not be influenced by the addition of a novel stimulus. To the extent that any data bearing on this prediction are available, they seem to confirm it. For example, Zavadsky (1908) found that the peak of the salivary CR occurred in the sixth 30-sec measurement interval, just before the presentation of the US, with no salivation at all occurring during the first two 30-sec intervals. When a metronome was added to the tactile

CS, salivary responding occurred during the first 30-sec interval, but the peak intensity of salivation was still found in the sixth 30-sec interval. In other words, onset latency was shortened by the operation of adding the novel disinhibitor (as a result of lowered response threshold), but CR peak latency was unchanged.

Similarly, Kimmel and Greene (1964) reported that the temporal locus of the peak of the disinhibited conditioned GSR was unchanged when the disinhibitor was added postasymptotically, occurring at or near US onset after either 25 or 50 conditioning trials. Amplitude of the disinhibited response increased substantially, however. Although more systematic evaluation of the proposed model is obviously required, presently available evidence seems to be in accord with it. To the extent that "disinhibition" may mean nothing more than those effects which result from a temporary lowering of CR threshold (producing shorter CR onset latency and larger CR amplitude), it probably should not be so labeled, since it does not result, in this view, from removal of inhibition generated during delay. Only a shift in the latency of the CR peak toward CS onset would justify the use of the term "disinhibition."

II. INHIBITION WITH REINFORCEMENT

Progressive movement of the onset of the CR away from the point of administration of the CS, even under condition of protracted constancy of the CS–US interval, was also reported by Pavlov, but he distinguished between this phenomenon and what he called "inhibition of delay." He based this distinction upon the fact that the phenomenon of continuous increase in CR onset latency was accompanied by reduction in CR strength and tended invariably to result in eventual total loss of the CR, whereas the more ubiquitous inhibition of delay (delayed CR onset and peak) often persisted for long training episodes without progressive changes. Once a gradual shift of response latency began to occur, ultimate total loss of the CR was apparently inevitable. This effect, although believed by Pavlov to be the inexorable end of all CRs, whether reinforced or not, did not occur in all animals after the same amount of training. In some dogs it took only days or weeks; in others it took years. Pavlov also reported that the ultimate total loss of the CR occurred sooner with thermal and tactile stimuli than with visual and auditory stimuli.

Even though he distinguished between this *inhibition with reinforcement* and inhibition of delay on the grounds described above, Pavlov considered the difference to be only a matter of degree. Although not fully worked out and evaluated experimentally, Pavlov's view was that inhibition without reinforcement (for example, extinctive inhibition) proceeded more rapidly than inhibition with reinforcement because the administration of the US in the latter case prevents the cortical center of the CS from exhaustion due to protracted activity. This reasoning was supported by his observation that progressive development of inhibition with reinforcement occurred more readily with long CS–US intervals than with brief ones.

Not long after the first publication of Pavlov's work in English (1927), researchers in the United States began to report phenomena similar to inhibition with reinforcement. The initial efforts involved studies using highly massed conditioning trials. Under these conditions of training, the CR in some cases diminished in strength relatively quickly even when consistently reinforced (Hilgard, 1933; Kantrow, 1937; Newhall & Sears, 1933; Wendt, 1930; Wolfe, 1932). Hilgard and Marquis (1935) studied adaptation, acquisition, extinction, reacquisition, and retention of the classically conditioned eyelid response in dogs, presenting 50 massed training trials per day for five days of acquisition. They found that CR amplitudes on nonreinforced test trials increased within training days only during the first three days. On the fourth and fifth days of acquisition, CR amplitudes declined within each daily session, although large increases in CR amplitude occurred between days throughout acquisition. The amount of increase in CR amplitude between days was negatively related to the size of the CR at the end of training on the previous day, suggesting that the increase was analogous to spontaneous recovery following extinction. Hilgard and Marquis (1935) interpreted the decrement in amplitude of CR within the fourth and fifth daily sessions as an effect of "repetitive work," and the recovery between sessions was attributed to "dissipation of some inhibitory or antagonistic process built up during the process of work [p. 54]." Reduction of the amplitude of the CR with reinforcement, which dissipated over time without training, was also found in an eyelid conditioning experiment with rhesus monkeys (Hilgard & Marquis, 1936), and with humans (Hilgard & Campbell, 1936).

Even when the "inhibition" was not great enough to produce immediately observable decremental effects on CR amplitude during conditioning, interruption of acquisition with a rest interval or the introduction of an extraneous stimulus sometimes resulted in enhancement of the strength of the CR immediately thereafter (Hilgard & Marquis, 1940). Actually, this effect was first reported by Switzer (1930) in his study of backward conditioning of the eyelid response in humans, although it was not immediately related to Pavlov's analogous results. Switzer found a large increase in the amplitude of the CR during the first three extinction trials, and decline in CR amplitude thereafter. Hilgard and Marquis (1935), on obtaining a "Switzer effect" in their eyelid conditioning study with dogs, concluded that the change in experimental conditions from acquisition to extinction acted as a "disinhibitor" that produced a temporary elevation of CR strength. Hovland (1936) appears to have been the first investigator to study inhibition with reinforcement systematically. Because he assumed that it resulted from massed training trials and immediate extinction, he conducted a human GSR conditioning study in which the subjects received either 8 or 24 training trials and were extinguished either immediately following acquisition or with a 30-min rest interpolated between acquisition and extinction. Only a group that received 24 massed reinforcements and immediate extinction showed the "Switzer effect" in the form of an initially rising extinction curve. Groups receiving either 8 massed trials and immediate extinction or 24 massed trials with a 30-min rest interval before extinction both had "normal" extinction curves. A fourth group, which received 24 trials in three sets of 8, with 30-min rest periods interpolated following the first and second sets of 8 trials but immediate extinction, also failed to show the increase in CR amplitude at the beginning of extinction.

Hovland (1936) gave the name "inhibition of reinforcement" to the process that he assumed was responsible for the Switzer effect. This reflected his emphasis upon the role played by massing reinforced trials, as opposed to spacing, in producing the effect. Hovland's fourth experimental group received a total of 24 training trials and underwent extinction training immediately following the last of these. But 30-min rest periods were interpolated between the first and second sets of 8 trials and between the second and third sets of 8 trials. These rest periods were assumed to be of sufficient duration to permit dissipation of the "inhibition of reinforcement" built up during each trial segment of training. This also could have been the case when the rest period followed 24 massed reinforcements. However, Hull (1943) was reluctant to attribute inhibition of reinforcement entirely to a temporary, unlearned condition, since he felt that it was possible that a more permanent, conditioned tendency toward nonresponse might have been established in Hovland's group that showed the Switzer effect.

Hull (1943) stated: "When conditioned reactions are set up by means of massed reinforcements, conditioned inhibition is generated which, at the outset of extinction, is disinhibited through the change in the functioning afferent impulses, with the result that the curve of experimental extinction shows an initial rise [p. 293]." It is quite clear that a learned, relatively permanent inhibition was intended by Hull, as opposed to something unlearned and temporary, both because of his use of the term "conditioned" to modify "inhibition" and because of his assumption that the rise in CR amplitude resulted from disinhibition. The disinhibiting stimulus change Hull referred to was the removal of the stimulus traces of the shock of the previous trial from the stimulus complex associated with nonresponse. This predicted that the Switzer effect would not occur until the second extinction trial, which was the case. However, Hovland's failure to find a Switzer effect in the group receiving 24 massed trials and a 30-min rest before extinction was not in accord with Hull's position, and he indicated that further study of the problem was needed.

Pavlov's finding that the CR ultimately tends to reduce in strength, increase in onset latency, and finally vanish altogether was not an isolated instance of even this extreme type of inhibition with reinforcement. The effect has been found in conditioned occipital electroencephalogram (EEG) desynchronization elicited by an initially indifferent auditory CS which has been paired with a visual US and in many GSR conditioning studies in humans, especially when longer than usual CS–US intervals are employed. Using a 4-sec CS–US interval, Kimmel (1959) found the largest CR to occur between 6 and 8 trials, with CR strength falling to near zero soon thereafter. Meryman (1953) reported that the largest conditioned GSR occurred within two or three trials when a very long (19-sec) interval was used. These data suggested the empirical generalization that "the number of trials required for the highest point in the curve to be reached appears to be inversely related to the CS–US interval employed" (Kimmel, 1966, p. 234). A systematic evaluation of this relationship, using four CS–US intervals ranging from 4 to 16 sec (Morrow & Keough, 1968), provided confirming evidence, at least for the conditioned GSR in humans.

As has been noted above, Pavlov (1927) came to the tentative conclusion that inhibition with reinforcement differed from other types of "internal" inhibition only in degree. He assumed that activity in the cortical cells associated with the CS, if prolonged or nonreinforced, resulted in their temporary exhaustion. Even though theorists from the United States have tended to invest in Pavlov's concept of internal inhibition a degree of permanence analogous to that assumed for other "learned" tendencies, it is not at all clear that Pavlov himself shared this belief. Speaking specifically to the relationship between inhibition *with* reinforcement and inhibition *without* reinforcement, he wrote:

> The rate at which cortical elements become subjected to inhibition in the case without reinforcement fits in with the extreme sensitivity which they exemplify in their extreme need for constant nutrition, being, as is well known, finally and irreparably destroyed by an arrest of blood supply far sooner than any other tissue of the body. It is in complete harmony also with the conception of the cerebral cortex as a signalling apparatus. The fact that the unconditioned stimulus which is signalled induces during its action an inhibition in the cortex is only an artistic finishing touch to the efficiency of the machine. I may permit myself to use the analogy of an efficient and watchful signalman who after having performed his responsible duties has to be provided with an immediate rest during which he is refreshed, so that he may afterwards perform his task again with the same efficiency as before [Pavlov, 1927, p. 244].

In spite of the foregoing suggestion of temporariness and potential recovery with rest, Pavlov reported evidence from an experiment by Speransky

(Pavlov, 1927) indicating that substantial retention of inhibition with reinforcement may be found as much as 24 and, even, 48 hr after it is first established. After a salivary CR had been conditioned to two different visual and auditory CSs (4 stimuli in all), using a 30-sec delayed paradigm and an intertrial interval of 10 min, one of the auditory stimuli, a metronome, was presented 25 times successively with reinforcement, with the intertrial interval reduced to 1.5 min. None of the other CSs was employed during this procedure. Under this massed training regimen, the CR to the metronome quickly reduced in strength, vanishing altogether on the 23rd, 24th, and 25th of these massed trials. In fact, the dog even refused food on the last three trials. One of the visual stimuli was presented on the next trial, again following a short intertrial interval. A small CR occurred and the animal took the food. Immediately subsequently, when food was given without any CS, it was taken and eaten avidly, demonstrating that the animal's hunger was not satiated. Twenty-four hr later the 10-min intertrial interval was reinstated, and all four CSs were presented as before with reinforcement. The metronome elicited a somewhat reduced response on its first presentation, a still smaller one on its second, four trials later, and zero response on its third presentation, an additional four trials later. The other three CSs elicited slightly smaller CRs than previously, but these responses showed no signs of gradual diminution. An additional 24 hr later, even with the intervening day of training with a 10-min intertrial interval, the metronome still showed rapid loss of its effectiveness after a few reinforcements.

Speransky's experiment illustrates the powerful effect of massing of reinforced trials in producing inhibition with reinforcement. It is of special interest because it shows that the inhibition is uniquely associated with the particular stimulus associated with massed training, rather than with any other stimuli which were conditioned to elicit the response. Perhaps even of greater significance is the evidence for substantial retention of this effect during a 24-hr period of removal from the experimental situation. The fact that the dog made a slightly reduced response to the metronome on the first trial following the 24-hr rest, but then rapidly ceased responding to that stimulus thereafter, suggests that proprioception from the first response is part of the stimulus complex governing the inhibitory effect.

The classical conditioning paradigm involves an invariant temporal sequencing of CS and US; the latter never occurs unless it is preceded by the former. These are the very features of the procedure that invest in it the possibility of acquisition of the CR. As Anokhin (1974) has pointed out, regardless of the ultimate "usefulness" of the CR as a preparatory response that may facilitate the organism's adjustment to the impending US, the initial coupling of the neural events elicited by the CS and US probably reflects nothing more than a primary protoplasmic chaining of chemical reactions underlying neural events which have occurred repeatedly in the past. From Anokhin's (1974) viewpoint, ". . . in the whole course of the evolution of living matter, the *principle of anticipatory reflection of the external world is an inalienable part of life and of its adaptation to surrounding conditions* [p. 15, italics in original]," in which the most complex organisms have ". . . acquired a special tool, the brain, the substance of which is highly specialized to the *'chemical coupling' of sequential and recurring influences of the external world* [p. 23, italics in original]." This is the basic meaning of the term "plasticity."

However, these primitive chemical couplings are not themselves adaptive. Only when some environmental adjustment becomes possible by means of these connections can they be consolidated, or, in Anokhin's words, "secured" (1974, p. 29). In the example of temporary acquisition of "conditioned" alpha blocking by an auditory stimulus given above, a large number of repetitions of the tone–light sequence eventually results in loss of the anticipatory cortical response to the tone. When the subject is required to make a response to the light, for example, when differently shaped visual stimuli must be followed by different skeletal responses, the auditory stimulus does not lose its acquired capacity to elicit occipital desynchronization (Karazina, 1958).

A somewhat similar point has been made regarding the conditioned GSR in humans (Kimmel, 1963). This response quickly rises in amplitude during the first few paired acquisition trials and, almost as quickly, begins a downward course that results eventually in its total loss. As Kimmel (1963) has noted, "While it is initially of adaptive value to S to learn which of the multitude of stimuli constantly impinging upon his sense receptors signal impending pain, this information can *ultimately* only be of adaptive value if a response is available that enables avoidance or reduction of the pain [p. 313, italics in original]." But, if the GSR is made effective in preventing the shock US, as in GSR avoidance conditioning (Kimmel & Baxter, 1964), the decline in GSR magnitude following its early rise, typically seen in GSR conditioning, does not occur.

It is one thing for the organism to learn to react emotionally to certain sporadic stimuli which have been associated with pain. But it would be inefficient for the organism to continue to make intense emotional reactions to stimuli that presage painful events regarding which nothing adaptive can be done. In such cases it may be adaptive to cease to respond to the sporadic CS, and rather to "manage" the learned fear (Kimmel, 1963). Alternatively, it may even be possible that the very adaptive factors that are responsible for movement of the peak amplitude of the CR toward the US may eventually result in the complete loss of that CR. This is essentially the notion that Pavlov (1927) entertained and that has been more elaborately treated by Kimmel (1966).

III. RESPONSE SHAPING

What is the mechanism by which the peak amplitude of the CR moves during conditioning away from the point of onset of the CS? Many theorists, from Pavlov and some of his Russian colleagues to current conditioners in the United States, have addressed themselves to this problem, but their efforts have not yet resulted in anything approaching agreement. In our view, the analysis and ultimate elucidation of the mechanism underlying the movement of the peak CR away from the CS (as well as other changes in the CR) has been impeded by methodological uncertainty regarding exactly what it is that changes during conditioning.

The different types of observed changes in the CR to which we have referred above, for example, changes in onset latency, peak latency, may be viewed micromolecularly (Logan, 1956), or more broadly. That is, one may approach the details of response change in piecemeal fashion, treating each identifiable quantitative feature of the response as if it were separately able to assume variable values depending upon the parameters of the particular conditioning paradigm, or one may wish to examine the topography of the total response as an integrated entity. Using the first approach, for example, responses with different onset latencies might be treated as if they were as "different" as are responses involving different effectors. In contrast, these might be viewed as topographic variations of the "same" response. Stewart, Stern, Winokur, and Fredman (1961), exemplifying the first of these approaches, have attempted to differentiate between original (unlearned) GSRs to the CS and "true" CRs on the basis of a latency criterion. Their application of this criterion led them to state: "In summary, we have put forward reasons for thinking that so far work on GSR conditioning has dealt with the adaptation and recovery of unconditioned responses rather than conditioning of responses" (Stewart et al., 1961, p. 66). In opposition to this view, Kimmel (1964) presented photographs of raw GSR records in support of his argument that CR topography changes gradually throughout conditioning, but with great variability, so that the different responses of Stewart et al. (1961) are actually early and late versions of the same response.

To some extent the question of micromolecularity versus topographic entity is empirical. In Logan's (1956) view, a micromolecular approach would prove fruitful (in instrumental conditioning) if it were shown that differential instrumental reinforcement for strong versus weak, late versus early, etc. responses resulted in responding in accord with the reinforcement contingency. However, in classical conditioning the experimenter does not explicitly introduce differential instrumental reinforcement contingencies, although the subject may behave as if such contingencies were present. Prokasy (1965) has cogently observed in this connection that whether or not there may be instrumental reinforcement in a classical conditioning situation depends upon what the subject does, not what the experimenter does. To this must be added that what the subject *may do* "for reinforcement" in the classical conditioning experiment is limited by what the experimenter *has done* in selecting the parameters of the paradigm used, for example, CS–US interval, US intensity.

It is clear that Pavlov (1927), from his physiological stance, treated phenomena such as inhibition of delay as if there could be no doubt that delayed CR onset and placement of peak CR amplitude near US delivery occur in the service of increased biological efficiency. It is obvious with hindsight that the biological function of the CR (to facilitate mastication and swallowing of food or to dilute acid) is best achieved by late CRs in a delayed conditioning paradigm. But, to agree with this proposition need not involve acceptance of the belief that an instrumental reinforcement, or *response shaping,* mechanism is its cause. It is just as likely, a priori, that differential classical conditioning is the basis of observed changes in CRs during conditioning.

A differential classical conditioning approach to the interpretation of CR movement away from CS onset has been suggested by Sheffield (1965), in his attempt to deal with the phenomenon of inhibition of delay in noninstrumental reinforcement terms. Belle, one of the first dogs whose salivary conditioning behavior he studied, showed a lengthening of CR onset latency during a 5.5-sec CS–US interval within the first few days of training. This animal had made its first anticipatory CR on the eighth acquisition trial and soon thereafter reached 100% frequency of responding. Nevertheless, the animal quickly displayed delayed responses and, on nonreinforced test trials, made salivary CRs at about the time that food was normally delivered. Sheffield interpreted this shift in the timing of the CR as resulting from differential association of food with the sound of the feeder mechanism (about 1.5 sec before the delivery of food) and no food with the onset and early portion of the CS. Even without the added auditory cues from the feeder, Sheffield argued, the temporal discrimination could be formed simply on the basis of temporal contiguity of stimuli and reinforcement. In his language (Sheffield, 1965), "At the outset of training the dog responds to the onset of the CS because it is similar to the cues present at the time the US is presented [generalization]. Later the dog discriminates the onset pattern from the cue-pattern present when the US is presented [pp. 308–309, parenthetical phrase added]." Sheffield suggests that this phenomenon might more properly be called "discrimination of delay," instead of "inhibition of delay," although no apparent difference in conceptual parsimony is evident.

Another Pavlovian conditioner who has recently opted for a classical discrimination explanation of changes in CR onset latency is Gormezano (1972). Analysis of the results of a number of studies of the effects of shifts in CS–US intervals led him to the conclusion that they ": . . strongly support the notion that a learned time discrimination may be a major component of what Ss learn in the classical conditioning situation" (Gormezano & Moore, 1969, p. 143). Further, ". . . some temporal mechanisms must be available to the organism to permit the CR peak to be accurately placed on test trials. Conceivably intensive variations in the stimulus trace could provide the necessary time base" (Gormezano, 1972, p. 169). It is appropriate to note that explanations of the type proposed by Sheffield (1965) and Gormezano (1972) either beg the question of what the "classical" conditioning mechanism underlying the proposed differentiation may be or, as in Gormezano's case, explicitly leave the door open to either classical or instrumental sources of reinforcement. Under either circumstance, an implicit assumption of difference between the basic classical- and instrumental-reinforcement mechanisms seems to be made, although this may be nothing more than verbal convention.

The notion that the CR reflects more of a *transaction* between the organism and its environment than is usually implied in theoretical discussions of classical conditioning, a transaction whereby the manner in which the response changes during conditioning depends upon the consequence of such changes, within the constraints of the particular paradigm employed, has been implied or directly suggested by a number of recent investigators (Jones, 1962; Kimmel, 1965; 1966; Martin & Levey, 1969). A common thread consisting of one or another version of the *law of effect* is woven among the fabrics of these otherwise quite different analyses. Jones (1962) has argued that classical conditioning involves two distinct sequential phases, in the first of which the determining *associative* factor is the temporal contiguity between the onset of the CS and the occurrence of the UR and, in the second, the main *reinforcing* factor is the temporal contiguity between the performance of the CR and the onset of the US. In Jones' second phase, the CR is reinforced to the extent to which it occurs in close temporal contiguity to the onset of the US. In this phase, presumably, response shaping would occur. Jones' use of the term "reinforcement" is explicitly empirical, rather than theoretical, it being an event "exhibiting the property of increasing the probability of occurrence of responses" (Jones, 1962, p. 178) it follows. Although Jones does not address herself specifically to changes in response topography, it seems clear that her CR–US gradient of reinforcement model generates the deduction of movement of the CR peak toward the US.

The response shaping analysis of eyelid conditioning offered by Prokasy (1965) comes somewhat closer to indicating a theoretical reinforcement commitment. According to Prokasy (1965), "The set of responses made by the subject on a particular trial, together with the resulting effect of the puff, determines whether, and to what degree, there is reinforcement. This has meaning only relative to what has occurred on previous trials.

Thus, the tensing of facial musculature when E_1 occurs as a kind of 'set' for the puff would very likely be reinforced relative to no such set at all [p. 216]." Although Prokasy's analysis is couched in operational language, it is apparent that both cognitive (for example, "set") and motivational (mitigation of "the effects of stimulation") concepts are involved. This observation is in no way intended critically, since the data discussed by Prokasy lend themselves to the interpretation he has tentatively offered. He makes no claim that response shaping accounts for all of the variations that have been observed, but only that it seems to operate significantly in the classical eyelid conditioning situation.

In Prokasy's subsequent mathematical analyses of changes in response probability in eyelid conditioning (1972), he clearly leans toward a more empirical and less theoretical position regarding "reinforcement" in classical conditioning. In this latter work he suggests that a two-operator, two-phase model accounts fairly well for response probability data under experimental conditions involving voluntary and classical responding with and without a masking task. He points out, however, that changes in CR latency and topography (form) continue to take place even *after* response probability is asymptotic, indicating that analysis of the latter changes remains substantially incomplete.

Martin and Levey (1969) have developed a highly original approach to the problem of analyzing CR modulation in eyelid conditioning, one that appears to incorporate the possibility of empirical determination both of what it may be that CR modulation actually achieves and how a particular "end point" defines response efficiency. They base their strategy on the premise that a priori definition of learning in terms of some expected change in behavior has the effect of a priori determination of the "learning curve" that will be obtained. They argue that changes in CR topography during conditioning tend to be independent of changes in response frequency or probability, as Prokasy (1972) has also observed. And they are quite unequivocal in their assertion that changes in the *way* the subject responds are what the "course" of learning comprises.

An "end point" of learning is assumed by Martin and Levey to be defined by whatever measure is maximized at the expense of others over a series of conditioning trials. This is then used as a criterion of efficiency for evaluating conditioning performance. In each subject correlation coefficients are computed among each of the several response measures chosen for study[2] and between each of the response measures and trial number

---

[2] Martin and Levey (1969) used 36 response measures for the analysis presented. These included CR amplitude at UR onset, CR peak amplitude, UR peak amplitude, CR latency, UR latency, etc., as well as complex measures such as "work ratio" (CR amplitude at UR onset divided by UR peak amplitude). The data employed came from 72 subjects who had conditioned above chance level during 48 acquisition trials using two CS–US intervals, two puff intensities, and two reinforcement schedules.

and ordinal number of each response.[3] In this variation of trend analysis, the square and the cube of the latter two values are also included in the correlation matrix in order to estimate quadratic and cubic trend components as well as linear ones. This analysis yields for each subject an estimate of the degree to which each measure increases. For comparisons among subjects, these measures are converted to z coefficients.

Most of the composite measures described by Martin and Levey tended to increase consistently throughout the 48 conditioning trials. Exceptions to this were "utility" measures, such as CR amplitude at US onset divided by peak CR amplitude. These measures increased rapidly within a few trials and then stabilized. Martin and Levey suggest that this means that the CR is quickly "placed" in an optimum relation to the US–UR complex, an indication that the whole response is being integrated even before its growth in strength has progressed very far. They further suggest that this integration is achieved by means of reciprocal adjustments of the separate response characteristics "in the interest of maximizing the effectiveness of the whole response" (Martin & Levey, 1969, p. 84). An increasingly larger proportion of CR amplitude was "used" in actual puff avoidance, as is shown in Figure 6. They point out that the changes shown schematically in Figure 6 reflect an increase in response efficiency, since in the final phase of their study a CR of somewhat reduced amplitude achieved the same degree of relative avoidance as a larger one had achieved earlier. The figure also shows compensatory decreases in CR latency in conjunction with increases in CR amplitude, an effect discussed above.

Martin and Levey (1969) draw attention to the possible relationship between the oscillation in CR topographic measures they observed during the process of movement of the CR toward an end point, or series of end points, and Pavlov's notion that the CR contributes to a developing equilibrium between the organism and its environment. Their preference, however, is to think analogically in terms of a steady state system, which, in order to change, must oscillate to find a stable level. To them, "It seems not impossible within the system represented by the integrated response, in which individual response elements are finely balanced, and in which the end point is defined by adaptation to constant environmental stimuli, that competing inhibitory and excitatory activities within the nervous system reach a state analogous to the velocity constant of a complex steady state" (Martin & Levey, 1969, p. 97). While this analogy may seem ambitious, it is actually no more so than their overall approach to the problem.

Systematic changes in certain classical CRs do not appear to lend themselves directly to an instrumental reinforcement, response shaping analysis.

---

[3] Trial numbers and ordinal response numbers were both used to permit evaluation of both *magnitude* and *amplitude* averages (Humphreys, 1943), that is, to assess both time and serial changes.

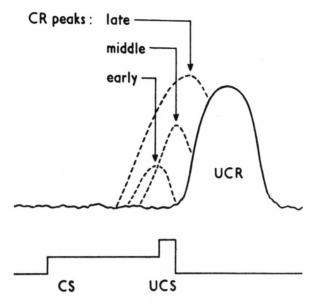

FIGURE 6: Schematic representation of increases in CR peak amplitude and decreases in CR onset latency accompanying movement of eyelid CR through three stages of conditioning. The "end point" in this hypothetical case is a compromise between puff avoidance and integration of CR and UR. (From Martin & Levey, 1969.)

For example, while the salivary CR may directly influence the manner in which the US, food or acid, is received and processed, and while the eye blink may succeed either in avoiding or reducing the aversiveness of an air puff (or possibly, via tensing of facial muscles, mitigating an infraorbital US), it is not immediately apparent by what mechanism modulation of a glandular response such as the GSR might influence reception and adjustment to the shock US. It is possible, of course, that what seems to be regulatory modulation of the conditioned GSR is actually similar to the loss of anticipatory occipital desynchronization to a tone, mentioned above. That is, the rapid appearance and growth of a conditioned GSR may simply reflect a primitive, preadaptive sequential coupling which vanishes fairly quickly because it is not "secured" by utilization in adaptive behavior. If this speculation is correct, it would be expected that the necessity of performing some task similar to the requirement of different motor responses to differently shaped lights in Karazina's (1958) experiment might prevent the rapid loss of the anticipatory GSR, much as happened with anticipatory occipital desynchronization to the tone in her study.

We know of only one classical conditioning study with paired stimuli in which an attentional-skeletal response to the US was required in some but not all subjects (Kimmel, 1967a). In the subjects required to judge the intensity of the US by moving a lever, the conditioned GSR was significantly larger than that in subjects conditioned without the judgment task. But neither group showed CR reduction in this study. Even when there is no explicit CS and the US is delivered at regular temporal intervals (as in temporal conditioning), the necessity of performing a motor response that indicates judged US intensity appears to result in maintenance rather than loss of anticipatory CRs (Pendergrass & Kimmel, 1968). Indeed, the subjects who received the regularly spaced USs without a judgment task made their largest anticipatory GSRs early in training (Trials 7 and 8) and did not differ from nonconditioning controls who received irregularly spaced USs. The results of these studies are thus in partial accord with the notion that modulation of the conditioned GSR (response decrement) may simply result from decoupling of a preadaptive sequential connection, in the absence of an explicitly adaptive task requirement.

An indirect instrumental reinforcement explanation of CR changes in GSR conditioning has been suggested by Kimmel (1963, 1965), based in part upon the futility of an early CR, or, possibly, any CR, and also upon the observation that the UR also changes in strength and, possibly, in latency during conditioning. Diminution of the UR is the subject of a subsequent section of this chapter, so Kimmel's hypothesis will be given only brief mention here, with emphasis upon CR changes. He has reported data from a study of 50 human subjects whose GSRs were conditioned with a CS–US interval of 7.5 sec. Of particular interest in connection with the foregoing discussion of shifts in the latency of the peak of the CR in Kimmel's finding, shown graphically in Figure 7, that this phenomenon characterizes human GSR CRs also. As can be seen in this figure, CR peak latency increases continuously over 50 trials, with an asymptote of 9.42 sec, approximately 1.98 sec *after* the onset of the US. Since nonresponse trials were scored as having peak latencies of 11.0 sec (2.0 sec more than an arbitrary maximum of 9.0 sec for CR onset latency), it is likely that this is an overestimate of the true asymptote. Omitting nonresponse trials, latency of the CR peak levels off at about 7.2 sec. In any case, it seems clear from data of this type that the peak of the CR moves to a point close to and possibly beyond US onset, so that an integrative fusion of the CR and UR may be the endpoint of this process.

Integrative fusion of the CR and UR, as an endpoint of the CR modulation process in GSR conditioning, would intuitively seem to be a more likely outcome than a slightly earlier placement of the CR so that its peak coincides with US onset (which would constitute maximal US avoidance in eyelid conditioning), since no established avoidance mechanism exists for the GSR case. However, the increase in skin conductance that defines the GSR also occurs at the site of the shock electrodes (in studies in our

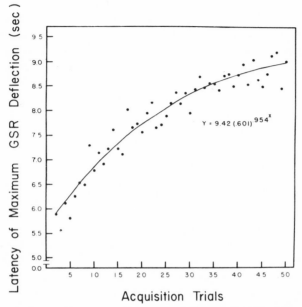

FIGURE 7. Average latency of peak conditioned GSR for 50 subjects receiving a 7.5-sec tone paired with .1-sec shock. Nonresponse trials were scored as 11.0 sec. (From Kimmel, 1965.)

laboratory this would be the volar surface of the forearm, which is known to be electrodermally active). Placement of the peak of the CR at the time of delivery of the shock US might, because of this, have a potentially reinforcing effect similar to puff avoidance in eyelid conditioning. Since the most common shock generators used in GSR conditioning research are designed to produce a constant-current stimulus, a shock delivered at the point of maximum drop in skin resistance at the site of the shock electrodes would necessarily have to be of lesser voltage in compensation for the reduced resistance. This adjustment is a simple consequence of Ohm's law. The net result of a compensatory drop in voltage to maintain constant current through a lowered skin resistance would also mean that power, the product of voltage and current, would be reduced. Comparative studies of the role of power, current, and voltage in influencing judgments of the subjective pain of electric shock (Green, 1962; Hill, Flanary, Kornetsky, & Wikler, 1952) have shown that variations in power are more closely tracked by subjective pain than either of the other shock parameters. In other words, when the peak amplitude of the conditioned GSR occurs at the point of administration of the US, the subjective pain of the US may be lower than it would be otherwise. The actual magnitude of this electrical "reinforcement" (relative reduction in power) would depend upon the size of the GSR in ohms of decrease in resistance, the shock intensity employed (the greater the intensity, the more potential reinforcement), and the manner in which the shock electrodes are attached (rubbing the skin to produce a slight abrasion and employing electrode paste combine to *reduce* basal resistance and resistance variations at the electrode site). All of this remains to be investigated in detail.

IV. DIMINUTION OF THE UNCONDITIONED RESPONSE

When Pavlov first described the phenomenon referred to above as *inhibition with reinforcement,* he made reference to concomitant effects beyond gradual increase in CR latency, reduction of CR amplitude, and eventual loss of the CR itself. When the inhibitory effect becomes extreme, "The animal grows inert in the stand during the experiment, and even declines the food which is given after application of the conditioned stimulus" (Pavlov, 1927, p. 239). In specific reference to the Speransky study (Pavlov, 1927), in which a series of 25 massed trials resulted in total loss of the CR, Pavlov added the comment, ". . . the dog even refusing food after the last three stimuli [p. 247]." Although no specific reference was made to the salivary UR on these occasions, it is obvious that the decremental process had spread to the point of implicating behavior associated with the food US. One may assume that the salivary UR, if the animal took the food at all, would have been reduced also.

Inhibition of the salivary UR resulting from pairing with a CS was serendipitously observed by Rikman, in an experiment in which daily feeding followed the administration of conditioning trials (Orbeli, 1949). The strength of the salivary UR during 1 min of normal feeding was greater than that during 1 min of eating the food reinforcement preceded by a CS. In addition, the UR was greater when the US followed weak CSs than when it followed strong ones. In the Wednesday discussion of December 18, 1929, Pavlov could give no satifactory explanation of these findings; indeed, he thought the reverse effects should have occurred (Orbeli, 1949)! Actual loss of the salivary UR to food has been described by Kupalov (1961), in a case he labeled "pathological irradiation of inhibition." Both the CR and the UR vanished in this animal, and it even ate its regular diet in the home cage without salivating, justifying the use of the term "pathological."

Specific identification of reduced strength of the UR as a potential concomitant of classical conditioning more generally was apparently first suggested by Kimble (1961) and Lykken (1959). These investigators approached the topic in somewhat different ways and studied different responses, but each noted that the UR was reduced in strength when the US was preceded by a CS, compared to its strength when the US was presented alone.

Lykken (1959) presented electric shocks to human subjects on a fixed-interval 30-sec schedule, or on a fixed-interval 30-sec schedule with a 5-sec tone preceding each shock. He found that the GSR elicited by shock was smaller on those occasions when the tone preceded it than when the tone was absent, presumably because the subjective aversiveness of the signalled shock was reduced by preparatory activity. He labeled the phenomenon *preception* and invested in it cognitive–preparatory characteristics governed by the warning signal. At about the same time, Kimble and Dufort (1956) were investigating the effects of an interpolated series of unpaired USs, following initial conditioning, on the terminal strength of eyelid conditioning. They noted that the UR increased dramatically in amplitude when the US was presented without the CS following paired trials. In describing this effect, Kimble (1961) presented photographs of selected eyelid URs, with and without paired CSs, to substantiate the claim that diminution of the UR may be a regular concomitant of classical conditioning, and that the recovery of the UR on US-only trials provides a measure of the degree of diminution.

To evaluate the proposition that the UR diminution effect is associative, Kimble and Ost (1961) varied the CS–US interval prior to presenting test trials with the US alone. They found that the largest amount of recovery of the amplitude of the UR occurred when the CS–US interval during conditioning was .5 sec, supporting their assumption that an associative process is involved. Because of the possibility that the UR on paired trials might be reduced because of fatigue resulting from an immediately preceding CR, they computed UR increments using as a base line only trials on which no CR occurred. This procedure is only partly effective, since subjects conditioned at "favorable" intervals provide few such trials late in conditioning and force the investigator to find no-CR trials which occurred early in conditioning. Nevertheless, Kimble and Ost (1961) concluded that the effect is associative and that it is probably related to Pavlov's inhibition of delay.

Follow-up of this approach to the analysis of diminution of the UR was undertaken by Kimmel and Pennypacker (1962), using the GSR. These investigators reported that both diminution and recovery of the UR in human GSR conditioning increase as a function of the number of reinforcements given prior to the US-only test trial. These results tended to support the conclusion that the diminution effect varies as a function of known conditioning parameters in the same way as do other, more traditional measures of the strength of conditioning. Subsequent studies of the UR diminution phenomenon indicated that it is weakened by the administration of extinction trials (Morrow, 1966), is greater when a delayed rather than trace conditioning paradigm is employed (Baxter, 1966; Kimmel, 1967a), and is greater in subjects receiving a temporal conditioning paradigm than in controls who received USs on a varying temporal schedule (Pendergrass & Kimmel, 1968).

The possibility that diminution of the UR results from the adoption of a perceptual–cognitive set by the subject, which enables preparation for the impending US and thus reduces the aversiveness or intrusiveness of the US has been suggested by Lykken (1959, 1972) and by Grings (1969). The available data on this issue are ambiguous. For example, Kimmel (1967a) varied the duration of the CS within a 5-sec CS–US interval and had the subjects judge the intensity of the US on each occasion of its presentation. She found that judged intensity of the US *increased* in a group receiving a CS duration of 5 sec (a delayed paradigm), whereas the size of the GSR *decreased*. In addition, omission of the CS on US-only test trials following conditioning resulted in large *increases* in the GSR to the US, accompanied by *decreases* in judged intensity of the US. The correlation between GSR amplitude and judged intensity of the US was significantly positive ($r = 0.52$) in a group of control subjects which received only USs, but in a group of subjects given paired conditioning trials with a .5-sec CS–US interval, the correlation was essentially zero. Results of this type do not seem to be compatible with a cognitive–perceptual explanation of UR diminution.

In contrast, Grings and Schell (1969a) have obtained diminution of the UR in *both* delayed and trace conditioning paradigms. Their study was an attempt to replicate the Baxter (1966) results mentioned above, since they noted that most of the difference between Baxter's delayed and trace paradigms was due to the performance of the unpaired groups in his study, not to the paired groups. Grings and Schell (1969a) offer no explanation of their results, other than to note that they are in disagreement with those of Baxter. Nor do they offer any explanation for the discrepancy between the two sets of results. Indeed, the only procedural difference we have been able to identify is the fact that Grings and Schell employed a "shock-workup" procedure in which the subject initially selects the intensity of shock to be employed during the conditioning trials. Baxter (1966) simply presented three preliminary shocks, in intensity increments ending with the intensity to be used thereafter. Baxter's US was an ac shock; Grings and Schell's US was dc. The shock workup procedure began with a threshold intensity and required the subject to indicate when the 4–6-V increments reached a shock level that was subjectively unpleasant. With no other differences between the two studies, perhaps the shock workup procedure has the effect of focusing the subject's attention on the shock, and on its intensity characteristics. It is possible that this could facilitate the UR diminution process.

In support of this speculation is the finding (Kimmel, 1967a) that diminution of the UR is more rapid when the subject is explicitly required to judge the intensity of the US than when judgments of US intensity are not required. Forcing the subject to attend to the US and make a psychophysical judgment of its intensity appears to facilitate UR diminution. A related line of support may be found in the fact (Morgenson, 1967) that subjects who are able to verbalize correctly regarding the CS–US temporal contingency ("aware" subjects) show substantially more rapid diminution of the UR than do "unaware" subjects, who are not able to verbalize the contingency. Diminution of the UR was found in both groups, but it was more rapid in the aware group. Peeke and Grings (1968) reported that instructing the subject regarding whether the CS–US interval would be regular (5.5 sec) or variable (varying around a mean of 5.5 sec) produced diminution of the UR on the very first paired conditioning trial in the regular interval condition. The variable interval group also showed diminution of the UR during conditioning, but the diminution was much more gradual in its development.

Although the mechanism is not known by which instructions or other procedures which increase the attention given by the subject to the US serve to facilitate diminution of the UR, there is no compelling reason to conclude that UR diminution *necessarily* depends upon cognitive factors. Further analysis of the finding that diminution occurs more rapidly in subjects who are required to judge the intensity of the US than in those who are not (Kimmel, 1967b) reveals that only those subjects who were conditioned with a *trace* paradigm (either with a 1- or 3-sec CS duration within a 5-sec CS–US interval) and did not judge the intensity of the US showed slower diminution of the UR. A group of subjects conditioned with a 5-sec *delayed* conditioning paradigm showed diminution of the UR which was just as rapid as that obtained in the judgment groups. Apparently, the facilitative effect of a judgment task on the development of diminution of the UR is observable only when experimental procedures are employed which are less than optimal for the establishment of classical conditioning in the first place (for example, *trace* versus *delayed* conditioning paradigms).

In spite of the differences among some of the results of these experiments, and regardless of theoretical conflict, the finding of UR diminution appears to be ubiquitous at the empirical level. We have concentrated on data obtained primarily in studies of human eyelid and GSR conditioning, because these preparations have been employed most often in studies directly aimed at theoretical analysis of the phenomenon. However, UR diminution has been reported in conditioned alpha blocking (Wells, 1959), with an auditory CS and a visual US, in cortical evoked responses (Lykken, Macindoe, & Tellegen, 1972), with an auditory CS and an electric shock US, in heart-rate conditioning in dogs (Fitzgerald, 1966), with an auditory

CS and shock US, and in salivary conditioning. Disagreement regarding interpretation appears to result as much from theoretical predeliction of the various researchers as much as from any other source. As was noted above, Kimble (1961) approached UR diminution as simply another manifestation of classical conditioning, suggesting that it might be related to Pavlov's inhibition of delay. This was by no means an acceptance on Kimble's part of Pavlov's theoretical account of inhibition of delay. Kimmel (1966) went somewhat beyond, simply drawing an empirical parallel between UR diminution and inhibition, since he explictly dealt with the possibility of an instrumental reinforcement explanation of both inhibition of delay and UR diminution. Grings (1969) and Lykken (1972), on the other hand, prefer a more cognitive–perceptual approach to the phenomenon, just as they do to classical conditioning generally (for example, Grings & Dawson, 1973).

Systematic evaluation of the possibility that a preparatory response to the CS in classical conditioning reduces the aversiveness of the shock, and consequently, the strength of the UR has been undertaken by Furedy and his collaborators (e.g., Biederman & Furedy, 1973; Furedy, 1970; Furedy & Klajner, 1972). Using the GSR and vasomotor response of humans and shock-preference behavior of rats, these investigators have reported that URs to shock were significantly smaller when the shock is signaled, but signaled and unsignaled shocks were not judged to be different in intensity. In addition, there was no correlation between CR strength and judged intensity, in agreement with the result previously reported by Kimmel (1967a). In a study which employed a complex procedure designed to "unconfound" the autonomic URs from responses to the CS, these investigators found no evidence that the unshocked part of the CS served as a "safety signal." The vasomotor response to the signaled shock was greater than that to unsignaled shock, in the opposite direction from both the GSR results and what a preparatory response theory would predict. Furedy and his colleagues have concluded that autonomic URs to shock do not provide unconfounded indices of the relative aversiveness of signaled and unsignaled shocks, and that the capacity of humans to gain informational cognitive control over responding is quite limited.

In the most recent extension of this line of research, Biederman and Furedy (1973) have shown that rats prefer signaled over unsignaled shock (a preference that has been assumed to provide a behavioral index of relative aversiveness of the shock) *only* when the physical intensity of the shock is actually modifiable by the animal. When unavoidable shocks are delivered either to the animal's tail or to its feet through scrambled foot grids, no preference for signaled over unsignaled shock is seen. When the unavoidable shocks are delivered via unscrambled foot grids however, preference for signaled over unsignaled shock was found. These results appear to limit the applicability of a preparatory response explanation of CR and UR modulation in classical conditioning.

Another potential contributor to observed diminution of the UR in classical conditioning is the fact that any response to the immediately preceding CS may interfere with the capacity of the US to elicit a UR (Badia & Defran, 1970; Grings & Schell, 1969b). If the subject responds to the CS in the interval immediately prior to the administration of the US, it is possible that a fatiguelike process may reduce the size of the UR. It was for this reason that Kimble and Ost (1961) employed trials on which no CR occurred as a base line in computing their UR-increment scores. Again we are confronted with the difference between necessary and sufficient conditions for observing some particular effect. Grings and Schell (1969b) have demonstrated that the strength of the GSR to the second of two successive stimuli is inversely related to the intensity of the first stimulus and the temporal interval between the two stimuli. The more intense the first stimulus, the larger is the response it elicits, and the smaller the response elicited by the second stimulus. Both the intensity and interval factors point to a response interference explanation of their results. However, the fact that *UR amplitude is attenuated on paired conditioning trials even when the subject makes no observable response to the CS* would suggest that the results of Grings and Schell's experiment are essentially irrelevant to the question of the source of this type of UR diminution.

Figure 8 shows an actual GSR conditioning record in a study employing a 4.9-sec CS–US interval, a 40-dB 1000-Hz pure tone as CS, and a 4.0-mamp shock as US. Two consecutive trials trials late in conditioning are shown in the figure, the earlier one containing no CR at all and the subsequent one indicating a CR of moderate strength. The size of the UR on the first of these two trials is slightly smaller than on the second one. Both URs are substantially smaller than the UR observed at the beginning of conditioning and on subsequent US-only test trials, both of these findings having been documented thoroughly in the past. If the UR is reduced on paired conditioning trials even when there is no observable basis for assuming response interference from an immediately preceding CR, the question still remains as to the source of this reduction. In Figure 8 two consecutive trials were selected because Grings and Dawson (1973) have explicitly criticized Kimble and Ost's procedure of using URs on no-CR trials to assess degree of relative UR recovery when the CS is omitted, on the grounds that, ". . . such restriction of analysis to trials on which the anticipatory response is absent could be interpreted as seriously biasing the sample of observed events in the direction of low performance learning trials [p. 226]." In eyelid conditioning the frequency of observed CRs becomes quite high in the late stages of conditioning, and it is difficult to locate any trials without CRs. But in GSR conditioning it is not uncommon

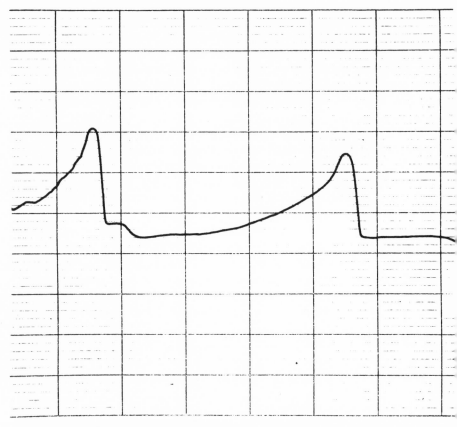

FIGURE 8. Photograph of actual GSR record showing two successive paired trials of 5.0-sec tone and 0.1-sec shock both terminating simultaneously). The earlier trial (right) contained no CR, whereas the later trial contains a CR of moderate amplitude. The UR on the later trial (containing a CR) is slightly larger than that on the earlier trial (not containing a CR). Event mark at top identifies CS delivery.

for the CR to be missing on half of the trials, especially late in conditioning (see Kimmel, 1965, pp. 157–162). If a response interference explanation of UR diminution were correct, one would expect the strength and probability of the UR to wax and wane inversely with those of the CR. This is manifestly not the case, as is shown in Figure 8 and can be observed in the records of almost any GSR conditioning study involving long CS–US intervals. Furthermore, Kimmel and Pennypacker (Kimmel, 1966) found a CS–US interval function for UR diminution that paralleled that of Kimble and Ost, using adjacent trials to assess UR recovery.

It was noted in the section on response shaping that one end point of CR modulation during conditioning may be an integrative fusion of the

CR with the UR. To the extent that this conjecture may be correct, it would not be unexpected to find trial-by-trial variations among occasions on which no CR at all occurs, others on which no CR is present but there is a UR with reduced latency, and still others in which the two responses fuse completely into a single, very late CR, which blends continuously with the UR. Figure 9 photographically reproduces a blended response of this type, selected from one of our recent GSR conditioning studies, with a 4.9-sec CS–US interval, a 40-dB 1000-Hz pure tone as CS, and a 4.0-mamp shock as US. The response shown in Figure 9 clearly begins before the onset of the US (and, thus, is a CR) and continues smoothly into the UR to the US. Although the type of quantitative analysis done by Martin and Levey (1969) on their eyelid CR data remains to be accomplished for the conditioned GSR, there is reason to believe that it would prove equally informative in the GSR case. For the present purpose, we wish to reemphasize the notion that the conditioning situation may involve more than simple input–output descriptors, and that this "transactionalist" approach may be fruitfully extended to include UR as well as CR modulation.

The argument has been made by Badia and Defran (1970) that omission of the CS on US-only test trials is an adequate stimulus for elicitation of an OR to the unpaired US, and, therefore, the UR on such tests is not a "pure" UR. Rejecting the idea that the increment of the UR on such

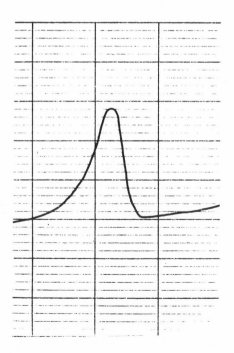

FIGURE 9. Photograph of actual GSR record showing blended CR–UR late in acquisition. Note that the response begins during the time of administration of the CS (event mark at top) and continues smoothly into the UR to the shock.

occasions results from the absence of CS-controlled inhibition, these authors state: "A more parsimonious interpretation, we believe, would hold that during training S learns *that* the UCS is always preceded by the CS" (Badia & Defran, 1970, p. 176, italics added). We emphasize their use of the word "that" in Badia and Defran's alternative to an explanation they judge to be inadequately "parsimonious," because we feel that it illustrates the point made previously regarding the influence of the different theoretical predelictions of different investigators. It has been well known for a long time that some conditioners attempt to deal with what the subject does while others speculate regarding what the subject knows. The explanation offered by Badia and Defran (1970) of UR diminution ("the S learns that . . .") is clearly of the latter type. Even if Badia and Defran are correct in emphasizing the participation of the GSR in the orienting reflex to stimulus change, however, it is hardly to be expected that the eyelid response, and other responses showing reduced URs during conditioning, equally reflect dishabituated orienting reflexes. They might argue that the elicitation of an OR may invigorate a variety of responses. But, then, could the reinstitution of the CS following a series of US-only trials in eyelid conditioning have the immediate effect of attenuating the UR to the puff (Kimble, 1961; Kimble & Dufort, 1956)?

There can be little doubt that omission of the CS and presentation of the US alone, following pairing, is an adequate elicitor of an OR, as Badia and Defran (1970) have pointed out. These authors have described a study in which the GSR to a light increased significantly when the tone that regularly preceded the light was omitted and the light presented alone. This is true even when the light was presented without the tone on five separate occasions interpolated among ten occasions of pairing of the two stimuli (Badia & Defran, 1970). From our viewpoint, data such as these complement rather than conflict with similar results in GSR conditioning studies using an electric shock as the US.

A priori distinctions regarding which combinations of stimuli may and may not comprise effective classical conditioning paradigms do not seem advisable, particularly in the light of Anokhin's (1974) suggestion that chemical coupling of sequential events occurs at least temporarily in the nervous system whether or not these sequences are "secured" via their utility in adaptation. Badia and Defran (1970) ask whether the GSR to the second of two repeatedly paired stimuli increases when the stimulus is presented alone, "when both stimuli were neutral (absence of conditioning) [p. 179]." Their own data show that the second stimulus, rather than being neutral, originally elicits the response in question and continues to do so for many trials. Rather than interpreting their finding that the second "neutral" stimulus does indeed elicit a larger response when the first stimulus is omitted to mean that UR diminution and recovery are not manifestations of conditioning, it might be more appropriate to examine the a priori distinction regarding what is and what is not "conditioning." Their tone–light paradigm would appear to qualify for inclusion on the basis of the results of their study.

If diminution of the UR in classical conditioning is a consequence of an integrative process that also involves modulations of the CR, it is possible that it would not occur under conditions in which the CR is instrumentalized experimentally, for example, in GSR avoidance conditioning. Kimmel and Baxter (1964) reported the first such study in which data indicating successful avoidance conditioning were found. Comparison of the CR magnitude curves of their avoidance and yoked control groups indicates that the former showed little, if any, tendency toward postpeak CR reduction, whereas the latter showed some response attenuation late in conditioning. Following acquisition, the subjects in both of these groups were given a single test trial with the US alone. Although there was a slight difference in UR recovery favoring the yoked control group over the avoidance group, it was not statistically significant, and its interpretation was complicated by the fact that a *trace* conditioning paradigm had been used in both groups. The possibility that recovery of the UR on US-only trials might be absent in avoidance GSR conditioning was examined directly in a subsequent study (Kimmel, 1965). Both trace and delayed paradigms were employed, with a 5-sec CS–US interval, a 1-sec or 5-sec CS duration, and the GSR preventing the shock and terminating the CS in the delayed condition for both avoidance and yoked control subjects. Diminution of the UR was absent in both avoidance groups and was present in both yoked control groups. The difference in UR recovery between the avoidance and control condition was significant only for subjects tested with a delayed conditioning paradigm. As in the earlier study, the difference was not significant in the trace groups. Followup of this question (Terrant, 1968), using a within-subject reciprocal yoked control technique, has shown that, at least for subjects above the median in conditioning scores, the URs late in acquisition are smaller in yoked classical controls than those in avoidance subjects. The fact that diminution and recovery of the UR occurs in classical conditioning but is absent in instrumental avoidance conditioning, if it does nothing else, indicates that the phenomenon is intimately associated with the classical conditioning process. Although its mechanism is not adequately understood and its function in conditioning only a matter of conjecture, diminution of the UR will very likely receive considerable further attention. As Martin and Levey (1969) have observed, attention to changes in the UR and related investigation of changes in the CR, "mark a rather more revolutionary way of considering conditioning . . . [p. 43]."

V. POSTACQUISITION CONSEQUENCES

It was noted above that massed classical conditioning trials tend to be followed by increases in the strength of the GSR and eyelid CR during the first few trials of extinction. This is the so-called "Switzer" effect, which was shown by Hovland (1936) to be absent when only 8 paired trials were run rather than 24 trials, or when either 30 min of rest was interpolated between the 8th and 9th and between the 16th and 17th trials, or a 30-min rest period followed the 24 trials of acquisition. Presumably these effects reflect the development of some kind of inhibition during massed acquisition. It is of some interest that the increase in CR strength in extinction does not occur until the third trial for the eyelid CR and the second trial for the GSR, *after* the US has been omitted on at least one immediately preceding trial. It is thus not the CS alone which controls this inhibition, but a more complex stimulus involving elements from the preceding UR. On the assumption that the eyelid CR involves more "work" than the GSR, it would be expected that the latter would recover more rapidly following US omission.

These early studies of postacquisition effects of paired conditioning trials were not immediately related to resistance to extinction. The similarity of *inhibition with reinforcement* and *extinctive inhibition* was implied by Pavlov (1927), but no experiments dealing directly with the question were done in his laboratory. Serendipitous discovery of a possible connection occurred in an experiment on retention of habituation and conditioning of the GSR (Bishop & Kimmel, 1969). These investigators examined the amount of savings between habituation and rehabituation, as a function of the temporal interval between the two, and compared this retention function with an analogous one obtained between conditioning and extinction. Because the criterion of habituation was two successive nonresponse trials, Bishop and Kimmel decided to terminate acquisition in their conditioning groups two trials after the largest GSR occurred. This seemed to be a reasonable index of maximal acquisition. More than half of their conditioning subjects failed to reach the extinction criterion within the 50 extinction trials employed. These subjects were equally distributed among groups that underwent extinction immediately, or following 20 min, 1 day, 1 week, 4 weeks, or 6 months. Compared to the rapidity of extinction in most GSR conditioning studies that use a fixed number of paired trials for all subjects (usually greater in number than the range of 5–9 trials in the Bishop and Kimmel study), these results strongly suggested that administering paired acquisition trials beyond the peak response has the effect of reducing resistance to extinction.

Two studies have been done to evaluate this generalization (Schramm & Kimmel, 1970; Silver & Kimmel, 1969). Their results indicate that resistance to extinction decreases in linear fashion as a function of postpeak acquisition trials. Control subjects who were given unpaired CSs and USs matched in number to those received by the conditioning subjects evidenced no relationship between resistance to "extinction" and number of unpaired CSs and USs. Sixteen postpeak paired trials reduced resistance to extinction to the level of the controls. Although Schramm and Kimmel (1970) commented that, "It is almost as if postpeak paired trials were the equivalent of extinction trials [p. 243]," group-by-group analysis showed that postpeak pairing had an even more attentuating effect on resistance to extinction than did actual extinction trials. Interestingly, the introduction of *unpaired* CSs and USs following reliable attainment of the peak CR is even more effective in reducing resistance to extinction (Kimmel & Owen, 1974), subjects run with this procedure extinguishing almost immediately following removal of the US. Apparently, the administration of initial paired trials potentiates the extinguishing effect of unpaired trials administered subsequently, as if some kind of "contrast" effect were occurring, although this suggestion needs further study.

In the Silver and Kimmel (1969) and Schramm and Kimmel (1970) studies extinction was begun immediately following acquisition, with an intertrial interval equal to the average acquisition intertrial interval. For this reason, the conclusion that reduction in resistance to extinction resulting from postpeak pairing reflects a *conditioned* inhibitory effect can only be tentative. Lanning and Yaremko (1971) conducted an experiment in which either 2 or 16 paired postpeak trials were run, and extinction was introduced immediately for one-half of the subjects but followed a 5-min rest period for the other half of the subjects. The rest period was filled with "soft music." They found a significant interaction in their trials to extinction data between Pairing (paired CS–US trials versus unpaired CSs and USs) and Rest (regular intertrial interval with no music versus 5 min with music). This interaction resulted from the fact that there was no difference due to rest following two trials past the peak, but a large difference favoring rest following 16 postpeak trials. Lanning and Yaremko interpreted these results to mean that the reduced resistance to extinction effect of the earlier studies must have resulted from a temporary inhibitory condition that dissipated with only 5 min of rest. However, as they pointed out, the rest period had no influence on resistance to extinction in their unpaired controls, which mitigates against a nonassociative interpretation.

The Lanning and Yaremko (1971) study may be questioned for other reasons, as well. In the Bishop and Kimmel (1969), Silver and Kimmel (1969), and Schramm and Kimmel (1970) experiments, groups who received only two postpeak paired trials averaged over 40 trials to criterion in extinction. Lanning and Yaremko's equivalent groups required only about 10 trials to extinguish. Even their group that was most resistant to extinction, the 16 postpeak-plus rest group, underwent extinction within 20 trials. These wide discrepancies between the data of the three separate Kimmel studies and the Lanning and Yaremko study, even in conditions intended to replicate earlier ones, raise reservations regarding the Lanning and Yaremko results. Furthermore, the use of music during the 5-min rest period may have added an even more significant complication to their situation. If the inhibitory effect is the result of an associative process, the introduction of a novel stimulus like music into the intertrial interval may have disinhibiting effects of its own.

Indeed, Hull (1943) suggested that even rest itself, by changing the intertrial stimulus situation grossly just before the beginning of extinction, may serve as a disinhibitor of *conditioned* inhibition as well as permitting the dissipation of possible temporary inhibition. To check on this possibility, we conducted an experiment[4] in which the subjects were given either 2 or 16 postpeak GSR conditioning trials, either paired or unpaired CSs and USs, extinction beginning immediately (with an intertrial interval between the end of acquisition and the first trial of extinction equaling the average of prior intertrial intervals, 1 min). One-half of the subjects heard "soft music" during the intertrial interval immediately preceding extinction, and half did not. In the paired groups the average magnitude of the CR on the first extinction trial was almost twice as large in the group receiving music than in the group that did not ($\bar{X} = 8.50$ versus $\bar{X} = 4.52$). In the unpaired groups, the average magnitude of the GSR in the group receiving music during the intertrial interval just before extinction was more than five times as large as in the no music group ($\bar{X} = 4.64$ versus $\bar{X} = 0.86$). This effect of music was statistically significant and did not interact with number of postpeak trials. It is obvious that these differences were not due to "rest" but to the novelty of the music that occurred for the first time just before the first extinction trial.

Substantial reduction of resistance to extinction resulting from overreinforcement has been demonstrated quite convincingly in a recent study using *Planaria* as subjects (Kimmel & Garrigan, 1973). The results of this study bear on the question of the phyletic generality of the phenomenon, the extent to which it may be related to the CS–US interval used during conditioning, and whether the attenuation of responding is temporary or relatively permanent. Several studies using *Planaria* have shown that highly reliable and large differences in response frequency during acquisition between paired and unpaired groups of subjects tend to vanish almost immediately when extinction is begun (Baxter & Kimmel, 1963; Kimmel & Yaremko, 1966; Yaremko & Kimmel, 1969). With continuous reinforcement

---

[4] This study was done by Richard Borden, Richard Burns, and Michael McCauley.

and 250 acquisition trials, response frequently in the animals receiving paired CS and US falls below the level of control animals within ten extinction trials. Kimmel and Garrigan (1973) compared resistance to extinction in groups receiving 150 and 250 paired acquisition trials, with either a 2- or a 4-sec CS–US interval. Figure 10 presents their data for the first day of 50 extinction trials. As is shown in Figure 10, substantially greater resistance to extinction was present following 150 than 250 reinforcements and, within the 150 reinforcements condition, the short CS–US interval was slightly superior to the long one.

We believe that this study is significant especially because of the fact that the paired conditioning trials were delivered in daily sessions of 50 trials, with a 23-hr rest between sessions, and the first 50 trials of extinction were preceded by a 23-hr rest period. It is difficult to imagine a *temporary* inhibitory condition that results from massed training, yet persists from day to day of training and, even transcends the day of rest before extinction. On the last day of conditioning all of the paired groups performed

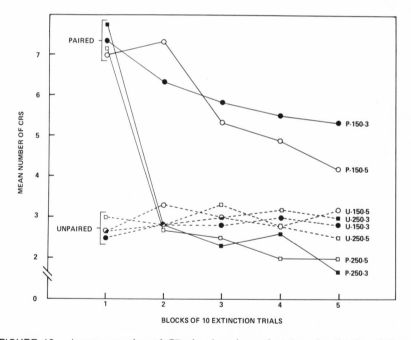

FIGURE 10.   Average number of CRs in planaria on first day of extinction, following either 150 or 250 paired conditioning trials with a 3- or 5-sec visual CS and a 1-sec shock US (CS–US interval of 2 sec or 4 sec) or unpaired CSs and USs equivalent in number to paired groups. The legend on the right hand edge of each group curve indicates pairing (P–U), number of trials (150–250), and CS duration (3–5). (From Kimmel & Garrigan, 1973.)

at about the 60–65% response level. During the first ten extinction trials, on the next day, responding rose slightly to the 70–75% level. Within the very next ten trials the animal that had received 250 paired trials dropped precipitously to below 30%, whereas the animals given only 150 paired trials remained near 70%.

These results suggest that response-produced cues must be part of the complex that governs the inhibitory effect (reduced resistance to extinction), since the groups did not differ during the first ten trials of extinction. The slight difference favoring the shorter CS–US interval over the longer one, however, implicates the CS as a contributing cue for inhibition also. Because of the fact that amplitude measurement has not yet become technologically feasible in classical conditioning in *Planaria,* the possibility of terminating acquisition immediately following each individual subject's peak CR has not been examined. The study by Kimmel and Garrigan (1973) simply shows that 250 reinforcements are too many relative to 150, but does note show whether the optimum number is closer to 250 or 150. Since response frequency does not appear to increase much beyond the third day of 50 trials per day within the parameters employed, it is likely that the optimum is not much beyond 150 paired trials.

The relationship between the effect of postpeak pairing on resistance to extinction and CR and/or UR regulatory modulations has not been investigated sufficiently to justify anything but tentative speculation. At a completely empirical level, it has been shown that resistance to extinction benefits from paired CS–US trials only up to some point and that, beyond that point, additional pairings result in reduced resistance to extinction. For the human GSR preparation, the level of technology of which is advanced sufficiently to permit trial-by-trial determination of CR amplitude, it has been found that no more than one or two trials beyond the attainment of the peak amplitude results in maximal resistance to extinction. It may be that a CR modulation process that tends toward the endpoint of CR–UR integration (presumably in the service of biological efficiency) also has the eventual effect of accelerating extinction when the US is removed. Protracted administration of paired stimuli under conditions of constant CS–US intervals and absolute certainty of CS–US predictability may finally result in uncoupling of the initial chemical sequence, if no adaptive adjustment to the US is available to the organism.

In the case of aversive USs, it is even possible that something akin to punishment may be involved, since an anticipatory CR is inevitably followed by the US in this situation. In the case of eyelid conditioning, Moore and Gormezano (1961) have suggested that the US is not "needed" when a CR has been performed. Indeed, the terminal level of CR performance in subjects receiving partial reinforcement is highly correlated with the percentage of USs given when no CR occurred (Kimmel, 1970). Beyond the suggestion that classical conditioning occurs only when the US is paired with the CS when no CR has occurred, it seems likely that conditioning may be retarded when unneeded USs are administered. This retardation may be signaled by reduction of the strength of the CR, and it may have the additional consequence of reducing resistance to extinction.

VI. OVERVIEW

We have attempted in this chapter to review those aspects of classical conditioning that may be characterized as adaptational insofar as they appear to enhance the organism's adjustment to its environment and reflect a continuous transaction between external stimuli and behavioral responses. Beyond the initial acquisition of the tendency to perform a CR, living organisms ranging across phylogeny from worms to humans appear to display regulatory modulations in both the temporal and topographical features of both the CR and the UR. It is apparent that many questions remain to be answered, the most significant of which pertain to the temporariness or relative permanence of these modulations and their underlying causes, and to the possibility that response-reinforcement as well as CS–US contingencies may apply. Nonetheless, the data presently available suggest that there is much more involved in classical conditioning than the formation of a new connection which results in the previously indifferent CS coming to elicit the CR. Although we have arbitrarily dealt with the various regulatory modulations of the CR and UR as if they occur *after* the initial association is formed, this aspect of our approach is admittedly simply a matter of convenience rather than a manifestation of a conviction that separate stages actually characterize the conditioning process.

To the extent that separate stages of conditioning have even this descriptive utility, in the sense that certain aspects of the phenomenon appear more reliably during, say, the first few trials, or the latter trials, the possibility must be considered whether *all* of the potentially observable characteristics of conditioning are implicated from the very outset of the process. We have tentatively assumed that a preconditioning potential of the nervous system enables the formation of a chemical "template" for subsequent utilization in environmental adaptation. Following Anokhin (1974), this assumption merely acknowledges the capacity of protoplasm, and especially neural protoplasm, to couple sequential events chemically, so that after several repetitions of these sequences of events, the occurrence of one member of the sequence is capable of activating the entire sequence. We refer to this stage of the process as a preconditioning stage because of its eventual reversability if not utilized adaptively. It seems possible that this may be mainly what is involved in the most simple occurrences of classical conditioning, as seen in conditioned desynchronization of occipital alpha or conditioning of electrodermal and vasomotor responses in humans, since in all of these instances the CR first appears and inevitably disppears following protracted repetition of the paired CS–US sequence.

Subsequent stages of conditioning are built upon this original template, in this view, depending upon the particular adaptive possibilities inherent in each different conditioning situation. Eye blinks may be placed in the CS–US interval so as to reduce the impact of the air puff; GSRs may be placed in the interval so as to reduce the effect of the shock; or post-US responses may be required that are facilitated by the advance signaling of the CS. In cases of this type, adaptive utility may have the effect of securing the initial sequencing. Similarly, integration of the CR and UR in a single, blended response may also have some biological advantage that could result in a somewhat different kind of securing of the sequence. We can only conjecture that the nature of this advantage lies in the increased efficiency in the performance of the UR it may permit. In all of these cases the conditioning process appears to involve a transaction between the organism and its environment and, in this respect, classical conditioning has some of the coloration of instrumental conditioning.

Throughout this chapter we have taken the position that an open attitude toward the foregoing possibilities is the only scientifically justified one. Whether experimental pursuits suggested by the present dynamic approach result in the emergence of a new view of classical conditioning will depend upon the findings of such experiments. Even at this early point it would appear that empirical questions beg answering that until recently would not have been asked. And even the asking has the effect of transforming the image of classical conditioning in a revolutionary way.

REFERENCES

Anokhin, P. K. *Biology and neuropsysiology of the conditioned reflex and its role in adaptive behavior*. Oxford and New York: Pergamon Press, 1974.

Badia, P., & Defran, R. H. Orienting responses and GSR conditioning: A dilemma. *Psychological Review*, 1970, **77**, 171–181.

Baxter, R. Diminution and recovery of the UCR in delayed and trace classical GSR conditioning. *Journal of Experimental Psychology*, 1966, **71**, 447–451.

Baxter, R., & Kimmel, H. D. Conditioning and extinction in the planarian. *American Journal of Psychology*. 1963, **76**, 665–669.

Biederman, G. B., & Furedy, J. J. Preference-for-signaled-shock phenomenon: Effects of shock modifiability and light reinforcement. *Journal of Experimental Psychology*, 1973, **100**, 380–386.

Bishop, P. D., & Kimmel, H. D. Retention of habituation and conditioning. *Journal of Experimental Psychology*, 1969, **81**, 317–321.

Coleman, S. R., & Gormezano, I. Classical conditioning of the rabbit's (*Oryctolagus cuniculas*) nictitating membrane response under symmetrical CS–US interval shifts *Journal of Comparative and Physiological Psychology*, 1971, **77**, 447–455.

Ellison, G. D. Differential salivary conditioning to traces. *Journal of Comparative and Physiological Psychology*, 1964, **57**, 373–380.

Fitzgerald, R. D. Some effects of partial reinforcement with shock on classically conditioned heart-rate in dogs. *American Journal of Psychology*, 1966, **79**, 242–249.

Furedy, J. J. Test of the preparatory adaptive response interpretation of aversive classical autonomic conditioning. *Journal of Experimental Psychology*, 1970, **84**, 301–307.

Furedy, J. J., & Klajner, F. Unconfounded autonomic indexes of the aversiveness of signaled and unsignaled shocks. *Journal of Experimental Psychology*, 1972, **93**, 313–318.

Gormezano, I. Investigations of defense and reward conditioning in the rabbit. In A. H. Black & W. F. Prokasy (Eds.), *Classical conditioning II: Research and theory*. New York: Appleton-Century-Crofts, 1972. Pp. 151–181.

Gormezano, I., & Moore, J. W. Classical conditioning. In M. T. Marx (Ed.), *Learning processes*. London: Macmillan, 1969. Pp. 121–203.

Green, R. T. The absolute threshold of electric shock. *British Journal of Psychology*, 1962, **53**, 107–116.

Grings, W. W. Preparatory set variables related to classical conditioning of autonomic responses. *Psychological Review*, 1960, **67**, 243–252.

Grings, W. W. Anticipatory and preparatory electrodermal behavior in paired stimulation situations. *Psychophysiology*, 1969, **5**, 597–611.

Grings, W. W., & Dawson, M. E. Complex variables in conditioning. In W. F. Prokasy & D. C. Raskin (Ed.), *Electrodermal activity in psychological Research*. New York: Academic Press, 1973. Pp. 203–254.

Grings, W. W., & Schell, A. M. Magnitude of electrodermal response to a standard stimulus as a function of intensity and proximity of a prior stimulus. *Journal of Comparative & Physiological Psychology*, 1969, **67**, 77–82. (a)

Grings, W. W., & Schell, A. M. UCR diminution in trace and delay conditioning. *Journal of Experimental Psychology*, 1969, **79**, 246–248. (b)

Hilgard, E. R. Reinforcement and inhibition of eyelid reflexes. *Journal of General Psychology*, 1933, **8**, 85–113.

Hilgard, E. R., & Campbell, A. A. The course of acquisition and retention of conditioned eyelid responses in man. *Journal of Experimental Psychology*, 1936, **19**, 227–247.

Hilgard, E. R., & Marquis, D. G. Acquisition, extinction, and retention of conditioned lid responses to light in dogs. *Journal of Comparative Psychology*, 1935, **19**, 29–58.

Hilgard, E. R., & Marquis, D. G. Conditioned eyelid responses in monkeys, with a comparison of dog, monkey and man. *Psychological Monographs*, 1936, **57**, 186–198.

Hilgard, E. R., & Marquis, D. G. *Conditioning and learning*. New York: Appleton-Century-Crofts, 1940.

Hill, H. E., Flanary, H. G., Kornetsky, C. H., & Wikler, A. Relationship of electrically induced pain to the amperage and the wattage of shock stimuli. *Journal of Clinical Investigation*, 1952, **31**, 464–472.

Hovland, C. I. Inhibition of reinforcement and phenomena of experimental extinction. *Proceedings of the National Academy of Sciences*, 1936, **22**, 430–433.

Hull, C. L. *Principles of behavior*. New York: Appleton-Century Crofts, 1943.

Humphreys, L. G. Measures of strength of conditioned eyelid responses. *Journal of General Psychology*, 1943, **29**, 101–111.

Jones, J. E. Contiguity and reinforcement in relation to CS–UCS intervals in classical aversive conditioning. *Psychological Review*, 1962, **69**, 176–186.

Kantrow, R. W. An investigation of conditioned feeding responses and concomitant adaptive behavior in young infants. *University of Iowa Studies in Child Welfare,* 1937, **13**, 337.

Karazina, S. A. The significance of novelty and of the differentiation of stimuli in the process of desynchronization of the cortical electrical activity. In L. G. Voronin (Ed.), *The orienting reflex and orienting-investigative activity.* Moscow: APN RSFSR, 1958. Pp 60–75.

Kimble, G. A. *Hilgard and Marquis' Conditioning* and *Learning.* New York: Appleton-Century-Crofts, 1961.

Kimble, G. A., & Dufort, R. H. The associative factor in eyelid conditioning. *Journal of Experimental Psychology,* 1956, **52**, 386–391.

Kimble, G. A., & Ost, J. W. P. A conditioned inhibitory process in eyelid conditioning. *Journal of Experimental Psychology,* 1961, **61**, 150–156.

Kimmel, E. Judgements of UCS intensity and diminution of the UCR in classical GSR conditioning. *Journal of Experimental Psychology,* 1967, **73**, 532–543. (a)

Kimmel, E. Non-associative factors in conditioning. *Ohio Psychologist,* 1967, **13**, 30. (Abstract) (b)

Kimmel, H. D. Amount of conditioning and intensity of conditioned stimulus. *Journal of Experimental Psychology,* 1959, **58**, 283–288.

Kimmel, H. D. Management of conditioned fear. *Psychological Reports,* 1963, **12**, 313–314.

Kimmel, H. D. Further analysis of GSR conditioning: A reply to Stewart, Stern Winokur, and Fredman. *Psychological Review,* 1964, **71**, 160–166.

Kimmel, H. D. Instrumental inhibitory factors in classical conditioning. In W. F. Prokasy (Ed.), *Classical conditioning: A symposium.* New York: Appleton-Century-Crofts, 1965. Pp. 148–171.

Kimmel, H. D. Inhibition of the unconditioned response in classical conditioning. *Psychological Review,* 1966, **73**, 232–240.

Kimmel, H. D. Essential events in the acquisition of classical conditioning. *Conditional Reflex,* 1970, **5**, 156–164.

Kimmel, H. D., & Baxter, R. Avoidance conditioning of the GSR. *Journal of Experimental Psychology,* 1964, **68**, 482–485.

Kimmel, H. D., & Garrigan, H. A. Resistance to extinction in planaria. *Journal of Experimental Psychology,* 1973, **101**, 343–347.

Kimmel, H. D., & Greene, W. A. Disinhibition in GSR conditioning as a function of the number of CS–UCS trials and temporal location of the novel stimulus. *Journal of Experimental Psychology,* 1964, **68**, 567–572.

Kimmel, H. D., & Owen, D. W. Resistance to extinction in classical GSR conditioning. *Bulletin of the Psychonomic Society,* 1974, **3**, 110–111.

Kimmel, H. D., & Pennypacker, H. S. Conditioned diminution of the unconditioned response as a function of the number of reinforcements. *Journal of Experimental Psychology,* 1962, **64**, 20–23.

Kimmel, H. D., & Yaremko, R. M. Effect of partial reinforcement on acquisition and extinction of classical conditioning in the planarian. *Journal of Comparative and Physiological Psychology,* 1966, **61**, 229–301.

Kupalov, P. S. Some normal and pathological properties of nervous precesses in the brain. *Annals of the New York Academy of Sciences,* 1961, **92**, 1046–1053.

Lanning, A. W., & Yaremko, R. M. Resistance to extinction in GSR conditioning: Effects of postpeak CR training and preextinction rest. *Journal of Experimental Psychology,* 1971, **88**, 433–435.

Logan, F. A. A micromolar approach to behavior theory. *Psychological Review,* 1956, **63**, 63–73.

Lykken, D. T. Preliminary observations concerning the "preception" phenomenon. *Psychophysiology Newsletter*, 1959, **5**, 2–7.

Lykken, D. T. Range correction applied to heart-rate and to GSR data. *Psychophysiology*, 1972, **9**, 373–379.

Lykken, D. T., Macindoe, I., & Tellegen, A. Preception: Autonomic response to shock as a function of predictability in time and locus. *Psychophysiology*, 1972, **9**, 318–333.

Martin, I., & Levey, A. B. *The genesis of the classical conditioned responses: International Series of Monographs in Experimental Psychology*. No. 8. Oxford, England: Pergamon Press, 1969.

Meryman, J. J. The magnitude of an unconditioned GSR as a function of fear conditioned at a long CS–UCS interval. Unpublished doctoral dissertation, State University of Iowa, 1953. Ann Arbor, Michigan: University Microfilms, 1953, No. A54-266.

Moore, J. W., & Gormezano, I. Yoked comparisons of instrumental and classical eyelid conditioning. *Journal of Experimental Psychology*, 1961, **62**, 522–559.

Morgenson, D. F. Cognitive factors in autonomic conditioning. Unpublished doctoral dissertation, University of London, 1967.

Morrow, M. C. Recovery of conditioned UCR diminution following extinction. *Journal of Experimental Psychology*, 1966, **45**, 62–91.

Morrow, M. C., & Keough, T. E. GSR conditioning with long interstimulus intervals. *Journal of Experimental Psychology*, 1968, **77**, 460–467.

Newhall, S. M., & Sears, R. R. Conditioning finger retraction to visual stimuli near the absolute threshold. *Comparative Psychology Monographs*, 1933, **9**, 25.

Orbeli, L. A. (Ed.), *Pavlovskie Sredy* (Pavlovian Wednesdays). Vol. I, *1929–1933*. Moscow-Leningrad: Akademiya Nauk SSSR, 1949.

Pavlov, I. P. *Conditioned reflexes*. London and New York: Oxford University Press, 1927.

Peeke, S. C., & Grings, W. W. Magnitude of CR as a function of variability in the CS–US relationship. *Journal of Experimental Psychology*, 1968, **77**, 64–69.

Pendergrass, V. E., & Kimmel, H. D. UCR diminution in temporal conditioning and habituation. *Journal of Experimental Psychology*, 1968, **77**, 1–6.

Prokasy, W. F. Classical eyelid conditioning: Experimenter operations, task demands, and response shaping. In W. F. Prokasy (Ed.), *Classical conditioning: A symposium*. New York: Appleton-Century-Crofts, 1965. Pp. 208–225.

Prokasy, W. F. Developments with the two-phase model applied to human eyelid conditioning. In A. H. Black & W. F. Prokasy (Ed.), *Classical conditioning II: current research and theory*. New York: Appleton-Century-Crofts, 1972, Pp. 119–147.

Schramm, C. F., & Kimmel, H. D. Resistance to extinction in GSR conditioning following different numbers of postpeak acquisition trials. *Journal of Experimental Psychology*, 1970, **84**, 239–243.

Sechenov, I. M. *Selected physiological and psychological works*. Moscow: Foreign Languages Publishing House. (n.d.—based on Russian edition dated 1952–1956)

Sheffield, F. D. Relation between classical conditioning and instrumental learning. In W. F. Prokasy (Ed.), *Classical conditioning: A symposium*. New York: Appleton-Century-Crofts, 1965. Pp. 302–322.

Silver, A. I., & Kimmel, H. D. Resistance to extinction in classical GSR conditioning as a function of acquisition trials beyond peak CR size. *Psychonomic Science*, 1969, **14**, 53–54.

Smith, M. C. Classical conditioning of the nictitating membrane response of the rabbit as a function of CS–US interval and US intensity. Unpublished doctoral dissertation, Indiana University, 1966.

Sokolov, Ye. N. *Perception and the conditioned reflex.* Oxford, England: Pergamon Press, 1963.

Stewart, M. A., Stern, J. A., Winokur, G., & Fredman, S. An analysis of GSR conditioning. *Psychological Review,* 1961, **68,** 60–67.

Switzer, S. A. Backward conditioning of the lid reflex. *Journal of Experimental Psychology,* 1930, **13,** 76–97.

Terrant, F. R. Effects of instrumental avoidance and punishment contingencies on the conditioned and unconditioned GSR. Unpublished doctoral dissertation, Ohio University, 1968.

Wendt, G. R. An analytical study of the conditioned knee jerk. *Archives of Psychology, New York,* 1930, **19,** 123.

Wells, C. E. Modification of alpha-wave responsiveness to light by juxtaposition of auditory stimuli. *American Medical Association Archives of Neurology,* 1959, **1,** 689–694.

Wolfe, H. M. Conditioning as a function of the interval between the conditioned and the original stimulus. *Journal of General Psychology,* 1932, **7,** 80–103.

Yaremko, R. M. The effects of direction and amount of change in stimulus intensity on magnitude of the orienting reflex and frequency of signal detection. *Dissertation Abstracts International,* 1969, **30B,** 1936.

Yaremko, R. M., & Kimmel, H. D. Two procedures for studying partial reinforcement effects in classical conditioning of the planarian. *Animal Behavior,* 1969, **17,** 40–42.

Zavadsky, I. V. An application of the method of conditioned reflexes to pharmacology. *Proceedings of the Russian Medical Society in Petrograd,* 1908, **75.**

4

Classical Conditioning: Some Methodological–Conceptual Issues

I. Gormezano
E. James Kehoe

University of Iowa

I. INTRODUCTION

In the years since Pavlov's work first became known in the United States (Pavlov, 1906; Yerkes & Morgulis, 1909), the least controversial assessment of his contributions is the recognition that he provided psychology with not only a method, but an elucidation of the many conditions affecting the formation and retention of learned responses and an objective terminology for their description (for example, conditioning itself, conditioned and unconditioned stimuli, reinforcement, stimulus generalization, extinction, spontaneous recovery, differentiation). Pavlov's terms are, in fact, still regarded by investigators of learning as being among the most basic descriptive units of behavior, applicable even in learning paradigms other than classical conditioning. Moreover, by virtue of his objective, deterministic, and Darwinian frame of reference, Pavlov's method of investigation, empirical findings, and concepts have had a persistent and broad impact not only upon learning psychologists, but also upon the wider psychological community. Unfortunately, this impact has been colored by numerous misconceptions of classical conditioning, which have accumulated and ramified to the point where even the mere specification of the method of classical conditioning has become ambiguous and controversial. The source of many of these misconceptions can be found in the wide and uncritical acceptance of the findings of Pavlov and his more psychologically oriented Russian contemporary, Bekhterev.

A. Historical Considerations

The work of Pavlov and Bekhterev became known to the psychological community of the United States in the midst of the functionalist revolt against the mentalistic theories and introspective methods of structuralism (see Boring, 1950). The revolt was characterized by three trends, all of which contributed to an enthusiastic and uncritical incorporation of classical conditioning into psychological thought in the United States. First, associationistic doctrines, especially the law of contiguity, were being recast into physiological terms (see James, 1890, p. 566), not unlike those terms used by Pavlov to describe cortical processes which he presumed to underlie conditioning. Second, the impact of the emphasis of Darwinian biology on adaptation, an orientation shared by Pavlov, vitalized interest in habit and learning, topics largely ignored by the structuralists. Third, under the influence of Loeb and other mechanists, objectivity as exemplified in Pavlov's mechanistic analysis, had become a criterion for the evaluation of psychological research. Watson (1913, 1916) brought these three trends to fruition with his behavioristic doctrines advocating conditioning as the objective method to replace introspection. Moreover, in his subsequent writings, Watson (1925) widely applied the conditioning principles to questions of emotion, mental disease, language, and, especially, learning. Furthermore, he employed the concept of conditioning as a central theoretical construct in which complex learning was considered to be simply the chaining, summation, and interaction of conditioned reflexes. In so doing, Watson shifted Western theoretical and, ultimately, empirical emphasis away from Pavlov's search for the laws and neural mechanisms of conditioning, toward the specification of conditioned-reflex combination rules that determine complex behaviors.

In retrospect, Watson, in advocating classical conditioning as the method and theory for behavioral analysis, distorted and constricted Pavlov's notions of conditioning. In setting down the behaviorist's dictum that one pursue stimulus–response associations, Watson fielded a methodology that required investigators in the United States to control and eliminate nonassociative effects. In contrast, Pavlov did not draw an associative–nonassociative distinction, but, rather, attempted to account for the occurrence of, and changes in, all responding. Therefore, an account of the formation of associations was only a part of Pavlovian theory and concerns. Further, Watson with few exceptions, viewed unconditioned reflexes as simple isolated reflexes. In contrast, Pavlov, while primarily examining isolated reflexes, hypothesized that some integrated actions could serve as unconditioned reflexes for the conditioning process. In addition, Watson's assumption of an invariant conditioned reflex carried with it the connotation of an automatic–stereotypic ("involuntary") process. Clearly, such an assertion is directly opposed to Pavlov's conception of determining agents and his recognition of the multitude of interacting factors that determine the course of conditioning and lend any given conditioned response great flexibility in its expression from instance to instance.

The decade following Watson's initial writings (1916) saw a broad and largely speculative application of conditioning to a wide range of behavior, extending from individual behavior to social action. Moreover, during this period, classical conditioning became so strongly identified with the associationistic law of contiguity (for example, Smith & Guthrie, 1921) that "conditioning" became synonymous with "association." However, the initial wave of enthusiasm ended with the appearance of detailed descriptions of Pavlov's (1927, 1928) work and reports of conditioning research in laboratories in the United States (for example, Cason, 1922; Hilgard, 1931) that revealed the complexities of conditioning. In addition, the initial American views of the conditioned reflex as the unit of habit and substitute for association came under strong attack (Hilgard, 1931; Robinson, 1932). Nevertheless, these initial views of conditioning have had a residual influence on American conceptions of conditioning. Specifically, there is still a prevalent tendency to regard any phenomenon deemed to be associative in nature as "classical conditioning," and hence, to blur the distinction between a specific phenomenon and a theoretical mechanism. The frequent usage of "classical conditioning" in a theoretical role, in the absence of any substantial body of research using Pavlov's method, has also created the illusion that Pavlov's findings are complete and well substantiated. Consequently, the tempering and sharpening influence that would be provided by data arising from active work with Pavlov's method has, until recently, been largely absent. Furthermore, the relative neglect of research in classical conditioning, conjoined with Watson's presentation of the conditioned reflex as isolated and stereotypic muscular movements and glandular secretions, has had the effect of leaving open to repeated attack the generality of classical conditioning phenomena as models for the undoubtedly, complex laws of behavioral adaptation.

B. Current Conceptions and Controversies

Although the above misconceptions have continued to exist in the common wisdom of American psychological thought, it is possible to discern three major issues surrounding the use of the term "classical conditioning" that evolved during the 1930s and still predominate as the source of today's theoretical controversies.

1. As originally conceived by Pavlov (1927), the classical-conditioning paradigm was viewed as a laboratory model for the mechanism of

behavioral adaptation. However, as procedural distinctions between classical and instrumental conditioning became commonly acknowledged, questions arose as to whether their respective laws represented a fundamental division in the laws of learning and, if so, which paradigm would serve as a more general model of behavioral adaptive mechanisms. As a consequence of the ensuing controversy, there has been a pervasive tendency to define classical conditioning in relation to instrumental conditioning rather than as an independent paradigm. In particular, classical conditioning has been commonly characterized as involving a "stimulus–stimulus" or "stimulus-reinforcer" contingency in order to contrast it with the "response–stimulus" or "response-reinforcer" contingency characteristic of instrumental conditioning. Unfortunately, such a superficial specification of the classical conditioning paradigm has commonly produced an inaccurate classical–instrumental distinction and frequently has led to an illusion of empirical convergence or divergence between the two paradigms.

2. Watson's assumption that all behavior consisted of conditioned reflexes was replaced by a more cautious approach in which the empirical laws of classical conditioning served as the source of axioms from which the laws of other behavior could be deduced (for example, Hull, 1930). However, the subsequent axiomatic use of classical conditioning by a variety of theorists have been troubled not only by the postulation of axioms which have not corresponded closely with the empirical laws of classical conditioning, but also by the postulation of axioms based upon the results of methodologically inadequate classical conditioning studies. Furthermore, in efforts directed at assessing the deductive consequences of postulated axioms, there has been a general failure to understand some of the unavoidable methodological hazards inherent in attempts to reveal the operation of putative conditioned reflexes in more complex learning situations.

3. As the identification of classical conditioning with the associationistic law of contiguity, often under the name of "stimulus substitution," underwent attack and some of the empirical complexities of conditioning became known, the conditioned reflex lost its status as a fundamental unit of habit. As a consequence, it became apparent that the phenomenon of conditioning itself was in need of explanation. The search for such explanation has been primarily directed at the issue of the mechanism of reinforcement in classical conditioning. However, the empirical assessment of theories regarding the mechanism of reinforcement in classical conditioning have been hindered by methodological limitations inherent in testing those theories which postulate events not subject to direct experimental manipulation within the procedural requirements of classical conditioning.

There is, of course, a fourth usage of the term "classical conditioning," which references the set of empirical findings arising from the application of the classical conditioning paradigm. However, provided that specification of the paradigm is methodologically adequate, the determination of its empirical laws raises few methodologically concerns falling within the scope of the present chapter. Accordingly, the following sections are addressed to some of the methodological problems and the attendant theoretical implications that have arisen in connection with the specification of the classical-conditioning paradigm, axiomatic application of the classical-conditioning paradigm, and proposed mechanisms of reinforcement in classical conditioning.

II. THE CLASSICAL-CONDITIONING PARADIGM

A. The Definitional Problem

There is a pervasive tendency to define the classical-conditioning paradigm solely in terms of the procedural distinction between classical and instrumental conditioning. Specifically, the classical conditioning paradigm is commonly depicted in terms of a "stimulus-reinforcer" contingency in counterpoint to the "response-reinforcer" contingency characteristic of the instrumental conditioning paradigm. Although such a stimulus-reinforcer contingency is the distinguishing feature of classical conditioning with respect to instrumental conditioning, the complete specification of the basic classical conditioning paradigm, to be detailed in the next section, contains further requirements regarding the presentation of stimuli and definition of the response. The general failure to recognize the additional requirements necessary for specifying the classical-conditioning paradigm appears to have arisen from the continuing controversy over whether or not the classical and instrumental conditioning paradigms are governed by different laws of learning. (See Hearst, Chapter 5 in this volume, for a detailed discussion of the classical–instrumental controversy). This classical–instrumental controversy has not only engendered an exclusionary emphasis on defining classical conditioning on the basis of the different contingencies operating in the two paradigms, but it has also led to inadvertent distortions in the commonly held conception of classical- and instrumental-conditioning paradigms. As a result of attempts to determine whether the two paradigms converge or diverge in their empirical outcomes, presumed empirical and theoretical dichotomies have tended to be incorporated into the conception of classical and instrumental conditioning paradigms as if such dichotomies were part of the definition of each paradigm. Thus, such nonprocedural characteristics as type of response system (autonomic versus skeletal) and mechanism of reinforcement (contiguity versus effect) have at times been treated as having equal status with procedural characteristics in distinguishing between classical and instrumental conditioning. However, the incorporation of these nonprocedural distinctions into the *definition* of classical and/or instrumental conditioning distorts their respective methodologies by confusing specification of a paradigm with empirical knowledge or theory about the outcomes of the so-specified paradigm.

The tendency to superficially specify the classical-conditioning paradigm solely in terms of the contingency relationship among stimuli by contrasting it to the response–stimulus contingency relationship characteristic of instrumental conditioning paradigms, as well as the occasional burdening of each of these paradigms by nonprocedural distinctions, has had at least two deleterious consequences. First, the utilization of such an incomplete specification of the classical-conditioning paradigm has led to the encompassing of paradigms that do not meet all of the procedural requirements necessary to specify them as classical conditioning. More particularly, and as is discussed more fully Section I.B, many procedures labeled "classical conditioning," because they ostensibly contain "stimulus-reinforcer" contingencies, are revealed on detailed analysis to be instrumental-conditioning procedures. The consequence is that by failing to employ a well-understood, carefully drawn specification of the basic classical conditioning paradigm, such investigations have impeded the resolving of the classical–instrumental controversy by producing a presumed empirical convergence or divergence between classical and instrumental conditioning where none may exist. Second, the utilization of an incomplete specification of classical conditioning by merely referencing a "stimulus–stimulus" contingency has led to a general failure to recognize and utilize the experimentally unique capabilities of the basic classical conditioning paradigm to address questions regarding the acquisition of associations. Specifically, employment of the fully specified basic classical conditioning paradigm permits the investigator complete control over presentation of the salient events to the organism, and thus provides the investigator with the unique ability to specify the stimulus antecedents to the target response. The consequence of failing to recognize this attribute of the classical-conditioning paradigm, as is detailed in Section I.B, has been a tendency in connection with "autoshaping" studies to presume that the associations studied are those of classical conditioning.

B.   The Defining of Classical Conditioning

The essential feature of classical conditioning is a set of experimental operations involving an unconditioned stimulus (US), which reliably produces a measurable unconditioned response (UR), and a conditioned stimulus (CS) that has been shown by test not initially to produce a response resembling the UR. The CS and US are then presented repeatedly to the organism in a specified order and temporal spacing, and a response similar to the UR develops to the CS that is called the conditioned response (CR). Although various temporal arrangements of the CS and US characterize the classical-conditioning paradigm, what distinguishs it from instrumental conditioning is that (a) presentation or omission of the UCS is independent of CR occurrence, and (b) the definition of a CR in restricted to the selection of a target response from among those effector systems elicited as URs by the US. We shall argue that adherence to both components of this definition is essential if we are to avoid common confusions and ambiguities in the use of conditioning terminology.

Unfortunately, the requirement that the administration of the CS and US be independent of CR occurrence has become the hallmark of the classical-conditioning paradigm to the exclusion of the second requirement of selection of a target response from among those effector systems elicited as URs. The tendency to emphasize the stimulus presentation procedure of classical conditioning, while ignoring selection of the target response, can be traced to at least two previously considered historical roots. First, the persistent identification of classical conditioning with associative mechanisms has produced a tendency to regard "classical conditioning" as an underlying process of which a CR is only a single manifestation. Second, the procedural distinction between classical and instrumental conditioning has been couched in terms of their respective stimulus-presentation procedures, with classical conditioning characterized in terms of a stimulus–stimulus contingency and instrumental conditioning characterized by a response–stimulus contingency (see Skinner, 1938). In addition, the observation that the topography of CRs do not exactly duplicate those of the UR has been used as a basis for dismissing target response selection as a portion of the specification of a classical-conditioning procedure (Zener, 1937). The last argument appears to have arisen from a confusion between the specification of the classical conditioning procedure and the theoretical expectation of CR and UR *identity* by the so-called stimulus substitution theory (Hilgard & Marquis, 1940; Terrace, 1973). In the vast majority, if not all classical-conditioning preparations, the topography of the CR differs from that of the UR in one or more dimensions (for example, latency, amplitude, duration). Yet, once differences between the CR and UR are allowed, it would appear that specification of the CR is on slippery grounds, ultimately allowing any response acquired as a result of CS–US presentations to qualify as a CR. However, an objective criterion for specifying a CR is obtained by requiring that the response to the CS appear in the same effector system as the UR. While such a criterion admits to a wide range of differences between the CR and UR, including so-called "compensatory" CRs (for example, a decelerative heart rate CR and an accelerative heart rate UR), it retains the historically elegant property of classical conditioning in which the original stimulus antecedents for the target response, in a general sense (that is, the US), are known and under experimental control. Advocacy of such a definition of a CR is not meant to deny the logical possibility that the procedure of presenting a CS and US may result in the acquisition of a response to the CS in an effector system not elicited by the UCS. However, if such a response were to be acquired, it should be distinguished from a CR since the original stimulus antecedents for the response remain to be specified and placed under experimental control.

In the basic classical conditioning paradigm, the effects of CS–US pairings are assessed by observation of the relationship between the CS and at least one of the response systems elicited by the US, that is to say, CS–CR functions are obtained. In contrast, the tendency to specify a classical-conditioning procedure simply in terms of the response-independent presentations of the CS and US has led to the aggregation of a broad set of learning phenomena under the heading of "classical conditioning." Common among these departures from the historic, basic classical conditioning paradigm are those in which the effects of CS–US pairings are assessed by superimposing the CS on a base line of instrumental behavior and observing changes in the behavior (for example, the conditioned emotional response or CER, paradigm). Accordingly, it may be said that conditioned stimulus–instrumental response (CS–IR) functions are obtained in these paradigms which purport to indirectly assess classical conditioning processes (see Rescorla & Solomon, 1967). We present a detailed critique of these conditioned stimulus–instrumental response studies later (Section III.C) for now it is necessary to more finely delineate the basic classical conditioning paradigm. In so doing, our concerns are to point out the methdological and theoretical pitfalls into which one can stumble if insufficient attention is paid to the additional specifications required of the basic paradigm.

1. Unconditioned Stimulus–Unconditioned Response Specification

Although USs are generally selected with reference to the response system to be conditioned, a number of USs can be found for evoking activity in any one response system. For example, the eyelid response commonly used in laboratories in the United States can be elicited by electric shock in the vicinity of the eye, a mechanical tap to the cheek, or an air puff to the cornea. Conversely, any given US usually elicits a constellation of URs, thus permitting the concurrent observation of conditioning in more than one response system. For example, a shock applied to a specific locus not only elicits local skeletal activity (for example, leg flexion), but also changes in heart rate, respiration, pupillary size, etc. Under such circumstances the investigator must decide which of these responses he wishes to observe. The decision is governed in part by the reliability of occurrence of the UR, the degree of instrumentation involved, the organism, and whether some response systems evoked by the US are more sensitive to change than others. For these, as well as theoretical reasons, some investigators concentrate upon measurement from one response system, whereas others may take concurrent measurement of several. Generally, however, the investigator will select, define, and measure responses that are maximally sensitive to parametric manipulation.

Under the basic classical conditioning procedure, a US is administered independently of the subject's behavior. This stricture is usually met by a combination of the proximal application of the US to the receptor surface and, in the case of distal USs (for example, a light source), restraint of the subject to maintain orientation to the source of the US. In the case of noxious USs, this requirement is usually met whereas, with appetitive USs, this stricture has been repeatedly violated with various degrees of severity. In early experiments, Pavlov himself frequently presented food in a bowl rather than injecting food or meat powder into the mouth of the subject.

The food-in-the-bowl procedure has been subsequently followed by investigators from the United States employing the salivary preparation (for example, Ellison, 1964; Shapiro, Sadler, & Mugg, 1971; Sheffield, 1965). In such a procedure, the subject is required to make an instrumental response of approaching and seizing the food before proximal application of the stimulating agent to the receptor surfaces of the mouth is achieved. While the food-in-the-bowl procedure does not violate the lesser requirement of classical conditioning that the US be delivered independently of the target response (that is, salivation), the procedure does reduce experimental control. By allowing the subject's instrumental response to determine actual receipt of the US, precise and uniform control the CS–US (UR) interval becomes impossible. A more severe violation of the classical conditioning procedure arises in connection with a "food-in-the-bowl" type of procedure in which the instrumental response necessary for the *receipt* of the US is mistakenly considered a UR. Such a mistaken identification of the UR can be found in several commonly employed purported classical-conditioning procedures. For example, Longo, Klempay, and Bitterman (1964) trained pigeons and Holland and Rescorla (1975) trained rats in a procedure involving paired presentations of a CS, with activation of a food magazine considered to be the US and stablimetric measures of activity being considered the UR and anticipatory activity the CR. Similarly, Boice and Denny (1965) paired presentation of a CS with activation of a liquid delivery well, and recorded the rat's licking as a UR and anticipatory licking as the CR. However, the classical-conditioning paradigm permits the specifying of responses to the CS as arising from CS–US pairings, and thus identified as CRs if, and only if, the target response (the

UR) has initially followed the US. Yet, in both these paradigms, the target licking or activity response had to precede the US before the US was received by the subject, whereas failure of the response to occur precluded receipt of the US. Consequently, the basis of the associative connections between the CS and the licking or activity response were established not by classical conditioning operations, but by those of instrumental conditioning.

A similar difficulty to the above, appears to arise in the majority of "autoshaping" procedures (see Brown & Jenkins, 1968). Generally, the autoshaping procedure consists of response-independent presentation of a lighted manipulandum (for example, a lighted key) as a "CS" and activation of a food magazine as the "US," with the target response being contact with the manipulandum (for example, key pecking). As in the previous cases considered, an instrumental response is necessary to actual receipt of the US, but, unlike the difficulty faced by the activity and licking measures, the target response per se is not instrumental to receipt of the US. While the target response is not an instrumental response, it does not by elimination qualify as a CR, since the target response is not a UR to the US (that is, food or water in the mouth). Since the molecular attributes of the target response do resemble those of the instrumental response necessary to receipt of the US (see Moore, 1973), the usual autoshaped response may represent the result of some concatenation of instrumental conditioning and some process of transfer that redirects the response (for example, pecking) from the food or water to antecedent stimuli (for example, the lighted key). However, there are some "autoshaping" data to suggest that a key-pecking target response may be acquired even when the reinforcing agent is proximally applied to the organism, without requiring an instrumental response (Wasserman, 1973; Woodruff, Morrison, & Williams, 1974). Yet, in these instances, the target response would still not qualify as a CR, but it may tentatively qualify as an instance of response acquisition in an effector system not affected by the US. In such cases, autoshaping would be considered a "new" learning phenomenon arising from only the *stimulus* presentation procedure of classical conditioning, with the acquired response having the interesting property of presumably having immediate stimulus antecedents separate from the US or possibly interacting with the US, but remaining to be specified.

2. Conditioned Stimulus–Conditioned Response Specification

The conditioned reflex denotes the regular relationship between a CS and designated target response, the CR, established on the basis of repeated presentation of the CS and US in some close temporal relationship.

In the ideal case, the single observation of a target response following a CS, after the CS–US pairings, would be sufficient to indicate the establishment of a CR. Not surprisingly, this ideal case has never been achieved. Early classical-conditioning studies in the United States (for example, Bernstein, 1934; Hilgard, 1931; Wendt, 1930) quickly revealed that not all responses observed in connection with the CS uniquely resulted from prior CS–US pairings. At a minimum, most response systems show some level of base-line activity, often raised by US presentations, that will produce spurious conjunctions of the CS and target response. Moreover, the CR is frequently masked by two other reflexes: the alpha reflex and pseudoconditioned reflex. The alpha response consists of a UR to the CS that is in the same response system as the target response, whereas the pseudoconditioned response consists of the occurrence of a response that resembles the CR, but depends only upon prior occurrence of the US, and not CS–US pairings. Accordingly, to ascertain the existence of a CR, it has been necessary to assess the contribution of these "nonassociative" sources of responding by specified control treatments.

The problem of the alpha response arises as a result of the violation of the ideal assumption that the CS is neutral with respect to the target response system under investigation. However, for many organisms the CS elicits a constellation of reflex responses, including response systems commonly employed in classical-conditioning studies (for example, GSR, eye blink, cardiac, and vascular reactions). Generally, a careful detailing of the latency, duration, and amplitude of the alpha response, as well as a determination of its course of habituation, can provide a basis for eliminating it from consideration as a CR. This can be accomplished by employing a control group given CS-alone presentations. Alpha responses are usually of a shorter latency than CRs; hence, if a sufficently long CS–US interval is employed, both the alpha response and the CR can be observed in the interval and scored accordingly. Further complexities can arise in distinguishing alpha responses from CRs (for example, sensitization) and the details of dealing with such complexities can be found elsewhere (see Gormezano, 1966; Gormezano & Moore, 1969).

Once the alpha response has been eliminated from consideration, the possible contribution of pseudoconditioned responses to CR measurement must be assessed. If the US is presented one or more times prior to the presentation of a CS (particularly if the UCS is noxious), the procedure may frequently result in the occurrence of a response to the CS, labeled a pseudo-CR, that may be quite indistinguishable from a CR. The mechanism producing the pseudo-CR is not known at present; however, it is traditionally treated as separate from those responses acquired by classical conditioning because of its occurrence in the absence of previous CS–US pairings. In any event, the pseudo-CR is clearly a result of US presentations and might therefore be expected to contribute to the responses scored as

CRs. While the US-alone procedure (see Gormezano, 1966) provides the clearest demonstration of the phenomenon, this procedure does not permit an assessment of the strength of a pseudo-CR on a trial-by-trial basis for comparison with the acquisition of a CR. To provide such a basis for comparison, a single control procedure has been employed for the assessment of both pseudo-CRs and base-line responses. Known as the "unpaired" control, this procedure involves presenting CS-alone and US-alone trials the same number of times as the experimental group is given CS–US pairings. However, the stimuli are presented in a random fashion (for example, Gormezano, Schneiderman, Deaux, & Fuentes, 1962), with any CS–US interval being variable and far exceeding the maximum interval believed to be effective in establishing a CR for the response system under observation. Under such a procedure, an examination of the responses occurring on CS trials (excluding responses in the alpha latency range) yields a summative measure of pseudoconditioned and baseline responses, or possibly some synergistic action of both stimuli.

C.   The Issue of "Unpaired" and "Truly Random" Controls

1.   "Pairings" and "Contingency" Hypotheses

In recent years, the status of the unpaired procedure as the best single control for assessing nonassociative contributions to CR measurement, has been challenged as being adequate only under a restricted set of theoretical assumptions derived from the so-called "pairings hypothesis." Specifically, use of the unpaired procedure is based on the assumptions that: (a) temporal contiguity of the CS and US is the necessary (and perhaps sufficient) condition for CR acquisition; and (b) any responding produced by the unpaired procedure is nonassociative in nature, since the randomized sequencing of CS and US presentations and extremely large intervals between stimulus events would preclude the operation of any CS–US contiguity effects. However, Prokasy (1965) has suggested that, in addition to CS–US pairings, other "correlations" between the CS and US may affect CR performance. To specify these "correlations," Prokasy proposed that any experimental session be considered divided into equal time units, usually the length of the longest stimulus, with each possible event, CS and US, occurring not more than once during the specified time unit. Furthermore, in the event of the joint occurrence of a CS and US in the time unit, a forward pairing restriction would apply. Thus, a 100% reinforcement schedule would be specified as one in which the conditional probability of a US in the presence of a CS is $p(US|CS) = 1.00$ and the conditional probability of a UCS in the absence of a CS is $p(US|\overline{CS}) = 0.00$. Conversely, the unpaired procedure produces a perfectly negative correlation etween the CS and US, with $p(US|CS) = 0.00$ and $p(US|\overline{CS}) = 1.00$. According to Prokasy then, this negative correlation would yield a biased underestimation of nonassociative contributions to CR measurement. In a theoretical extension of Prokasy's arguments, Rescorla (1967) proposed a "contingency hypothesis," from which he has argued that the unpaired control produces inhibitory associative effects. Moreover, as an alternative to the unpaired control, Rescorla has recommended programming CS and US presentations independently of one another to yield what he has called the "truly random" procedure as an unbiased control for nonassociative contributors to responding.

While CS–US contiguity is of prime theoretical interest to the pairings hypothesis, Rescorla's (1967) contingency hypothesis focuses on the degree to which the CS "predicts" or carries "information" about the US, as specified in terms of the relative frequency or probability of US occurrence in the presence and absence of the US. Furthermore, the contingency hypothesis assumes that there are symmetric excitatory and inhibitory associative contributions to responding to the CS arising from CS and US presentations. Specifically, if the probability of a US is greater in the presence of the CS than in its absence, a "positive contingency" would prevail and "excitatory" associative effects would accrue to the CS. Conversely, "inhibitory" associative effects would presumably accrue if the probability of a US were higher in the absence of the CS than in its presence to yield a "negative contingency." Since the unpaired procedure consists entirely of presentations of the US in the absence of the CS, the contingency hypothesis asserts that the unpaired procedure constitutes a perfectly negative and, thus, inhibitory contingency, rendering it inappropriate as a nonassociative control. Accordingly, Rescorla (1967) has contended that the appropriate control procedure would be a "truly random" procedure in which the CS carries no "information" regarding the occurrence and nonoccurrence of the US. This "truly random" or zero contingency condition was variously specified by Rescorla in terms of independent programming of the CS and US (Rescorla, 1967, p. 74) or, more precisely, in terms of approximately equal probabilities of UCS occurrence in the presence and absence of the CS (p. 76). In any event, the "truly random" control would presumably produce no associative effects since the CS is "irrelevant" to the US. In contrast, under the pairings hypothesis, the "chance" CS–US pairings occurring with the "truly random" control procedure would be expected to produce positive associative effects.

The challenge to the unpaired control procedure on the basis of the above considerations might appear to be incongruous in view of the common conception that control methodology is relatively devoid of theoretical concerns. In the "testbook" case, the variable of interest is usually depicted as a discrete physical event, and, accordingly, the control treatment for assessing the effects of that variable merely involves the elimination of the event. However, for the classical-conditioning paradigm, the variables of interest are not the physical events of the CS and US per se, but are rather the sequence and temporal relationship between these events. Unless either the CS or US is removed, the best that can be done in the way of a contro condition would be to alter the sequential and temporal relationships be tween the two events. Since the variables of interest cannot be eliminate but only altered, it becomes necessary to consider the contentions of th pairings and contingency hypotheses as to what may be effects of th altered sequential and temporal relationships on responding of their respec tive control groups. In the case of the unpaired control, a "long" tempora relationship is arranged between the CS and US as well as successive CS or USs. Here, "long" is defined as being longer than the longest CS–US interval thought to be effective in producing conditioning for the respons system under observation. In contrast, the "truly random" control pro cedure arranges for a variable temporal relationship between the CS and US as well as successive CSs or USs, involving, according to the unpaired control methodology, an unspecified mix of both "short" and "long" inter vals between events.

Hence, the theoretical controversy arises from concerns over the possibl learned consequences of the respective procedures. Advocates of the un paired control would generally assert that the "long" temporal relationshi between CSs and USs, in falling outside the "contiguity gradient," woul have only nonassociative effects, and, conversely, any occasional close tem poral contiguity between the CSs and USs in the "truly random" contro would lead to the addition of some associative effects, and hence, to a overestimation of nonassociative effects. In contrast, as indicated earlier Rescorla (1967) has argued that the "long" temporal relationship betwee CSs and USs in the unpaired control, because of the negative contingency produces an inhibitory associative effect, and accordingly, leads to an un derestimation of nonassociative effects. Furthermore, he maintained tha the "truly random" control produces neither an excitatory nor inhibitor associative effect to provide an unmasked assessment of nonassociativ contributions to responding.

2. Empirical Considerations

Although the challenge to the unpaired methodology arises from th theoretical controversy between the pairings and contingency hypotheses the origin of the unpaired control methodology is not completely theoretica in nature but is grounded in independent empirical findings. Recall tha the associative–nonassociative distinction, originally generated by Watso (1916), was subsequently substantiated by observations of responding no attributable to combined presentations of the CS and US in any sequenc of temporal relationship. In particular, alpha responses were demonostrated in procedures employing only CS presentations (for example, Hilgard, 1931), and pseudoconditioned CRs were demonstrated strictly on the basis of prior UCS presentations (for example, Grant, 1943). Thus, by the use of the "textbook" control methodology of eliminating any CS–US relationship through removal of one of the physical events, nonassociative contributions were defined independently of the unpaired procedure. However, the CS-alone and US-alone procedures were not suitable for a trial-by-trial comparison with the experimental CS–US procedure, nor did these procedures provide the possibility of assessing the synergistic effects of the CS and US upon responding. Accordingly, the unpaired procedure was instituted as a conjunction of the two procedures, with the sequence and temporal relationships between the CS and US specified with reference to a "contiguity gradient" empirically determined on the basis of the observed relationship between response frequency and the CS–US interval for the response system under observation (for example, Schneiderman, & Gormezano, 1964). More generally, for the few response systems in which the CS–US interval-response frequency function has been repeatedly demonstrated (see Gormezano & Moore, 1969), the outer boundary of the CS–US "contiguity gradient" can be defined as the point on the function beyond which increasingly long CS–US intervals have no differential effect on responding (that is, the "flat" portion of the function). Moreover, the level of responding characteristic of the "flat" portion of the function would be attributed to nonassociative factors. Accordingly, with the empirical "contiguity gradient" so defined, the associative contributions to responding could be precluded or minimized by setting the shortest interval between any two stimulus events, particularly any CS–US sequence, to some value *well in excess* of the outer boundary of the empirical "contiguity gradient." By such a procedure, the "unpaired" nonassociative control has been defined and implemented not only on the basis of theoretical associative assumptions, but on the basis of converging empirical outcomes.

The empirical basis for the unpaired control methodology was developed within the domain of the basic CS–CR classical-conditioning paradigm. However, the attack on the unpaired control methodology and, conversely, the original justification for the "truly random" control methodology is based on findings obtained with a CS–IR paradigm (that is, classical–instrumental transfer studies purportedly assessing a covert "fear" CR through its effects on instrumental responding). Specifically, in two studies, Rescorla (1966) and Rescorla and LoLordo (1965), a CS previously presented in an unpaired fashion with a shock US was found to produce depression of "fear-motivated" avoidance responding, indicating the acquisition of inhibitory properties by the CS. Furthermore, Rescorla (1966) found that a "truly random" procedure yielded a CS which had no effect upon avoidance responding, indicating that no associative properties, either excitatory or inhibitory, had accrued to the CS. The observation of a "zero" effect produced by a "truly random" procedure was taken by Rescorla as strong evidence that the "neutral" contingency between the CS and US, rather than the "chance" CS–US pairings, determined associative strength. More particularly, in the case of the "truly random" control, the associative strength was now presumed to be invariably zero. However, subsequent CS–IR studies have revealed that the "truly random" procedure can produce substantial conditioning ("excitatory") effects on responding depending upon the placement of "chance" CS–US pairings within the overall schedule of events (Benedict & Ayres, 1972) and on the number of "chance" CS–US pairings (Ayres, Benedict, & Witcher, 1975; Kremer & Kamin, 1971; Quinsey, 1971). Since these effects are consistent with the "pairings" hypothesis rather than the "contingency" hypothesis, they constitute a substantial erosion in the empirical support for a "truly random" control methodology.

The empirical difficulties that have arisen for the "truly random" control arises largely from an ambiguous treatment of the effects of temporal relationships between the CS and US. Despite Rescorla's (1967) acknowledgement of the importance of the interval between the CS and US in the determination of both positive and negative dependencies between the CS and US, the contingency hypothesis is basically formulated in a time-free fashion, referencing only the relative probabilities of US occurrence in the presence and absence of the CS. In principle, an adequate "truly random" procedure could consist of a mixture of "short" CS–US intervals, constituting excitatory "pairings" and "long" CS–US intervals constituting inhibitory "unpairings." Yet, in the absence of an empirically defined boundary between shorter CS–US intervals constituting "pairings" and longer CS–US intervals constituting "unpairings," it becomes impossible to specify unequivocally an appropriate mixture of CS–US intervals that would yield a zero contingency and thus, leave nonassociative contributions unmasked.

3. The Reassessment

In addition to the above difficulties with the "truly random" control under the assumptions of the contingency hypothesis, there are several general theoretical problems with the contingency hypothesis. Specifically, it would appear that the contingency hypothesis assumes a one-to-one correspondence between the experimenter-defined contingency and the "subjective" (cognitive) contingency which the organism extracts from expsoure to CS and US presentations. Moreover, as stated, the contingency hypothesis would apparently require the organism to possess a complex computational apparatus to calculate the CS–US contingency, and, since the organism cannot be supplied directly with this contingency, the scope of this hypothesis is largely limited to asymptotic predictions of performance after sufficient time and events have interceded to permit the organism to calculate the CS/US contingency. Taking note of these objections, Rescorla (1972, p. 28) has relegated CS/US contingency from the status of a fundamental variable to the realm of an "intuitive" guide and derives the asymptotic relations between responding and the correlational variable from a *contiguity-based* hypothesis of excitatory and inhibitory associative effects (see Rescorla & Wagner, 1972).

The Rescorla and Wagner (1972) model and a subsequent elaboration (Rescorla, 1972) assumes that individual "pairings" and "unpairings" of the CS and US are the theoretically relevant variables having incremental and decremental effects on associative strength, leading potentially to the observation of excitatory and inhibitory effects. Specifically, under the model all conditioning occurs through temporal contiguity of the CS (on "paired" trials) and/or background stimuli (on "unpaired" trials) with the US; and in general, excitatory and inhibitory effects are derivative from the relative associative strength of the CS and background stimuli. Moreover, it is still contended that the "truly random" procedure would be the appropriate nonassociative control, because it would presumably balance excitatory and inhibitiroy effects, thus revealing nonassociative contributions to responding. However, to obtain a net associative strength of zero under the "truly random" procedure, it would still be necessary to know the relative magnitudes of excitatory incremental and inhibitory decremental associative effects produced by "paired" and "unpaired" presentations, respectively. In an attempt to deal with this problem, Rescorla (1972) contented himself with the selection of arbitrary values for the incremental and decremental parameters of the quantitative model. Most recently, apparently recognizing the logical, empirical, and theoretical difficulties involved in the use of a "truly random" control, Rescorla and his associates (Holland & Rescorla, 1975; Rescorla, 1973; Rizley & Rescorla, 1972) have reverted to the more traditional unpaired control, associated with contiguity-based formulations, to assess nonassociative effects.

III. AXIOMATIC USE OF CLASSICAL CONDITIONING

Theoretically, any instrumental learning situation has within it the stimulus conditions for the development of classically conditioned responses. The reinforcing event (for example, food), although response contingent, occurs in a specific situation; and since these situational stimuli are regularly associated with reinforcement in the "manner" of classical conditioning, it has been speculated that CRs may concurrently develop. Learning theorists (for example, Amsel, 1958; Hull, 1943; Konorski, 1967; Mowrer,

1960; Sheffield, 1966) have given formal recognition to the possibility of CR accompaniments of instrumental conditioning by such concepts as secondary reinforcement, secondary drive, and incentive motivation. In the application of these concepts to instrumental conditioning it is assumed that two different learning processes are involved. One process consists of the acquisition of the specific instrumental response, whereas the second consists of the acquisition of collateral CRs conditioned to situational stimuli and/or proprioceptive stimuli arising from the instrumental responses of the organism. It is then assumed that these CRs modulate the instrumental response tendency by their action as *motivators* (incentive motivators and secondary drives) or *reinforcers* (secondary reinforcers) of the instrumental response.

To investigate the above purported influences of situational CRs on instrumental performance, two research strategies have been employed (see Gormezano & Moore, 1969; Rescorla & Solomon, 1967). Some investigators have concurrently recorded presumed situational CRs and instrumental responses (IRs) to ascertain whether the empirical relationship between situational CRs and IRs corresponds to theoretical expectations. Other investigators have resorted to the use of classical–instrumental transfer paradigms. However, in using transfer designs, usually no attempt is made to isolate mediating situational CRs. Instead, changes in instrumental performance resulting from presentation of the previously established CS is attributed to the effects of covert CRs presumed to be elicited by the CS.

A. Concurrent Measurement Designs

Under the concurrent measurement procedure, observation is made of the IR and a situational CR selected from one or more of the response systems elicited as URs to the reinforcing event (for example, food or shock). Under the specific hypothesis that CRs operate as instigators or motivators of the IR, CRs would be expected to precede the instrumental response, whereas CRs acting as reinforcers would be expected to follow the instrumental response. Consequently, a number of investigators have also attempted to examine the temporal sequence of IRs and CRs.

Historically, the initial use of the concurrent measurement design can be traced to the investigations of Konorski and Miller (1930), who found that a paw-movement response (IR) for food reinforcement consistently preceded an increase in salivary flow (CR). Subsequently, the concurrent measurement design has been applied in a variety of instrumental conditioning situations (for example, the discriminative operant reward paradigm, discriminative avoidance paradigm, appetitive runway paradigm) with measurement taken of diverse situational CRs (heart rate, licking, salivating, respiration, etc.). However, the overall pattern of results from concurrent measurement studies has revealed no consistent temporal relationship between IRs and presumed indicants of situational CRs (see Gormezano & Moore, 1969; Rescorla & Solomon, 1967; Scavio,1972).

The lack of any consistent temporal pattern between situational CRs and IRs would appear to weaken the validity of the theoretical notion that peripheral CRs operate as mediators of responses in the instrumental conditioning situation. Moreover, the discrepant findings of concomitant measurement studies seem to have been an important factor in the formulation of the hypothesis that CR mediational effects are totally executed by "central nervous system" CRs (for example, Konorski, 1967; Miller, 1963; Rescorla & Solomon, 1967). However, these assumptions may be unwarranted, owing to the methodological issues surrounding interpretation of concurrent measurement studies. First, since any selected indicant response is only an individual reaction in a complex of somatic and visceral responses elicited by reinforcing events, rejection of the peripheral CR mediational hypothesis could be accomplished only by delineating the relationship between all responses elicited by reinforcing events and the possible combinations of these responses with the IR. Practical considerations, as well as the possibility of becoming engaged in an infinite regress of testing increasingly refined CRs, would appear to preclude such a research program. Second, it is possible that whatever response system is chosen to represent situational CRs, it would be subject to a variety of influences beyond its acquired stimulus determinants. For example, the frequently used heart rate response may also reflect metabolic requirements of executing the IR (Black & Dalton, 1965; DeToledo, 1971) or it may simply be a part of the orienting reflex (Sokolov, 1963). Third, even if an unconfounded and appropriate situational CR could be chosen, the inability to specify the eliciting CS in most concomitant measurement studies complicates an analysis of the temporal relations between the eliciting stimulus, the situational CR, and the IR. Fourth, it is possible on occasion to obtain different temporal relationships between situational CRs and IRs simply by the employment of different response criteria (see Shapiro & Miller, 1965). Fifth, and finally, even if all these methodological questions could be resolved, the correlational nature of concurrent measurement studies have the unavoidable limitation that they cannot by themselves indicate a causal relation between CRs and IRs or vice versa. Accordingly, although these studies are provocative, they have the logical limitation of being unable to reject the hypothesis that situational CRs are inconsequential concomitants of the instrumental conditioning situation.

B. Transfer Designs

The above theoretical and methodological considerations have unquestionably led to a decline in the use of concurrent measurement designs. Accordingly, classical–instrumental transfer designs involving the examination of CS–IR functions are now the most commonly used means of assessing the possible motivational and/or reinforcing effects of CRs on instrumental performance. In the prototypic transfer experiment, the stimulus pairings of classical conditioning are carried out either "on the base line" (that is, during instrumental training) or "off the base line" (that is, in a situation separate from the instrumental training). Then, in the test phase of the experiment the CS, used in the stimulus pairings of classical conditioning, is interpolated during instrumental training with the usual result of an augmentation or decrement in the rate of instrumental responding. The interpretation commonly attached to such CS–IR functions is that the changes in instrumental performance are directly due to the covert CRs elicited by the interpolated CS (a CR–IR interaction).

By permitting the manipulation of classical conditioning parameters and, presumably, the strength of covert CRs in a fashion independent of instrumental responding, the classical–instrumental transfer paradigms would appear to offer an ideal means for experimentally assessing CR mediational theories without becoming entangled in the complexities of using correlational techniques and identifying situational CRs. However, several difficulties mitigate acceptance of the conclusion that the result of classical–instrumental transfer studies reflect the properties of the CS-elicited covert CRs. First, examination of the stimulus presentation procedures employed in the majority of classical–instrumental conditioning studies reveals the methodological possibility that instrumental responses are adventitiously acquired to the CS during the classical-conditioning phase, and these IRs when evoked by the CS in the test phase operate to modulate the instrumental target response (that is, an IR–IR interaction). Specifically, in "classical" aversive training the US is generally delivered to an unrestrained organism (for example, shock through an electrified grid) and hence, the opportunity exists for the organism to acquire instrumental escape-like responses. Furthermore, in "classical" appetitive training, the organism is generally required to make instrumental approach responses to obtain the food or water "US." Trapold and Overmier (1972) have cogently argued that a number of studies conducted to foster the acquisition of specific instrumental responses during the stimulus pairing stage (for example, Trapold & Carlson, 1965; Trapold & Fairlie, 1965) failed to support the notion that instrumental response mediators govern the outcomes of classical–instrumental transfer studies. Nevertheless, for the majority of transfer studies, the failure to control for instrumental response mediators questions a CR-mediated interpretation of their outcomes.

In some classical–instrumental transfer studies, the stimulus presentation procedures requisite of classical conditioning have been met through the use of restrained subjects (for example, Overmier & Seligman, 1967) and by direct application of either a liquid US into the subject's oral cavity (for example, Gross, Trapold, & Hyde, 1968) or by brain stimulation (for example, Azrin & Hake, 1969). However, even when the stimulus presentation requirements of classical conditioning are met, a second difficulty arises in the interpretation that the CS–IR functions obtained in classical–instrumental transfer studies reflect the mediating properties of the CS-elicited CRs. The central proposition of CR mediational theories is that situational CRs develop concurrently with IRs in instrumental training. Hence, in the test phase of classical–instrumental transfer designs instrumental performance should already be under the influence of situational CRs. Accordingly, when the CS is introduced, these situational CRs might be expected to interact with the CS-elicited CRs, with their product ultimately influencing instrumental performance. Although the possibility of a CR–CR–IR interaction in classical–instrumental transfer experiments is a logical consequence derived from the general mediational view that situational CRs control instrumental performance, there has been no explicit reference to such an interaction. Such an oversight is surprising, given the fact that recent CR-mediational theories (for example, Bindra, 1968; Konorski, 1967; Miller, 1963; Rescorla & Solomon, 1967) have been predicated on the general assumption that appetitive and aversive motivational systems algebraically summate to affect overt responding. Specifically, these theories presume that appetitive and aversive motivational systems are mutually inhibitory, canceling by subtraction each other's influence on responding. Accordingly, these formulations commonly express the expectation that a CS previously paired with an aversive shock US would suppress appetitive food-reinforced instrumental responses but facilitate aversive shock-reinforced instrumental responses. Likewise, a CS previously paired with an appetitive US would be expected to facilitate appetitive and suppress aversive instrumental responses. In point of fact, however, these writers have failed to acknowledge that CR-mediational theories would dictate that the situational CRs and their stimulus consequences would be the source of the motivational state purportedly operating during instrumental responding in the classical–instrumental transfer design.

The coupling of the theoretical notions of algebraic summation of motivational states with explicit recognition of the possibility of CR–CR–IR interactions would appear to account for the outcomes of a large number of classical–instrumental transfer studies (see Trapold & Overmier, 1972). However, the pattern of results has not been completely consistent with such expectations. In particular, facilitation and suppression have been found within the same transfer paradigm depending on: (a) reinforcement schedule during instrumental training (for example, Blackman, 1968); (b) the order in which classical and instrumental training were administered (for example, Overmier & Seligman, 1967; Seligman & Maier, 1967); and

(c) parameters of classical conditioning, particularly when stimulus pairings have been administered "on the base line" (for example, Meltzer & Brahlek, 1970; Scobie, 1972). Yet, the fact that variables have been isolated that appear to play a role in producing diametrically opposed CS–IR functions should not be surprising in view of the complexities that can exist in classical–instrumental transfer paradigms (see Scavio, 1972). Analytically, classical–instrumental transfer paradigms can be regarded as involving the permutation of three events that occur in the test phase: (a) the CS-elicited CR (CR_1); (b) the situational CR (CR_2); and (c) the instrumental response (IR). These three events can have six possible permutations: CR_1–CR_2–IR; CR_2–CR_1–IR; CR_1–IR–CR_2; CR_2–IR–CR_1; IR–CR_1–CR_2; and IR–CR_2–CR_1. Hence, the relatively straightforward CR–CR–IR interaction in classical-instrumental transfer designs is predicted on the assumption that the first or second (CR_1–CR_2–IR or CR_2–CR_1–IR) sequence of events is present in the test phase. However, in all other possible permutations, the IR occurs before or after one or both CR events. The presence of the former or latter permutations within the same type of transfer paradigm may well be the factor producing diametrically opposed CS–IR functions. In any event, the common assumption that classical–instrumental transfer paradigms provide a simple means for assessing the mediational effects of CS-elicited CRs on instrumental responding would appear to be unwarranted, owing to the complexities that are deducable from the very theories which these paradigms were designed to test.

C. Conditioned Stimulus–Instrumental Response Functions

In a curious transposition of theory and method, the classical–instrumental transfer paradigms, originally designed to ascertain modulating effects of classical covert CRs on instrumental performance, have become regarded in some quarters as "classical conditioning" paradigms in their own right (Kamin, 1965; Rescorla & Solomon, 1967) and thus a testing ground for theories of classical conditioning (for example, Rescorla & Wagner, 1972) to the exclusion of the historic, basic classical conditioning paradigm. Specifically, Kamin (1965) has argued that the CS–IR functions generated by the CER paradigm correspond closely with the CS–CR functions observed in the basic paradigm. Moreover, Rescorla and Solomon (1967) have gone so far as to suggest that classical–instrumental transfer paradigm may produce CS–IR functions that are more sensitive to changes in "classical conditioning" here regarded as a central state, than the CS–CR functions produced by the basic paradigm. However, in view of the issues raised in the previous section of possible IR–IR interactions and the numerous possible interactions of a CS-elicited CR, situational CR, and the IR in classical–instrumental transfer paradigms, one might expect to observe disparities between the CS–CR functions obtained under the basic paradigm and the CS–IR functions obtained with the transfer paradigm.

The possible methodological or theoretical expectations of divergence between CS–CR and CS–IR functions would, of course, be superseded by their demonstrated empirical convergence. Although, CS–IR and CS–CR functions appear sensitive to many of the same parameters, there are sufficient disparities between them as to question the perception of equivalence. For example, substantial behavioral effects have been obtained with the CER paradigm when CS–US intervals of several minutes have been used (for example, Annau & Kamin, 1961; Kamin, 1965; Stein, Sidman, & Brady, 1958). Furthermore, in the most extreme case, behavioral effects have been obtained in the taste aversion paradigm with CS–US intervals extending to several hours (see Garcia, McGowan, & Green, 1972). (In the prototypic taste aversion study, the classical training phase consists of the presentation of a distinctly flavored food CS followed by a poison UCS, as, for example, an injection of lithium chloride. Subsequently, the test phase consists of presenting the flavored food CS and the acquisition of a conditioned taste aversion is defined as a suppression of the instrumental consummatory response to the flavored food CS, that is, a CS–IR function.) In contrast, there are no experimental findings with CS–CR paradigms that indicate CR acquisition at CS–US intervals of several minutes or several hours (see Gormezano & Moore, 1969). Although Pavlov (1927) reported the *maintenance* of salivary CRs at CS–US intervals of several minutes, initial CR acquisition training required a substantially shorter CS–US interval, generally about 5 sec or less, after which the CS–US interval was gradually increased over the course of extended periods of training.

It may be argued that the above disparities largely represent a difference in the sensitivity to experimental parameters shown by the response systems directly observed in CS–CR paradigms and those only indirectly observed in CS–IR paradigms. Historically, it has been argued that CS–IR paradigms reflect the strength of mediating "emotional" CRs generally specified in terms of autonomic CRs. However, taking the hypothesis of autonomic CR mediators of CS–IR functions seriously, it would not appear plausible to attribute the disparities between CS–CR and CS–IR functions solely to any purported greater sensitivity of autonomic response systems over skeletal response systems. While there are experimental data to suggest that autonomic CRs may show a broader range of effective CS–US intervals than skeletal CRs (see Schneiderman, 1972), the maximal effective CS–US intervals for autonomic CRs do not nearly approach the large effective CS–US intervals obtained in CS–IR paradigms.

On the basis of the failure of autonomic situational CRs to correla with instrumental responding in concurrent measurement designs, Rescor and Solomon (1967) attempted to free CR-mediational theories from the anchoring in autonomic response systems. Accordingly, Rescorla and Sol mon (1967) have argued that CS–IR functions reflect the motivational co sequences of "central CRs" with the clear implication that "central CR were more sensitive to experimental parameters than the peripheral Cl observed in CS–CR paradigms. Unlike the hypothesis of autonomic C mediators, the "central CR" hypothesis precludes the possibility of dire observation of the mediating CRs due to their hypothetical nature. The it is not possible to assess their presumed sensitivity to experiment parameters independent of a CS–IR paradigm, since "central CRs" posse no status beyond their presumed mediating influence in CS–IR paradign. Accordingly, the presumed sensitivity of "central CRs" is a postulat simply redescribing known CS–IR functions, and, although not requir to do so, the formulation provides no basis of explaining disparities b tween CS–IR and CS–CR functions.

The above arguments are not meant to denigrate the more gener hypothesis that CS–CR and CS–IR functions may reflect in some degr common associative laws (see Rescorla & Wagner, 1972). Rather, the arguments are presented to serve only as a caution against an overly e thusiastic identification of CS–CR and CS–IR paradigms, which blinds its to diverging empirical outcomes. Moreover, it is hoped that the reade attention has been drawn to the fact that CS–IR transfer paradigms a "classical" only in the tentative theoretical sense that CS–IR functions a presumed to reflect the consequences of mediating CRs. Accordingly, a tempts to merge CS–IR and CS–CR paradigms on a paradigmatic level equivalent "classical conditioning" procedures, involves the a priori a sumption that CR-mediational theory is true. However, the paradox of su an assumption is that there is a very high likelihood of divergences betwee CS–CR and CS–IR functions based upon the very expectations of Cl mediational accounts (that is, interactions of situational CRs, CS-elicit CRs, and the IR).

IV. MECHANISMS OF CONDITIONED STIMULUS– CONDITIONED RESPONSE ACQUISITION

A. Variants of Effect Theory

Despite the early and persistent identification of classical conditioning wi the associationistic principle of contiguity (see Robinson, 1932), the mec anism of reinforcement for the CR remains a subject of continued debat

At an empirical level the US is the reinforcer for the acquisition and maintenance of a CR, but the mechanism by which the US provides a reinforcing state of affairs remains a matter of theoretical controversy. Nevertheless, the principal formulations have been contiguity and effect accounts. In contiguity formulations (for example, Estes, 1959; Guthrie, 1952; Sheffield, 1965) the role of the US is presumed to assure the occurrence of the UR in an appropriate temporal relationship to the CS, whereas effect theories hold that the US must also have motivational consequences. However, within the realm of effect theories, there have been numerous proposals regarding the character of the motivational consequences arising from the US. These latter proposals may be divided into two broad classes on the basis of whether CR acquisition is determined (*a*) by the presumed motivational properties of the US per se or (*b*) through CR-produced modification of the sensory consequences of the US.

The first effect principle, which postulates that the US itself has reinforcing motivational properties, represents a relatively straightforward application of Thorndike's (1911) "Law of Effect." Although the Law of Effect was formulated in connection with an attempt to account for behavioral changes in what were only subsequently recognized as instrumental conditioning paradigms, its application to classical conditioning does no violence to the procedural distinction between classical and instrumental conditioning. As stated, the Law of Effect only requires that, within a stimulus situation, a response and "satisfying state of affairs" occur in close temporal conjunction; no mention is made of the presence or absence of an instrumental relation between the target response and reinforcing state of affairs. Moreover, the Law of Effect is an associationistic principle stating the conditions for strengthening a S–R "connection," manifested by the tendency for a response to recur in a situation. Under the Law of Effect as applied to classical conditioning, the necessary close conjunction of a target response and satisfying state of affairs is assured in that the US is presumed to serve a dual function as the source of the UR and source of the necessary motivational consequences. With UR-reinforcement contiguity assured in this way, the pairing of a CS with the US is all that is experimentally necessary to establish a connection between the CS and target response. This effect principle has been held by a number of theorists who have differed, however, on the proposed mechanism by which the motivational properties of the US operate to serve their reinforcing role (for example, Hull, 1943; Konorski, 1967; Miller, 1963; Mowrer, 1960; Spence, 1956).

The second major form of effect theory, which postulates that CR acquisition arises through CR-produced modification of the sensory consequences of the US, is based on a strong identification of the Law of Effect with instrumental procedures. Consequently, this application of the Law of Effect to classical conditioning has involved blurring the procedural distinction between classical and instrumental conditioning by the fundamental contention that a hidden instrumental contingency is intrinsically embedded in classical conditioning procedures. Accordingly, we reference this persistent theme in the conditioning literature (see Hebb, 1956; Martin & Levey, 1969; Perkins, 1955, 1971; Prokasy, 1965; Schlosberg, 1937) as instrumental "law of effect" accounts of classical conditioning. In so doing, it should be readily recognized that these formulations essentially assert that the mechanism of reinforcement in classical conditioning can be reduced to the same process of "effect" presumed to govern instrumental conditioning.

B.   Instrumental "Law of Effect" Accounts

In its most general form, the instrumental "law of effect" tradition holds that a CR is acquired in classical conditioning because it is capable of so affecting the stimulus consequences of delivery of the US that execution of a CR is "rewarding" relative to a failure to make a CR. Specifically, CR–US overlap is presumed to provide the source of differential reinforcement of CRs through its attenuation of the noxiousness of the aversive US in classical defense conditioning or by enhancement of the "attractiveness" of the appetitive US in classical reward conditioning. Historically, this tradition can be traced to the purported methodological assessment of classical conditioning paradigms by Schlosberg (1937), whose views can be considered a logical extension of Hull's (1929) analysis of avoidance conditioning.

Hull (1929) conceptualized the avoidance paradigm as one of repeated cycling of conditioning and extinction. However, such a cyclical phenomenon seemed to Hull biologically unadaptive, since reacquisition could occur only by reexposure to the dangerous event. The unsatisfactory explanatory solution offered by Hull consisted in postulating a suspension of the weakening tendencies of experimental extinction in the avoidance conditioning situation. Subsequently, the biological paradox of the avoidance response provided Schlosberg (1937) with the theoretical justification for postulating that the law of success learning (that is, Thorndike's "law of effect") overrides the Pavlovian law of extinction of CRs. Specifically, Schlosberg suggested that the avoidance response developed under CS–US contiguity and was maintained under the Law of Effect, and hence, two processes affected the time course of development of a *single* response. Generalizing beyond the avoidance paradigm Schlosberg offered criteria for what appears to be the first "law of effect" interpretation of classical conditioning, although the criteria were stated as a methodological device for determining whether experiments carried out ostensibly by classical conditioning had in fact succeeded in minimizing the CR's operation of "success" or "effect" upon the US. Schlosberg's (1937) criteria were ". . . a conditioned response will be considered successful if it prevents or terminates a nociceptive unconditioned stimulus or . . . increases a beneceptive unconditioned stimulus [p. 382]." A CR found to modify the reception of the US would then be said to reflect not merely the laws of Pavlovian conditioning, but also the Thorndikian Law of Effect, tied as it was to instrumental conditioning. Schlosberg examined the conditioned eyelid, knee jerk, and salivary response preparations and found none for which he could hold with certainty that the law of success had no application. By an imaginative reconstruction of the possible consequences of a CR for receipt of the US, Schlosberg reasoned that the eyelid CR may avoid the air puff, the anticipatory knee jerk may decrease the stimulating value of the tap on the tendon, and the salivary CR may enhance the stimulating value of a dry meat powder US and decrease that of an acid US.

Thus, with Schlosberg (1937), Thorndike's Law of Effect was applied in a decisive shift, consistently honored by subsequent adherents to the instrumental "law of effect" tradition, from a purely extrinsic relation between the CR and reinforcement (presence of the US) to a presumed intrinsic causal relation (CR-produced modification of the US). Obviously, this shift was necessitated by the fact that in the classical conditioning situation the delivery of the US is not CR contingent. Accordingly, an instrumental "law of effect" interpretation must provide "events," the occurrence of which is contingent upon the occurrence (and topographical features) of the CR. The only available contingent event is the presumed effect of a CR upon the sensory consequences of the US. However, the logic of Schlosberg's appeal (and subsequent adherents to the position) to Thorndike's Law of Effect is questionable, especially in its application to classical defense conditioning. Thorndike's Law of Effect was originally defined in instrumental reward and escape conditioning paradigms in which the target response was followed by an on-trial change in stimulus conditions, presumed to be accompanied by a change in the motivational state of the organism from a "less satisfying" to a "more satisfying" state of affairs. Yet, within classical defense conditioning, the presumed on-trial changes in stimulus conditions following a CR would not appear to lead to a "more satisfying" state of affairs, for if CR–US overlap does not fully attentuate the US, the organism would experience some of the noxious consequences of the US. Furthermore, if CR–US overlap fully attentuates the US, the organism would experience no on-trial change in stimulus conditions and, accordingly no change in motivational state. Conceivably, "law of effect" accounts could argue that the organism possesses some mechanism for cross-trial comparisons of the presumed less aversive motivational consequences of a CR–US overlap trial with the more aversive motivational consequences of a trial without CR–US overlap. As yet, there has been no delineation of the laws governing such a comparator mechanism. In contrast, application of Thorndike's Law of Effect to classical appetitive conditioning would not appear to require postulation of a comparator mechanism, for, on trials with or without CR–US overlap, there is an on-trial change to a "more satisfying" state of affairs accompanying US presentation. The difference between the two types of trials would presumably be the effective magnitude of this on-trial change, with CR–US overlap producing the greater change to a "more satisfying" state of affairs.

It should be noted, that by emphasizing the possible "adaptive" value of the execution of each CR for the organism, Schlosberg (1937) departed from the broad Darwinian focus upon survival of the species displayed in the conception of conditioning held by Pavlov (1927) and Hull (1929). Instead, he shifted to Skinner's (1938) subsequently held local and individually oriented conception of adaptation, which rested entirely on the presumed consequences of a response for the individual organism. It is likely that Schlosberg's shift fathered the rise of subsequent local adaptive interpretations of the presumed consequences of the CR upon the US (see Hebb, 1956; Kimble, 1961; Perkins, 1955, 1971, pp. 78–79). Recently, the instrumental "law of effect" account has turned to a more refined phase in the guise of the response shaping hypothesis (for example, Kimmel, 1965; Prokasy, 1965). Essentially, the response shaping hypothesis extends the "law of effect" formulation by making the additional assumption that the dependence of the source of reinforcement on CR–US overlap provides a mechanism of differential reinforcement for shaping CR topography. Accordingly, evidence in support of the operation of the "law of effect" is sought in an examination of a large number of dependent variable measures. While a number of such studies have appeared in the literature, they have essentially attempted to provide evidence in descriptive accord with the response shaping hypothesis by examination of topographical characteristics of the CR (for example, CR latency and CR duration) and then inferring the operation of the "law of effect."

Because criteria for determining the presence of CR modification of the US and its presumed reinforcing consequences wait upon operationalization, there has been no procedure proposed for deciding unequivocally either upon the range of application of the "law of effect" or the legitimacy of its application in any particular instance. As a result, it has been particularly difficult to demonstrate the inapplicability of the "law of effect" in any selected classical conditioning preparation. Indeed, the local adaptive framework exemplified in the "law of effect" tradition has sustained the expectation that every classical-conditioning situation not only does but *must* operate under the "law of effect." Otherwise, so the reasoning goes, why is the CR acquired at all? Various imaginative reconstructions of the local adaptive consequences of CRs have been readily produced by such theories to make local adaptive interpretations seem reasonable. Yet, given the lack of operational content to such adaptive interpretations, the applicability of the "law of effect" to any classical conditioning situation has been as difficult to prove as to disprove. Specifically, as yet, no procedure exists which simultaneously permits the manipulation of CR–US overlap and adherence to classical conditioning's procedural requirement that the US be delivered independently of the CR. Hence, an intrinsic CR–US overlap reinforcement contingency cannot be given a procedural specification similar to that of an extrinsic instrumental contingency. Lacking such a procedural specification, three research strategies have been pursued to assess the plausibility of the contention that an intrinsic CR–US overlap reinforcement contingency operates in classical conditioning.

First, attempts have been made to determine the reinforcing effects of CR-produced US attenuation in aversive conditioning through the use of explicit response-contingent alterations in US intensity, thus making completely extrinsic the presumed relation between the CR and its effects upon US sensory consequences. While the introduction of such a contingency would designate the paradigm as one of instrumental conditioning, it would not constitute a confounding of the procedural and theoretical distinctions under consideration, since such a procedure would bring under experimental control what has been the speculative source of reinforcement in classical conditioning for instrumental "law of effect" accounts. Considering this tactic, human eyelid experiments comparing conventional classical conditioning, and response-contingent US omission (avoidance) conditions have uniformly revealed lower levels of the performance under the avoidance procedure (see Gormezano, 1965).

Moreover, Coleman (1975), using the rabbit nictitating membrane preparation, further dimensionalized the effects of the CR upon the US. At one end of the dimension, a classical-conditioning group received no contingent US intensity reduction; at intermediate points, two other groups each received a specified magnitude of contingent US intensity reduction; and, at the other end of the dimension, an avoidance group received the largest magnitude of contingent US intensity reduction, that is, contingent US omission. Coleman (1975) observed that CR frequency decreased with increases in the magnitude of CR-contingent US intensity reduction, with the avoidance group showing the lowest CR frequency. Both sets of results are contrary to expectations from the "law of effect," since the failure of response-contingent US intensity reduction to be more efficacious than a fixed US intensity procedure (that is, conventional classical conditioning) questions the assertion that any presumed US attenuation occurring during CR–US overlap is the mechanism of reinforcement in classical defense conditioning. In a similar fashion, "law of effect" accounts would not expect conditioning to occur in omisson training with appetitive USs. Yet, successful acquisition of CRs under an appetitive omission procedure has been reported for the dog's salivary response (Sheffield, 1965), the rat's licking response (Patten & Rudy, 1967), and the rabbit's jaw movement response (Gormezano & Hiller, 1972). Hence, by precluding any possible CR–US overlap, and yet still producing CR acquisition with both appetitive and aversive USs, these investigations clearly fail to support the tenability of a CR–US overlap mechanism of reinforcement.

Second, assessments have been made on the implication of the response shaping formulation that the noxiousness of the US should be negatively correlated with CR magnitude. Such an implication derives from the assumption that a larger CR attenuates the noxious sensory consequences of the US more fully than a smaller CR. For example, Furedy (1970), using the galvanic skin response, and Furedy and Doob (1971), the vasomotor response, obtained a verbal rating of the US intensity on each trial. Counter to the expectations of response shaping formulations, the correlation between CR magnitude and US intensity rating was not significantly different from zero. (Even if the negative correlation expected by response shaping formulations had obtained, such a correlation, while suggestive, would not permit one to specify the CR as the causal agent for a low rating of US noxiousness.)

Third, adherents to response shaping formulations have attempted to identify putative measures of CR topographical classes which reflect the differentially reinforcing effects of CR–US overlap. However, CR characteristics indicative of the operation of CR–US overlap have never been precisely specified. Such a lack of specificity may be attributed in part to the response inferred nature of the CR–US overlap contingency, for response-shaping formulations possess no means for predicting which CR measures should reflect the presumed operation of the differential reinforcement mechanism. Hence, in the absence of a precise definition of a CR–US overlap indicant, response shaping theorists have had to rely on post hoc determinations of the correspondence between the expectations of their formulation and a variety of topographical measures (for example, CR latency). However, the support which such data lend to response shaping formulations lacks the strength that would accrue if it were possible to manipulate the presumed contingency between the selected CR topographical feature and the degree of US modification.

V. SUMMARY

In contemporary usage, the term "classical conditioning" has become the source of extensive ambiguity. As presently detailed, "classical conditioning" has in different contexts referred to a specific learning paradigm, a set of empirical laws, a source of axioms for more general learning theories, and a phenomenon of theoretical interest in its own right. The central thrust of the chapter has been directed at distinguishing among these usages of "classical conditioning" and delineating some of the methodological issues that arise.

The basic classical conditioning paradigm, herein designated the "CS–CR paradigm," has been specified as consisting of: (a) administration of the CS and US, independent of all responding; and (b) selection of a target response from among the effector systems elicited by the US. The first feature of the CS–CR paradigm has the unique property of permitting the experimenter to retain absolute control over the timing and sequence of stimulus events to the organism, and the second feature allows the identification and manipulation of the stimulus antecedents to the target response from the outset of training. It has been indicated that the CS–CR paradigm in providing complete experimental control over stimulus events, and especially the stimulus antecedents to the target response, provides the analytical power for discovering the precise conditions of stimulation under which the acquisition of responding based upon associative and nonassociative factors occurs. Moreover, when the classical-conditioning paradigm is so specified, it becomes more clearly distinguishable from instrumental conditioning paradigms. The sharpened distinction markedly facilitates the identification of instrumental contingencies in paradigms commonly referenced as "classical" (for example, autoshaping, CS–IR, and "food-in-the-bowl" type paradigms).

In addition to the presentation of issues surrounding the paradigmatic usage of "classical conditioning," consideration was given to the axiomatic application of the empirical laws of classical conditioning by theories postulating that CRs mediate more complex behaviors, particularly instrumental response sequences. In the assessment of CR-mediational theories, the research strategies of concurrent measurement of situational CRs in instrumental conditioning and the utilization of CS–IR transfer paradigms have evolved. It was noted that neither paradigm has yielded results entirely consistent with CR-mediational theories, but, due to methodological failings or as yet unresolved theoretical issues, the disparate findings cannot be interpreted unambiguously as either supporting or denying CR-mediational accounts.

In brief, the failure of concurrent measurement designs to yield consistent temporal relationships between the indicant situational CR and IR may arise from such methodological difficulties as differences in the criterion for CR detection, inability to specify the eliciting stimulus for the indicant CR, and the misidentification of the indicant CR as the mediating CR. In any event, it was indicated that the correlational nature of the data arising from concurrent measurement studies precludes their serving as definitive evidence for any causal relationship between a CR and IR. The failures of CS–IR transfer studies to reflect uniformly a one-to-one-correspondence between the strength of a CS–IR relationship and the strength of a presumed covert CS-elicited CR may arise from the possible interactions of the CS-elicited CR, the situational CR, and the IR. In addition, another source of response interaction may arise from the opportunity of IRs to be established in the so-called "classical" training stage of many CS–IR transfer studies.

In the assessment of theories of classical conditioning itself, interest was focused upon the methodological issues that arise in connection with instrumental "law of effect" accounts of the mechanism of reinforcement in classical conditioning. When the "law of effect" formulation is taken for what it is, that is a theory, the methodological difficulty is the inability to test the theory by the experimental manipulation of the hypothesized CR–US overlap contingency, except by the use of explicit instrumental procedures. Moreover, in those instances in which explicit instrumental procedures have been used as analogs to the hypothetical CR modification of the US, the experimental findings have been inconsistent with expectations of the "law of effect" account.

ACKNOWLEDGMENTS

The preparation of this chapter was supported by NSF Grant GB-41531 to the first author and by NIH Training Grant MH 08333-12 to the second author.

REFERENCES

Amsel, A. The role of frustrative nonreward in noncontinuous reward situations. *Psychological Bulletin,* 1958, **55,** 102–119.

Annau, Z., & Kamin, L. J. The conditioned emotional response as a function of intensity of the US. *Journal of Comparative and Physiological Psychology,* 1961, **54,** 428–432.

Ayres, J. J. B., Benedict, J. O., & Witcher, E. S. Systematic manipulation of individual events in a truly random control in rats. *Journal of Comparative and Physiological Psychology,* 1975, **88,** 97–103.

Azrin, N. H., & Hake, D. F. Positive conditioned suppression: Conditioned suppression using positive reinforcers as the unconditioned stimuli. *Journal of the Experimental Analysis of Behavior,* 1969, **12,** 167–173.

Benedict, J. O., & Ayres, J. J. B. Factors affecting conditioning in the truly random control procedure in the rat. *Journal of Comparative and Physiological Psychology,* 1972, **78,** 232–330.

Bernstein, A. L. Temporal factors in the formation of conditioned eyelid reactions in human subjects. *Journal of General Psychology,* 1934, **10,** 173–197.

Bindra, D. Neuropsychological interpretation of the effects of drive and incentive-motivation on general activity and instrumental behavior. *Psychological Review,* 1968, **75,** 1–22.

Black, A. H., & Dalton, A. J. The relationship between the avoidance response and subsequent changes in heart rate. *Acta Biologicae Experimentalis,* 1965, **25,** 107–119.

Blackman, D. Conditioned suppression or facilitation as a function of the behavioral baseline. *Journal of the Experimental Analysis of Behavior,* 1968, **11,** 53–61.

Boice, R., & Denny, M. R. The conditioned licking response in rats as a function of the CS–UCS interval. *Psychonomic Science,* 1965, **3,** 93–94.

Boring, E. G. *A history of Experimental Psychology.* (2nd ed.) New York: Appleton-Century-Crofts, 1950.

Brown, P., & Jenkins, H. M. Auto-shaping of the pigeon's key peck. *Journal of the Experimental Analysis of Behavior,* 1968, **11,** 1–8.

Cason, H. The conditioned eyelid reaction. *Journal of Experimental Psychology,* 1922, **5,** 153–196.

Coleman, S. R. Consequences of response-contingent change in unconditioned stimulus intensity upon the rabbit (*Oryctolagus cuniculus*) nictitating membrane response. *Journal of Comparative & Physiological Psychology,* 1975, **88,** 591–595.

DeToledo, L. Changes in heart rate during conditioned suppression in rats as a function of US intensity and type of CS. *Journal of Comparative and Physiological Psychology,* 1971, **77,** 528–538.

Ellison, G. D. Differential salivary conditioning to traces. *Journal of Comparative and Physiological Psychology,* 1964, **57,** 373–380.

Estes, W. K. The statistical approach to learning theory. In S. Koch (Ed.), *Psychology: A study of a science.* Vol. 2. New York: McGraw-Hill, 1959. Pp. 380–491.

Furedy, J. J. Test of the preparatory adaptive response interpretation of aversive classical autonomic conditioning. *Journal of Experimental Psychology,* 1970, **84,** 301–307.

Furedy, J. J., & Doob, A. N. Classical aversive conditioning of human digital volume–pulse change and tests of the preparatory—adaptive—response interpretation of reinforcement. *Journal of Experimental Psychology,* 1971, **89,** 403–407.

Garcia, J., McGowan, B. K., & Green, K. F. Biological constraints on conditioning. In A. H. Black & W. F. Prokasy (Eds.), *Classical conditioning II: Current theory and research.* New York: Appleton-Century-Crofts, 1972. Pp. 3–27.

Gormezano, I. Yoked comparisons of classical and instrumental conditioning of the eyelid response; and an addendum on "voluntary responders." In W. F. Prokasy (Ed.), *Classical conditioning: A symposium.* New York: Appleton-Century-Crofts, 1965. Pp. 48–70.

Gormezano, I. Classical conditioning. In J. B. Sidowski (Ed.), *Experimental methods and instrumentation in psychology.* New York: McGraw-Hill, 1966. Pp. 385–420.

Gormezano, I., & Hiller, G. W. Omission training of the jaw-movement response of the rabbit to a water US. *Psychonomic Science,* 1972, **29,** 276–278.

Gormezano, I., & Moore, J. W. Classical conditioning: Beyond the basic parameters. In M. M. Marx (Ed.), *Learning: Processes.* Toronto and New York: Macmillan, 1969. Pp. 169–203.

Gormezano, I., Schneiderman, N., Deaux, E., & Fuentes, I. Nictitating membrane: Classical conditioning and extinction in the albino rabbit. *Science,* 1962, **138,** 33–34.

Grant, D. A. Sensitization and association in eyelid conditioning. *Journal of Experimental Psychology,* 1943, **32,** 201–212.

Gross, D. M., Trapold, M. A., & Hyde, T. S. A simple technique for delivering liquids directly to the mouth of an unrestrained rat. *Journal of the Experimental Analysis of Behavior,* 1968, **11,** 191–195.

Guthrie, E. R. *The psychology of learning.* (rev. ed.) New York: Harper, 1952.

Hebb, D. O. The distinction between "classical" and "instrumental". *Canadian Journal of Psychology,* 1956, **10,** 165–166.

Hilgard, E. R. Conditioned eyelid reactions to a light stimulus based on the reflex wink to sound. *Psychological Monographs,* 1931, **41,** No. 184.

Hilgard, E. R., & Marquis, D. G. *Conditioning and learning.* New York: Appleton-Century-Crofts, 1940.

Holland, P. C., & Rescorla, R. A. Second-order conditioning with food unconditioned stimulus. *Journal of Comparative and Physiological Psychology,* 1975, **88,** 459–467.

Hull, C. L. A functional interpretation of the conditioned reflex. *Psychological Review,* 1929, **36,** 498–511.

Hull, C. L. Knowledge and purpose as habit mechanisms. *Psychological Review,* 1930, **37,** 511–525.

Hull, C. L. *Principles of behavior.* New York: Appleton-Century-Crofts, 1943.

James, W. *Principles of psychology.* New York: Holt, 1890.

Kamin, L. J. Temporal and intensity characteristics of the conditioned stimulus. In W. F. Prokasy (Ed.), *Classical conditioning: A symposium.* New York: Appleton-Century-Crofts, 1965. Pp. 118–147.

Kimble, G. A. *Hilgard and Marquis' conditioning and learning.* New York: Appleton-Century-Crofts, 1961.

Kimmel, H. D. Instrumental inhibitory factors in classical conditioning. In W. F. Prokasy (Ed.), *Classical conditioning: A symposium.* New York: Appleton-Century-Crofts, 1965. Pp. 148–171.

Konorski, J. *Integrative activity of the brain: An interdisciplinary approach.* Chicago: University of Chicago Press, 1967.

Konorski, J., & Miller, S. Methode d'examen de l'analysateur moteur par les réactions salivomatrices. *Compte Rendu Hebdimadaire des Séances et Memoires de la Société de Biologie,* 1930, **104,** 907–910.

Kremer, E. F., & Kamin, L. J. The truly random control procedure: Associative or nonassociative effect in rats. *Journal of Comparative & Physiological Psychology,* 1971, **74,** 203–210.

Longo, N., Klempay, S., & Bitterman, M. E. Classical appetitive conditioning in the pigeon. *Psychonomic Science,* 1964, **1,** 19–20.

Martin, I., & Levey, A. B. *The genesis of the classical conditioned response.* Oxford: Pergamon Press, 1969.

Meltzer, D., & Brahlek, J. A. Conditioned suppression and conditioned enhancement with the same positive UCS: An effect of CS duration. *Journal of the Experimental Analysis of Behavior,* 1970, **13,** 67–73.

Miller, N. E. Some reflections on the law of effect produce a new alternative to drive reduction. In M. M. Jones (Ed.), *Nebraska symposium on motivation.* Lincoln: University of Nebraska Press, 1963. Pp. 65–112.

Moore, B. R. The role of directed Pavlovian reactions in simple instrumental learning in the pigeon. In R. A. Hinde & J. Stevenson-Hinde (Eds.), *Constraints on learning.* New York: Academic Press, 1973. Pp. 159–206.

Mowrer, O. H. *Learning theory and the symbolic processes.* New York: John Wiley & Sons, 1960.

Overmier, J. B., & Seligman, M. E. P. Effects of inescapable shock upon subsequent escape and avoidance responding. *Journal of Comparative and Physiological Psychology,* 1967, **63,** 28–33.

Patten, R. L., & Rudy, J. W. The Sheffield omission training procedure applied to the conditioning of the licking response in rats. *Psychonomic Science,* 1967, **8,** 463–464.

Pavlov, I. P. Scientific study of so-called psychical processes of higher animals (Thomas Huxley Lecture). *Lancet,* 1906, **84,** 911–915.

Pavlov, I. P. *Conditioned reflexes.* (Translated by G. V. Anrep.) London and New York: Oxford University Press, 1927.

Pavlov, I. P. *Lectures on conditioned reflexes.* (Translated by W. H. Gantt.) New York: International Press, 1928.

Perkins, C. C., Jr. The stimulus conditions which follow learned response. *Psychological Review,* 1955, **62,** 341–348.

Perkins, C. C., Jr. Reinforcement in classical conditioning. In H. H. Kendler & J. T. Spence (Eds.), *Essays in neobehaviorism.* New York: Appleton-Century-Crofts, 1971. Pp. 113–136.

Prokasy, W. F. Classical eyelid conditioning: Experimenter operations, task demands, and response shaping. In W. F. Prokasy (Ed.), *Classical conditioning: A symposium.* New York: Appleton-Century-Crofts, 1965. Pp. 208–225.

Quinsey, V. L. Conditioned suppression with no CS–US contingency in the rat. *Canadian Journal of Psychology/Review of Canadian Psychology,* 1971, **25,** 69–82.

Rescorla, R. A. Predictability and number of pairings in Pavlovian fear conditioning, *Psychonomic Science,* 1966, **4,** 383–384.

Rescorla, R. A. Pavlovian conditioning and its proper control procedures. *Psychological Review,* 1967, **74,** 71–80.

Rescorla, R. A. Informational variables in Pavlovian conditioning. In G. H. Bower & J. T. Spence (Eds.), *The psychology of learning and motivation.* New York: Academic Press, 1972. Pp. 1–46.

Rescorla, R. A. Second-order conditioning: Implications for theories of learning. In F. J. McGuigan & B. D. Lumsden (Eds.), *Contemporary approaches to conditioning and learning.* Washington, D.C.: Winston, 1973. Pp. 127–150.

Rescorla, R. A., & LoLordo, V. M. Inhibition of avoidance behavior. *Journal of Comparative & Physiological Psychology,* 1965, **59,** 406–412.

Rescorla, R. A., & Solomon, R. L. Two-process learning theory: Relationships between Pavlovian conditioning and instrumental learning. *Psychological Review,* 1967, **74,** 151–182.

Rescorla, R. A., & Wagner, A. R. A theory of Pavlovian conditioning: Variations in the effectiveness of reinforcement and nonreinforcement. In A. Black & W. F. Prokasy (Eds.), *Classical conditions II: Current theory and research.* New York: Appleton-Century-Crofts, 1972. Pp. 64–99.

Rizley, R. C., & Rescorla, R. A. Associations in second-order conditioning and sensory preconditioning. *Journal of Comparative and Physiological Psychology,* 1972, **81,** 1–11.

Robinson, E. S. *Association theory to-day: An essay in systematic psychology.* New York: Century, 1932.

Scavio, M. J. Classical–classical transfer: Effects of prior classical aversive conditioning upon classical appetitive conditioning. Unpublished doctoral dissertation, University of Iowa, 1972.

Schlosberg, H. The relationship between success and the laws of conditioning. *Psychological Review,* 1937, **44,** 379–394.

Schneiderman, N. Response system divergences in aversive classical conditioning. In A. H. Black & W. F. Prokasy (Eds.), *Classical conditioning II: Current theory and research.* New York: Appleton-Century-Crofts, 1972. Pp. 341–376.

Schneiderman, N., & Gormezano, I. Conditioning of the nictitating membrane of the rabbit as a function of CS–US interval. *Journal of Comparative and Physiological Psychology*, 1964, **57**, 188–195.

Scobie, S. R. Interaction of an aversive Pavlovian conditional stimulus with aversively and appetitively motivated operants in rats. *Journal of Comparative and Physiological Psychology*, 1972, **79**, 171–188.

Seligman, M. E. P., & Maier, S. F. Failure to escape traumatic shock. *Journal of Experimental Psychology*, 1967, **74**, 1–9.

Shapiro, M. M., & Miller, T. M. On the relationship between conditioned and discriminative stimuli and between instrumental and consummatory responses. In W. F. Prokasy (Ed.), *Classical conditioning: A symposium*. New York: Appleton-Century-Crofts, 1965. Pp. 269–301.

Shapiro, M. M., Sadler, E. W., & Mugg, G. J. Compound stimulus effects during higer order salivary conditioning in dogs. *Journal of Comparative and Physiological Psychology*, 1971, **74**, 222–226.

Sheffield, F. D. Relation between classical conditioning and instrumental learning. In W. F. Prokasy (Ed.), *Classical conditioning: A symposium*. New York: Appleton-Century-Crofts, 1965. Pp. 302–322.

Sheffield, F. D. New evidence on the drive-induction theory of reinforcement. In R. N. Haber (Ed.), *Current research in motivation*. New York: Holt, Rinehart, & Winston, 1966. Pp. 111–122.

Skinner, B. F. *The behavior of organisms: An experimental analysis*. New York: Appleton-Century-Crofts, 1938.

Smith, S., & Guthrie, E. R. *General psychology in terms of behavior*. New York: Appleton-Century-Crofts, 1921.

Sokolov, E. N. Higher nervous functions: The orienting reflex. *Annual Review of Physiology*, 1963, **25**, 545–580.

Spence, K. W. *Behavior theory and conditioning*. New Haven, Connecticut: Yale University Press, 1956.

Stein, L., Sidman, M., & Brady, J. V. Some effects of two temporal variables on conditioned suppression. *Journal of the Experimental Analysis of Behavior*, 1958, **1**, 153–162.

Terrace, H. S. Classical conditioning. In J. A. Nevin (Ed.), *The study of behavior*. Glenview: Scott, Foresman, 1973. Pp. 70–112.

Thorndike, E. L. *Animal intelligence*. New York: Macmillan, 1911.

Trapold, M. A., & Carlson, J. G. Proximity of manipulandum and foodcup as a determinant of the generalized *SD* effect. *Psychonomic Science*, 1965, **2**, 327–328.

Trapold, M. A., & Fairlie, J. Transfer of discrimination learning based upon contingent and noncontingent training procedures. *Psychological Reports*, 1965, **17**, 229–246.

Trapold, M. A., & Overmier, J. B. The second learning process in instrumental conditioning. In A. H. Black & W. F. Prokasy (Eds.), *Classical conditioning II: Current theory and research*. New York: Appleton-Century-Crofts, 1972. Pp. 427–452.

Wasserman, E. A. Pavlovian conditioning with heat reinforcement produces stimulus-directed pecking in chicks. *Science*, 1973, **181**, 875–877.

Watson, J. B. Psychology as the behaviorist views it. *Psychological Review*, 1913, **20**, 158–177.

Watson, J. B. The place of the conditioned reflex in psychology. *Psychological Review*, 1916, **23**, 89–116.

Watson, J. B. *Behaviorism*. New York: Norton, 1925.

Wendt, G. R. An analytical study of the conditioned knee-jerk. *Archives of Psychology*, 1930, **19**, No. 123.

Woodruff, G., Morrison, R. R., & Williams, D. R. Consummatory fixed action patterns underlying conditioned keypecking. Paper presented at a meeting of the Psychonomic Society, Boston, November, 1974.

Yerkes, R. M., & Morgulis, S. The method of Pavlov in animal psychology. *Psychological Bulletin*, 1909, **6**, 257–273.

Zener, K. The significance of behavior accompanying conditioned salivary secretion for theories of the conditioned response. *American Journal of Psychology*, 1937, **50**, 384–403.

5

The Classical–Instrumental Distinction: Reflexes, Voluntary Behavior, and Categories of Associative Learning

Eliot Hearst

Indiana University

> The question of whether the most voluntary of all voluntary actions of man depend on external and internal conditions has been answered in the affirmative. From this it inevitably follows that *given the same internal and external conditions the activity of man will be similar.* Choice of one of the many possible ends of the same psychical reflex is absolutely impossible; its apparent possibility is merely a delusion of self-consciousness.... *The initial cause of any human activity lies outside man.*
>
> IVAN M. SECHENOV (1863, p. 105)

I. INTRODUCTION

Whenever a psychologist or physiologist of today states an opinion like Sechenov's he can expect a general reaction similar in tone, if not in intensity, to the response elicited by the unconventional comments of this influential Russian physiologist and anatomist. The St. Petersburg Censors' Committee brought legal action against Sechenov for his book, *Reflexes of the Brain,* which contained numerous passages of this kind. Their indictment included the charges that his theory reduced man to the level of a machine devoid of free will, swept away good and evil by destroying the

concept of human responsibility, corrupted the moral foundations of s
ciety, and subverted the religious doctrine of life after death.

The view that all the various behaviors of man and lower organisr
are controlled by specific prior stimulation—and therefore become pote
tially predictable—remains a very controversial opinion today. It evok
disbelief, repulsion, or anger from large segments of society, as well
from contemporary psychologists who embrace humanistic values. Son
experimental psychologists who publicly assert such a deterministic vie
point have been known to suffer lingering, private doubts about its legi
macy; almost no "civilized" human being can easily conceive of hims
or his child or even his dog as anything faintly resembling a puppet
a robot.[1]

Our cultural heritage and the maxims of popular psychology suppc
the common-sense view that behavior can be classified into two major cat
gories, reflexive and voluntary. The first of these generally conforms
the formula offered by Sechenov: some of our relatively simple actioi
and habits are triggered by very specific external stimuli. These reactioi
which often involve isolated parts of the body, appear to be performe
unthinkingly, automatically, immediately, and inevitably. Voluntary beha
ior, on the other hand, is thought to comprise most of our daily activitie
especially the important ones. These organized and integrated activiti
are apparently acquired through experience and do not seem to be rigid
controlled or evoked by definite external events; they appear spontaneou
flexible, modifiable, intelligent, and farsighted. Once initiated, a volunta
action can still be stopped or delayed—presumably unlike involuntary
reflexive behavior. Sometimes an originally voluntary act (for exampl
tying one's shoelaces or driving a car) is practiced so often that it is sa
to become automatic, unconscious, and involuntary (see Kimble & Perlm
ter, 1970).

This basic distinction between reflex and voluntary action is deep
ingrained into most of our thinking about behavior and is specifically er
bodied in our legal and moral systems. When a person is not able to su
press certain antisocial or compulsive behaviors that the rest of us c
control by an "effort of the will," he is often confined to a prison or ment
hospital. Distinctions between voluntary and involuntary manslaughte
manslaughter and murder, and first- and second-degree murder have the
roots in the notions of voluntary and involuntary behavior and relat
terms such as "intent." We easily forgive the behavior of the student wi

---

[1] As many chapters in this Handbook will attest, however, the view that m
resembles a modern-day computer is apparently not so abhorrent, even thou
such a conception of man is also deterministic and mechanistic. Is it because
computer is more complex, "organized," and "intelligent" than a puppet or simp
robot, and can "calculate" faster than man?

a cold who coughs and sneezes throughout our lecture, but not the same fellow, completely recovered a few weeks later, when he chats with his neighbor or rustles the newspaper he is reading in class.

The general distinction between voluntary and involuntary behavior has played an important role in the history of the biological sciences, although it is often camouflaged through the use of presumably "objective" terminology. Major theoretical controversies in physiology and experimental psychology have revolved around points related to the distinction. This chapter focuses on the question of whether associative learning[2] can justifiably be categorized into two fundamental processes whose properties correspond in several ways to those implied by the dichotomy between reflex and voluntary activity. Konorski, Skinner, Schlosberg, and Mowrer agreed that there are two different kinds of associative learning. On the other hand, Pavlov and Bekhterev, and the American learning theorists Guthrie and Hull, thought that all learning was basically of one kind and involved the attachment of responses to stimuli via the particular explanatory mechanism each theorist favored. Some authors, such as Tolman and Razran at various points in their careers, talked about six or more different fundamental types of learning. However, most contemporary textbooks on learning are organized according to the "two-factor" or "two-process" approach that distinguishes two basic categories of learning, classical and instrumental conditioning. Skinner's terms, "respondent" and "operant" conditioning, are for practical purposes synonymous with "classical" and "instrumental" conditioning, respectively, and will also be used frequently in this chapter.

Although the classical–instrumental distinction refers to categories of learning, there is much behavior that does not seem to involve learning. Nature endows an organism with a variety of behaviors that are evoked by rather specific stimuli. The learned behavior of an organism is thought to develop out of these basic, innate patterns by the action of environmental dependencies that parallel the types of conditioning procedures studied in the psychologist's laboratory. The role of innate behavioral factors in the acquisition of new responses and in the attachment of previously established responses to new stimulus situations was stressed in the pioneering experimental work of both Pavlov and Thorndike, performed during the early years of the twentieth century. These two outstanding scientists used different procedures to study learning in lower organisms—procedures that

---

[2] The present author would not restrict the term "learning" to associatively induced changes. Habituation, pseudoconditioning, and sensitization (see Gormezano & Kehoe, Chapter 4 of this volume; Kimble, 1961; Mackintosh, 1974, for relevant discussions), for example, do not involve "association" in the usual sense of correlated events, but I would consider them examples of learning. However, for purposes of this chapter, the discussion is limited to cases of learning that are the outcome of certain correlations among stimuli, responses, and reinforcers.

correspond to classical and instrumental conditioning and account for the terms "Pavlovian" and "Thorndikian" conditioning, another way of labeling the distinction with which this chapter is concerned.

In a typical experiment Pavlov repeatedly paired a stimulus that did not originally elicit salivation with one that did. The ticking of a metronome, for example, which does not produce salivation in an untrained dog, soon came to evoke many drops of saliva when it was consistently followed by the delivery of meat powder to the hungry dog's mouth. Pavlov called the food → salivation connection the *unconditioned reflex,* composed of the *unconditioned stimulus* (US, food) and the *unconditioned response* (UR, salivation). This unconditioned (innate) stimulus–response link provided the raw material from which the salivary response could be transferred to a formerly ineffective stimulus. The new stimulus–response link was called the *conditioned reflex,* composed of the *conditioned stimulus* (CS, metronome beats) and the *conditioned response* (CR, salivation).

In his research, Thorndike used an arrangement that was relatively crude compared to the experimental setup, surgical procedures, and measuring devices employed by Pavlov. Thorndike constructed wooden "puzzle boxes" from which cats, by performing some response, could escape and reach a piece of food located outside. For example, they might have to pull a string or turn a button. Like Pavlov, Thorndike stressed what he called the "helping hand of instinct," reactions which an animal makes to a situation "without experience" because of the "inherited nature of its reception-, connection-, and action-systems." When restrained for the first time, most cats clawed all over the box and struck anything loose and shaky. These instinctive reactions provided the raw material from which a particular response could be selectively strengthened and made more precise by its "satisfying consequences" (Thorndike's famous *Law of Effect*).

Thus, both Thorndike and Pavlov emphasized the importance of unlearned stimulus–response links or reflexes as the basis for the learning of new connections or reflexes. Pavlov's procedure, however, did not require any response from the subject to produce the food; the sound of the metronome and delivery of food occurred in regular sequence on every trial, regardless of the dog's behavior. On the other hand, Thorndike's procedure permitted escape from confinement and access to food only after a particular response was made. Thus, the experimental dependency or "contingency" established in Pavlov's situation was between two environmental events—food delivery occurred if and only if the metronome had just been turned on. In Thorndike's situation, however, the contingency was between a response and some subsequent environmental change—a door opened and access to food occurred if and only if the "correct" response had just been made. It seemed as if salivating at the sound of the metronome reached high levels in Pavlov's setting *even though* the response was not required for food, whereas string-pulling became very likely in Thorndike's setting *because* the response was required.

Since Pavlov's and Thorndike's work, the laboratories of American behaviorists and of Soviet physiologists studying "higher nervous activity" have been the scene of numerous investigations of initial learning and subsequent performance under the two basic kinds of conditioning procedures. Researchers were justifiably reluctant to limit themselves to a mere description of experimental results; they also sought explanations for the findings. Theories have proliferated and, as already noted, a common contemporary view holds that learning via the two procedures is governed by different fundamental processes or laws. To preview some of the topics stressed in this chapter, it seems worth listing here a few of the differences that have been considered important in distinguishing the two processes.

Some writers have argued that Pavlovian conditioning is confined mainly, if not exclusively, to responses of the autonomic (involuntary) nervous system, and operant conditioning to responses of the somatic nervous system. Accordingly, visceral and glandular responses, which include many of the responses popularly called "emotional" (stomach- and heart-muscle contractions, sweating, crying, blushing, etc.), were said to be conditionable via Pavlov's procedure but not via Thorndike's. On the other hand, skeletal movements (uttering a word, handling a knife and fork, turning toward one's mother, etc.) were considered trainable and modifiable almost exclusively via Thorndike's procedure. Some writers contended that in the Pavlovian arrangement the CR resembles the UR, whereas in operant conditioning the acquired behavior (e.g., string pulling) need not bear any necessary relation to URs in the situation (e.g., eating food when available). Pavlovian CRs have been described as "elicited" in reflexive fashion by very specific stimuli, whereas operant responses are "emitted" in the sense of being uncorrelated with any obvious prior stimulation. Certain phenomena associated with the partial or complete removal of the US (intermittent reinforcement and extinction) were suspected to hold for one type of conditioning and not the other. The "consequences" of responding were thought important in operant but not in Pavlovian conditioning; string-pulling was strengthened by a satisfying outcome, whereas salivation was not. Other researchers have sought the neurophysiological, anatomical, or phylogenetic factors that underlie and differentiate the two types of learning. It is revealing that many writers contrast classical *conditioning* with instrumental *learning,* and thereby imply that one process involves a relatively passive subject (the *experimenter* does the "conditioning") whereas the other process involves a relatively active, problem-solving subject (the *subject* does the "learning").

The list of proposed differences includes other points, and a major part of this chapter will be devoted to reassessing the accuracy or validity of the most important of them. For extensive reviews of specific findings and additional critical commentary, the reader should consult Mackintosh (1974), Rescorla and Solomon (1967), and Seward (1970). The present chapter concentrates on problems and issues rather than on experimental details and summaries of the relevant literature.

If there *are* two basic categories of learning, is one more important than the other in real-life situations? Skinner (1953) declared that Pavlov's conditioned reflexes "are mainly concerned with the internal physiology of the organism. We are most often interested, however, in behavior which has some effect upon the surrounding world. Such behavior raises most of the practical problems in human affairs [p. 59]." Strangely enough, Skinner's major predecessor as a vociferous spokesman for behaviorism, John B. Watson, was not of the same mind. Writing on "the heart or the intellect," Watson (1928) asserted that "we may earn our bread with the striped muscles but we win our happiness or lose it by the kind of behavior our unstriped muscles or guts lead us into [p. 349]." Contemporary behaviorists engaged in practical matters, such as modifying behavior in the classroom or mental hospital or psychotherapeutic situation, usually emphasize one or the other of the two conditioning procedures: for example, the reconditioning of emotional responses (phobias, anxiety, etc.) mainly by means of Pavlovian procedures, or the strengthening or weakening of motor responses (eating habits, disruptive school behavior, tics, stuttering, etc.) by means of response-produced reward or punishment. Patients under medical treatment for cardiac or circulatory abnormalities are being trained to control their heart rhythms or blood pressure by techniques of "biofeedback." A knowledge of basic conditioning procedures, as well as an appreciation of the historical and theoretical issues that surround them, therefore ought to be useful for the clinically inclined professional psychologist as well as for the scientist studying animal and human behavior.

Since several issues from the history of philosophy and the biological sciences have, in this writer's opinion, greatly influenced the original statements and persistence of the classical–instrumental distinction in psychology, a very brief discussion of these issues seems appropriate first. The experimental and logical basis for the distinction, as psychologists have described it, is assessed later. There is one major question the reader should bear in mind throughout the chapter: Does the existence of two different *procedures* for modifying behavior necessitate the conclusion that fundamentally different *processes* or *mechanisms* are operating in each? Since there are an indefinitely large number of different procedures available for an experimenter to use, on what grounds does he decide that some are *basically* different from others? At the end of the chapter, a few tentative suggestions are offered concerning potentially profitable future directions for research and theory, based on evaluation of the current status of the classical–instrumental distinction.

II. SOME HISTORICAL PERSPECTIVES

A. Philosophy and Physiology

The history of psychology as a science has two major roots, one derived from philosophy and the other from the biological sciences. Although there is the danger of oversimplifying complex issues, questions concerning associative learning, and particularly its subdivision into classical and instrumental conditioning, may be illuminated by viewing them in the context of the history of philosophy and biology. Philosophers and physiologists of the seventeenth to the nineteenth centuries shared two problems about behavior that can perhaps best be encompassed by the word *etiology,* which refers both to "causes" *and* to "origins." Writers in both disciplines attempted to analyze the immediate causes of behavior, and these discussions often concerned problems of involuntary (reflexive) versus voluntary action: Did some external stimulus trigger the bodily activity or was the behavior "willed?" Writers in both disciplines also examined the question of general origins: Were ideas (for the philosopher) or responses (for the physiologist) innate or acquired? This second question (nativism versus empiricism) had an important corollary: If responses or ideas were acquired, how was such learning achieved? In both philosophy and physiology the concept of association, in one form or another, provided an answer to the problem of learning. The involuntary–voluntary and innate–learned distinctions were usually mixed together, implicitly or explicitly, in discussions of the etiology of behavior. There was, however, a general belief that, although all voluntary behavior was learned, involuntary behavior could be either innately determined or acquired via past experience.

Within each discipline, philosophy and physiology also developed opposing views about these problems. For example, in the seventeenth century the philosopher Descartes made a clear distinction between the machine-like, stimulus–response nature of certain behaviors (which he believed to be characteristic of all actions of animals and some of the actions of man) and other activities, occurring independently of external stimulation and controlled by the Mind or Soul (which only human beings were thought to possess). However, several later writers, for example, La Mettrie, argued that man was a machine, too, with the implication that all behavior is triggered by some form of stimulation.

Analogously, early workers (e.g., Marshall Hall) interested in the physiological mechanisms of bodily activity felt that there was a difference between reflex action, which involved highly reliable and invariant correlations between certain stimuli and certain responses, and voluntary action, which seemed to occur "spontaneously" without identifiable prior stimulation. Voluntary behavior was often said to involve the cerebrum, and reflexive behavior to be mediated by other regions of the nervous system. Yet, as we noted at the beginning of this chapter, Sechenov wrote a book entitled *Reflexes of the Brain* and argued that all behavior was reflexive in nature.

As one reviews the arguments concerning the general distinction between classical and instrumental conditioning, it becomes increasingly evident that the distinction is not based on compelling experimental and theoretical considerations. The distinction has its roots buried deeply in the past and its tenacity appears traceable to a variety of sources, many outside psychology. The two-factor approach in contemporary experimental psychology seems to serve as a repository for many long-standing concerns about voluntary versus involuntary activity and innate versus acquired behavior.

B. Psychology

By the time Pavlov and Thorndike began their work, the question of whether reflex or involuntary activity was clearly distinguishable from some other category of organismic activity had been debated by philosophers and by biological scientists for at least two centuries. A great deal of experimental work had been performed on elicited movements in special "preparations"—such as decapitated frogs, and cats with their brains sectioned at various levels—but research with normal, intact subjects had been neglected. Not only did techniques for investigating innate reaction patterns in normal organisms have to be further refined, but experimental methods for assessing the acquisition and maintenance of learned behavior also had to be devised. The work of Pavlov and Thorndike proved very relevant to these issues, even though neither of these men developed his procedures for the specific purpose of answering the above philosophical and biological questions.

Pavlov regarded behaving organisms as aggregates of reflexes, which could be released by more or less interchangeable stimuli. The idea of the *interchangeability* of stimulation placed Pavlov several steps ahead of the workers who had previously studied reflexes. The response that was a part of some inborn reflex could be transferred to another, apparently unrelated stimulus by pairing the unrelated stimulus with the stimulus eliciting the inborn response. Presentation of the latter stimulus, a biologically significant event (US), was said to *reinforce* the conditioned reflex.[3] By means of Pavlov's procedures, the learning of "associations" could be studied objectively in the laboratory.

---

[3] Throughout the rest of this chapter the terms US and "reinforcer" are used more or less interchangeably (but see page 210 for discussion of this usage).

Since Pavlov's original work, a variety of CSs, USs, responses, organisms, and control techniques have been employed in classical conditioning experiments (see Gormezano & Kehoe, Chapter 4 of this volume). Almost always, subjects in these experiments are restrained in some way; for example, the human undergoing eyelid conditioning may sit in a dental chair with his head fixed in a relatively immobile position. Pavlov's dogs were harnessed on a stand. The reasons for such restraint are usually practical: to enable the experimenter to present the CS and US in a very precise and consistent manner from trial to trial, and to prevent movements of the subject that might interfere with or loosen the electrical or mechanical devices attached to the subject for measurement of CR and UR.

This feature of classical conditioning methodology differs from instrumental conditioning situations, where most often the subject is relatively free to move around, and directed skeletal movements rather than autonomic or undirected movements are studied. Of course, the difference in freedom of movement is one of degree, since subjects in instrumental conditioning experiments are usually observed in some enclosure rather than in their natural habitats. However, the point is worth the reader's attention because the arrangements used traditionally to study classical and instrumental conditioning reflect the experimenter's preconceptions about what kinds of responses should be measured in each, and may be responsible for some of the "differences" claimed to exist between the two. Suppose we released the dog from its harness in a Pavlovian situation and recorded its motor reactions directed toward or away from the CS and US locations. Or suppose we carefully tried to condition glandular or visceral responses by presenting reinforcers contingent on appropriate behavior in a situation where the subject is restrained. It is only in the last decade that researchers have broken with tradition and attempted serious and extensive investigations of these kinds. The results have important implications for evaluating the classical–instrumental distinction.

Early studies of maze learning in animals, and Thorndike's experiments with the puzzle box, initiated laboratory research on instrumental conditioning. Several major subcategories of this procedure exist (see Mackintosh, 1974, and Woods, 1974, for an extensive summary of taxonomy, methodology, and findings). The general procedure is defined as one in which some outcome is contingent upon the occurrence of a certain response. And a response can have these outcomes: (a) it can produce or prolong some appetitive reinforcer (e.g., food); this outcome should increase the likelihood of the response over its preexperimental levels; (b) it can remove or prevent delivery of some appetitive reinforcer; this outcome should decrease the likelihood of the response; (c) it can produce or prolong some aversive reinforcer (e.g., painful electric shock); this outcome should decrease the likelihood of the response; or (d) it can remove or prevent delivery of some aversive reinforcer; this outcome should increase the likelihood of the response. Psychologists have usually applied the labels *reward* training, *withdrawal* or *omission* training, *punishment* training, and *escape* or *avoidance* training to (*a*) through (*d*), respectively.

Considerable research had been conducted in a variety of classical- and instrumental-conditioning situations (see Hilgard & Marquis, 1940, for a review) before the development of specific conceptions of learning that treated the two conditioning procedures as *theoretically* distinct. Prior to 1928, no one seems to have taken this possibility very seriously; experimenters frequently did not even distinguish between the *procedures*. For example, in Russian laboratories "defensive conditioning" procedures were employed in which a neutral stimulus preceded shock. The shock US elicited flexion responses, which eventually occurred during the CS, before shock was actually delivered. Sometimes the shock was withheld if flexion occurred during CS, and sometimes the flexion response was required to terminate the shock; both of these procedures were instrumental (avoidance or escape). On other occasions, or in other experiments, the shock was delivered on every trial regardless of the subject's behavior—a classical conditioning procedure. Early American researchers using similar arrangements often failed to state which procedure they had used or, if they did comment on it, gave little or no indication that they thought anything fundamental was at stake.

Miller and Konorski (1928), two Polish investigators, were the first to make an explicit distinction between the two procedures and to propose that different associative mechanisms were operating in each. A few years later, Skinner described what he called two types of conditioned reflex,[4] *Type S* and *Type R,* depending on whether the reinforcer was contingent on a prior *S*timulus or a prior *R*esponse.

In his major analysis Skinner (1938) was careful to discuss the two types of conditioning procedure (S and R), and their associated behaviors (respondent and operant), without resort to the use of any physiological constructs or theoretical associative mechanisms. He stated that respondent behavior, which is evoked by a known stimulus, was conditioned according to the Type S paradigm. Operant behavior, on the other hand, seemed to be emitted spontaneously (it involved, Skinner (1937) said, "responses uncorrelated with observable stimuli–a statement which must not be made lightly but cannot, so far as I can see, be avoided [p. 273]"), and was conditioned according to the Type R paradigm. Thus, salivation, invariably evoked by placement of food in the subject's mouth, is an example of respondent behavior and is conditionable via the Type S procedure. The

---

[4] In his later writings, Skinner abandoned the term "reflex" as applied to operant responses—presumably because of the lack of correlation between ("emitted") operant behavior and prior stimulation.

lever pressing of rats in a Skinner Box, however, is not correlated with any known stimulus and is therefore an example of operant behavior, conditionable via the Type R procedure. The distinction between *behaviors,* operant versus respondent, is more general than that between forms of conditioning because the distinction between behaviors includes unconditioned as well as learned responses.

Skinner (1938) stated: "I do not mean that there are no originating forces in spontaneous behavior but simply that they are not located in the environment. We are not in a position to see them, *and we have no need to* [p. 20, italics mine]." He believed that prior attempts to analyze behavior into stimulus–response connections, or to fit all procedures into the Pavlovian paradigm, were cumbersome and inappropriate, because many responses are emitted which cannot be demonstrated to be controlled by specific stimuli. Skinner decided to make a clean break with previous approaches, abandon the stimulus–response- and classical-conditioning formlas, and study operant behavior in its own right, without searching for or hypothesizing stimuli that originally evoked it. The large amount of work on operant behavior that was performed in the next 35 years proved the heuristic value of his approach. However, as the years passed, the question of whether the operant–respondent distinction was a fundamental one or a heuristically useful one seemed no longer an empirical matter. For example, Skinner (1953) said: "Operant reinforcement is *therefore a separate process* [from the Pavlovian variety] *and requires a separate analysis* [p. 65, italics mine]." He did not leave open the possibility that the "originating forces" or stimuli for operant behavior might eventually be identified, an outcome that could allow a reduction of all forms of conditioning to a single type.

Although Skinner's distinction between elicited and spontaneous behaviors was empirically based and was developed in quite a different context, the reader will recognize its similarity to (a) Descartes' breakdown of activity into the type evoked by specific external stimuli and the type controlled by the Soul, and (b) the early physiologists's distinction between reflex and voluntary action depending on whether identifiable prior stimuli could be found in a particular case. For all these approaches, the difference between types of behavior was mainly based on knowledge versus ignorance of the originating stimuli. This chapter suggests that a search for these stimuli in operant behavior may be profitable and that current research supports that course of action.

While not disagreeing with Skinner's central lines of analysis [as expressed in the articles (Skinner, 1935a, b) that set forth the theoretical positions he later developed at length in *The Behavior of Organisms*], Konorski and Miller (1937a) speculated that operant conditioning is confined to striped-muscle movements, whereas classical conditioning can apply also to the activity of smooth muscles and glands. They guessed that "being a glandular reaction, salivation cannot by any means" be conditioned according to the operant procedure. Subsequently, Skinner agreed that "a strict topographical separation of types" may follow the skeletal–autonomic distinction (1938, p. 112), but that he was "not prepared to assert" whether responses of smooth muscles or glands may or may not be conditioned via the operant paradigm; "it is a question for experiment" (Skinner, 1937, p. 279).

In the late 1930s and the 1940s, so-called "two-process" learning theories developed. Their theoretical superstructure and basic assumptions went far beyond Skinner's analysis. Schlosberg (1937) stated that Pavlovian procedures produce associations between afferent elements (stimulations) and that the responses involved in Pavlovian conditioning are emotional, diffuse, and preparatory; Thorndikian conditioning, on the other hand, involves precise, adaptive motor responses, and the underlying principle of learning is "success," the improvement of the subject's hedonic state. In 1947 Mowrer extended Schlosberg's analysis and argued that Pavlovian CRs provide the motivation or "problem" that is solved by the precise, adaptive skeletal reactions. In other words, emotional states established by Pavlovian conditioning act principally as *mediators* of instrumental responses. Mowrer concentrated almost exclusively on aversive-conditioning situations in his analysis, and he proposed that the laws of Pavlovian conditioning apply only to visceral (autonomic) responses and the laws of Thorndikian conditioning apply only to skeletal responses. Some years later, modified versions of Mowrer's two-process theory were advanced by R. L. Solomon and his colleagues (see Rescorla & Solomon, 1967, for a summary).

This chapter does not dwell on the specific details and hypotheses that constitute "two-process learning theory." Our interest is in the more basic question of whether evidence and logic support the prevalent belief that fundamental differences exist in the processes that underlie the two conditioning arrangements. However, experimental work conducted within the context of two-process theory provides some of the data and interpretations to be considered now.

III. CLASSICAL VERSUS INSTRUMENTAL CONDITIONING

A. Preview of Complications

In classical conditioning the delivery of a reinforcer is dependent on some prior stimulus, and in instrumental conditioning it is dependent on some prior response of the organism. This simple statement concerning different experimenter operations is rather trivial in itself, although it may help to classify or label procedures used in various experiments. The significance of the distinction arises from prevailing views that, out of the many criteria potentially available for distinguishing experimental procedures, the classical–instrumental dichotomy is truly basic. Different laws or processes are thought to operate under each type of procedure, as indicated by differences in kinds of stimulus control, response systems, reinforcement processes, associative mechanisms or principles, and physiological mediators. It is potential differences of this sort that are controversial and will concern us for the remainder of this chapter. Our conclusion will be that none of them is extremely convincing and that the persistence of the classical–instrumental distinction is based at least as much on philosophical–cultural prejudices and traditions as on behavioral experimentation and psychological theories.

Unfortunately, research on classical or instrumental conditioning does not provide us with a simple case of either type. Consider a rat pressing a lever for food in a Skinner Box. As far as the experimenter is concerned, food delivery depends only on a particular response of the subject. However, if we measured responses besides lever pressing, we would probably obtain evidence that the rat salivates or displays other autonomic activity as he approaches or touches the lever or food chute; the visual, auditory, or tactual cues provided by the lever and chute, as well as sensory feedback from the subject's own movements, have been closely associated with delivery of the food pellet. The rat might even exhibit these autonomic responses as we carry him down the hallway to the laboratory or as we place him in the Skinner Box. Even though the experimenter did not explicitly say so, the important features of classical conditioning (stimulus-reinforcer correlations) must be involved in this operant conditioning situation; a pellet appears only after the subject receives stimulation from the lever, only after the noise of the food dispenser occurs, and only after he is placed in the general confines of the Skinner Box.

Our example suggests that standard operant tasks always involve concurrent classical conditioning. The converse is also a distinct possibility. Suppose we removed the lever from the box, placed a new rat in it, and sounded a tone 2 sec before each food delivery. This procedure fulfills the definition of classical conditioning; food is dependent on a prior stimulus and not on any behavior of the subject. Our new rat will soon begin salivating to the tone. But some writers would argue that salivation makes dry food more palatable and, since the degree of palatability is thereby controlled by a prior response, the definition of operant conditioning is implicitly fulfilled. Furthermore, salivation comes to consistently precede food delivery—which could establish a (fortuitous) link between this response and subsequent US delivery. And if the subject does not approach the food chute, he will not obtain the pellet; therefore, receipt and consumption of the food are dependent on a response, as well as on the stimulus (tone) the experimenter presented. The subject may even approach the loudspeaker when the tone is sounded, and these approach responses are also followed by the reinforcer. This conjunction of events establishes still another relation between specific behaviors and the reinforcer, even though food would have been delivered regardless of the subject's behavior toward the location of the loudspeaker.

From these simple illustrations, we can anticipate that "pure" examples of operant or classical conditioning are practically impossible to arrange. The details of the procedure as stated by the experimenter probably do not include a number of important dependencies established by the procedure; these unstated correlations may be as important, or more important, than the ones the experimenter has explicitly stated. Whether the procedure is labeled "classical" or "operant," responses occurring in the presence of some stimulus are followed by a reinforcer. A variety of responses will be conditioned on either procedure and may interact with, interfere with, or facilitate each other. They constitute a whole pattern of behavior, and it seems misleading to call any one of them *the* conditioned "response." As we analyze the classical–instrumental distinction, the reader ought to keep in mind the above complications and interactions.

B. Response Characteristics

1. Type of Response

a. Problems and Issues.   The belief that classical and instrumental conditioning are procedures which reflect fundamentally different learning processes is most often justified by reference to the kinds of behavior that seem particularly susceptible to modification by each procedure. The most common distinction of this sort is the one made between autonomic (visceral–glandular) and somatic (skeletal) responses. Besides this distinction, other writers have, for example, differentiated between responses supplying weak sensory feedback and those supplying rich feedback (Konorski, 1948) or between diffuse-emotional and precise-adaptive responses (Schlosberg, 1937); in each case, classical conditioning is presumed to provide the means for conditioning or modifying the former and instrumental conditioning the latter. Since most other response distinctions closely parallel the autonomic–somatic one, they are not explicitly discussed here. Furthermore, compared to the others, the autonomic–somatic distinction is easier to objectify. Since the autonomic and somatic systems are defined neuroanatomically and not behaviorally, arguments about which class a particular response belongs to are minimized. However, the two kinds of responses influence and interact with each other in a normally functioning organism, and therefore the analysis is more complex than it may appear on the surface.

Let us review the general beliefs of those who have maintained that autonomic and somatic behaviors are differentially sensitive to classical and operant procedures. A most extreme claim would be that autonomic responses can *only* be conditioned by classical conditioning procedures and skeletal responses can *only* be conditioned by operant procedures. More than ten years ago, however, there was reason to challenge such an unqualified statement. Human experiments had apparently shown that such autonomically controlled behaviors as heart rate and galvanic skin responses (GSRs) could be modified by operant procedures, and that such skeletal responses as the knee jerk, flexion of the hand, and blinks of the eye could be conditioned by Pavlovian methods.

Nevertheless, alternative interpretations of these results were difficult to rule out and the importance of the findings was questioned. In the case of apparent classical conditioning of skeletal responses, these CRs were said to have "instrumental" effects; for example, hand flexion conditioned to a tone preceding shock to the hand was presumed to reduce the effectiveness of the forthcoming shock, or an eye blink in anticipation of a forthcoming air puff was presumed to decrease the aversiveness of the air puff. Moreover, the responses in most conventional studies of instrumental conditioning involve organized movements of the whole organism that are directed at external objects, whereas eye blinks and flexion responses are relatively isolated bits of behavior and are not directed at any external point of reference. Therefore, these examples of the classical conditioning of skeletal responses were often viewed as only minor exceptions to the proposed dichotomy.

On the other hand, in cases in which autonomic responses had apparently been modified by application of instrumental conditioning, a persistent counterproposal was that some skeletal response had actually been conditioned, and that this response mediated (i.e., preceded and itself evoked) the acquired autonomic response. Skinner (1938) pointed out that, if food were delivered to a hungry man only when his blood pressure increased to a certain level, the subject would not be said to exhibit "voluntary control" of blood pressure if he learned to stick a pin in his arm and thereby indirectly produce a blood pressure change. The response under voluntary control was pin-sticking, an operant response—not blood pressure change, a form of respondent behavior. Moreover, the same hungry man might jump up and down, or look at pictures of nude women, or whisper obscene poems to himself—behaviors which would probably accomplish the same goal of raising his blood pressure. In these cases, too, conditioning of some skeletal response could be the crucial factor.

How can mediating skeletal movements like exercise, tension of muscles, or control of breathing be ruled out as explanations of apparent instrumental conditioning of autonomic responses? The main experimental technique

for evaluating this alternative has been to paralyze subjects by injecting chemical agents, such as curare. Pharmacologists have long known that
the drug acts by blocking transmission at neuromuscular junctions and
paralyzes the peripheral skeletal musculature without eliminating consci-
ousness, sensations of pain, or neural control of smooth or cardiac muscles
in human beings. However, since the breathing apparatus is paralyzed, subjects under high levels of curare have to be kept alive by means of artificial
respiration. Although human beings have occasionally been used in research with curare (e.g., Birk, Crider, Shapiro, & Tursky, 1966), the possible risks have led to the almost exclusive use of nonhuman subjects; this
type of experiment will be discussed shortly.

Even the use of curarelike substances does not completely eliminate
mediational explanations of successful operant conditioning of autonomic
responses. Proponents of the mediation hypothesis could argue that the
peripheral skeletal musculature was not *completely* paralyzed (permitting
mediation by responses of the muscles that remained unparalyzed or partially paralyzed), or they could contend that the subject was acquiring
"central" mediators (thoughts, or other "responses" not involving motor
movement) that themselves produced the peripheral autonomic changes.
Despite these interpretive problems, recent research on these topics has
yielded many provocative results, and has stimulated development of some
potentially significant practical applications, as described below.

b. Operant conditioning of autonomic responses. In a review article
(1969) on which the following summary of Neal Miller's work is based,
he pointed out that neuroanatomists have generally thought that the autonomic nervous system is "inferior" to the cerebrospinal nervous system
because of the presumed diffuseness of autonomic action. Evaluating the
corresponding belief of psychologists that the operant conditioning of autonomic responses is either impossible to achieve or wholly explainable by
skeletal mediation, he concluded that it is "only against a cultural background of great prejudice that such weak evidence could lead to such
a strong conviction" (Miller, 1969, p. 434). We have described several
aspects of this cultural, philosophical, and biological heritage. Miller commented that preconceptions of this kind made it almost impossible for him
to persuade students and assistants to work with confidence and enthusiasm
on the problem.

However, Miller and Carmona did succeed in training thirsty dogs to
increase or decrease their salivation, depending on whether water reward
was contingent on bursts or pauses in their ongoing (spontaneous) rate
of salivation; water itself had no consistent effects on salivation. In these
initial studies the subjects were not curarized, and dogs trained to increase
salivation seemed more active than those trained to decrease salivation.

Therefore, the learning of skeletal responses, including panting, chewing, etc. might have mediated the apparent conditioning of the salivary response.

Unfortunately, curarized subjects could not be used to assess possible skeletal mediation in the salivation experiments, because curare itself elicits constant and excessive salivation. Therefore, Miller and his colleagues had to select some other autonomic response for study. They successfully increased or decreased heart rate in curarized rats by rewarding appropriate heart-rate changes with the delivery of electrical stimulation to a reward center of the brain (since the early 1950s, stimulation of certain brain areas has been known to act as a very powerful reinforcer of operant behavior). Because brain stimulation might be a very special type of reinforcer, however, later experiments in Miller's laboratory were performed in which appropriate heart-rate changes permitted curarized rats to avoid or escape mild electric shock to their tail. Those experiments were successful, too, as were studies involving brain-stimulation reward, curarized rats, and different autonomically controlled responses such as (a) intestinal contractions or relaxations, (b) rate of urine formation in the kidney, (c) blood pressure, and (d) amount of blood in the stomach wall or tail. Rats could even learn to dilate the blood vessels in the pinna of one ear relative to the condition of the blood vessels in the pinna of the other ear; these blood vessels are believed to be almost completely under autonomic control and had been thought to function, nonspecifically, as a unit.

The specificity of these findings (control of vascular dilation in the pinnae could not have resulted from overall changes in heart rate or blood pressure, because these changes would have affected both ears equally) argued against explanations in terms of conditioned mediators—as did other experiments in which, for example, subjects rewarded for changes in intestinal contractions did not show concurrent changes in heart rate, and vice versa. Miller concluded that the autonomic nervous system is not the diffuse, nonspecific system it previously had been thought to be.

Kimmel (1974) reviewed work with normal human beings on the instrumental conditioning of autonomic responses: for example, heart rate, GSR, vasomotor responses, and salivation. To evaluate possible skeletal mediators in this research, experimenters have concurrently measured muscular and respiratory activity while attempting to condition autonomic responses. Since no obvious correlations have usually been obtained between skeletal and autonomic responses in cases of autonomic conditioning, Kimmel concluded that the mediation hypothesis is a weak one. Schwartz, Shapiro, and Tursky (1971) found that "man can learn to increase both his blood pressure and his heart rate, lower both his blood pressure and his heart rate, or raise and lower his blood pressure or his heart rate [p. 62]." Subjects can also learn to raise their blood pressure while simultaneously lowering their heart rate. Such specificity of response also provides evidence against skeletal or "cognitive" mediation. Like Miller, Kimmel believes that cultural and scientific preconceptions about classes of involuntary and voluntary behavior provide the main reasons for the persistence of several unparsimonious and often far-fetched explanations. The word "involuntary" would presumably refer to responses that cannot be modified by operant conditioning procedures.

Miller (1969) pointed out how operant conditioning of autonomic responses could be involved in the development of psychosomatic symptoms in human beings. A child's fear of attending school may initially display itself in certain autonomic symptoms (queasy stomach, faintness, headache). If his mother permits him to stay home when he exhibits such symptoms, they may recur because of their role in avoiding school attendance. Differential reinforcement of various autonomic responses could account for the well-established differences in patterns of autonomic behavior that occur between individuals within a society and between societies themselves.

Today, the possibilities for using autonomic-operant techniques in therapeutic work with humans are being widely explored in medical settings (see the annual volumes on *Biofeedback and Self-Control,* edited by Barber, DiCara, Kamiya, Miller, Shapiro, & Stoyva, 1970–1974). Subjects strongly motivated to eliminate or reduce such symptoms as high blood pressure, cardiac arrhythmias, or asthmatic reactions receive visual–auditory feedback or verbal praise for successful approximation of more adaptive patterns of response. In these practical situations, neither the researcher nor the patient frets about the theoretical question of whether some mediating response is indirectly producing the appropriate effect. Improvement in the subject's symptomatology is the only crucial "result."

Despite promising prospects, it must be noted that Miller (1974) has recently reported difficulty in his and his colleagues' attempts to repeat some of the most important and most convincing of their original experiments with curarized rats. He has frankly admitted the problems, but at the present time can offer nothing definite to account for them; in various presentations, he has suggested that perhaps new breeding and shipping techniques of rat suppliers or differences in the type of curare might be involved in some way. Furthermore, the statistically significant effects in many experiments on this topic were not large in an absolute sense. There is a real question as to whether the techniques will succeed in producing the more substantial changes probably required for effects of great practical benefit in humans.

Although a number of studies have yielded convincing findings, clinical research along these lines has been somewhat uneven up to now. Findings have frequently been reported from human studies in which control treatments or groups were lacking to evaluate (*a*) fluctuations in auto-nomic-response levels that would have occurred without use of feedback procedures, (*b*) the effects of suggestion by the experimenter (placebo effects), (*c*) the permanence and reversibility of the obtained conditioning, (*d*) the degree of transfer of the learned behaviors from laboratory to real-life situations, and (*e*) the specificity rather than diffuseness of the con-ditioned responses. These problems are among those listed by Miller (1974), who advises investigators in this field "to be bold in what they try but cautious in what they claim."

c. *Classical conditioning of skeletal movements.* It is time to consider the frequent claim that skeletal responses, for example, directed movements of the whole organism, are conditionable primarily, if not exclusively, via operant procedures. In contrast to this view, Pavlov believed that such movements could be conditioned according to the general procedures and rules that control salivary conditioning. Unfortunately, his standard prac-tice of restraining dogs in a harness prevented extensive investigation of the subject's spatial or manipulative behavior. Nevertheless, he did report some interesting but seldom cited observations about the motor behavior of his dogs during presentations of the CS:

> The first reaction elicited by the established conditioned stimulus usually consists in a movement toward the stimulus, i.e., the animal turns to the place where the stimulus is. If the stimulus is within reach, the animal even tries to touch it, with his mouth. Thus if the conditioned stimulus is the switching on of a lamp, the dog licks the lamp; if the conditioned stimulus is a sound the dog will even snap at the air.... [He appears] to eat the sound, that is, licking his lips and making the noise of chewing with his teeth as though it were a matter of having the food itself.... The condi-tioned stimulus actually stands for the food. In the case of several con-ditioned stimuli coming from different directions the animal turns toward each of them [Pavlov, 1941, pp. 120 and 150].

If Pavlov had not been primarily a physiologist, perhaps the classical conditioning of directed movements would have much sooner become an important object of study by experimental psychologists. Pavlov was forced to harness his subjects in order to accurately measure salivation, a response that he had used for several decades in his physiological and pharmacologi-cal research and continued to employ in his later work on conditioned re-flexes. However, if he had released his dogs from the harness after salivary conditioning, he might have observed some dramatic effects. The anecdotal account of such an experiment, reported by Liddell to Lorenz, was de-scribed in the following context by the distinguished ethologist:

> The system of physiological mechanisms that undergoes an adaptive modification through conditioning never is "one reflex," as Pavlovian ter-minology implies. Even the classical salivary response is really only one

part of a complicated system of feeding behavior, *all* of which is activated
by the conditioned stimulus and which, in the experiment, is prevented
from being performed only by the simple means of tying the dog to a
frame. My late friend, Howard Liddell, told me about an unpublished
experiment he did while working as a guest in Pavlov's laboratory. It
consisted simply in freeing from its harness a dog that had been conditioned to salivate at the acceleration in the beat of a metronome. The dog
at once ran to the machine, wagged its tail at it, tried to jump up to it,
barked, and so on; in other words, it showed as clearly as possible the
whole system of behavior patterns serving, in a number of Canidae, to beg
food from a conspecific. It is, in fact, this whole system that is being
conditioned in the classical experiment [Lorenz, 1969, p. 47].

This comment reflects one of the central themes of the present chapter:
a pattern of functionally related behaviors, not a single response, is being
conditioned in any classical or operant conditioning experiment. The artificial restrictions of a particular laboratory setup (restraint of the subject,
measurement of only one type of response, failure to tabulate or even observe other behaviors of the subject), although easing the experimenter's
task because they permit simple automation of the experiment, have led
to neglect of some important effects.

In the above examples provided by Pavlov and Liddell, there were no
explicit instrumental contingencies involved. Despite the absence of any
dependency between food delivery and the subject's behavior, some writers
would argue that the licking of the lamp by Pavlov's dog was followed
by food and was therefore "superstitiously" reinforced (superstitious conditioning will be discussed in more detail later). Such an account would not
explain why the dog licked the lamp for the first time, but it could handle
the progressive development and later maintenance of the response.
However, this type of explanation obviously cannot explain Liddell's observation, since approach and contact of the metronome had never been
permitted before the dog was released from the harness.

The first extensive study of the classical conditioning of directed movements was performed by Brown and Jenkins (1968). They employed
pigeons, a standard operant conditioning chamber, and the most popular
response used today in studies of operant behavior (pecking at a circular
disk or key). In contrast to standard procedures with pigeons, keys, and
grain reinforcement, however, Brown and Jenkins delivered grain regardless of the bird's behavior. Every minute or so, the key was illuminated
for 8 sec and immediately followed by grain delivery. As pairings of CS
(key illumination) and US (grain) continued, the birds first exhibited an
increase in activity and oriented toward the lighted key, then began to approach it, and finally pecked at it. The first peck occurred, on the average,
after approximately 40 pairings of light and grain. As in many classical
conditioning experiments, the CS eventually evoked responses (pecks) resembling those that occur to US.

Numerous subsequent experiments have demonstrated that the acquisition of key pecking in this type of situation depends on a positive contingency between key illumination and grain delivery. For example, birds rarely peck keys that are illuminated randomly with regard to grain presentations. Brown and Jenkins gave the name "autoshaping" to the phenomenon whereby approach and contact behavior develops toward a stimulus that predicts the arrival of a reinforcer. The procedure is *auto*matic and the pigeon shapes it*self* to peck the key. In these ways, the procedure is different from conventional "operant" methods of training a pigeon to peck a key, which require the experimenter's continuous monitoring of the bird's behavior; the experimenter shapes the key peck by providing grain for responses that successively approximate the desired response, for example, glances at the key → approaches toward it → pecks at it (the same sequence of behaviors, incidentally, that typically occurs during autoshaping).

Although Skinner (e.g., 1953, p. 93) was cautious in his evaluation of the representativeness of the pigeon's key peck, a popular belief has been that the response is relatively arbitrary, convenient for use in studies of operant behavior. However, the auto-shaping experiments suggest that the key peck is not very arbitrary at all. It consistently develops toward a localized visual signal that predicts grain, even though the response is not required for grain.

Since Brown and Jenkins' initial work, "autoshaping" has been reported in studies employing a variety of species, CSs, responses, reinforcers, and general situations. Hearst and Jenkins (1974) reviewed and evaluated these findings but used the term "sign tracking" to cover a variety of behavioral effects, including autoshaping. Sign tracking appears to be a rather pervasive phenomenon and

> ... refers to behavior that is directed toward or away from a stimulus as a result of the relation between that stimulus and the reinforcer, or between that stimulus and the absence of the reinforcer.... The word "tracking" is meant to be flexible in its application; it can refer to an organism's orientation, approach, or contact responses directed toward signs of particular reinforcers, as well as to an organism's withdrawal responses directed away from signs that a reinforcer is not coming. [If illumination of a key signals that grain is not coming for some time, pigeons consistently move away or stay away from the lighted key and virtually never peck it]. Among other advantages, the word "sign" implies the importance of stimulus-reinforcer correlations, rather than the traditional Law of Effect. A sign predicts the presence or absence of some other environmental event [Hearst & Jenkins, 1974, p. 4].

The sign or CS apparently achieves its capacity to control directed movements of the whole organism via procedures operationally the same as those used in conventional classical conditioning.

An important similarity between sign-tracking experiments of the Brown–Jenkins variety and conventional studies of classical conditioning lies in the resemblance of CRs and URs that usually occurs in both. When one key-light stimulus (e.g., a red light) signaled grain delivery and another stimulus (e.g., three vertical stripes) signaled water delivery in pigeons that were both hungry and thirsty, the subjects generally displayed brief and forceful pecks at the food-predictive key and sustained, weak, irregularly spaced pecks at the water-predictive key (Jenkins & Moore, 1973). Human observers reported that the pigeons seemed to "eat" the food signal and "drink" the water signal. Similarly, Peterson, Ackil, Frommer, and Hearst (1972) found that rats gnawed and licked a lever, the insertion of which into the chamber signaled food, but sniffed and "explored" a lever, the insertion of which signaled rewarding brain stimulation (the most frequent response to the brain stimulation itself was sniffing and exploring).

After key pecking has begun to occur in an autoshaping experiment, approach and pecking of the lighted key are consistently followed by food. Of course, these conjunctions of responses and food are entirely fortuitous but they could play an important role in the strengthening and maintenance of key pecking. There are several methods available (see Hearst & Jenkins, 1974) to determine whether *response*-reinforcer or *stimulus*-reinforcer relations are more important in the control of behavior in this situation.

One general method, which has often produced dramatic results, involves procedural arrangements in which the two correlations oppose each other. For example, stimulus-reinforcer pairings may be permitted to occur *only* if the subject does not approach or contact the key. Thus, a reinforcer would never closely follow the "response" (negative response-reinforcer correlation) but would always occur in close conjunction with the prior stimulus (positive stimulus-reinforcer correlation). If the approach or contact response persisted under conditions in which its occurrence could only *prevent* the reinforcer, then the greater importance of the stimulus-reinforcer relation would be demonstrated. Sheffield (1965) established such an *omission* contingency during standard salivary conditioning experiments with dogs. He found that salivary CRs were maintained even when the occurrence of one or more drops of saliva during CS had the effect of preventing the scheduled food US.

Williams and Williams (1969) performed the first auto-shaping study that included an omission contingency for key pecking. Any peck during CS canceled the grain scheduled to occur after CS. Despite this negative consequence, pigeons continued to peck the illuminated key on many trials and therefore lost a large number of the reinforcers that they would have received if they had not pecked. Jenkins subsequently showed that birds would approach and peck a predictive key light 3 ft away from the grain dispenser, even though this behavior prevented the subject from returning to the dispenser in time to consume most of the available grain (access to grain lasted only 4 sec on each trial). When a prevention (omission) contingency was specifically established for key approach (rather than key pecking), Browne, Peden, and Hearst (described in Hearst, 1975) found that birds continued to "approach" (within 14 inches of the key) on approximately half the trials, even though each instance of this response canceled the reinforcer that was scheduled after CS. Thus, the positive relation between *stimulus* and reinforcer is mainly controlling and directing the subject's approach and contact behavior in these situations, since conjunctions of such *responses* and reinforcers are never permitted to occur.

Hearst and Jenkins (1974; see also Hearst, 1975) presented data from a variety of procedures to further document the conclusion that perception of a relation between stimulus and reinforcer mainly controls sign-tracking behavior. For example, pairings of a stimulus (key light) and reinforcer (grain) presented to an "observing" bird that is physically prevented from reaching the source of the stimulus or reinforcer results in a tendency to approach and contact the stimulus when the barrier is removed (see also the above quotation from Lorenz). Furthermore, Hearst and Jenkins (1974, pp. 34–44) argued that sign tracking probably plays an important role in many other experimental arrangements and effects, including several phenomena often classified under the category of "operant behavior."

The food-predictive signal in the autoshaping situation seems to have a status very similar to that of the token or object in the situations so vividly described by Breland and Breland, (1961, 1966) in discussions of the "misbehavior of organisms." In their animals, consummatory-like behaviors developed and persisted toward objects that had to be manipulated to obtain reinforcement, *even though* these behaviors delayed or prevented the delivery or reinforcers. For example, racoons taught to insert coins in a box for food reward began to "wash" the coins in the way they wash food. These prolonged forms of behavior delayed receipt of food; nevertheless, they became *more* frequent as training progressed. As in sign-tracking "omission" experiments, certain behaviors directed toward a surrogate of food persisted despite their negative consequences in terms of access to food.

d. Conclusions. An appreciable number of studies indicate that both autonomic responses and skeletal movements of the whole organism can be conditioned via either classical conditioning or instrumental conditioning procedures. Simple "mediational" explanations of the operant conditioning of autonomic responses and "superstitious reinforcement" accounts of sign tracking receive relatively weak support. On these grounds, can one conclude that there is little or no basis for a distinction between classical and instrumental conditioning in terms of the types of responses they are capable of modifying?

Certainly, the findings contradict any extreme position that limits modification of autonomic responses to Pavlovian conditioning and modification of skeletal responses to operant conditioning. However, someone who believes in the importance and heuristic value of the operant–respondent distinction could maintain that (a) relatively few cases currently exist of skeletal movements that have been modified by Pavlovian procedures, and (b) the evidence for substantial modification of a variety of autonomic responses by operant techniques is not completely convincing yet. In other words, there may be exceptions to the rule, but the correlation between autonomic or skeletal response classes and modifiability by Pavlovian or operant procedures, respectively, is generally high.

Part of the reason for this relatively high correlation, however, probably lies in the fact that, until the last 5 to 10 years, there have not been many careful attempts to test the limits of the correlation. Certain kinds of experiments were simply not performed very often before 1960. How many contradictory examples are needed before one would abandon the autonomic–skeletal dichotomy as it relates to conditioning procedures? Traditional beliefs have hindered experimentation along these lines and the successes of recent years suggest that additional positive instances of the classical conditioning of skeletal responses and the operant conditioning of autonomic responses are likely to be obtained in the future. However, the safest current statement seems one that regards the whole question as unsettled.

2. Resemblance of the Conditioned Response and Unconditioned Response

The assertion is often made that the CR in classical conditioning resembles the UR, whereas in operant conditioning the relationship between the conditioned response and reinforcer is arbitrary. Choice of food as the US in Pavlov's standard situation is said to limit the selection of a CR to be measured, whereas in a Skinner Box the adoption of food as a reinforcer presumably does not constrain the experimenter in his choice of a response to strengthen by the contingent delivery of food. From our earlier comments, the reader will recognize that distinctions of this kind are not likely to be particularly valuable. First, a trivial reason why CRs may resemble URs in classical conditioning research is that the experimenter usually arranges to measure the same type of response during CS and US. Conceivably, he could establish a classical conditioning procedure and examine responses during CS that did not originally occur as responses to US (e.g., specific responses originally elicited by CS; movements toward CS).

Furthermore, the skeletal response usually selected for study in operant conditioning is not as arbitrary or randomly selected as many experimenters have implied. Pigeon keys and rat levers, the two most popular response devices in operant studies, support behaviors (e.g., pecking, gnawing, grasping) that resemble responses to food itself or are highly probable in situations where food is delivered and animals are hungry (Segal, 1972). If a different type of skeletal response is chosen, conditioning often proves difficult. For example, Blough (1958; see also Breland & Breland, 1961; Hinde & Hinde, 1973; Shettleworth, 1972, for other examples and relevant comments) reported that the task of "standing still" in order to obtain food was not an easy one for pigeons. Sevenster (1973) found that stickle-backs did not learn to bite a glass rod at a high rate to gain access to a female although they would swim frequently through a ring to reach her; they did bite the rod at a high rate, however, when this response produced opportunities to fight with another male. With noxious USs, Bolles (1971) has demonstrated the difficulty of training certain types of behavior as avoidance responses. He argued that only those responses that occur as natural reactions to painful stimuli ("species-specific defense reactions," for example, running away) are easily established as instrumental avoidance responses. Anyone who has ever attempted to train an experimentally naive rat to press a lever, or a pigeon to peck a key, to avoid shock is aware of the often insurmountable difficulty of such a task. In other words, the choice of a US affects the experimenter's likelihood of successfully conditioning particular responses on *both* classical and instrumental procedures.

In any event, the question of whether CR and UR must greatly resemble each other in order for an outcome to qualify as an example of classical conditioning has never been clearly answered. On the basis of experimental results using Pavlovian procedures, many writers have been impressed by the similarity between CR and UR, whereas others conclude—principally on the basis of studies with noxious USs and respiratory, cardiac, or eye-blink responses—that Pavlov's concept of *stimulus substitution,* whereby a new stimulus comes to substitute for some old one in evoking a particular response, is untenable (see Mackintosh, 1974, for a balanced presentation of the two views, although he concludes that experimental findings generally support the stimulus-substitution concept). In this area of research, qualitative differences between CR and UR are usually considered the crucial ones; quantitative differences (e.g., number of drops of saliva during CS versus US, latency and magnitude of eye blinks) may merely reflect variations in the strength of a single response, such as might be produced by changes in CS or US intensity. However, the observation that salivary URs are more viscous than salivary CRs, and differ in their chemical constituents—although apparently "qualitative"—is not particularly damaging to the stimulus-substitution notion. The precise composition of the salivary UR itself changes depending on the nature and strength of the US (Gormezano, 1966).

If one views classical conditioning as modifying a variety of behaviors, failures to obtain substantial resemblance between CR and UR are not surprising. Shock US, for example, elicits widespread and sizable autonomic changes as well as struggling behavior and increases in general activity, which interact with and affect cardiac and respiratory activity. Preparation for receipt of such a US probably involves a number of functionally related responses that are not the same as those evoked by the US. Certain responses that occur during CS and not during US (e.g., the tensing of certain muscle groups as the time for a painful US approaches) may minimize the effects of US delivery, and thereby be controlled at least partially by their "successful" consequences—a problem described above as inherent in most classical conditioning designs. These skeletal responses, in turn, may indirectly affect autonomic measures and account for instances in which respiratory or cardiac CRs do not greatly resemble their respective URs. Culler (1938) made the interesting observation that the CR does *begin* as a copy of the UR, but gradually develops into a different ("preparatory") response.

In summary, available evidence suggests that the choice of a reinforcer influences the occurrence and conditionability of various response classes in both classical and instrumental conditioning situations. Respondent *and* operant responses often resemble, or include components of, behaviors that occur to the reinforcer itself.

3. Comparisons of "Respondents" and "Operants" from the Same Response System

In contrast to the work described previously in this section on response characteristics, most of which involved the testing of some hypothesis about how classically conditioned responses differ from instrumentally conditioned responses, a more empirical approach to the analysis of response properties has been adopted by several groups of researchers. This strategy involves (a) selecting an appropriate response, and (b) conditioning some subjects to perform it via Pavlovian procedures and other subjects to perform it via operant procedures. Then the experimental results are compared to determine whether the "response" differs in latency, form, ease of conditioning, etc., under the two types of procedure.

This kind of research has a long history, extending back to Starytzin (1926, cited in Razran, 1956). He found that leg-flexion responses during CS in dogs reached a high level in 30–50 trials if this response avoided the shock US; in contrast, the same response was difficult to condition and maintain if a strictly Pavlovian procedure was used (CS always followed by shock to the leg). A superiority for instrumental (avoidance) over Pavlovian procedures was also obtained for a running response in guinea pigs by Brogden, Lipman, and Culler (1938). Later experimenters employed different response systems, for which URs to shock do not compete with the CR, as appeared to be the case in most of the previous studies. Logan (1951) and Kimble, Mann, and Dufort (1955) selected the human eye-blink response for investigation. Competing responses ought to be minimized in the case of eye-blink conditioning, since a shock delivered during a blink closes the eyelid further rather than opens it. Both these experiments produced clearly superior conditioning for the classical group, the opposite result from the earlier studies with locomotor and flexion responses, and a finding repeated many times since then in the eyelid-conditioning situation.

Rather than to describe other results, necessary control treatments, and conclusions that characterize this empirical approach to comparing classically and instrumentally conditioned responses, our preference is to comment on the logic of the strategy as specifically applied to the question of whether classical and instrumental conditioning are fundamentally different. Although the approach is appealing because of its simplicity and relative lack of theoretical preconceptions, and the associated experimental designs do provide valuable information about the possible role of response consequences in different learning situations, the general strategy seems questionable insofar as its systematic implications about the significance of the classical–instrumental distinction are concerned.

One reason for pessimism is related to our prior comments that "pure" examples of classical and instrumental conditioning cannot be arranged for comparison. Consider two conditions, which include different groups of subjects: Situation A ("classical"), in which CS is always followed by US, regardless of the subject's behavior, and Situation B ("instrumental") in which the occurrence of the CR measured in Situation A affects the delivery of US (produces or prevents its occurrence at the end of CS). Although operational definitions of the two conditioning procedures are being followed, it seems somewhat misleading to imply that classical contioning is simply being compared with instrumental conditioning. Situation B also includes the main ingredients of classical conditioning, since USs are contingent on the presence of CS in that situation as well as in Situation A; in both situations USs never occur in the absence of CS. And there is the possibility in Situation A that occurrence of the CR will somehow influence the effectiveness of the US.

Therefore, such experiments may provide valuable data concerning the influence of explicit response-reinforcer contingencies above and beyond possible effects of response-reinforcer conjunctions occurring in the classical-conditioning situation itself,[5] but they do not seem to tell us very much about basic differences between classical and instrumental conditioning.

---

[5] However, the fact that explicit response-reinforcer contingencies can be demonstrated to modify behavior when added to a classical conditioning procedure does not necessarily mean that response-reinforcer conjunctions act similarly and have substantial influence during conventional classical conditioning.

Possibly, if the two procedures produced more or less identical results (cf. Gormezano & Coleman, 1973), one could conclude that the presumed instrumental factors are not important and that there is no need to posit two learning processes, at least for that specific type of test situation. However, when the results differ for the two procedures, conclusions about the classical–instrumental distinction seem ambiguous or impossible to reach. As suggested later in this chapter, a more reasonable approach might be to attempt to analyze these situations, as well as all others, in terms of the relative effects of both stimulus-reinforcer and response-reinforcer correlations—rather than to attempt a categorization of situations as simply "classical" or "instrumental."

C. Stimulus Control

Although Skinner's original distinction between Type S and Type R *conditioning* was precisely stated in terms of stimulus-reinforcer or response-reinforcer dependencies established by the experimenter, his distinction between respondent and operant *behavior* was not so clearcut. Respondent behavior was said to be elicited by definite environmental stimuli, whereas operant behavior was described as occurring spontaneously. According to Skinner, the "originating forces" for such spontaneous behavior are not "located in the environment."

Other writers, for example, Konorski and Miller (1937b) and Guthrie (1952), insisted that we must assume that every behavior has its controlling stimuli, whether we can identify them or not. Guthrie (1952) added that such an assumption "encourages search for the signals of emitted behavior" and "we can often discover them if we look [p. 280]." Some writers regarded the lever as a CS in the Skinner Box situation. These views recall the quote of Sechenov that opened this chapter.

As we noted earlier, Skinner had heuristic as well as systematic reasons for adopting the view that operant behavior was "emitted"; he could pursue its analysis without worrying about specification of controlling stimuli and without implying that operant behavior could be fit into the stimulus–response or classical conditioning paradigms popular at the time. In his most recent work (Skinner, 1974) he still maintains that "to distinguish an operant from an elicited reflex, we say that the operant response is 'emitted'. . . . The principal feature is that there seems to be no necessary prior causal event. . . . The apparent lack of an immediate cause in operant behavior has led to the invention of an initiating event [pp. 52–53]." He goes on to deplore (justifiably) the use of terms like "ideas" or "will," which are such inventions. Then he says that "operant behavior is called voluntary, but it is not really uncaused; the cause is simply harder to spot" (Skinner, 1974, p. 54). Prior positive reinforcement contingent on the response is the critical "cause," not immediately prior stimulation.

Skinner's distinction between "elicitation" and "emission" seems meaningful, in the present writer's opinion, only when applied to *unconditioned* responses. Skinner (1937) implied this restriction when he stated that the concept of emitted behavior is "a necessary recognition of the fact that in the unconditioned organism two kinds of behavior may be distinguished [p. 274]"—the kind of response that constitutes part of a reflex in the traditional physiological sense, and the kind of response that occurs spontaneously. Behavior is respondent if the experimenter can consistently produce it by presenting a specific discrete stimulus to an experimentally naive subject. All other behavior is operant.

However, Skinner also applies the terms operant and respondent to learned behavior. He differentiates between "eliciting" and "discriminative" stimuli, which characterize the control of (conditioned) respondent and operant behavior, respectively. These terms are closely linked to his original distinction between elicitation and emission, as a few examples may make clear.

Once an operant response, such as a lever press in the rat or some verbal utterance such as "Good morning" in a human being, is initially conditioned (by arranging for a reinforcer to follow it), the response can easily be and almost always is brought under the control of external stimuli. If rewarded for pressing a lever only when a light is on, the rat soon begins to press the lever *promptly and reliably* whenever the light is turned on. Likewise, we do not greet someone with "Good morning" as we sit down for dinner, but we promptly and reliably do when we see our secretary at 9 A.M. On the surface, these behaviors seem as much controlled by prior stimulation as is salivation upon seeing an orange. However, Skinner would call our secretary in the office a "discriminative stimulus," who merely "sets the occasion" for a particular verbal utterance, whereas he would call the orange an "eliciting stimulus."

The distinction between these two functions of a stimulus is not based on our current observations of learned behavior—in both cases we observe an immediate and reliable response to a stimulus—but apparently on our knowledge that you can evoke salivation in an untrained human by placement of food in his mouth and that there is no US which elicits "Good mornings." Developing Skinner's analysis, Keller and Schoenfeld (1950) stated that "all responses, conditioned or unconditioned, that are elicited by known stimuli, we call respondent [p. 49]." However, they do not tell us how to distinguish elicited CRs from responses that promptly and reliably follow onset of discriminative stimuli; discriminative stimuli are "known," too.

If elicitation is a stimulus function applicable to both unconditioned and conditioned behavior, in what sense is the *conditioned* response in respondent conditioning elicited? When the CS was first presented, it did not evoke the CR (if it had, it would not have been used as a "neutral" stimulus). However, after several pairings of CS and US, the CR reliably occurs to the CS. Why is this CR any more "elicited" than lever pressing under the discriminative control of a light? Both generally require extinction of responses that occur in the absence of the controlling stimulus. But Skinner maintained (1953, p. 112) that eliciting stimuli appear to be more "coercive" than discriminative stimuli, a point to be reconsidered in a moment.

Another problem with the distinction arises when we consider, for example, bursts of salivation or other forms of respondent behavior that may take place in dogs in the absence of identifiable prior stimulation. When such "respondents" occur spontaneously, are they "operants"? One cannot assume that eliciting stimuli must have been present without greatly weakening the original basis for the distinction between operant and respondent behavior.

Thus, the distinction between elicitation and emission as characterizing the control of two different types of conditioned response (respondent versus operant) is apparently not very helpful. It is rarely mentioned by non-Skinnerians who, like Skinner, maintain a two-process approach. Possibly, Skinner's distinction is related to another potential behavioral criterion for distinguishing categories of learning: the degree of inhibitability of the conditioned response. Can we learn to refrain from salivating to a CS for a desirable food less easily than we can learn to refrain from saying "Good morning" to our secretary? Perhaps Skinner implied a certain outcome in such cases when he labeled a CS more "coercive" than a discriminative stimulus. We shall return later to the question of the relative inhibitability of responses under different experimental arrangements.

D. Reinforcement and Motivational Factors

Throughout this chapter the terms "unconditioned stimulus" (or US) and "reinforcer" have been used more or less interchangeably. Although Pavlov was the first to describe the US as a reinforcer or strengthener of the link between CS and CR, the word "reinforcer" is today used primarily in operant, conditioning research and the term "US" is preferred in classical conditioning research. We have been sidestepping some important issues by using the terms interchangeably, and several writers have suggested that the reinforcers effective for classical conditioning are not exactly the same as those effective for operant conditioning—even though they grant that the overlap between the two is substantial. For example, Schlosberg (1937) and Mowrer (1947) suggested that reinforcers for instrumental learning must be pleasant or unpleasant (emotion or motivation arousing), whereas they need not be in Pavlovian conditioning (although, ironically,

Pavlovian conditioning is often described as a method for conditioning the "emotions"). However, precise definitions of hedonic or affective quality are not available, and even loose definitions of "affect" cannot easily encompass the fact that operant conditioning is possible in animals with such reinforcers as mere sensory change (e.g., light or tone onset) or the opportunity to explore a novel environment. Moreover, it is hard to think of any effective Pavlovian US toward which a subject would be totally "neutral."

An example of a US that is supposedly effective for classical conditioning but not for operant conditioning is electrical stimulation of the motor cortex, which produces leg flexion and successful conditioning to a CS paired with such cortical stimulation. When a situation was established in which bar presses produced cortical US as well as their usual consequence (food), the rate of bar pressing was unchanged (Doty & Giurgea, 1961). However, Wagner, Thomas, and Norton (1967) suggested that instrumental reinforcement may have been important even in the classical-conditioning procedure; their argument, like several we have already alluded to, was that the CS might have permitted the subjects to prepare for US and thus lessen any aversive effects that unexpected delivery of US might have. Wagner and his colleagues observed that their subjects (dogs) stood poised during CS in a way which might have altered the effect of US. These experimenters subsequently found that dogs, given a choice between obtaining signaled and unsignaled USs, learned to select the signaled USs. Apparently stimuli correlated with information about the impending delivery of this type of US can act as operant reinforcers.

Thus, the overlap between Pavlovian USs and operant reinforcers is considerable, if not complete. At least, there is no clear evidence of a reinforcer that works in one type of arrangement and not in the other.

Closely related to the concept of reinforcement is the concept of motivation or drive. One of the effects of depriving a subject of food (appetitive motivation) is the potentiality for using food delivery as a reinforcing event, and one of the effects of delivering a noxious US to a subject (aversive motivation) is the potentiality for using prevention or termination of this US as a reinforcing event. Skinner argued that in respondent conditioning a close relationship exists between USs, URs, and certain drives; in contrast, operant behaviors are not necessarily related to any particular drive. For example, one could presumably train a subject without difficulty to press a bar to obtain food, to obtain water, or to escape shock, but one presumably could not condition salivation in classical conditioning experiments using many different USs. However, both of these presumptions are questionable. We have already pointed out (Section III.B) that the conditioned response in most conventional operant studies is not really so arbitrary; its base level, conditionability, topography, and persistence depend on the US and drive. And, in classical-conditioning studies, salivation may be induced by a variety of USs. In any event, the point at issue does not imply a strict distinction between respondent and operant conditioning, but merely states that operant behaviors can be conditioned in a broader range of situations than can respondent behaviors.

Drive manipulations affect both classical and instrumental conditioning. Pavlov pointed out that salivary CRs were almost impossible to form and maintain in food-satiated dogs. In water-satiated rats, DeBold, Miller, and Jensen (1965) failed to obtain classical conditioning of licking responses to a buzzer CS that was followed by injections of water directly into the rat's mouth; thirsty rats, however, were easily conditioned. Analogous results are also typically found in operant conditioning research: the degree of motivation affects the ease of initial conditioning and later performance.

E. Empirical Phenomena and Laws

The question of whether the procedures used in conventional classical and operant conditioning affect behavior through basically different processes or mechanisms can be approached in yet another way. If different processes or mechanisms are involved in each, certain phenomena should be observed under one procedure and not under the other, or certain laws relating independent and dependent variables should hold for one type of procedure and not the other. Discovery of such irregularities or divergences often leads scientists to suspect the involvement of more than one process or mechanism.

Do certain phenomena or laws hold for classical conditioning and not for operant conditioning, and vice versa? The overwhelming conclusion from the experimental literature is negative on this question. Almost every phenomenon studied by Pavlov has its clear counterpart in operant conditioning; for example, extinction, spontaneous recovery, stimulus generalization and discrimination, blocking and overshadowing, induction effects, conditioned inhibition, inhibition of delay, and disinhibition. Laws relating amount and delay of reinforcement, length of intertrial interval, motivation level, intensity of CS, etc. to behavioral measures do not differ in any obvious way between the two arrangements (see, for example, the comments of Kimble 1961; Rescorla & Solomon, 1967; Seward, 1970).

Some researchers maintain that partial reinforcement (i.e., the use of procedures in which not every CS is followed by US in Pavlovian conditioning, or not every response is followed by a reinforcer in operant conditioning) has a greater (weakening) effect on the learning of classically conditioned responses than of operant responses. Other writers believe that the phenomenon of greater resistance to extinction after partial reinforcement as compared to continuous reinforcement is easier to obtain following oper-ant conditioning. However, these conclusions are based on comparisons of a large number of studies from operant conditioning with a collection of studies from classical conditioning—usually without any real attempt to equate a variety of factors (stimuli, responses, reinforcers, species, and situations) as closely as possible—and are not very convincing (see Mack-intosh, 1974; Rescorla & Solomon, 1967; Seward, 1970, for reviews and comments about these experiments). Besides, the difficulty, if not the im-possibility, of establishing pure cases of classical or operant conditioning in the laboratory may prevent acceptable comparisons along these lines. Thus, there is little evidence to support the belief that the "laws of Pavlo-vian conditioning" are different from the "laws of operant conditioning."

F. Transfer and Interaction Experiments

All the strategies described thus far for evaluating whether Pavlovian and operant conditioning are governed by different basic processes have en-tailed a comparison of the effects of specific factors (response, stimulus, reinforcer, drive) or general laws or phenomena that might differentiate the two. Other than the experimenter's rule that reinforcers are contingent on prior stimulation in one case and on prior responding in the other, there appears to be no point that can clearly distinguish them.

   Two-process learning theories (Rescorla & Solomon, 1967) assume that Pavlovian conditioning and instrumental learning involve two distinct pro-cesses, "each governed by its own appropriate sets of operations and laws [p. 170]." The laws of Pavlovian conditioning are "probably *the laws of emotional conditioning or laws of acquired drive states*" and these states *"can serve either as motivators or reinforcers* of instrumental responses" (Rescorla & Solomon, 1967, p. 172). The claim that the laws of Pavlovian conditioning differ from those of instrumental learning, and the implicit assumption that responses can be measured or inferred which are either Pavlovian or instrumental, do not receive convincing support from the arguments and evidence summarized in the present chapter. Rescorla and Solomon (1967) themselves concluded that the relevant results are "inade-quate" to justify the "claim that two independent processes are acting [p. 163]." Furthermore, the successful recent work on the operant conditioning of autonomic responses and on the classical conditioning of directed movements (autoshaping), performed since their 1967 paper, would pre-sumably make it now even more difficult for Rescorla and Solomon to distinguish between Pavlovian and instrumental responses. Despite these problems, experiments based on two-process learning theory have prolifer-ated since the publication of their paper and have yielded very interesting results. As a prelude to examining their implications for the classical–instrumental distinction, a brief examination of the types of experiments prompted by this approach and some of the general findings seems in order.

If Pavlovian CRs mediate (instigate or reinforce) instrumental behavior, as two-process theory assumes, then concurrent measures of the two presumed types of behavior—for example, of salivary CRs during operant conditioning of lever pressing for food, or of fear CRs (heart rate, respiration) during instrumental avoidance learning—should reveal close correspondences between the acquisition curves for each and between the sequences in which they appear on a given trial after acquisition is complete. Evidence (see Rescorla & Solomon, 1967) is inconsistent on these points: sometimes autonomic CRs reliably precede the occurrence of the instrumental response on each trial, sometimes the opposite effect occurs and sometimes no reliable sequence is observed. In some experiments autonomic CRs are acquired first and then the instrumental response, but in other experiments the reverse effect occurs. Prevention or blockage of peripheral autonomic ("fear") responses by means of surgical procedures or various drugs does not importantly affect avoidance performance. Therefore, the notion that some peripheral (Pavlovian) CR is necessary for the maintenance or guidance of ongoing operant behavior is not supported by the findings of these studies.

In any case, "concurrent measurement" studies of this kind are beset with technical and interpretive problems. The "state" conditioned to a Pavlovian CS, as Rescorla and Solomon pointed out, may not be adequately indexed by measurement of one or two specific responses; in fact, research has indicated that supposedly different emotional states are hard to separate even on the basis of a constellation of different autonomic measures. Skeletal activity itself, such as that occurring during operant behavior, affects various autonomic measures, for example, heart rate. Attempts to determine whether certain autonomic responses precede or follow the operant responses that they presumably mediate are fraught with problems: different response systems have different intrinsic properties (latency, recovery time) and incommensurate units; decisions as to when each "response" has begun and finished are difficult to make when graded changes in some continuous base line (such as for heart rate or salivation) are compared to relatively discrete responses (such as the closing of a switch when a rat presses a lever); the technical devices used to measure onset and magnitude of each response may not be equally sensitive; and it may be that some unknown correlate or consequence (feedback) of the measured response is really the crucial "mediator," anyway. These problems, as well as the inconsistency of the data amassed thus far, suggest that the oncurrent-measurement technique is not likely to prove very profitable, s far as tests of two-process theory are concerned.

Another, more fruitful, strategy proposed by Rescorla and Solomon to ssess two-process theory has yielded a large number of provocative and onsistent findings, many of which they review in their article. In these tudies, subjects receive Pavlovian conditioning of one kind or another, nd are subsequently presented with the Pavlovian CSs while they are per- orming some operant response. If Pavlovian "conditioned emotional tates" do serve as mediators of instrumental behavior, they ought to have efinite and reliable effects on ongoing operants. Results confirm this eneral hypothesis. Pavlovian signals for unavoidable shock facilitate instru- iental avoidance behavior, whereas Pavlovian safety signals (which indi- ate a shock-free interval) depress avoidance behavior. Other experiments ave examined the effects of Pavlovian CSs associated with aversive USs n operant behavior controlled by appetitive consequences like food, and ice versa. Additional important research has revealed effects that differ epending on whether Pavlovian conditioning precedes operant condition- ig, or operant conditioning precedes Pavlovian conditioning (relevant are xperiments on "learned helplessness" and "learned laziness" by Seligman, laier, & Solomon, 1971, and Engberg, Hansen, Welker, & Thomas, 1972).

From these studies and many others, Rescorla and Solomon (1967) oncluded that Pavlovian conditioning produces effects that can be used ɔ control instrumental responding. These writers suggested that instru- iental responding may be "as sensitive, or perhaps even more sensitive, measure of the effects of Pavlovian conditioning procedures than are ie traditionally measured conditioned visceral or motor reflexes them- elves [p. 178]." They believe that the success of these experiments sup- orts the main assumption of their version of two-process theory, namely, hat Pavlovian procedures result in conditioning of a "central state" to 'S, which can and does mediate instrumental responding.

What do these experiments and findings imply about the classical–instru- iental distinction? The work demonstrates that exposure of subjects to wo different procedures produces very interesting and consistent interac- ons, but it does not tell us whether the procedures involve fundamentally ifferent processes. We could separately train subjects on two *operant* pro- edures (for example, to press a lever for food and to turn a wheel for rater) and then obtain behavioral interactions when these subjects are iven the opportunity to perform both responses simultaneously; or we ould separately train subjects on two *classical* procedures (for example, ɔ salivate to a tone that precedes food, and to flex their paw to a light hat precedes shock) and then test them with both CSs simultaneously. 'he mere fact that interactions occur between the effects of our procedural manipulations does not seem to warrant the postulation of separate under lying processes. We might then have to postulate a separate process for every different effective procedure we could think of.

In the present writer's opinion, different "processes" can justifiably be posited only if one can show that different laws, phenomena, or mecha nisms underlie each procedure. Rescorla and Solomon talk about the "law of Pavlovian conditioning," and include among them various phenomen of excitation and inhibition—all of which, however, have clear counterpar in operant conditioning. They call "salivation, cardiac changes, licking, an swallowing" Pavlovian CRs, but research suggests that each of these re sponses can also be modified via operant procedures. Evidence and logi do not appear to support the strong positions taken by Rescorla and Solo mon and other two-process theorists on the classical–instrument; distinction.

IV. CONCLUSIONS AND PROSPECTUS

A. General Evaluation

Kimble (1964) concisely stated the main questions to be resolved in diffe. entiating among types of learning: "The problem of establishing a satisfac tory taxonomy of learning is a definitional problem involving the sam issues as other problems of this type: (1) there must be a clear operation; distinction among categories of learning, and (2) these operationally estab lished categories must have some significance for behavior [p. 44]." Th classical–instrumental distinction can fulfill the first of these requirement in terms of the contingency, or lack of it, between response and reinforce However, even though the distinction may have had heuristic value, then is no strong evidence that it satisfies the second.

A recent assessment by Kimble (1971) agrees in general with that c the present chapter:

> As the evidence accumulates, it begins to appear that even two-factor theory is an unrealistic oversimplification. Classical and instrumental conditioning are both much more complicated than . . . two-process theory treated them as being. A strong argument can be made that cognitions [expectancies] and stimulus–response connections are formed in any learn ing situation and that the results of learning experiments depend upon con tributions of both types [p. 75].

In addition, it is noteworthy that even the *operational* distinction be tween classical and operant conditioning has not been consistently followe by some of its main proponents. For example, throughout his career Skinner has maintained that respondent conditioning involves the contingency of a reinforcer upon a prior stimulus, and operant conditioning involves the contingency of a reinforcer upon a prior response. In his influential research on superstitious conditioning, in which pigeons received grain regularly every x seconds regardless of their behavior, Skinner (1948) observed the acquisition of specific movements in most subjects. These behaviors included pecking directed toward the floor, thrusting of the head into one of the upper corners of the cage, etc.—responses that had rarely occurred prior to the periodic presentation of grain. He stated that the "conditioning process is usually obvious. The bird happens to be executing some response as the [grain] hopper appears; as a result it tends to repeat this response" (Skinner, 1948, p. 168). Additional conjunctions of response and grain serve to strengthen the behavior still further, until it achieves a considerable state of strength.

In describing the results, Skinner maintained that "operant conditioning usually takes place" even when grain is presented "at regular intervals *with no reference whatsoever to the bird's behavior*" (italics Skinner's). Such a statement means that Skinner is willing to extend the concept of response-reinforcer contingency to cases that involve mere conjunctions of responses and reinforcers. In that article Skinner explicitly stated that the term "contingency" may refer to nothing more than conjunctions of this kind. However, one procedure used by Pavlov in studies of salivary conditioning was the so-called time reflex, in which food was regularly presented every x seconds and salivation was observed to increase as the time for food delivery approached. Pavlov's procedure was virtually the same as Skinner's, except that an autonomic rather than skeletal conditioned response was measured. Can conventional Pavlovian salivary conditioning also be labeled "superstitious"? If not, why not? In any case, the extension of the concept of contingency to apply to mere conjunctions of response and reinforcer, rather than to an actual dependency of reinforcer upon response, nullifies the original procedural distinction between respondent and operant conditioning.

Despite the current lack of strong support for the notion that a basic difference exists between classical and instrumental conditioning, it seems likely that the distinction will continue to be endorsed by many psychologists. These researchers and writers will argue that even though the categories are not perfectly distinct, there is a generally high correlation between the sensitivity of autonomic and skeletal responses to classical versus instrumental procedures, respectively. Furthermore, they might contend that the range and importance of the behaviors which can be conditioned by means of the application of operant reinforcement (the Law of Effect) are much greater than the range and importance of the responses that can be directly elicited by Pavlovian USs and thereafter transferred, even in modified form, to formerly neutral CSs. Other workers will insist that the classical conditioning paradigm provides a totally inappropriate vehicle for understanding how precise motor (and verbal) skills develop from the originally undifferentiated skeletal movements that organisms possess. Adherents of the operant–respondent distinction will also argue for its heuristic value in organizing the data from learning experiments and in directing research; they will probably feel the distinction ought to be maintained, despite exceptions and weaknesses, at least until more attractive alternative approaches come along. In addition, supporters of the two-process approach could contend that experimental techniques are at fault; the processes or mechanisms underlying classical and instrumental conditioning, or involuntary and voluntary action, are fundamentally different, but our current behavioral and physiological techniques are simply unequal to the task of separating them. Future refinements, perhaps from research on the neurophysiology of learning, may reveal data about localization of nervous-system function that can be used in support of the two-process approach.

This chapter has suggested that the tenacity of the classical–instrumental distinction is as much based on deeply ingrained philosophical and cultural beliefs as on research and theory in the psychology of learning. Until recently, many experimenters have taken the distinction for granted and not even performed careful experiments that would test the limits of the criteria believed to support the distinction, for example, the operant conditioning of autonomic responses and the classical conditioning of directed movements of the whole organism. The partial, if not complete, success of recent work on these topics indicates that belief in the classical–instrumental distinction may have impeded as much as stimulated research. It would seem a good idea to shed, as far as possible, some of our preconceptions and biases about behavioral categories and take a new look at how one might study and interpret the phenomena of learning and behavioral change.

B.   Some Directions for Research and Theory

Several strategies and topics appear likely to provide information of the type needed to further evaluate two-process theory and to construct viable alternatives to the approaches outlined and criticized in this chapter. Perhaps listing a few such directions would be helpful.

1. The interactions between and relative effectiveness of stimulus-reinforcer and response-reinforcer contingencies ought to be examined empirically in a variety of learning tasks, embodying many different stimuli,

reinforcers, responses, and species. Of particular interest is the use of the *omission* procedure, in which certain responses are actually programmed to prevent delivery of scheduled reinforcers, that is, stimulus-reinforcer and response-reinforcer correlations are pitted against each other. As noted earlier, key-pecking and CS-approach responses in pigeons continue even on procedures in which these responses prevent grain on a given trial—evidence that the response-reinforcer correlation is relatively unimportant in that situation—but it is unclear how general this type of finding will prove to be.

Such manipulations are relevant to the question of whether certain kinds of responses are more sensitive to negative consequences than are others. One would not expect a clear-cut dichotomy between response classes, as the involuntary–voluntary or classical–instrumental distinctions generally imply, but a continuum of effects. Some responses, such as pecking in the pigeon or salivation in the dog or human in the presence of signs of food, may be extremely difficult to eliminate, whereas other responses may be easy to abolish by arranging appropriate negative consequences (including punishment procedures). As suggested earlier, the "inhibitability" of a response provides one of the common-sense criteria for calling it voluntary or involuntary (cf. Kimble & Perlmuter, 1970); the statement "I couldn't help it" often accompanies pleas that an action was involuntary. Skinner (1953) remarked that evidence for the view that reflexes were involuntary "was not so much that they could not be willed as that they could not be willed against [p. 111]." The belief that voluntary behavior involves a "choice" also suggests that certain responses can be inhibited. Actually, "inhibitability" may prove easier to define operationally and study experimentally than the property of "elicitation" offered by Skinner; application of negative response-reinforcer contingencies like those indicated above, may be useful in this connection.

2. A deeper analysis of the *biology* of learning and behavioral change seems needed. A psychologists's comment that "in any operant situation, the stimulus, the response, and the reinforcement are completely arbitrary and interchangeable" is simply not true (cf. Hinde & Hinde, 1973; Seligman & Hager, 1972; Shettleworth, 1972). A more biological approach to behavior than has been characteristic of major learning theories may force us to reconsider and reanalyze topics such as inborn reflexes, instincts, and organized species-specific patterns of behavior within the context of theories of learning. A large part of the repertoire of most organisms is probably not "learned," and the stress on learning over 50 years of behavioristic experimentation may have been unwarranted, although understandable in terms of its practical implications.

The influence of associationism in the history of philosophy and early psychology has led to a deemphasis of such modifications of behavior as are found under the headings of habituation, sensitization, and pseudocon-ditioning (see Kimble, 1961; Gormezano & Kehoe, Chapter 4 of this vol-ume). Because they do not involve correlated events, these phenomena are often labeled "nonassociative," and relegated to a minor position in the objective analysis of learned behavior; they frequently provide only control procedures against which "true" learning is evaluated. Biological research, however, suggests that phenomena of these kinds are ubiquitous and should be included as major topics in the psychology of learning. If our definition of learning were broadened in this way, it would be clear that classical and instrumental conditioning would not comprise even all the *procedural* possibilities.

3. In studies of operant conditioning, careful analysis and observation may isolate or narrow the range of stimuli responsible for initial emission of the response. Echoing Sechenov, Konorski, and Guthrie, we may be able to discover the stimuli controlling emitted behavior if we look hard enough for them. Significantly, Skinner's (1948) research on superstitious conditioning indicated that the subject's responses were almost always directed toward some feature of the experimental chamber: "The effect of the reinforcement was to condition the bird to respond to some aspect of the environment rather than merely to execute a series of movements [p. 169]." Such observations suggest that accidental *stimulus*-reinforcer conjunctions may guide the development of particular superstitious behav-iors, as sign-tracking (autoshaping) experiments would imply (Hearst & Jenkins, 1974).

One could formulate hypotheses about the stimuli (including internal stimuli, from drive or hormonal manipulations, for example) that increase the probability of certain "operants." Then one could vary aspects of these potential stimuli to determine their effects on response frequency and form, in situations that do not involve experimental contingencies. Detailed etho-logical observation of subjects in typical operant situations should also help in the formulation of hypotheses about which stimulus factors might be crucial in controlling the emission of particular responses. If such stimuli can be identified, it is conceivable that classical and instrumental condition-ing may be combined into one conceptual framework. Perhaps all condi-tioning involves the shift of certain behavioral elements or patterns from one stimulus to another (a variant of classical conditioning?).

If information were accumulated on these and other related points, one might be able to propose new categories of behavior modification that would be based exclusively on behavioral and biological data rather than on a variety of extraexperimental criteria and traditional ways of thinking. It is difficult to predict the type of classificatory framework that might emerge and whether it would resemble the two-process approach assessed n this chapter. However, the deficiencies of that approach require some resh attempts at reorganizing the data in the psychology of learning.

ACKNOWLEDGMENTS

The preparation of this chapter was supported by a Guggenheim Fellowship and National Institute of Mental Health Research Grant MH-19300 during 1974–1975. The Indiana University Cognitive Institute and Department of Psychology provided ecretarial assistance and moral support during this period. I thank the colleagues nd students who commented critically on early drafts of this chapter. Herbert M. enkins and Conrad G. Mueller have greatly influenced my thinking on many topics discussed here.

REFERENCES

Barber, T., DiCara, L., Kamiya, J., Miller, N. E., Shapiro, D., & Stoyva, J. (Eds.). *Biofeedback and self-control.* Chicago: Aldine-Atherton, 1970–1974. (5 vols.)

Birk, L., Crider, A., Shapiro, D., & Tursky, B. Operant electrodermal conditioning under partial curarization. *Journal of Comparative and Physiological Psychology,* 1966, **62,** 165–166.

Blough, D. S. New test for tranquilizers. *Science,* 1958, **127,** 586–587.

Bolles, R. C. Species-specific defense reactions. In F. R. Brush (Ed.), *Aversive conditioning and learning.* New York: Academic Press, 1971. Pp. 183–233.

Breland, K., & Breland, M. The misbehavior of organisms. *American Psychologist,* 1961, **16,** 681–684.

Breland, K., & Breland, M. *Animal behavior.* New York: Macmillan, 1966.

Brogden, W. J., Lipman, E. A., & Culler, E. A. The role of incentive in conditioning and extinction. *American Journal of Psychology,* 1938, **51,** 109–117.

Brown, P. L., & Jenkins, H. M. Autoshaping of the pigeon's key peck. *Journal of the Experimental Analysis of Behavior,* 1968, **11,** 1–8.

Culler, E. A. Recent advances in some concepts of conditioning. *Psychological Review,* 1938, **45,** 134–153.

DeBold, R. C., Miller, N. E., & Jensen, D. D. Effect of strength of drive determined by a new technique for appetitive classical conditioning of rats. *Journal of Comparative and Physiological Psychology,* 1965, **59,** 102–108.

Doty, R. W., & Giurgea, C. Conditioned reflexes established by coupling electrical excitation of two cortical areas. In J. Delafresnaye (Ed.), *Brain mechanisms and learning.* London: Blackwell Scientific Publ. 1961. Pp. 133–151.

Engberg, L. A., Hansen, G., Welker, R. L., & Thomas, D. R. Acquisition of key pecking via auto-shaping as a function of prior experience: "Learned laziness"? *Science,* 1972, **178,** 1002–1004.

Gormezano, I. Classical conditioning. In J. B. Sidowski (Ed.), *Experimental methods and instrumentation in psychology.* New York: McGraw-Hill, 1966. Pp. 385–420.

Gormezano, I., & Coleman, S. R. The law of effect and CR contingent modification of the UCS. *Conditional Reflex,* 1973, **8,** 41–56.

Guthrie, E. R. *The psychology of learning.* New York: Harper & Brothers, 1952.

Hearst, E. Pavlovian conditioning and directed movements. In G. H. Bower (Ed.), *The psychology of learning and motivation.* Vol. 9. New York: Academic Press, 1975.

Hearst, E., & Jenkins, H. M. *Sign-tracking: The stimulus-reinforcer relation and directed action*. Austin, Texas: The Psychonomic Society, 1974.

Hilgard, E. R., & Marquis, D. G. *Conditioning and learning*. New York: Appleton Century, 1940.

Hinde, R. A., & Hinde, J. S. *Constraints on learning*. New York: Academic Press 1973.

Jenkins, H. M., & Moore, B. R. The form of the auto-shaped response with food or water reinforcers. *Journal of the Experimental Analysis of Behavior*, 1973, **20**, 163–181.

Keller, F. S., & Schoenfeld, W. N. *Principles of psychology*. New York: Appleton Century-Crofts, 1950.

Kimble, G. A. *Hilgard and Marquis' conditioning and learning*. (2nd ed.) New York: Appleton-Century-Crofts, 1961.

Kimble, G. A. Categories of learning and the problem of definition. In A. W. Melton (Ed.), *Categories of human learning*. New York: Academic Press, 1964. Pp 32–45.

Kimble, G. A. Cognitive inhibition in classical conditioning. In H. H. Kendler & J. T. Spence (Eds.), *Essays in neobehaviorism*. New York: Appleton-Century-Crofts, 1971. Pp. 69–87.

Kimble, G. A., Mann, L., & Dufort, R. H. Classical and instrumental eyelid conditioning. *Journal of Experimental Psychology*, 1955, **49**, 407–417.

Kimble, G. A., & Perlmuter, L. C. The problem of volition. *Psychological Review*, 1970, **77**, 361–384.

Kimmel, H. D. Instrumental conditioning of autonomically mediated responses in human beings. *American Psychologist*, 1974, **29**, 325–335.

Konorski, J. *Conditioned reflexes and neuron organization*. Cambridge, England: Cambridge University Press, 1948.

Konorski, J., & Miller, S. On two types of conditioned reflex. *Journal of General Psychology*, 1937, **16**, 264–272. (a)

Konorski, J., & Miller, S. Further remarks on two types of conditioned reflex. *Journal of General Psychology*, 1937, **17**, 405–407. (b)

Logan, F. A. A comparison of avoidance and nonavoidance eyelid conditioning. *Journal of Experimental Psychology*, 1951, **42**, 390–393.

Lorenz, K. Z. Innate bases of learning. In K. Pribram (Ed.), *On the biology of learning*. New York: Harcourt, Brace, & World, 1969. Pp. 13–93.

Mackintosh, N. J. *The psychology of animal learning*. New York: Academic Press, 1974.

Miller, N. E. Learning of visceral and glandular responses. *Science*, 1969, **163**, 434–445.

Miller, N. E. Introduction: Current issues and key problems. In N. E. Miller, T. X. Barber, L. DiCara, J. Kamiya, D. Shapiro, & J. Stoyva (Eds.), *Biofeedback and self-control, 1973*. Chicago: Aldine Publ., 1974. Pp. xi–xx.

Miller, S., & Konorski, J. Sur une forme particuliere des reflexes conditionnels. *Compte Rendu Hebdomadaire des Séances et Mémoires de la Societé de Biologie*, 1928, **99**, 1155–1157.

Mowrer, O. H. On the dual nature of learning—a re-interpretation of "conditioning" and "problem-solving." *Harvard Educational Review*, 1947, **17**, 102–148.

Pavlov, I. P. *Lectures on conditioned reflexes. Vol. 2: Conditioned reflexes and psychiatry*. (Translated by W. H. Gantt.) New York: International Publ., 1941.

Peterson, G. B., Ackil, J., Frommer, G. P., & Hearst, E. Conditioned approach and contact behavior toward signals for food or brain-stimulation reinforcement. *Science*, 1972, **77**, 1009–1011.

Razran, G. Avoidant vs. unavoidant conditioning and partial reinforcement in Russian laboratories. *American Journal of Psychology*, 1956, **69**, 127–129.

Rescorla, R. A., & Solomon, R. L. Two-process learning theory: Relationships between Pavlovian conditioning and instrumental learning. *Psychological Review*, 1967, **74**, 151–182.

Schlosberg, H. The relationship between success and the laws of conditioning. *Psychological Review*, 1937, **44**, 379–392.

Schwartz, G. E., Shapiro, D., & Tursky, B. Learned control of cardiovascular integration in man through operant conditioning. *Psychosomatic Medicine*, 1971, **33**, 57–62.

Sechenov, I. M. *Reflexes of the brain.* (Translated by S. Belsky.) Cambridge, Massachusetts: MIT Press, 1965 (Originally published 1863).

Segal, E. F. Induction and the provenance of operants. In R. M. Gilbert & J. R. Millenson (Eds.), *Reinforcement: Behavioral analysis.* New York: Academic Press, 1972. Pp. 1–34.

Seligman, M. E. P., & Hager, J. L. *Biological boundaries of learning.* New York: Appleton-Century-Crofts, 1972.

Seligman, M. E. P., Maier, S. F., & Solomon, R. L. Unpredictable and uncontrollable aversive events. In F. R. Brush (Ed.), *Aversive conditioning and learning.* New York: Academic Press, 1971. Pp. 347–400.

Sevenster, P. Incompatibility of response and reward. In R. A. Hinde & J. S. Hinde (Eds.), *Constraints on learning.* New York: Academic Press, 1973. Pp. 265–283.

Seward, J. P. Conditioning theory. In M. Marx (Ed.), *Learning: Theories.* New York: Macmillan, 1970. Pp. 49–117.

Sheffield, F. D. Relation between classical conditioning and instrumental learning. In W. F. Prokasy (Ed.), *Classical conditioning.* New York: Appleton-Century-Crofts, 1965. Pp. 302–322.

Shettleworth, S. J. Constraints on learning. In D. S. Lehrman, R. A. Hinde, & E. Shaw (Eds.), *Advances in the study of behavior.* Vol. 4. New York: Academic Press, 1972. Pp. 1–68.

Skinner, B. F. The generic nature of the concepts of stimulus and response. *Journal of General Psychology*, 1935, **12**, 40–65. (a)

Skinner, B. F. Two types of conditioned reflex and a pseudo-type. *Journal of General Psychology*, 1935, **12**, 66–77. (b)

Skinner, B. F. Two types of conditioned reflex: A reply to Konorski and Miller. *Journal of General Psychology*, 1937, **16**, 272–279.

Skinner, B. F. *The behavior of organisms.* New York: Appleton-Century-Crofts, 1938.

Skinner, B. F. 'Superstition" in the pigeon. *Journal of Experimental Psychology*, 1948, **38**, 168–172.

Skinner, B. F. *Science and human behavior.* New York: Macmillan Co., 1953.

Skinner, B. F. *About behaviorism.* New York: Alfred Knopf, 1974.

Wagner, A. R., Thomas, E., & Norton, T. Conditioning with electrical stimulation of motor cortex: Evidence of a possible source of motivation. *Journal of Comparative & Physiological Psychology*, 1967, **64**, 191–199.

Watson, J. B. The heart or the intellect? *Harper's Monthly Magazine*, 1928, **156**, 345–353.

Williams, D. R., & Williams, H. Auto-maintenance in the pigeon: Sustained pecking despite contingent nonreinforcement. *Journal of the Experimental Analysis of Behavior*, 1969, **12**, 511–520.

Woods, P. J. A taxonomy of instrumental conditioning. *American Psychologist*, 1974, **29**, 584–597.

6

Perspectives on the Behavioral Unit: Choice Behavior in Animals

Charles P. Shimp

University of Utah

I. DECISION MAKING AND CONSERVATIVE BEHAVIORISM

The experimental analysis of choice behavior in animals is rewarding to theorists and behavioral engineers alike. Nowhere else in the behavioral sciences is there a better-developed methodology for predicting and controlling with mathematical precision the behavior of an individual organism. This methodology is descended from the schedules of reinforcement developed by B. F. Skinner in the 1930s. Skinner's positions remain highly influential in the area, but new methods and data are challenging nearly all of the traditional theoretical and methodological assumptions in the laboratory basis for Skinner's radical behaviorism. Because of the traditional preference in this area for inductive research, Estes (1962) was able correctly to write of it that "theoretical publication has been largely confined to criticism of other approaches [p. 108]." The antitheoretical position began quickly to fade, however, after workers in the area began to obtain empirical results susceptible to a mathematically elegant description. New theories, especially simple algebraic theories dealing with a small set of phenomena of a special type, are now appearing in this area about as quickly as quantitative models have for 20 years elsewhere in experimental psychology.

In this chapter, is described part of the area known as the analysis of "schedules of reinforcement," with an emphasis on results that inspire the urge to theorize. There has been no effort to make the area appear more unified than it really is. In fact, there has been a deliberate effort to describe puzzling complexities and opposing viewpoints, in order to focus attention on points where progress seems needed. Space limitations have, of course, ensured a selective rather than exhaustive discussion. In particular, of all possible species, here the data come exclusively from pigeons. Of all possible combinations of reinforcers and motivational states, the data are only for mixed grain given to organisms deprived to 80% of their free-feeding weights. Before the reader turns from this chapter in dismay at its limited generality, let him be assured that the author duly acknowledges, in all humility, just how severe these limitations are. However, while the data certainly are not sufficient to characterize a general theory of behavior, they do raise many issues with which a general theory must come to grips.

To understand the contemporary analysis of choice behavior in animals one must have some understanding of the behavior of scientists studying choice behavior in animals. The behavior of these scientists tends to depend on a few assumptions about science in general and about a science of behavior in particular. Unfortunately, some of these theoretical assumptions are covert (Rozeboom, 1974). Thus, our first task is to uncover these assumptions and to state them explicitly so that they may be evaluated and contrasted with alternative assumptions.

An assumption held in the highest regard is that a good psychological explanation shows how to control some feature of an individual organism's behavior: the highest premium is put on the effective control of observable behavior. Explanations therefore tend to involve experimental methods by means of which some feature of behavior may be varied; the more precise the control, the better is the explanation. This assumption historically has been associated with, but is logically independent of, a radical, behavioristic reaction against psychological explanations in terms of unobservable, hypothetical events and processes. Skinner's arguments that theoretical quantities should be observable are well known (Skinner, 1950), and his arguments have had immeasurable impact on the behavior of scientists in the area. This writer should acknowledge his skepticism regarding these arguments. He finds it difficult to understand why all theoretical quantities must be observable in the behavioral sciences when they are not in the physical sciences (Einstein, 1973). But, one need not rest with appeals to authority. More important, the data reviewed below have refused to succumb to theoretical analysis in terms of purely observable events and processes. The criterion of observability seems so wholesome, so entirely benevolent, that this turn of events may be surprising to some. But the criterion of observability turns out to have remarkably specific implications for the interpretation of choice behavior and decision making. Some of these implications seem incorrect in at least some contexts. Fortunately, the influence of the strictest interpretation of the criterion of observability seems generally to be waning, even within the most conservative reaches of behaviorism (see Section V.A). Let us examine some of the implications that follow from an insistence that legitimate theoretical quantities must be observable.

A. The Law of Effect

When one studies schedules of reinforcement, one studies behavior that is under the control of its consequences. This is simply a truth about the methodology: one sets up a rule that prescribes the way the delivery of a reinforcer is contingent upon behavior. One then sees what behavior is established and maintained by this rule, that is, the schedule of reinforcement. This truth by itself states little or nothing about why a given schedule of reinforcement generates a particular behavior. The statement, being purely methodological, provides no general concepts from which the effects of a given schedule may be derived. The Law of Effect, during the formative stage of this research area, was given the task of providing the central concepts regarding the role of reinforcement. The Law of Effect admirably satisfied the criterion of observability that has been so influential in guiding theoretical research in this area. The Law of Effect, in its simplest version, may be said to consist of two components: (a) the delivery of a reinforcer after a response directly increases the subsequent frequency of that response; (b) the response, called an operant, which is strengthened, and learned, is the behavior temporally contiguous with the delivery of the reinforcer. Thorndike (1931), Skinner (1938), Estes (1950), and many others, developed theories incorporating these two components of the Law of Effect. Observe that this account of the effect of reinforcement equates what is learned with what an organism is seen to do at the moment a reinforcer is delivered: it equates learning and performance. Accordingly, "learning," as distinct from changes in the frequency of occurrence of the behavioral unit, or operant, becomes superfluous (Skinner, 1950).

Each component of the Law of Effect has been largely abandoned outside the borders of radical behaviorism. Thus, these two components are mostly of historical interest to most experimental psychologists. However, as described in Section I.B, they still play commanding roles in the analysis of operant behavior by virtue of their influence during the birth of what are to this day the standard experimental paradigms and methods of data analysis.

B. The Behavioral Unit and the Fundamental Datum

According to the Law of Effect, the behavioral unit, or operant, is the behavior one can see an organism performing when the reinforcer is delivered. This behavioral unit satisfies both components of the Law of Effect;

it is temporally contiguous with the reinforcer, and it is observable. The pigeon's key-pecking response, with which we are concerned here, admirably suits the Law of Effect. So, of course, does the rat's lever-pressing response. The experimental analysis of behavior rests to a remarkable degree on the rather ephemeral foundation provided by these virtually instantaneous behaviors. It does so in large part because of an interdependence between the temporal-contiguity component of the Law of Effect and the procedures developed in the 1930s. These two separate issues, the theoretical issue of temporal contiguity and the methodological paradigms that determine the data, have been locked together so that they correlate almost perfectly.

Standard paradigms make the delivery of a reinforcer contingent upon the occurrence of an essentially instantaneous response that is temporally contiguous with the delivery of the reinforcer. The rule describing the contingency between behavior and its consequences, that is, the schedule of reinforcement, is arranged in terms of the behavior that the temporal-contiguity component of the Law of Effect specifies as the behavioral unit. Contingency and contiguity are confounded.

We have now seen three properties of the key-peck response that induce us to accept it as the behavioral unit in terms of which data should be expressed: (a) it satisfies the observability criterion associated with the Law of Effect; (b) it satisfies the temporal-contiguity component of the Law of Effect; and (c) it is by convention the behavior upon which the delivery of a reinforcer is contingent. Let us then momentarily adopt the key peck as the behavioral unit, and ask what dependent variable may constructively be based upon it. If one allowed a key peck to occur at any moment, perhaps the simplest datum one could image would be the frequency of occurrence of the key peck over a period of time sufficiently long to give a reliable estimate of its long-term mean rate of occurrence. This dependent variable, mean rate of occurrence of an essentially instantaneous response, is widely held to be the fundamental datum in the experimental analysis of behavior. Originally, it was regarded as an estimate of response probability (Skinner, 1938), but more recently it is viewed simply to be the appropriate datum in its own right (Skinner, 1966). It comes close to being the defining property of the experimental analysis of behavior (Blough & Millward, 1965). It surely is the most widely used dependent variable: most issues of the *Journal of the Experimental Analysis of Behavior* contain more than twice as many articles reporting mean response rate as those reporting all other dependent variables combined.

The observability criterion, response-reinforcer contiguity, the assumption that essentially instantaneous responses are meaningful behavioral units, the methodological confounding of contiguity and contingency, and the use of mean response rate; together, these decades-old methods and theoretical assumptions characterize much of the experimental analysis of

behavior to this day. The implications of this collection of views for decision making are immediate and specific. According to these views, a decision
is an observable behavior: we should be able to look into the experimental
chamber and to see it occur. If one sees a pigeon peck, then it chose to
peck. If one sees it not peck, then it chose not to peck. The reader will
note that this decision-making interpretation adds nothing whatever to the
observed fact that the subject sometimes pecks and sometimes does not.
And in this lies one of the crowning achievements of radical behaviorism:
the proof that, for all intents and practical purposes, decision making does
not exist.

There is, however, one unsettling possibility. This demonstration that
the notion of decision making is unnecessary required some assumptions
about the importance of observability, temporal contiguity, the nature of
the behavioral unit, and the like. What if one or more of these assumptions
is wrong? The implications of this possibility will be considered in some
ddetail, for, as Sections II, III, and IV show, there are cogent reasons
to doubt each of the assumptions of conservative behaviorism.

II. DECISION MAKING AND LIBERAL BEHAVIORISM

We have seen that response-reinforcer temporal contiguity is a component
of the Law of Effect, is built into standard schedules of reinforcement,
and is a justification for the belief that behavioral units are instantaneous.
What if response-reinforcer temporal contiguity were not necessary for
learning to occur? What if a subject could remember details both of its
preceding environment and of its preceding behavior? What if a reinforcer's
effects were determined in part by a subject's memories for these things?
Before one can meaningfully explore the answer to this latter question,
one must first inquire into the extent to which a pigeon can remember
recent events. Thus, we must now look into the literature on short-term
memory in the pigeon. A fundamental assumption throughout this brief review of work on memory in the pigeon is that there is a positive virtue
in providing an alternative to the temporal-contiguity component of the
Law of Effect and its corollary (see Section II.A.1 below), "mediating
chains," in that a theory may sometimes be more constructively evaluated
by means of comparison with another theory than by comparison with an
arbitrary, absolute standard.

A. Short-Term Memory

Most experiments on short-term memory in pigeons use one of three procedures, a delayed matching-to-sample procedure, a delayed pair-comparison

procedure, or a probe technique in which a subject is presented with a list of items one of which it later is asked to remember. Each of these procedures is described in turn.

1. Delayed Matching-to-Sample Paradigms

In this procedure, a subject is presented with a stimulus, often one randomly selected from a set of two. This stimulus is then removed, and the subject is required to wait through a period after which the original stimulus and some other stimulus are presented simultaneously on different keys. The task requires the subject to peck the key with the stimulus that is the same as the original stimulus. It is found that correct performance in this task drops sharply as the delay increases. Smith (1967) found that the probability of a correct response after a delay of 1 sec ranged over three pigeons from about .75 to .90 and decreased on the average to about .60 to .65 after a delay of 5 sec. What do these results mean? They mean different things depending on whom one asks. Let us first consider an interpretation in terms of memory. Smith's results, as well as more recent results (Grant & Roberts, 1973; Roberts, 1972; Zentall, 1973), may be conceptually integrated by means of an assumption that a nonassociative short-term memory for the sample stimulus decays over time and that the decay rate is a function of interfering stimuli present during the delay.

Even the earliest radical behaviorists rejected this kind of memory interpretation because it admits theoretical quantities not directly observed (Watson, 1924). At the present time, Skinner continues to reject it for the same reason. An experiment by Blough (1959) nicely illustrates an alternative interpretation designed to preserve the observability and temporal-contiguity components of radical behaviorism.

Blough in some instances observed a subject engage during the delay in one behavior after one sample stimulus and in another behavior after another sample stimulus. The probability of a correct response tends in such cases to be higher than otherwise. For example, Blough (1959) in one case observed nearly perfect performance after a 10-sec delay. The Law of Effect can "explain" this result without any appeal to unobservable memory processes. It is assumed that these behaviors are stimulus–response chains the properties of which conform to the Law of Effect: each link in the chain is assumed to consist of observable behavior, to provide conditioned reinforcement for the previous link, and to set the occasion for the next link. Such a chain would "mediate" the delay via a sequence of behaviors both observable and satisfying the temporal-contiguity requirement. This view appears to have been implicit in much of the thinking about delayed matching-to-sample research. However, the demonstration that mediating chains sometimes seem to appear is quite different from showing that they always appear. There are cases, even in Blough's experiment, in which no mediating chain is detected. Thus, the position of the mediating-chain notion presently is analogous to the position at an earlier time of Watson's (1924) idea that thought may be viewed as subvocal speech: investigators were able to find subvocal speech in some cases but not in all cases. The idea therefore fell into disuse: the idea that only observable behavior is permissible as a theoretical quantity in a science of behavior was not satisfactorily supported by subvocal speech that only occasionally could be observed. Similarly, the mediating-chain idea fails to serve its intended purpose, which is to insure that all theoretical quantities are always directly observable. Note also that the raison d'être of the mediating-chain concept is removed if for any reason at all one abandons the temporal-contiguity component of the Law of Effect.

2. Delayed Pair-Comparison Paradigms

The psychophysical method of pair comparisons has been used constructively in the analysis of perceptual short-term memory in humans (Massaro, 1970) and in pigeons (Moffitt, 1972). As this method is applied with pigeons, the animal is briefly presented on each of a series of trials with a visual stimulus in the study phase, and then, after a retention interval, is presented with a second stimulus in the test phase. Depending on whether the stimuli in the study and test phases of a trial are the same or different, the subject is to peck a left key or right key, respectively. Moffitt (1972) found that the probability of a correct response was about .9 after 1-sec retention intervals and was still slightly above chance after 16 sec, provided that the chamber was dark during the retention interval. The probability of remembering the study-phase stimulus was less if visual material was presented between study and test. Similarly, subsequent experiments in the writer's laboratory have degraded performance by visual stimuli presented in advance of a study phase.

3. A "Probe" Paradigm

The procedures described in the two preceding sections provide information about short-term memory for visual stimuli. A probe technique has extended data on short-term memory in the pigeon to a broader category of remembered events: stimulus–response associations (Shimp & Moffitt, 1974) and judgments of temporal order. The latter judgments seem fundamental to the development of any general theory of memory (Estes, 1973; Tulving & Madigan, 1970). The paradigm used to obtain them was as follows. In each of a sequence of discrete trials, a study phase was separated from a test phase by a retention interval during which the three-key experimental chamber was darkened. The study phase consisted of three successive left- or right-key pecks. First, one key would be illuminated and the subject would be required to peck it. The peck would turn that key light off; then .1 sec later, a second (perhaps the same) key would be illuminated; and so on. The presentation of the entire "list" of three pecks to lighted keys consumed roughly 2 sec. Over trials, all eight possible lists appeared: left, left, left; left, left, right; . . . ; right, right, right. During the study phase, whenever a side key was illuminated, a dim, white "×" appeared on it. Also the center key was always dark during the study phase. The test phase of a trial began with the illumination of the center key by one of three colors: red, blue, or white. A peck on the center key then turned the light off and turned on both side keys with the same color that had been on the center key. Red side keys meant "Remember the first side key that was lighted and pecked in the study phase of this trial and now peck that key." Blue side keys meant "Remember the second side key pecked in the study phase and now peck that key." White meant "Peck the third, or most recently pecked, side key." That is, in the test phase, a reinforcer was presented if a subject pecked the side key that had appeared originally in the study phase in the ordinal position corresponding to the test-phase color. A recency effect was obtained: the probability of correctly recalling an item was directly correlated with its position in the list: the probability was highest for the most recent and lowest for the least recent item. But even the least recent item was recalled better with a retention interval of 4 sec than would be expected by chance. Thus, one may probe a pigeon's short-term memory and find that the pigeon can remember at least part of the temporal organization of recent events. Alternatively, one might wish to say that a pigeon can establish a different mediating chain for each of the eight study-phase lists. The latter interpretation, one that a theorist might prefer if he wished to retain the temporal-contiguity component of the Law of Effect, seems to this writer to suffer the handicap of a complexity perhaps as great as that of the phenomenon it is designed to explain: there are no data indicating that eight such chains can be established and maintained under the conditions required here.

B.   Short-Term Memory and the Law of Effect

The short-term memory data reviewed above suggest an alternative to the temporal-contiguity component of the Law of Effect. Short-term memory might interact with reinforcing events in at least two ways. First, short-term memory for recent events, especially for a subject's own behavior, could expand the time frame over which a reinforcer might directly affect behavior: a reinforcer might strengthen the behavior a subject remembers

having recently emitted, rather than only the behavior temporally contiguous with the reinforcer. This possibility is elaborated in Section I.C.1,
where it is described as a potential mechanism for the establishment of
organized behavioral patterns functioning as integrated behavioral units.
Second, short-term memory for recent events could form part of the
functional stimulus in the "presence" of which a subject chooses among
behavioral units. This possibility offers a mechanism by means of which recent events could provide the stimulus basis for differential reinforcement
of sequences of behavioral units.

C. Organization in Long-Term Memory, the Behavioral Unit, and the Fundamental Datum

We have raised the possibility that the delivery of a reinforcer may affect
more than the behavior that is both temporally contiguous with it and observable to us. More specifically, we have suggested a reinforcer might
affect the behavior that subject remembers having recently emitted. If the
remembered behavior and the actually emitted behavior are different, reinforcement might more plausibly affect what a subject remembers of its
previous behavior than the behavior itself.

1. Organization in Memory and the Behavioral Unit

We have seen that radical behaviorism focuses on the rate of occurrence
of a simple, instantaneous response that is contiguous with a reinforcing
stimulus. This focus reveals an inheritance from associationism. From Ari-
stotle to this day, the main variables responsible for determining the
strength of an association between two events have been assumed to be
the extent to which they are temporally contiguous and the frequency or
rate with which they are repeated together. For approximately a hundred
years, association theorists have been measuring the strengths of associations by counting the frequency of occurrence of the simplest responses
they could invent or find, ranging from recall of nonsense syllables (Ebbinghaus, 1885) to pigeon's key pecks (Herrnstein, 1970).

Students of human memory have suggested that the familiar tools of
association theory fail to attack fundamental issues, such as that of organization in memory. Miller (1967), Tulving (1962), and many others, have
suggested that the effects of the repetition of to-be-remembered material
is not summarized by noting that the frequency of simple responses increases with greater repetition. Instead, they interpret this increase in frequency as a by-product of a more fundamental process, the establishment

with repetition of a new structure in memory, that is, an organization of the material into new, higher-order functional units. These new response units consist of clusters of the simple responses that are taken as the functional response units by classical association theory.

Let us suppose that the repeated delivery of a reinforcer after the same remembered pattern of behavior can establish that pattern as an organized "chunk" of behavior in long-term memory (Miller, 1956; Tulving, 1962). One property of an integrated chunk of behavior is that it would function as a unit. Thus, the memory literature provides an alternative definition of a behavioral unit or operant. According to this view, the behavioral unit is not necessarily the behavior contiguous with reinforcement, except when that is the only behavior a subject remembers. Neither is the behavioral unit necessarily the behavior on which reinforcement is contingent, unless that behavior also happens to be the same as that which the subject remembers when the reinforcer is delivered.

When more than one behavioral pattern frequently precedes the delivery of a reinforcer, one could expect the establishment of corresponding behavioral units. It will be especially important in subsequent sections (IV.A and B) to consider the situation in which different behavioral units terminate with the same response topography, such as a key peck. In such a case, a subject would be confronted with a choice among these different reinforced behavioral patterns functioning as behavioral units. In contrast, observe that in terms of the Law of Effect, the delivery of a reinforcer would establish only a single behavioral unit, unless one appealed to hypothetical mediating chains, because all of the patterns preceding reinforcement terminate in the same behavior that is contiguous with reinforcement.

2. The Fundamental Datum

We have seen that the fundamental datum is, according to radical behaviorism, the mean rate of occurrence of a simple response. But if one fails to accept the assumptions of radical behaviorism, then the fundamental datum consists simply of a sequence of behavioral units from an individual organism. The sequence of behavioral units ultimately is that which should be controlled and understood. If one understood the sequential structure of an individual subject's protocol, one could derive gross features of the data such as the total number of responses, the overall percentage of choices of a particular behavioral unit, or the percentage of time allocated to a particular unit.

Decision making is not trivial if behavioral patterns function as behavioral units. In such a case it would be likely that we could not always identify the most recent decisions by observing the organism. In the following sections instances are given in which the decision between behavioral units at any given moment is ambiguous to an external observer. Thus, there no longer is a one-to-one correspondence between behavior at each moment and decisions. Abandonment of response-reinforcer contiguity implies that decisions are not always observable at the moment at which they occur.

Outlines now have been presented of two radically different theoretical views differing in terms of the importance of observability, response-reinforcer temporal contiguity, the nature of the behavioral unit, and the fundamental datum. The reader now has been given a theoretical perspective sufficient for progress to the description of methods and data in the analysis of choice behavior of animals.

III. CHOICE BEHAVIOR: DATA FROM DISCRETE-TRIALS PARADIGMS

The behavior of an organism seldom if ever can be described in terms of a single behavioral unit. Even the simplest environments where there is only a single key to peck or lever to press are now widely assumed to involve choice, although there is little or no agreement on what it is that is chosen or when a subject chooses (Herrnstein, 1970; Rachlin, 1973; Shimp, 1969a). There is no theory sufficient to guide this discussion, so we resort to a methodological categorization of data. The two major methodological categories are discrete-trials paradigms and free-operant paradigms.

In a discrete-trials procedure, a subject's opportunity to engage in a behavior that can lead to a reinforcer is limited to certain periods of time, either by brute force or by more subtle means. In the former case, the "operanda" are only presented occasionally. In the latter, the operanda are always available, but a subject is taught that a reinforcer is available only at specific times or in the presence of certain stimuli. There may be little or no difference between the latter situation and that prevailing in free-operant procedures in which a subject can emit an instantaneous response such as a key peck at any time. The free operant seems to depend on the existence of an instantaneous behavioral unit. As is suggested with the following material, there is grave doubt that behavioral units in standard free-operant situations are in fact instantaneous, as traditionally imagined to be. The determination of the behavioral unit or units and the correct interpretation of free responding in terms of decision making and response strategies is essential for a unification of discrete-trials and free-operant paradigms in terms of common behavioral processes.

A discrete-trials procedure that is particularly useful in the analysis of choice behavior is one in which a pigeon is occasionally presented with two lighted keys, a peck on one of which will deliver a reinforcer with some probability. It is easy and useful to vary this probability of reinforcement. Any respectable theory, it has long seemed, should predict the percentage of choices of a given key as a function of the percentage of reinforcements for responses to that key. Some special cases of this probabilistic-reinforcement paradigm will be discussed in a sequence of increasing complexity.

A. Reinforcement Arranged on Every Trial

The basic discrete-trials procedure is quite simple. At the beginning of each trial a pigeon confronts two lighted keys. A peck on a key for which reinforcement has been arranged delivers a food hopper for a brief duration and then initiates an intertrial interval during which the experimental chamber is usually darkened. In contrast, a peck on a key for which reinforcement has not been arranged either ends the trial and directly initiates the intertrial interval (if a "noncorrection procedure" is used) or initiates a "correction interval" at the end of which the same trial is repeated, and so on until a correct response occurs and is reinforced (if a "correction procedure" is used). An experimental session usually consists of as many such trials as may be delivered without introducing contaminating effects such as satiation.

In the simplest case, reinforcement is available on every trial for a probabilistically selected one of two alternatives. Whether a reinforcement is, in fact, delivered on every trial depends on whether or not a "correction procedure" is used. If there is no correction procedure, a reinforcer is delivered on a trial only if the subject chooses the alternative to which reinforcement is arranged. Without a correction procedure, a subject tends ultimately to respond very nearly exclusively to one alternative, almost always to the alternative which over trials is more frequently reinforced (Bullock & Bitterman, 1962; Graf, Bullock, & Bitterman, 1964). Occasionally a subject is seen always to choose the other, poorer alternative. The noncorrection procedure does not ensure that a subject is provided information about the way in which arranged reinforcements are distributed across left and right keys. This failure of the noncorrection procedure to control the way in which reinforcements are actually distributed over the two alternatives has encouraged experimenters to use a correction procedure that ensures on each trial that the reinforcer arranged is collected: by any of a number of means, a trial is continued until a response to the "correct" alternative occurs and is reinforced. Under most conditions that have been employed, the "choice" response must be carefully distinguished from subsequent responses under control of the correction procedure. That is, the first response in a trial, the choice response, is controlled by one set of parameters, and the subsequent correction response, or responses, is controlled by a different set. Adding the two classes of responses together is therefore rather like adding together apples and oranges, and is only rarely done (but see Herrnstein, 1970). The following discussion applies exclusively to choice responses obtained when a correction procedure is used.

1. Constant Probability of Reinforcement

This special case is commonly called a "probability-learning" procedure (Estes, 1964, 1972). In comparison with the voluminous literature on probability learning in humans, scarcely anything is known about it in pigeons. Especially little is known about acquisition. Admittedly, acquisition is quite difficult to analyze, since innumerable variables associated with pretraining, including how a pigeon is taught to eat from a food hopper and to peck the keys, no doubt influence early performance. Investigations therefore have tended to concentrate on steady-state performance, which probably can be assumed to obtain, when a correction procedure is used, after a few thousand trials (Graf et al., 1964; Shimp, 1966, 1973a). Steady-state behavior may be reached somewhat earlier with noncorrection procedures (Graf et al., 1964).

Interest in this steady-state performance has focused on the percentage of trials when a subject chooses a particular alternative, and to a much lesser extent on a few simple sequential statistics. A number of theories make different predictions for the preference function relating percentage choice to percentage reinforcement. Two predictions of great historical importance are matching and maximizing. Matching is said to obtain when the percentage of trials on which a subject chooses a given alternative approximately equals the percentage of trials when food is delivered for that alternative. Maximizing is said to obtain when a subject nearly exclusively chooses the alternative with the higher reinforcement probability.

Matching was at one time of great interest because of its prediction by certain linear models (Estes, 1964) and maximizing was of interest because of its prediction from the age-old view that behavior is adaptive, rational, and optimal. Neither of these theoretical predictions is accurate in the present context. Actual data tend to lie somewhere in between: the choice of the "better" alternative tends to deviate from the matching value in the direction of, but sometimes not very far in the direction of, maximizing (Graf et al., 1964; Hale & Shimp, 1975; Shimp, 1966, 1973a). No great imagination is required to realize that the extent of the deviation depends on many variables. One important variable is the extent to which a subject attends to the cues correlated with different reinforcement probabilities: inattentiveness generally will tend to drive performance away from maximizing (Mackintosh, 1969). Lack of attention does not seem to be the whole story, however, since conditions in which stimulus control should be good still do not produce maximizing (Shimp, 1966), and conditions across which stimulus control presumably varies produce similar deviations from maximizing (Shimp, 1966, 1973a).

The term "steady-state performance" does not mean that performance does not vary from trial to trial. It is a sad commentary on the crudity of most data analyses in this area that sequential properties of steady-state behavior in pigeons are nearly lacking entirely, despite the clear trend in the corresponding human literature to focus on sequential statistics as a source of information on fundamental processes (Anderson, 1964; Myers, 1970; Restle, 1961). The lack of sequential data is less a testimony to their lack of value than to the power of theoretical preconceptions in favor of molar data analyses to determine the behavior of behavioral scientists working in this area. The little numerical evidence that is available suggests the presence of response perseveration and positive recency (Shimp, 1966). That is, the probability of choosing an alternative is greater if that alternative was chosen on the previous trial, and also is greater if that alternative was reinforced on the previous trial.

2. Variable Probability of Reinforcement

The molar perspective of conservative behaviorism may well have retarded the analysis of schedules in which the reinforcement probability for an alternative varies over trials according to some simple rule: such schedules require an analysis of sequential statistics foreign to the molar approach of conservative behaviorism. However, even the correction component of the procedures already described is an instance in which local reinforcement probability varies, and the correction procedure generates what may be viewed as a simple response strategy, a lose–shift strategy. The correction procedure provides that the probability of reinforcement for one response is unity after a nonreinforced response to the other alternative, regardless of the probability of reinforcement for choice responses. The correction procedure as often arranged requires a subject to remember its last response if it was unreinforced.

Williams (1972) investigated the conditions under which a win–stay, lose–shift strategy could be established. The lose–shift component corresponded to the strategy generated by a correction procedure: after a nonreinforced response, the probability of reinforcement for the other response was one. The win–stay response component was reinforced only probabilistically, rather than deterministically. As one would therefore expect, the lose–shift component was learned more readily than the win–stay component. It was also found that requiring a subject to emit more responses to an alternative on a trial assisted the learning of a response strategy, as it should have, because this requirement lengthened the presentation time of a to-be-remembered cue. Presumably, a subject can better remember its response on the previous trial if it is required to emit that response several times.

The way in which a win–stay response strategy is dependent upon memory for the previous response is illustrated further by an experiment conducted in the writer's laboratory. In this experiment, a trial began with the illumination of left and right keys. The probability of reinforcement for a peck on the left key depended on which response was reinforced on the previous trial. If the left response had been reinforced, left and right responses had reinforcement probabilities of .8 and .2, respectively. If the right response had been reinforced, left and right responses had reinforcement probabilities of .2 and .8, respectively. Thus, the probability of reinforcement for the win–stay strategy was .8, and that for the lose–shift component was .2. A within-trial correction procedure ensured that each trial ended with a reinforced response. The probability of choosing a key depended on the intertrial interval, which may be viewed as a retention interval during which the subject was to remember the response reinforced on the previous trial. The probabilities of choosing the left key, averaged over 13 pigeons, were .94, .85, and .74, for .5-, 2.0-, and 4.0-sec retention intervals, respectively. To the extent to which a subject could remember the relevant cue, that is, the response reinforced on the previous trial, choice behavior was highly adaptive and, for retention intervals less than 2 sec, choice probability deviated from matching in the direction of maximizing. It will be observed that no one function relating overall percent choice and percent reinforcement can accommodate even the simplest facts about response strategies in pigeons.

B. Intermittent Reinforcement

The analysis of choice behavior is much more difficult when reinforcement on some trials is not arranged for a response on either alternative and reinforcement probability varies as a function of the behavior of an organism. Indeed, the analysis is so difficult that there is no general agreement about the nature of the independent and dependent variables. One view holds that fundamental processes are revealed by the relationship between the percentages of choices of an alternative and of reinforcements for that alternative. This view, a molar view, denies any importance to local effects (Herrnstein, 1961, 1970). A second view holds that choice probability is sensitive to local changes in reinforcement probability. According to this view, the overall percentage choice of an alternative is an average over different behaviors controlled by different contingencies, and adding the different behaviors has no meaning. Experimenters with response-strategy views typically subscribe to the latter position (Shimp, 1969a).

Consider in detail one version of the commonest intermittent reinforcement paradigm. This schedule is particularly instructive because it illustrates how the value of an experimental paradigm depends on one's theoretical views. Here, results appear simple and meaningful from a molar viewpoint based on conservative behaviorism. The simplicity of the molar data encourages the belief not only that the molar view is the correct view but also that the schedule is of great analytical value in the development of a science of behavior. In contrast, the results appear complex and even uninterpretable from a molecular view based on considerations interrelating short-term memory and reinforcement. From this viewpoint, the schedule has analytical value only insofar as it directs us to thinking about alternative schedules by means of which one could uncover the simple, fundamental relations at the molecular level. In the particular discrete-trials schedule now under consideration, there is a constant probability that a reinforcement is arranged on a trial. Once arranged, a reinforcement is held until collected and no more can be arranged until it is collected. When a reinforcement is arranged, it is assigned with a constant probability to a given alternative, with the complementary probability to the other alternative. This procedure has the property that the probability of reinforcement for the choice of an alternative increases as a subject successively chooses the other alternative and is not rewarded. Nonreinforcement of an alternative implies either that reinforcement was not arranged at all, or that it was arranged for the other response. The latter event has a relatively increasing probability as a subject successively chooses an alternative and is not rewarded. The reader may be asking why anyone would wish to use such a complicated procedure. The answer certainly is not that it gives ready answers to important questions, because we have noted already that there is no general agreement about even the appropriate independent and dependent variables. The answer is twofold. First, the procedure closely resembles that of an even-more-complicated but standard free-operant paradigm. That is, the method, complicated as it is, is yet a simplification of a widely used paradigm, the concurrent variable-interval variable-interval schedule (see Section IV.B). Second, as noted previously, the results are wonderfully simple at a molar level of analysis. The steady-state matching result that elsewhere is so elusive with discrete trials paradigms is obtained consistently: the percentage of pecks on a key closely approximates the percentage of reinforcements for that key (Nevin, 1969; Experiment III in Shimp, 1966). The very existence of this elegant relationship at the molar level supports the molar view holding that this relationship is a preference function measuring the value of an alternative as a function of the percentage of reinforcements associated with it (Herrnstein, 1970)

An alternative view holds that this matching is an unimportant by-product of behavioral control by local processes (Shimp, 1966, 1969a;

Silberberg & Williams, 1974). This view requires one to look for sensitivity of choice to local changes in reinforcement probability and then to derive the molar matching relation from these local processes. As a start, Shimp (1966) found that obtained sequential statistics roughly approximated those expected if behavior conformed to an optimal strategy in which each response was made to the alternative having at the moment the greater probability of reinforcement. Consider the specific example in which reinforcement is arranged with probability of .25 and in which 75% of the reinforcements are arranged for a peck on the left key. Recall that once arranged, a reinforcement is held until collected and once a reinforcement is arranged for a peck on one key, no more can be arranged for pecks on either key until the previously arranged one is collected. In this case, the optimal strategy is to peck left, left, right, left, left, right, ... That is, after two successive unreinforced left-key pecks, the local probability of reinforcement is higher on the right than on the left. Observe that this optimal strategy depends only on programmed reinforcement probability and therefore can be calculated in advance of an experiment. Behavior was seen to approximate this optimal strategy. What does this strategy predict for the molar outcome? What should be the overall percent of pecks on the left key? Within a single sequence, the fraction of left-key pecks is two-thirds, but reinforcement is more likely after some run lenghts than after others. When this is taken into account, one finds that the predicted overall percentage of pecks on the left key is about .75, which is the percentage of reinforcements on the left key: the optimal response strategy predicts an approximation to the matching that was observed at the molar level, More generally, local changes in choice probability were shown in this experiment to depend on local changes in reinforcement probability even if not quite to the extent required by perfect maximizing. This result is in line with the discrete-trials results described earlier, but quite at odds with a molar view.

The optimal strategy discussed thus far defines the optimal response at a moment to be that response for which the reinforcement probability is greater at that moment, with reinforcement probability for a response in turn meaning the long-term average number of reinforcements expected for a large number of occurrences of that response. But what if the response does not occur? Let us take the following extreme example to illustrate the point. Suppose a subject invariably switches to the right only after two successive nonreinforced responses on the left. Such a subject would be exposed only to the contingencies for this response sequence. In particular, it never would be reinforced for a switch to the right except after two left responses: all of the reinforced right responses would be preceded by exactly two left responses. The general problem, one that makes this procedure difficult to analyze, is that the point at which a subject is rewarded for switching from one key to another depends on the point at which it *does* switch. Recall that a dependency between percentage pecks on a key and percentage reinforcements on that key led to the adoption in discrete-trials probability-learning experiments of a correction procedure by means of which an experimenter can control the percentage of reinforcements on a key (see Section III.A.1). But no methodological device allows an experimenter to control the distribution of reinforced runs in the paradigm presently under discussion. Here, the distribution of reinforced runs of different lengths depends on the distribution of runs a subject produces. In fact, this dependency is a matching function! The percentage of time a subject allocates to runs of a given duration must necessarily equal, except for sampling fluctuation, the percentage of reinforcements obtained by switches terminating runs of that duration. An equivalent matching function obtains in the free-operant version of the present method, a concurrent variable-interval variable-interval schedule. There, an "interchangeover time" corresponds to a run length, and the percentage of time allocated to a given interchangeover time approximately equals the percentage of reinforcements delivered for changeovers terminating interchangeover times of that duration (Menlove, 1972, 1975).

As a consequence of this automatic and inescapable matching relation, one cannot look for meaningful sequential statistics relating choice probabilities after different run lengths to the corresponding obtained reinforcement probabilities. This fact has not been appreciated until recently. Sequential data that originally were viewed as support for a molar view of behavior maintained by these schedules, and contrary to a molecular view (Figure 3 in Nevin, 1969), apparently do not describe anything but a schedule itself. Neither the discrete-trials nor free-operant versions of the paradigm discussed here are adequate to let one evaluate a molecular theory attributing major importance to the relation between emitted and reinforced patterns of choices. This example illustrates a problem all too common in the debate over molar versus molecular analyses. Elegant results obtained at the molar level are held up as support for a molar analysis, but these results are obtained with methods that deny an opportunity to prove or reject the possibility that the molar results are derived from molecular laws. This peculiar, built-in bias of the methods maintains support for molar analyses in the absence of knowledge that molar results are fundamental and not derived from molecular laws.

Data presently are not available on the issue of whether or not the distribution of reinforced runs determines where a subject tends to switch, and as a by-product, the overall percent choices of an alternative. Stated more generally, there are no data to state the extent to which the temporal patterning of choices is generally determined by the distribution of reinforced temporal patterns. By analogy with a very nearly identical situation described below in Section IV.A, one can probably anticipate that, when the appropriate experiments are performed, one will find that pigeons tend to emit the temporal distributions of choices that are required for, or adventitiously precede, reinforcement. However, this tendency presumably is operative only within the limitations imposed by such variables as a subject's short-term memory for its own recent patterns of choices.

C. Summary of Discrete-Trials Data

An analysis of discrete-trials choice behavior requires, of course, a choice by the experimenter of the independent and dependent variables. This choice has been guided by either of two sets of pretheoretical assumptions. These different viewpoints have been called the "molar" and the "molecular" analyses. A molar analysis focuses on the way in which the overall, average frequency of occurrence of a peck on one key depends on the average frequency of reinforcement for pecks on that key (Herrnstein, 1970). A molecular analysis regards this average relationship to be derived from more local effects (Estes, 1964, 1972; Shimp, 1969a). That is, a molecular analysis focuses on how the temporal patterning of pecks on different keys depends on local reinforcement contingencies. The strength of each of these viewpoints in the present empirical context presently lies more on the side of behavioral engineering than on the side of theoretical understanding. Present practical knowledge is sufficient to enable an experimenter to establish any desired quantitative degree of average preference by an organism for one of two alternatives, and also, to control fairly precisely some simple aspects of temporal patterning of choices. Unfortunately, no theory has yet been elaborated to the point where it can handle available data, although an outline of a theory that offers some hope of doing so is given in Section V.B.

Let us now summarize some of the established results. In probability-learning experiments, where the reinforcement probability for an alternative is constant for a given physical stimulus, overall preference for an alternative deviates from probability matching in the direction predicted by maximizing. The extent of this deviation can be modulated by the level of attention to and the discriminability of the cues correlated with different reinforcement probabilities (see Hale & Shimp, 1975; Mackintosh, 1969). Thus, no single preference function relates overall percent choices of a key to overall percent reinforcements for that key. In other experiments, local reinforcement probability on a trial varies. It has been made dependent on the response on the previous trial (Nevin, 1969; Shimp, 1966), and on the reinforcing event on the previous trial (see Williams, 1972; Section III.A.2 of this chapter). It would seem at an engineering level that any desired first-order sequential dependency could be established by a judicious combination of variables such as the dependencies in the sequence of reinforcing events, those variables determining memory for these dependencies, and discriminiability of visual or temporal cues correlated with different reinforcement contingencies. There is no evidence at all to support the assumption implicit in molar analyses that local reinforcement contingencies can be ignored in discrete-trials experiments on choice behavior, and that fundamental processes generally are revealed by a function relating the overall percentage of choice to overall percentage of reinforcement. All available evidence bearing on this issue is consistent instead with a molecular view holding that this molar function is a byproduct of temporal patterning of behavior over trials, and that this patterning in turn depends on numerous trial-by-trial contingencies and variables.

IV. CHOICE BEHAVIOR: DATA FROM FREE-OPERANT PARADIGMS

In Section III, a molecular analysis revealed that local variations in reinforcement probability generated local variations in choice probability. The molar dependent variable favored by conservative behaviorism, that is, overall percentage of choice of a key, only obscured these controlling relationships. To be fair to a molar analysis, however, one must admit that it was established in the context of free-operant, rather than discrete-trials, paradigms. It will be recalled that the notion of a "free operant" has both methodological and theoretical components. A free operant is an instantaneous response that is therefore "free" to occur at any moment. It is also the response contiguous with reinforcement and the response on which reinforcement is contingent in standard paradigms. It cannot be overemphasized that this notion of a free operant rests on theoretical assumptions that may be wrong. In particular, the free operant is supposed to be the behavioral unit in terms of which behavioral laws are best expressed. A behavioral unit that is not instantaneous, however, and instead is a behavioral pattern extending over time, cannot be "free" to occur at any moment in time. Accordingly, it is of fundamental importance to determine the conditions under which behavioral units are instantaneous behaviors and when they are behavioral patterns. Situations nominally free operant in nature will be examined in which behavioral units are patterns rather than instantaneous.

A. One-Key Schedules of Reinforcement

One-key data in an order of increasing numbers of behavioral units and of increasing complexity of preference are discussed here.

1. One Reinforced Behavioral Pattern

There is a fairly common schedule in which every occurrence of a single, very elementary, behavioral pattern is reinforced. In a differential reinforcement of low rate schedule (commonly abbreviated as DRL), a reinforcer is delivered for a key peck if a subject sufficiently spaces that peck from the preceding peck. Thus, in a DRL schedule, a reinforcer is delivered for a peck terminating an interresponse time longer than some minimum required value. In much of the work with this schedule, experimenters have sought to determine the extent to which the behavior it maintains resembles that required for reinforcement. It is only a slight oversimplification to say that the distribution of interresponse times maintained by the schedule tends to approximate the interresponse time necessary for reinforcement. This approximation is especially close if one measures it in terms of the percentage of the time allocated to interresponse times similar to the criterion interresponse time, because very little time is consumed by the very short interresponse times that may appear to be an important source of maladaptive behavior in terms of a frequency distribution of interresponse times. Further research on the extent to which reinforced patterns and emitted patterns resemble one another might profitably advance to more complex patterns than simple interresponse times (Hawkes & Shimp, 1975; Shimp, 1973c).

Not every pattern satisfying the DRL requirement has to be reinforced: patterns may be reinforced intermittently. In a paced variable-interval schedule, interresponse times in some specified class are reinforced according to a variable-interval schedule. For example, interresponse times between 2 and 3 sec in duration might be reinforced on an average of once every minute, but with interreinforcement intervals varying randomly about this average. Such schedules, like DRL schedules, establish and maintain patterns resembling those required for reinforcement (Shimp, 1967).

2. Two Reinforced Behavioral Patterns

When we begin to ask what is known about preference between two functional units that are behavioral patterns, we find that answers are available only for extremely simple measures of patterning, such as interresponse times. Two different intermittent reinforcement schedules are available to study preference between two interresponse times; a concurrent variable-ratio variable-ratio schedule and a concurrent variable-interval variable-interval schedule. In the former, a reinforcer is delivered after the completion of a variable number of interresponse times in a given class

(Malott & Cumming, 1966). The average number required for one class may be the same or different from the other. This schedule does not control the distribution of reinforced patterns, with the consequence that obtained preference functions are very difficult to interpret. Most of the data on preference between two reinforced patterns have been obtained with a concurrent variable-interval variable-interval schedule for two classes of interresponse times. This schedule is very similar to that used by Shimp (1966) and Nevin (1969) described in Section III.B. However, in this case, reinforcers are arranged for two patterns (interresponse times) rather than for a peck on a left or right key. With this schedule, the longer a subject continues to emit one pattern, that is, interresponse times in one class, and is not rewarded, the higher becomes the reinforcement probability for the other behavioral pattern, that is, an interresponse time in the other class. Preference is involved in two interrelated ways in a concurrent variable-interval variable-interval schedule of reinforcement for two behavioral patterns. One preference function plots total time allocated to either pattern as a function of, say, total reinforcements per hour. This function presumably measures motivational effects, and may be said to show a subject's preference for food-related activities over all others. This function is a monotonically increasing, negatively accelerated curve with an asymptote of 80–100% of the time allocated to food-related activities for reinforcement rates greater than about 20 per hour (Shimp, 1970; Shimp & Hawkes, 1974). A second preference function, dependent on the first, plots the percentage of time allocated to either class that is allocated to a particular one, say the shorter, as a function of any of numerous variables. A convenient frame of reference for the effects of these variables is a time-allocation matching function, according to which the percentage of time a subject allocates to a pattern approximates the percentage of reinforcements the experimenter allocates to that pattern. With preference at this matching level, the local reinforcements per hour for the two patterns are equal. According to time-allocation matching, if a pigeon allocates, say 80% of the time to two reinforced patterns receiveing 60 and 40% of the reinforcements, respectively, the subject will partition the 80% of the time spent responding in a 60:40 ratio. Such matching obtains within boundary conditions that can be specified moderately well. Specifically, time-allocation matching is obtained, provided that the duration of the shorter pattern, or behavioral unit, is about 2 sec (Shimp, 1968, 1969b); Staddon, 1968). (Time-allocation matching becomes apparent for Staddon's data only after they are replotted in terms of the coordinate system under discussion here.) If the duration of this unit is greater or less than two seconds, preference for the preferred unit is greater or less than that predicted by matching, respectively (Hawkes & Shimp, 1974). Also, matching obtains only if the total reinforcement density is above about

20 per hour (Shimp, 1970; Shimp & Hawkes, 1974). For lower reinforcement densities, preference approaches indifference. Also, matching is dependent upon which sequences of behavioral units precede the delivery of a reinforcer (Shimp, 1973c): when shorter and longer units are reinforced equally often, matching obtains only if the shorter unit almost invariably precedes the reinforced one. Indeed, sequential statistics reveal a pattern similar to those described by Shimp (1966). This similarity suggests that choice between behavioral patterns on a single key and choice between side keys may conform to approximately the same response strategies, so long as reinforcement contingencies for patterns and side-key pecks are equivalent.

How can one unify all these facts about preference between reinforced patterns? Presently no one knows, although an outline of a theory to do so is sketched below in Section V.B. It is clear that matching, at least as now conceived, is not a sufficient unifying concept for behavioral units that are patterns. The deviations from matching may, however, give some clues to the conditions under which matching may not obtain in other concurrent-reinforcement paradigms (see Section IV.B). In any event the present results give some insights into the general nature of choice behavior in operant settings. For instance, the term "free operant" is clearly a misnomer here. This is so despite the fact that the paradigm satisfies all the traditional criteria for a free-operant setting: a single key is continuously available and a reinforcer is always contiguous with an instantaneous key peck. A cumulative record would reveal only a straight line, the slope of which traditionally would be said to estimate the strength of a key-pecking operant. Obviously, however, the key peck is not the behavioral unit here. There is no one behavioral unit at all. There are two units, and each is a behavioral pattern. Thus, these data seem incompatible with the temporal-contiguity component of the Law of Effect, unless one would wish to appeal to hypothetical mediating chains. They also seem incompatible with a rigid requirement that all theoretical quantities be observable, because decisions between two behaviors functioning as integrated units presumably must occur when the subject initiates a unit. However, it is impossible to observe a pigeon peck a key and to observe at the same time whether the next peck will terminate one behavioral unit or the other, that is, a shorter or longer interresponse time.

3. Several Reinforced Behavioral Patterns

Much of the work on temporal patterning of responses traces its origins to a very innovative experiment by Anger (1954). He developed a schedule, called a "synthetic variable-interval" schedule, the most important property of which was that it allowed for the first time an experimenter to control the distribution of reinforced patterns, in Anger's case, interresponse times. He successfully demonstrated (Anger, 1954) that the distribution of reinforced patterns affected the distribution of all patterns produced by the organism. It was left to the future, however, to determine the functions relating properties of the distributions of reinforced and emitted patterns. The concurrent variable-interval variable-interval schedule for two patterns discussed in Section IV.A.2 is a simplified synthetic schedule, and the preference functions described there are special cases of the functions now considered. Synthetic schedules have recently been generalized from two patterns to ten, .5-sec classes of reinforced interresponse times ranging from 1.0 to 6.0 sec. The preference functions described previously generalize remarkably well to this more complex situation involving preference for ten rather than only two reinforced patterns. Time-allocation matching appears to obtain within the same boundary conditions previously specified, and the effects of total reinforcements per hour on the two separate time-allocation preference functions seem equivalent (Shimp, 1973b, 1974). The results from this synthetic schedule that closely resembles the standard variable-interval paradigm described in the next section (IV.A.4) fully support the conclusions described above: response-reinforcer temporal contiguity is unessential in the establishment of a behavioral unit; the observability criterion for decisions must be relaxed; and mean response rate of an instantaneous response fails to reveal the controlling relationships, and indeed, does not even involve the functional behavioral units. Much of this can be summarized by noting that there seems to be no free operant when behavioral patterns function as units.

4. Classical Paradigms: Uncontrolled Numbers and Types of Reinforced Behavioral Patterns

We have just seen that the notion of a free operant does not apply when behavioral patterns function as behavioral units. One immediately wonders what the conditions are that favor the development of patterns versus instantaneous responses as behavioral units. What has been demonstrated thus far suggests that behavioral patterns are established as behavioral units when the delivery of a reinforcer depends on patterns, that is, on more behavior than that which is contiguous with the delivery of the reinforcer. Such an arrangement favors the establishment of units that resemble the patterns required for reinforcement. Thus, if there are conditions in which instantaneous behaviors function as units, they presumably require that the behavior on which the delivery of a reinforcer depends be the behavior contiguous with the reinforcer. Standard schedules control only the last small fraction of a second of whatever behavioral sequence precedes a reinforcer. That is, the reinforcer is contingent upon and contiguous with a key peck. This confounding was described in Section I in some detail. It seems to the present writer to be truly remarkable and not a little ironic that an almost total lack of control over reinforced patterns remains so highly esteemed in a science ostensibly dedicated to the refinement of means to control behavior.

Space limitations prevent the discussion of any but a single standard one-key paradigm. The paradigm selected for consideration here, the variable-interval schedule, is the one most commonly serving as a component schedule in analyses of complex schedules, and it is very often used as a base-line schedule. In this schedule, a reinforcer is delivered for the first peck to occur after a variable time since the last reinforcement. Thus, in a variable-interval 1-min schedule, reinforcement occurs once per minute on the average, but the interreinforcement interval may range from perhaps zero to many minutes. The probability of reinforcement for a key peck increases as a function of the time since the last peck, and time-allocation matching is a necessary consequence of responding: the percentage of a session allocated to a class of interresponse times will approximate the percentage of the reinforcers delivered for interresponse times in that class (Shimp, 1967). The schedule maintains a moderately high rate of key pecking that varies considerably fom subject to subject but which viewed on a cumulative record is nearly always "steady." That is, the schedule generates a straight-line cumulative record. It is the slope of this line, mean response rate, that is the fundamental dependent variable according to the molar view of conservative behaviorism. The behavior maintained by this schedule may be viewed in terms of choice and preference in several different ways, three of which are described below. The following sections (IV.A.4.a, b, c) are designed more to illustrate that one cannot make sense of behavior maintained by this standard free-operant schedule without a theory of the nature of that behavior, than it is designed to review the gigantic number of articles on this particular standard schedule.

a. *Simple go, no-go choice behavior.*   The oldest interpretation is that described in Section I, according to which a subject decides in each moment whether or not to emit what is assumed to be the behavioral unit, the key peck. According to this view, any curve showing how mean response rate depends on some experimental variable shows how a subject's preference for the behavioral unit over all other behavior depends on that variable. Hundreds of such curves have been obtained over the past few decades. According to this view, classic presentations of results obtained with standard operant methods, as in Ferster and Skinner (1957), may be interpreted as studies of choice behavior. At the same time, however, "choice" is superfluous here.

b. *A generalized two-state model.*   Gilbert (1958) and Rachlin (1973) generalized the first interpretation but retained the key peck as the behavioral unit and rate of key pecking as the fundamental datum. According to their view, time during which a subject responds and is reinforced by a variable-interval schedule can be partitioned into two parts: time during which a subject key pecks at a "steady rate" or "constant tempo," and time during which a subject does not key peck. The steady-rate component has been variously identified as a straight-line cumulative record (Gilbert, 1958) or as a constant interresponse time (Rachlin, 1973). This view has never been evaluated, and it is not clear how to do so. Given most interresponse-time distributions, it would not be obvious how to sort either time or interresponse times into two categories. Also, it is interesting that this view, preserving as it does some of the assumptions of conservative behaviorism, nevertheless abandons the observability criterion: transitions (decisions?) between the two modes of responding generally would be unobservable at the moments at which they occur. This view of choice in a variable-interval schedule has been used more as a theoretical convenience in attempts to unify different kinds of data than as a view having any cogent support in its own right. Rachlin (1973) was able, through its use, to correlate perfectly time allocated to responding and mean response rate, but the references he cited to support this dichotomous view of behavior dealt only with nonquantitative data from continuous reinforcement situations or situations having no reinforcement at all. An additional difficulty with this two-state analysis is that it is incompatible with results obtained with synthetic schedules. This two-state analysis demands that it be sufficient to look at the way a subject partitions time between food-related and non-food-related activities. In Sections IV.A.2 and IV.A.3, however, it was shown that preference between these two activities is only one of two preference functions determining mean response rate: this two-state analysis omits the possibility that within the key-pecking state various behavioral patterns may be functioning as behavioral units.

c. *Reinforced behavioral patterns.* A picture of behavior very different from those described in Sections IV.A.4.a and b emerges as soon as one contemplates implications of the literature on short-term memory (Section II). Compatible both with the short-term memory literature and with the behavioral patterning literature is the possibility that behavioral patterns are accidentally established and maintained by standard schedules, such as variable-interval schedules. Imagine a continuum of "precision of behavioral control" with complex reinforced patterns exquisitely controlled at the top and with the "superstitition" paradigm at the bottom. The latter paradigm simply delivers a reinforcer with no control over the preceding behavior (Skinner, 1948). Where would a standard schedule be placed on this continuum? A standard schedule controls only the last fraction of a second of behavior preceding reinforcement so it would have to be placed scarcely above the superstition paradigm at the bottom. Even tradition allows that the superstition paradigm can establish and maintain behavior by the chance occurrence of that behavior contiguously with reinforcement (Skinner, 1948). If one widens the time interval over which reinforcement is assumed to operate as suggested by the short-term memory literature, one would have to conclude by the same logic as Skinner's that standard schedules can establish and maintain behavioral patterns by the chance occurrence of those patterns before the delivery of a reinforcer. According to this view, variable-interval schedules, and indeed all standard schedules, are ineffective tools to study behavioral control since they are little better than the superstition paradigm. This view predicts much variability in the behavior maintained by variable-interval schedules. The great variety of shapes of interresponse-time distributions and the considerable variations in rates of key pecking maintained by the same schedule (Catania & Reynolds, 1968), tend to confirm this prediction.

B. Two-Key Schedules of Reinforcement

The standard operant paradigm for the analysis of choice behavior is the two-key concurrent variable-interval variable-interval schedule. This schedule and modifications of it have generated a great part of the data that in recent years have revolutionized the theoretical analysis of schedules of reinforcement.

1. Controlled Reinforced Patterns

Consider the case in which there is only a single reinforced pattern per key. This situation, with the patterns being interresponse times, is equivalent in terms of the nature of the behavioral units to the one-key situation described in Section IV.A.2, except that here the sequence of behavioral units a subject produces has some of its units on one key and all the others on the other key. In both situations, the probability of reinforcement for one unit increases with the time since that unit was last emitted. An experiment by Moffitt and Shimp (1971) illustrates the effects of two separate contingencies: (a) the interresponse-time contingency that establishes the behavioral patterns emitted on each key, that is, establishes the behavioral units; and (b) the contingency determining preference between those behavioral units, that is, determines the way in which a subject partitions its total behavioral output between the two behavioral units. Separate control by these same two within-key and between-key contingencies also was obtained in a two-key experiment in which there were two behavioral units (interresponse times) established on each key rather than only one (Shimp,

1971). This experiment showed that preference between the two units for a given key was the same as if there had not been a second key to which a subject allocated time in accordance with the time-allocation matching rule. These results encourage the belief that various kinds of temporal patterns can be imposed on pecking on one or both keys without affecting the way a subject allocates time between keys. Stated differently, different kinds of behavioral units can be established for one key without affecting the total time allocated to that key.

2. Uncontrolled Reinforced Patterns

Standard two-key paradigms exert minimal control over the within-key behaviors: In a standard concurrent variable-interval variable-interval schedule, the delivery of a reinforcer depends upon the occurrence only of a key peck, that is, the schedule controls only the terminal fraction of a second of behavior preceding a reinforcer. Thus, much is left for chance to determine what behavioral units are established on a key. The discussion of the behavior maintained by this schedule is organized around four interrelated issues.

a. *Matching.* An outcome that inspired literally hundreds of subsequent experiments was that obtained by Herrnstein (1961), who found that the percentage of all pecks that occurred on a given key approximated the percentage of all reinforcements that were delivered for pecks on that key. It has also been found that the percentage of time allocated to a key, or component, approximates the percentage of reinforcements delivered while that component is in effect (Catania, 1966; Shull & Pliskoff, 1967). But a recent review of the matching literature from concurrent variable-interval variable-interval schedules concludes that this approximation is not as close as was once thought (Myers & Myers, in press). Myers and Myers have shown that the slope of the function relating percent pecks on a key to the percentage of reinforcements on that key is typically closer to about .8 than to the 1.0 of the matching function.

b. *The changeover delay.* It has always been acknowledged that an approximation to matching obtains only for a "changeover delay" greater than 1.5 or 2.0 sec (Herrnstein, 1961). That is, approximate matching is obtained only when a peck in one component is ever followed by a reinforced peck in the other component in less than 1.5 or 2.0 sec. The traditional interpretation of the changeover delay is that it ensures "independence" of pecks on the two keys (Herrnstein, 1961). It is designed to ensure that pecking on one key is not accidentally maintained by reinforcements delivered for pecks on the other key. Two seconds is judged a sufficiently long delay only because approximate matching is obtained for delays longer than 2 sec, not because 2 sec is known to be a sufficiently long delay to have the desired properties. All the relevant evidence clearly points the other way. First, we have seen that a pigeon can remember the order of recent events for longer than two seconds. Second, delay-of-reinforcement gradients obtained with concurrent variable-interval variable-interval schedules show that a reinforcer has quite strong effects on behavior temporally separated from it for more than 2 sec (Chung, 1965; Herbert, 1970). Third, reinforcement after a behavioral pattern 5 sec in duration is capable of quite precisely determining the structure of behavior throughout the 5 sec (Hawkes & Shimp, 1975). There is no more widespread misconception than that pecking on two keys is "independent" when matching is obtained.

   c.   *The rate-constancy phenomenon.*   Soon after the discovery of approximate matching at the molar level, an additional discovery was made that supported the molar over the molecular position. Catania (1962, 1963b) found that mean rate of pecking on a key was constant, regardless of variations in the temporal patterning of that behavior. Such an outcome obviously is a difficulty for a molecular analysis: it suggests that the real invariances are at the molar level and that molecular data represent little more than noise. However, it has subsequently been found that this rate constancy holds only in a few scattered cases (Catania, 1971; Shimp, 1971; Hawkes & Shimp, 1974). Further, balancing this molar invariance over different temporal patterns are data showing relationships involving temporal patterns that are invariant over different mean response rates (see Sections IV.A.2 and 3). The latter data seem quite unexplainable in terms of the molar analysis, while an occasional molar invariance is to be expected from chance according to a molecular analysis. Thus, the rate-constancy data in general seem to pose more of a problem for a molar than for a molecular analysis.

   d.   *The relative sensitivity of rate and choice.*   Skinner's early advocacy of response rate over choice is well known. He maintained that the mean rate of occurrence of an instantaneous behavior had to be more informative than choice: the former measured absolute response strength while the latter measured only relative response strength (Skinner, 1938). When operant data on the problem became available, they tended to support the opposite position, and the standard view now is that choice is a more sensitive measure than rate (Herrnstein, 1970; Kling, 1971). This view in turn, however, seems likely to be wrong, at least for steady-state data. It rests largely on results such as those obtained by Herrnstein (1961) and Catania (1963a) who obtained matching results involving choice (percentage of key pecks on one of two keys) but almost no effects involving total key pecks per minute. Keesey and Kling (1961) also obtained results testifying to the insensitivity of total responses per minute. This insensitivity of rate should surprise the reader of Section IV.A.2 and IV.B.1, in which the same preference function was obtained with one and two keys. How is one to resolve the inconsistency? The answer is not yet certain, but one issue seems important. Neuringer (1967) and Shimp (1968) have suggested that one must not overlook the contingency relating a behavioral measure to reinforcement. Comparison between one-key and two-key results would seem to require comparable contingencies, but comparable contingencies have seldom been studied. The experiment by Moffitt and Shimp (1971) is an exception. In the experiments in which "choice" has been sensitive and "rate" has not, the two keys were correlated with different reinforcement parameters, but the total responses per minute was not (for example, Catania, 1963a). It is therefore scarcely surprising that the reinforcement parameter affected preference between the two keys but not the total rate of pecking. Thus, there is no cogent evidence that either rate or choice is more sensitive than the other.

C.   Summary of Free-Operant Paradigms

The analysis of free-operant behavior requires, just as does the analysis of discrete-trials behavior, a selection of independent and dependent variables. The same two pretheoretical views have guided this selection in the case of both free-operant and discrete-trials behavior. First, the molar view holds that one should look at how mean rate of occurrence of instantaneous key pecks and lever presses depends on such variables as the mean rate at which reinforcers are delivered. Second, the molecular view holds that molar results are by-products of more fundamental relations involving behavioral patterning, or organization of behavioral output. The molecular view focuses, in other words, on behavioral patterns acting as functional units, and on the sequence in which these units are emitted. To the extent to which a molecular analysis is successful, a molar analysis becomes superfluous. What would it mean to measure a variation in the mean rate of key pecking or lever pressing if the key peck or lever press is not the behavioral unit? The answer may well be "precious little" in a context where one strives to uncover fundamental concepts, that is, in a science dedicated to the development of better methods and theories by means of which one can control and understand the behavior of an individual organism. In contrast in a context of behavioral engineering having fairly immediate and crude but practical objectives, one may find, of course, not only that molar variables are sufficient for his purposes but indeed that they are the only ones that can be controlled or even measured.

Let us summarize the results obtained with one of the most effective methods, a concurrent variable-interval variable-interval schedule. This schedule can make reinforcement contingent upon two general types of behaviors: (*a*) instantaneous key pecks appropriate to the traditional molar analysis and (*b*) behavioral patterns such as interresponse times appropriate to the molecular analysis. The percentage of instantaneous pecks on a key roughly equals, or matches, the percentage of reinforcements earned by pecks on that key, provided that a changeover delay is greater than 1.5 or 2.0 sec. But the slope of the regression line between percent pecks and percent reinforcements is actually approximated better by .8 than by the 1.0 of the matching function: matching seldom describes regression lines for individual subjects. Evidence on the issue of the relative sensitivity of rate of key pecking versus choice between pecks on different keys indicates neither is more sensitive than the other, provided that reinforcement contingencies for rate and choice are comparable. Evidence on the rate-constancy phenomenon requires an interpretation different from the original one. That is, some evidence originally was obtained that indicated that the mean rate of pecking a key depended only on the reinforcement rates for pecking on both keys: mean rate of key pecking remained constant while local patterning of pecking varied. Thus, it was concluded that a molar analysis based on the frequency of instantaneous responses might be constructed without recourse to the temporal organization of behavioral output. Recent data cast doubt on this earlier conclusion, because the rate-constancy phenomenon apparently has very limited generality: in several settings mean response rate depends almost exclusively on the way in which behavioral output is patterned. This finding leads us to the second type of behavior on which reinforcement may be made to depend in a concurrent variable-interval variable-interval schedule.

When reinforcement is contingent upon temporal patterns of behavior, such as interresponse times, behavioral units often are established that approximate the behavior required by the contingency. However one might wish to explain how these units are established, as stimulus–response chains or as products of organized functional units in memory, one cannot make sense out of the behavior maintained by these contingencies by ignoring that the behavioral units are indeed patterns and not instantaneous key pecks. It has been shown how overall preference for one such behavioral unit over another depends on the percentage of reinforcements delivered for that unit, the absolute and relative durations of the units, and total reinforcement density. A beginning has been made on understanding the variables determining the sequence in which these units are emitted. A beginning also has been made on the analysis of patterns more complex than interresponse times.

Sad to say, no theory presently available accounts for the behavior maintained by both contingencies, that is, contingencies for instantaneous behaviors and contingencies for patterns of behaviors. In Section V.B a theory is outlined that ultimately may do so.

The analysis of free-operant behavior in terms of behavioral patterns may lead to a unification of free-operant and discrete-trials paradigms. In the latter, a subject is physically denied an opportunity to emit a response except at restricted times. In the former, he is taught not to respond except at restricted times by means of contingencies determining the temporal spacing of responses. Perhaps one may identify equivalent paradigms by finding the "free-operant" paradigm that establishes behavioral units and preference relations among these units such that the temporal sequence of key pecks on one or two keys is precisely the same as that produced by a given discrete-trials paradigm. Stated differently, equivalent free-operant and discrete-trials paradigms are those that produce the same sequence of choices among the same behavioral patterns functioning as units.

V.   CHOICE BEHAVIOR: THEORIES

The brief survey of theories for the data described above is organized into two categories, depending on the nature of the theoretical behavioral units. Molar theories, described first, deal with the mean rate of occurrence of instantaneous behavioral units, whereas molecular theories deal with behavioral patterns functioning as units. These two categories parallel conserative and liberal behaviorisms, as described in Sections I and II. The distinction between these two viewpoints on the nature of operant behavior in animals resembles a distinction between two viewpoints on the nature of human learning and memory. A viewpoint that resembles conservative behaviorism and is historically closely linked to it is the well-known stimulus–response association viewpoint (Hull, Hovland, Ross, Hall, Perkins, & Fitch, 1940; Thorndike 1931), whereas a second viewpoint more closely resembling the analysis of patterns of operant behavior is that which emphasizes organization of behavioral output in terms of higher-order functional units (Miller, 1956; Tulving, 1962; Tulving & Donaldson, 1972).

It would be well to emphasize here that this writer does not subscribe to the prevailing opinion (Herrnstein, 1970) that in the study of operant behavior the phrases "molar level of analysis" and "molecular level of analysis" do, in fact, refer to a difference in levels of analysis, that is, to a situation where the notion of reductionism applies. The distinction between molar and molecular analyses in the study of operant behavior may have originated in the use of cumulative records, in which mean rate of occurrence of an instantaneous response is clearly visible as the average slope of a curve, and other features of performance, such as interresponse times, are invisible: they are thoroughly obscured by the low standard rate at which cumulative-recorder drums revolve. But the actual response protocol from an organism is a sequence of interresponse times whether or not one's apparatus is sufficient to record it. Mean response rate is the reciprocal of the mean of the distribution of interresponse times.

Clearly the only reductionism involved in passing from the molar to the molecular "level" is a statistical one: the molar analysis assumes that the mean of the distribution of interresponse times contains all the important information in the original sequence of interresponse times. This assumption seems equivalent to the assumption that everything else about this sequence is simply noise that an analysis ought to disregard or filter out (Honig, 1966). This assumption is scarcely ever tested. Catania (1963b) obtained data consistent with it in his "rate-constancy" phenomenon, but it has been shown that this result has little generality (see Section IV.B.2.c). There is a potentially more convincing way to demonstrate that the mean of the distribution of interresponse times contains all the useful information in the distribution. One could manipulate the distribution of reinforced inter-response times, at the same time keeping constant the molar independent variable, the total number of reinforcements. If the molar position is correct, one ought to find a constant relation between molar independent and dependent variables while reinforced patterns are varied. This writer is not aware of a single experiment of this type that has supported the molar position. What happens instead is that the relation between molar dependent and independent variables, far from remaining constant, can be shown to depend almost exclusively on the molecular reinforcement contingencies (Shimp, 1974; Shimp & Hawkes, 1974).

A. Instantaneous Responses as Behavioral Units

With rare exceptions, theories based on the traditional assumptions of conservative behaviorism have as their objective the conceptual unification of functions showing how the mean rate of instantaneous behaviors depends on various reinforcement parameters in a variety of standard paradigms. The following discussion very briefly examines only three of many such theories (Baum, 1973; Blough, 1975; Catania, 1973; Herrnstein, 1970; Killeen, 1975; Rachlin, 1973; Skinner, 1938; Staddon, 1974).

1. Herrnstein's Theory

Herrnstein (1970) developed a theory that has had impressive success not only in interrelating data from several contexts but also in predicting phenomena in advance of their discovery (for example, Shimp & Wheatley, 1971). The theory continues to be broadened in its coverage of data from different contexts (Herrnstein & Loveland, 1974). According to this theory, behavior maintained by a standard schedule, such as a variable-interval schedule for food, can be partitioned into two categories: food-related activities and everything else. A subject's partitioning of its behavior between these two categories is measured by the mean rate of occurrence of the instantaneous behavior contiguous with the delivery of food. The theory predicts a monotonically increasing, negatively accelerated curve relating mean response rate to reinforcements per hour. The theory requires the estimation of two free parameters to enable it to describe a set of points from an individual organism. Catania and Reynolds (1968) reported several such sets of points, and the theory summarizes quite well the data points for each of six birds. The theory predicts matching in standard concurrent variable-interval variable-interval schedules as a theorem derived from the basic assumption relating mean response rate to reinforcement rate. However, the matching theorem does require a few additional assumptions about the equivalence of response topographies in the two component schedules and about reinforcement interactions between components. Matching is assumed to hold when a changeover delay ensures independence of responding in the two components (see Section IV.B.2.b); this situation peculiarly is the same as that for which reinforcement interactions between components are assumed to be maximal (Herrnstein, 1970). The theory handles discrete-trials probability learning data by interpreting the outcome to be maximizing, and by adding together choice responses and correction responses, in which case perfect maximizing is matching. As seen in Section III.A, maximizing is not in fact obtained, only an approximation that varies widely as a consequence of numerous variables. Herrnstein's theory handles neither this fact nor the sequential data obtained in probability-learning experiments. With an additional assumption relating reinforcement interactions to component duration, the theory can handle to some extent contrast phenomena (Reynolds, 1961; Shimp & Wheatley, 1971). De Villiers (1974) has extended Herrnstein's theory to a shock avoidance situation. De Villiers found that the relationship between response rate and shock-frequency reduction in a successive discrimination paradigm conformed to the predictions of Herrnstein's theory. An algebraically similar but conceptually different theory has been proposed by Catania (1973). These two theories presently are difficult to distinguish.

2. Rachlin's Theory

Rachlin (1973) developed a theory designed to cover a somewhat different set of data compared to Herrnstein's theory: he deleted probability learning but added autoshaping. According to this theory, there is an element of Pavlovian conditioning when different stimuli are correlated with different reinforcement values: transitions between stimuli having different reinforcement values may generate classically conditioned key pecks that sum with operant key pecks to determine mean response rate. Rachlin regarded matching in two-key concurrent schedules not as a theorem derived from more primitive assumptions but as a fundamental relation between response strength and reinforcement value. We have noted already that he subscribed to a two-state analysis of behavior maintained by variable-interval schedules: he partitioned time into that allocated to responding at a steady rate and that allocated to not responding at all. As previously noted, there are no cogent data to support this view, though it will no doubt remain attractive to some theorists because of its simplicity.

3. Baum's Theory

Baum (1973) seems at first glance to have abandoned the temporal-contiguity component of the Law of Effect, for his theory holds to be fundamental a "molar correlation" between behavior and reinforcement, such as that between response rate and reinforcements per hour, and he explicitly denies the importance of temporal contiguity. Yet, just as did Herrnstein (1970) and Rachlin (1973), Baum retained standard reinforcement contingencies defined in terms of response-reinforcer temporal contiguity. Thus, the rationale for Baum's advocacy of rejecting temporal contiguity collapses if the molar correlation between response rate and reinforcement per hour is not fundamental. Ironically, we have seen that reinforcement contingencies in which response-reinforcer temporal contiguity is absent demonstrate that temporal contiguity is not essential. From this finding it was concluded not that molar correlations are fundamental but rather that they are derived (Section IV).

4. General Comments on Molar Theories

The focus of most theoretical work in the experimental analysis of behavior continues to be the traditional molar datum. Molar theories as a class, however, are obviously not without their difficulties. None has yet handled temporal-patterning data in which behavioral patterns function as integrated functional units. As a class they seem limited to "free-operant" situations involving instantaneous responses, that is, to situations confounding contingency and contiguity. But reasons have been given to doubt that the behavioral unit is ever an instantaneous response (Section IV.A.4.c). The failure of molar theories to accomodate behavioral patterns in the free-operant case is parallel to their failure to accommodate sequential effects in the discrete-trials case. The emphasis on molar functions blinds the theories to the presence of a sensitivity of behavior to local variations in reinforcement probability. Also, it nearly goes without saying that molar theories fail to interface with data on short-term memory. Last, molar theories based on specific instantaneous behavioral units such as the pigeon's key peck are open to the charge that they lack generality across species, because the pigeon's key peck apparently has some species-specific properties, making it unsuitable as a unit of behavioral analysis in general.

In particular, the topography of the pigeon's key peck may have rather limited plasticity, and it seems peculiarly susceptible to becoming associated with certain classes of stimuli (Brown & Jenkins, 1968; Moore, 1973; Smith, 1974). The key peck therefore seems not to have properties often attributed to the optimal behavioral unit (Skinner, 1938). But these species-specific limitations of the key peck offer fewer problems for a behavioral analysis based not directly on the key peck itself as the behavioral unit, but instead one based upon temporal patterns of key pecks. In such an analysis, the lack of plasticity of the topography of the key peck may not seriously interfere with the establishment and maintenance of patterns by a reinforcement contingency that attempts only to modify the way in which key pecks are distributed in time. Generally speaking, a reinforcement contingency may be said to overcome any species-specific peculiarities of the key peck to the extent to which patterns of pecking emerge and resemable those preceding reinforcement. This is, of course, not to say that a wide range of species-specific issues do not impose upper bounds on the structure of patterns that can be established and maintained.

B. Behavioral Patterns as Behavioral Units

A theory assuming that behavioral patterns may function as behavioral units shares some of the features of modern theories of human memory and requires the abandonment of nearly all of the most characteristic properties of radical behaviorism. It requires the abandonment of a rigid opposition to all unobservable theoretical quantities, the abandonment of response-reinforcer contiguity, and therefore, of mean rate of occurrence of an instantaneous behavioral unit as the fundamental datum. What such a pattern theory retains of the constellation of viewpoints defining radical behaviorism is a focus on the control of behavior of an individual organism. Let us try to sketch the outline of a pattern theory that seems to be emerging within a liberalized behaviorism. Assume a nonassociative short-term memory and an associative long-term memory (Estes, 1973; Konorski, 1967). It was suggested in Section II that a pigeon can remember the structure, that is, temporal patterning, of recent events, at least for a few seconds. Perhaps, therefore, it sometimes can remember the previous few interresponse times in free-operant settings, or the previous few pecks on left or right keys in discrete-trials settings. And, perhaps it can remember the order in which it emitted these behaviors. The precision of these aspects of a pigeon's short-term memory depends on numerous variables that can both facilitate and degrade memory, as seen in Section II.

The effects of reinforcement, that is, presentation of food to a hungry organism, may be tentatively interpreted as follows. The repeated delivery of a reinforcer after the same remembered pattern of behavior may establish and maintain that pattern as an integrated "chunk" or functional unit in long-term memory. Thus, reinforcement induces the subject to develop "subjective units" (Tulving, 1962) in long-term memory, and these units will tend to resemble the behavioral patterns preceding reinforcement. Seldom will a reinforcer always be delivered after the same remembered behavioral pattern. Therefore, more than one behavioral unit frequently will be established. Assume further that a subject builds up in long-term memory estimates of the likelihood that reinforcement follows different behavioral units in the presence of some functional stimulus. One component of the functional stimulus at the moment of choice among behavioral units would be a subject's short-term memory for recent events. Estes (1972) has described several specific ways in which these probability estimates for a given functional stimulus could develop in long-term memory. In a choice situation, a subject would be assumed to scan the behavioral units previously established in that situation, retrieve from long-term memory the likelihood of reinforcement for each, and then, let us say, maximize by choosing the alternative with the highest likelihood of leading to reinforcement (with such things as expected delays to reinforcement and the like being equal). Some such model as this appears to offer a realistic possibility of accommodating all the data described in this chapter. Of course, one cannot quantitatively evaluate this model at the present time: essential data required to adequately specify the model in detail are not presently available. More information is needed on issues such as the extent to which a subject can remember various details about recent events in diverse contexts, the way in which reinforcement forms organized units in long-term memory, and so on.

The model just outlined resembles previous models for operant behavior. In particular, the model is related to one based on expected utility theory (Shimp, 1969a). The present model retains a maximizing response rule, but the overall level of optimization is limited here by various limitations on memory processes and by the nature of the learning of reinforcement likelihoods. The present model and the earlier one are alike in that both assume that behavioral patterns can function as behavioral units. Finally, without describing details, one may note that the model outlined here bears a family resemblance to decades-old "expectancy" theories in general (Tolman, 1932) and specifically to a recent model for avoidance learning developed by Seligman and Johnston (1973).

VI. CONCLUSIONS

Choice behavior in animals may be viewed from two radically different perspectives. The first and traditional perspective, conservative behaviorism, is that of a "molar" analysis holding that the fundamental datum is the mean rate of occurrence of an instantaneous behavioral unit. This datum has its theoretical foundation in the assumption of response-reinforcer temporal contiguity in the Law of Effect, and, even more broadly, in the criterion of observability. Standard paradigms in the experimental analysis of behavior are deeply embedded within this traditional theoretical framework. These standard paradigms, however, confound the behavior contiguous with a reinforcer and the behavior upon which the delivery of the reinforcer is contingent. When these behaviors are experimentally unconfounded, patterning data are obtained that suggest that the temporal-contiguity assumption is generally incorrect. Short-term memory for behavioral patterns poses additional difficulties for the response-reinforcer, temporal-contiguity assumption. One must acknowledge, however, that the mediating-chain idea of conservative behaviorism seems sufficiently general to offer some hope for success of methods and theories based on response-reinforcer temporal contiguity. However, the mediating-chain idea has yet to handle either patterning data or short-term memory data from operant contexts.

A second and much more recent perspective on choice behavior in animals is a "molecular" analysis related to ideas dominant in contemporary analyses of human learning and memory. Thus, short-term memory for recent events may form part of the functional stimulus. And, the repeated delivery of a reinforcer after the same remembered pattern of behavior might establish that pattern as an organized functional unit in long-term memory. Thus, an intrinsic feature of such a molecular analysis is its capability of dealing with behavioral patterns functioning as units. A molecular analysis seems capable of handling data that are outside the scope of traditional analyses in terms of the mean rate of occurrence of instantaneous behavioral units. Data amenable to a molecular analysis include short-term memory data, temporal patterning of behavior, and response strategies resembling optimal strategies. A theory based on behavioral patterns functioning as behavioral units must emphasize the extent to which behavior is sensitive to local changes in reinforcement probability, as it is the way in which reinforcers are differently presented after various patterns that presumably establishes and maintains those patterns. Such a theory seems to imply that in certain cases important processes, including decision making, are not at every moment observable. Thus, the rigid requirement that all theoretical quantities must be observable may need to be relaxed. A molecular analysis also implies that the mean rate of occurrence of an instantaneous behavior, such as a key peck, affords little or no insight into fundamental controlling relationships that are in fact stated in terms of patterns, that is, temporal distributions of key pecks.

This writer shares the belief expressed by Jenkins (1970) that the study of behavioral patterning, of the temporal organization of behavior, may lead to a level of understanding unobtainable by an analysis only of the frequency of simple responses. Indeed, the improvement in understanding of operant behavior that may be gained by a study of temporal organization and patterning may resemble the improvement in understanding of human verbal behavior that earlier was gained by studying organization and patterning instead of the mere frequency of occurrence of simple responses (Tulving, 1962). As was the case in the analysis of organization in human verbal behavior, the study of temporal organization of operant behavior requires new experimental paradigms, new methods of data analysis, and new theoretical perspectives. The situation both in the analysis of human memory and of choice in animals is rather well described by the idea of a "paradigm shift" in the development of a science (Hanson, 1958; Kuhn, 1970). Over the years, there have been intermittent cries for the unification of the experimental analysis of behavior with the rest of experimental psychology. A molecular analysis based on a liberalized behaviorism may offer a greater promise of this unification than does the molar analysis of conservative behaviorism.

ACKNOWLEDGMENTS

This chapter could not have been written without the support provided to the author in recent years by NIMH Grants 14715, 16928, 19901 and 24537, and by a fellowship from the Center for Advanced Study in the Behavioral Sciences.

REFERENCES

Anderson, N. H. An evaluation of stimulus sampling theory: Comments on Professor Estes' paper. In A. W. Melton (Ed.), *Categories of human learning.* New York: Academic Press, 1964.

Anger, D. The effect upon simple animal behavior of different frequencies of reinforcement. Document No. 7779, ADI Auxiliary Publications Project, Photoduplication Service, Library of Congress, 1954.

Baum, W. M. The correlation-based law of effect. *Journal of the Experimental Analysis of Behavior*, 1973, **20**, 137–153.

Blough, D. S. Delayed matching in the pigeon. *Journal of the Experimental Analysis of Behavior*, 1959, **2**, 151–160.

Blough, D. S. Steady-state data and a quantitative model of operant generalization and discrimination. *Journal of Experimental Psychology: Animal Behavior Processes*, 1975, **104**, 3–21.

Blough, D. S., & Millward, R. B. Operant conditioning and verbal learning. In P. R. Farneworth (Ed.), *Annual review of psychology*. Vol. 16. Palo Alto: Annual Reviews, 1965.

Brown, P. L., & Jenkins, H. M. Auto-shaping of the pigeon's key-peck. *Journal of the Experimental Analysis of Behavior*, 1968, **11**, 1–8.

Bullock, D. H., and Bitterman, M. E. Probability-matching in the pigeon. *American Journal of Psychology*, 1962, **75**, 634–639.

Catania, A. C. Independence of concurrent responding maintained by interval schedules of reinforcement. *Journal of the Experimental Analysis of Behavior*, 1962, **5**, 175–184.

Catania, A. C. Concurrent performances: Reinforcement interaction and response independence. *Journal of the Experimental Analysis of Behavior*, 1963, **6**, 252–263. (a)

Catania, A. C. Concurrent performances: A baseline for the study of reinforcement magnitude. *Journal of the Experimental Analysis of Behavior*, 1963, **6**, 299–300. (b)

Catania, A. C. Concurrent operants. In W. K. Honig (Ed.), *Operant behavior: Areas of research and application*. New York: Appleton, 1966.

Catania, A. C. Reinforcement schedules: the role of responses preceding the one that produces the reinforcer. *Journal of the Experimental Analysis of Behavior*, 1971, **15**, 271–287.

Catania, A. C. Self-inhibiting effects of reinforcement. *Journal of the Experimental Analysis of Behavior*, 1973, **19**, 517–526.

Catania, A. C., & Reynolds, G. S. A quantitative analysis of the behavior maintained by interval schedules of reinforcement. *Journal of the Experimental Analysis of Behavior*, 1968, **11**, 327–383.

Chung, S. H. Effects of delayed reinforcement in a concurrent situation. *Journal of the Experimental Analysis of Behavior*, 1965, **8**, 439–444.

de Villiers, P. A. The law of effect and avoidance: a quantitative relationship between response rate and shock-frequency reduction. *Journal of the Experimental Analysis of Behavior*, 1974, **21**, 223–235.

Ebbinghaus, H. On memory. Leipzig: 1885. (Rev. ed., Translated by H. Ruger & C. Bussenius.) New York: Teacher's College, Columbia University, 1913.

Einstein, A. As quoted in *The secrets of the old one*, Part II, p. 69. *The New Yorker*, March 17, 1973.

Estes, W. K. Toward a statistical theory of learning. *Psychological Review*, 1950, **57**, 94–107.

Estes, W. K. Learning theory. In P. R. Farnsworth (Ed.), *Annual review of psychology*. Vol. 13. Palo Alto: Annual Reviews, 1962.

Estes, W. K. Probability learning. In A. W. Melton (Ed.), *Categories of human learning*. New York: Academic Press, 1964.

Estes, W. K. Research and theory on the learning of probabilities. *Journal of the American Statistical Association*, 1972, **67**, 81–102.

Estes, W. K. Memory and conditioning. In F. J. McGuigan & D. B. Lumsden (Eds.). *Contemporary approaches to conditioning and learning.* New York: Wiley, 1973.

Ferster, C. B., & Skinner, B. F. *Schedules of reinforcement.* New York: Appleton-Century-Crofts, 1957.

Gilbert, T. F. Fundamental dimensional properties of the operant. *Psychological Review,* 1958, **65,** 272–282.

Graf, B., Bullock, D. H., & Bitterman, M. E. Further experiments on probability-matching in the pigeon. *Journal of the Experimental Analysis of Behavior,* 1964, **7,** 151–157.

Grant, D. S., & Roberts, W. A. Trace interaction in pigeon short-term memory. *Journal of Experimental Psychology,* 1973, **101,** 21–29.

Hale, J. M., & Shimp, C. P. Molecular contingencies: reinforcement probability. *Journal of the Experimental Analysis of Behavior,* 1975 (in press).

Hanson, N. R. *Patterns of discovery.* Cambridge, England: Cambridge University Press, 1958.

Hawkes, L., & Shimp C. P. Choice between response rates. *Journal of the Experimental Analysis of Behavior,* 1974, **21,** 109–115.

Hawkes, L., & Shimp, C. P. Reinforcement of behavioral patterns: shaping a scallop. *Journal of the Experimental Analysis of Behavior,* 1975, **23,** 3–16.

Herbert, E. W. Two-key concurrent responding: response-reinforcement dependencies and blackouts. *Journal of the Experimental Analysis of Behavior,* 1970, **14,** 61–70.

Herrnstein, R. J. Relative and absolute strength of response as a function of frequency of reinforcement. *Journal of the Experimental Analysis of Behavior,* 1961, **4,** 179–184.

Herrnstein, R. J. On the Law of Effect. *Journal of the Experimental Analysis of Behavior,* 1970, **13,** 243–266.

Herrnstein, R. J., & Loveland, D. H. Hunger and contrast in a multiple schedule. *Journal of the Experimental Analysis of Behavior,* 1974, **21,** 511–517.

Honig, W. K. Introductory remarks. In W. K. Honig (Ed.), *Operant behavior: Areas of research and application.* New York: Appleton-Century-Crofts, 1966.

Hull, C. L., Hovland, C. I., Ross, R. T., Hall, M., Perkins, B. T., & Fitch, F. B. *Mathematico-deductive theory of rote learning.* New Haven, Connecticut: Yale University Press, 1940.

Jenkins, H. M. Sequential organization in schedules of reinforcement. In W. N. Schoenfeld (Ed.), *The theory of reinforcement schedules.* New York: Appleton-Century-Crofts, 1970.

Keesey, R. E., & Kling, J. W. Amount of reinforcement and free operant responding. *Journal of the Experimental Analysis of Behavior,* 1961, **4,** 125–132.

Killeen, P. On the temporal control of behavior. *Psychological Review,* 1975, **82,** 89–115.

Kling, J. W. Positive reinforcement. In J. W. Kling & L. A. Riggs (Eds.), *Woodworth and Schlosberg's experimental psychology.* New York: Holt, Rinehart & Winston, 1971.

Konorski, J. *Integrative activity of the brain.* Chicago: University of Chicago Press, 1967.

Kuhn, T. S. *The structure of scientific revolutions.* (2nd ed.) Chicago: University of Chicago Press, 1970.

Mackintosh, N. J. Habit-reversal and probability learning: Rats, birds, and fish. In R. M. Gilbert & N. S. Sutherland (Eds.), *Animal discrimination learning.* New York: Academic Press, 1969.

Malott, R. W., & Cumming, W. W. Concurrent schedules of IRT reinforcement: Probability of reinforcement and the lower bounds of the reinforced IRT intervals. *Journal of the Experimental Analysis of Behavior,* 1966, **9,** 317–325.

Massaro, D. W. Retroactive interference in short-term recognition memory for pitch. *Journal of Experimental Psychology,* 1970, **83,** 32–39.

Menlove, R. L. Local patterns of responding maintained by concurrent and multiple schedules. Unpublished doctoral dissertation, University of Utah, 1972.

Menlove, R. L. Local patterns of response maintained by concurrent and multiple schedules. *Journal of the Experimental Analysis of Behavior,* 1975, **23,** 309–337.

Miller, G. A. The magical number seven, plus or minus two: some limits on our capacity for processing information. *Psychological Review,* 1956, **63,** 81–97.

Miller, G. A. *The psychology of communication.* New York: Basic Books, 1967.

Moffitt, M. Short-term memory in the pigeon: Retroactive interference. Unpublished doctoral dissertation, University of Utah, 1972.

Moffitt, M., & Shimp, C. P. Two-key paced VI paced VI schedules of reinforcement. *Journal of the Experimental Analysis of Behavior,* 1971, **16,** 39–49.

Moore, B. R. The role of directed Pavlovian reactions in simple instrumental learning in the pigeon. In R. A. Hinde & J. Stevenson-Hinde (Eds.), *Constraints on learning.* New York and London: Academic Press, 1973.

Myers, J. L. Sequential choice behavior. In G. H. Bower (Ed.), *The psychology of learning and motivation: Advances in research and theory.* Vol. 4. New York: Academic Press, 1970.

Myers, D. L. & Myers, L. E. Undermatching: A reappraisal of performance on concurrent variable-interval schedules of reinforcement. *Journal of the Experimental Analysis of Behavior,* in press.

Neuringer, A. Effects of reinforcement magnitude on choice and rate of responding. *Journal of the Experimental Analysis of Behavior,* 1967, **10,** 417–424.

Nevin, J. A. Interval reinforcement of choice behavior in discrete trials. *Journal of the Experimental Analysis of Behavior,* 1969, **12,** 875–885.

Rachlin, H. C. Matching and contrast. *Psychological Review,* 1973, **80,** 217–234.

Restle, F. *Psychology of judgment and choice: a theoretical essay.* New York: Wiley, 1961.

Reynolds, G. S. Relativity of response rate and reinforcement frequency in a multiple schedule. *Journal of the Experimental Analysis of Behavior,* 1961, **4,** 179–184.

Roberts, W. A. Short-term memory in the pigeon: Effect of repetition and spacing. *Journal of Experimental Psychology,* 1972, **94,** 74–83.

Rozeboom, W. W. The learning tradition. In E. C. Carterette & M. P. Friedman Ed.), *Handbook of perception.* Vol. 1. New York: Academic Press, 1974.

Seligman, M. E. P., & Johnston, J. C. A cognitive theory of avoidance learning. In F. J. McGuigan & D. B. Lumsden (Eds.), *Contemporary approaches to conditioning and learning.* Washington, D.C.: Winston, 1973.

Shimp, C. P. Probabilistically reinforced choice behavior in pigeons. *Journal of the Experimental Analysis of Behavior,* 1966, **9,** 443–455.

Shimp C. P. The reinforcement of short interresponse times. *Journal of the Experimental Analysis of Behavior,* 1967, **10,** 425–434.

Shimp, C. P. Magnitude and frequency of reinforcement and frequency of interresponse times. *Journal of the Experimental Analysis of Behavior,* 1968, **11,** 525–535.

Shimp, C. P. Optimal behavior in free-operant experiments. *Psychological Review,* 1969, **76,** 97–112. (a)

Shimp, C. P. The concurrent reinforcement of two interresponse times: the relative frequency of an interresponse time equals its relative harmonic length. *Journal of the Experimental Analysis of Behavior*, 1969, **12**, 403–411. (b)

Shimp, C. P. The concurrent reinforcement of two interresponse times: absolute rate of reinforcement. *Journal of the Experimental Analysis of Behavior*, 1970, **13**, 1–8.

Shimp, C. P. The reinforcement of four interresponse times in a two-alternative situation. *Journal of the Experimental Analysis of Behavior*, 1971, **16**, 385–399.

Shimp, C. P. Probabilistic discrimination learning in the pigeon. *Journal of Experimental Psychology*, 1973, **97**, 292–304. (a)

Shimp, C. P. Synthetic variable-interval schedules of reinforcement. *Journal of the Experimental Analysis of Behavior*, 1973, **19**, 311–330. (b)

Shimp, C. P. Sequential dependencies in free-responding. *Journal of the Experimental Analysis of Behavior*, 1973, **19**, 491–497. (c)

Shimp, C. P. Time allocation and response rate. *Journal of the Experimental Analysis of Behavior*, 1974, **21**, 491–499.

Shimp, C. P., & Hawkes, L. Time-allocation, matching, and contrast. *Journal of the Experimental Analysis of Behavior*, 1974, **22**, 1–10.

Shimp, C. P., & Moffitt, M. Short-term memory in the pigeon: stimulus–response associations. *Journal of the Experimental Analysis of Behavior*, 1974, **22**, 507–512.

Shimp, C. P., & Wheatley, K. L. Matching to relative reinforcement frequency in multiple schedules with a short component duration. *Journal of the Experimental Analysis of Behavior*, 1971, **15**, 205–210.

Shull, R. L., & Pliskoff, S. S. Changeover delay and concurrent schedules: Some effects on relative performance measures. *Journal of the Experimental Analysis of Behavior*, 1967, **10**, 517–527.

Silberberg, A., & Williams, D. R. Choice behavior on discrete trials: a demonstration of the occurrence of a response strategy. *Journal of the Experimental Analysis of Behavior*, 1974, **21**, 315–322.

Skinner, B. F. *The behavior of organisms*. New York: Appleton-Century-Crofts, 1938.

Skinner, B. F. "Superstition" in the pigeon. *Journal of Experimental Psychology*, 1948, **38**, 168–172.

Skinner, B. F. Are theories of learning necessary? *Psychological Review*, 1950, **57**, 193–216.

Skinner, B. F. Operant behavior. In W. K. Honig (Ed.), *Operant behavior: Areas of research and application*. New York: Appleton-Century-Crofts, 1966.

Smith, L. Delayed discrimination and delayed matching in pigeons. *Journal of the Experimental Analysis of Behavior*, 1967, **10**, 529–533.

Smith, R. F. Topography of the food-reinforced key peck and the source of 30-millisecond interresponse times. *Journal of the Experimental Analysis of Behavior*, 1974, **21**, 541–551.

Staddon, J. E. R. Spaced responding and choice: a preliminary analysis. *Journal of the Experimental Analysis of Behavior*, 1968, **11**, 669–682.

Staddon, J. E. R. Temporal control, attention, and memory. *Psychological Review*, 1974, **81**, 375–391.

Thorndike, E. L. *Human learning*. New York: Appleton-Century-Crofts, 1931.

Tolman, E. C. *Purposive behavior in animals and men*. New York: Appleton-Century-Crofts, 1932.

Tulving, E. Subjective organization in free recall of "unrelated" words. *Psychological Review*, 1962, **69**, 344–354.

Tulving, E., & Donaldson, W. *Organization of memory*. New York: Academic Press, 1972.

Tulving, E., & Madigan, S. A. Memory and verbal learning. In P. R. Farnsworth (Ed.), *Annual review of psychology*. Palo Alto, California, Annual Reviews, 1970.

Watson, J. B. *Behaviorism*. New York: Norton, 1924.

Williams, B. Probability learning as a function of momentary reinforcement probability. *Journal of the Experimental Analysis of Behavior*, 1972, **17**, 363–368.

Zentall, T. R. Memory in the pigeon: retroactive inhibition in a delayed matching task. *Bulletin of the Psychonomic Society*, 1973, **1**, 126–128.

7
Stimulus Selection in Associative Learning

Jerry W. Rudy

Princeton University

Allan R. Wagner

Yale University

I. INTRODUCTION

Several generations of theorists concerned with associative learning have wrestled with issues of "stimulus selection." In this chapter we describe the essential problem that has required such persistent attention and discuss certain of the theoretical attempts to deal with it. We do not intend to provide a comprehensive historical treatment of the problem area nor an exhaustive survey of the relevant data. For this purpose recent discussions by Mackintosh (1965a), Sutherland and Mackintosh (1971), and Trabasso and Bower (1968) are especially commendable. Nor do we intend to offer a brief for some particular theoretical position. In writing about the issues today we are less impressed with any single definitive solution to the problem of stimulus selection (or even with any continuous progress toward consensual resolution) than we are with the more general theoretical insights that have been spawned by the persistent obligation to somehow deal with the facts of stimulus selection. As different theorists have approached the different faces of the problem, they have developed theoretical machinery that has remained to form much of the workings of our theories of learning. Thus, we have chosen to illustrate some of the past

269

and present attempts to deal with the problem of stimulus selection so as to emphasize the theoretical legacy that is involved and the current implications for our understanding of the associative process.

A. The Stimulus Selection Problem

"Associative learning" is a very general abstraction. It may be said to have occurred whenever an organism acts as though it had acquired some knowledge of the relationship between two or more stimuli. In equally general terms the stimulus selection problem arises from the fact that the behavioral indexes of association between particular experienced events, for example, E_1 and E_2, appear to be influenced by other stimuli contemporaneously experienced during training. That is, it appears that the association between E_I and E_2 does not simply mirror the isolated relationship that is experienced between the two events, but is determined by other concurrent event relationships. The problem therefore becomes one of specifying the rules whereby a relationship will or will not appear to be learned about depending upon the context of environmental events in which it is imbedded. The theoretical task is one of identifying the orderly process whereby the experienced relationship between E_1 and E_2 does or does not appear to be abstracted (selected) for association, as expressed in subsequent responding to the individual stimuli.

In practice, the laboratory investigation of associative learning suggests a more specific characterization of the problem. First, although associative learning may in principle involve any manner of relationship between events, it should be recognized that there has been a preoccupation with temporal relationships wherein one event, for example, E_1, presages the occurrence of another event, for example E_2. Thus, the research that we examine is in Pavlovian conditioning, in which a conditioned stimulus (CS) is presented in controlled temporal relationship to an unconditioned stimulus (US); in selective discrimination learning, in which a discriminandum announces the availability of reward; and in human paired-associate learning, in which a stimulus term antedates a response term. In these situations the different response measures indexing association are typically focused on some tendency for E_1 to be acted toward as though it were a "signal" for E_2. Second, although the contextual influence upon association might, in principle, involve any manner of additional stimulus relationships, it should be recognized that the problem of stimulus selection has generally been seen in regard to a particular influence. That is, what is often witnessed is *variability in the degree to which E_1 comes to act as a signal for E_2, depending upon the presence or absence of other events during training which have had a similar relationship to E_2 as did E_1.*

A relatively informal set of observations from Pavlov's laboratory led to one of the first explicit references to the problem of stimulus selection (Pavlov, 1927, pp. 141–144) and still remains adequate to exemplify the common ingredients. The studies of interest employed two separable stimuli (for example, a thermal CS, A, and a tactual CS, B), which were otherwise known in Pavlov's laboratory to be potentially adequate conditioned stimuli: with sufficient experience with either A followed by food or B followed by food, a dog would come to salivate upon presentation of the respective individual CS. That is, it could be assumed that the subject would come to appreciate that A signaled food or that B signaled food if there were no other cues present during training. The interesting phenomenon Pavlov then reported was this: if, during training, A and B were always presented *together,* and the compound followed by food, the subject might subsequently salivate to A alone, but not to B alone, or salivate to B alone, but not to A alone. When trained in compound, one cue might be "obscured" or "overshadowed" by another, that is, one otherwise adequate cue might appear not to have become associated with the US as an apparent consequence of the concurrent experiencing of another cue in a similar temporal relationship to the US.

This kind of dependence of the index of association between E_1 and E_2 upon the context of relationships in which E_1 and E_2 are imbedded during training has been seen in hundreds of investigations (see Sutherland & Mackintosh, 1971; Trabasso & Bower, 1968; Wagner, 1969a). The challenge is in how to accommodate the phenomena of stimulus selection in our theories of associative learning.

B. Theoretical Approaches to Stimulus Selection

Although there is a large number of specific theories addressed to the phenomena of stimulus selection there are certain affinities that can be recognized. First, one can classify some approaches as being "elementistic" as opposed to those approaches that are "configural." This distinction concerns the vocabulary for describing the events that are taken to enter into association, that is, whether it is theoretically useful to conceptualize a training episode as promoting multiple associations each involving separable "elements" (aspects, dimensions) of the total experience, or whether it is preferable to treat associative learning as involving a singular pattern (configuration) of stimulation. Second, one can classify some approaches as involving a special "selective" theoretical process as opposed to those approaches that appeal to no such identifiable mechanism. This distinction becomes meaningful only in the context of some theoretical prescription for association formation. Then, it can be asked whether stimulus selection can be accounted for via a concantination of the basic principles (whatever these may be), or whether it requires the addition of some further theoretical process. Examples of the latter would be "cue neutralization" as added to statistical association theory (e.g., Restle, 1955) or "observing responses" as added to conditioning-extinction theory (e.g., Lawrence, 1949).

Taken together, the two distinctions mentioned above result in a fourfold classification of the major approaches to the problem of stimulus selection, that is, nonselective elementistic, selective elementistic, nonselective configural, and selective configural. We describe theories that exemplify each type, although our treatment is more or less detailed, in keeping with the influence that the several approaches have had.

II. NONSELECTIVE ELEMENTISTIC THEORY

The prototypical example of a nonselective elementistic approach has been Spence's classic "continuity" theory of discrimination learning (e.g., Spence, 1936). A more recent example is the "modified-continuity theory" (Wagner, 1969a) as proposed by Kamin (1968) and Wagner (1969a) and more formally developed by Rescorla and Wagner (e.g., Rescorla & Wagner, 1972; Wagner & Rescorla, 1972).

A. Spence's Continuity Theory

Spence's theoretical treatment of discrimination learning was developed as a direct response to a problem of stimulus selection as posed by Lashley (1929) and Krechevsky (e.g., 1932). In describing the behavior of the rat in solving a two-choice visual discrimination problem Lashley called attention to two common characteristics. First, he noted that choice between the relevant discriminanda often remained at a chance level for individual subjects over some period of training before changing abruptly to virtually errorless responding. Second, he noted that, while choice behavior was at a chance level with respect to the correct versus incorrect alternatives, it was systematically related to other stimuli in the environment. Behavior during the so-called "presolution period" seemed to be in response to such features as position of the cues, movements of the experimenter, or the animal's response on the previous trial, features that were not, in fact, well correlated with the occasions for reward. Lashley (1929) concluded that these characteristics "strongly suggest that the actual association is formed very quickly, and that the practice preceding and errors following are irrelevant to the actual formation of association [p. 135]." Krechevsky (1932), on the basis of similar, but more detailed, observations proposed that discrimination learning "consists of changing from one systematic purposeful way of behaving to another until the problem is solved [p. 532]." Both Lashley and Krechevsky leap from the descriptive characteristics of choice behavior during training to an assertion involving stimulus selection: it appears as though the subject does not learn the association between the relevant discriminanda and reward during the presolution period *because* of the concurrent influence of other cues which from trial to trial may occasionally stand in a similar relationship to reward. It appears that only when the subject focuses upon the relevant cue, rather than others, does it learn the association between that cue and reward.

Spence's response to this problem was elementistic (as was that of Lashley and Krechevsky), the stimulus complex the animal experienced during training was assumed to be usefully analyzed into a number of elementary components (for example, position, brightness, size, shape). What Spence attempted to show, however, was that the apparent selectivity of association might be accounted for by assuming (*a*) that the relationship of *each* of the stimulus elements to the occasion of reward and nonreward is learned about *on each trial* according to the exact schedule of stimulation that is experienced, and (*b*) that choice behavior on each trial is determined by the combination of associative tendencies that have accrued to the several constellations of cues facing the animal at the choice point.

To be more specific, Spence (e.g., 1936) assumed that the tendency to approach any stimulus *component* was a monotonic function of its "excitatory strength," which, in turn, was an algebraic function of the association between that component and the occurrence of reward minus the association between that component and nonreward. The association between each stimulus component and reward was assumed to be increased by each sequential experience of the component followed by reward, whereas the association between each of the same stimulus components and nonreward was assumed to be increased by each sequential experience of the component followed by nonreward. Quantitatively, it was proposed that the net increment in excitatory strength of a stimulus component followed by reward was a bell shaped function of its current excitatory strength, whereas the net decrement in excitatory strength of a stimulus component followed by nonreward was a linear function of its current excitatory strength. Later Spence (1952a) expressed a preference for linear assumptions in either case which in terms of his 1936 model would allow the simple expression of the change in excitatory value (V) of any component, i, consequent to a reward or nonreward experience to take the form

$$\Delta V_i = \theta_i (\lambda_j - V_i), \tag{1}$$

where λ_j would be replaced by the asymptotic excitatory value that would be produced by continued reward or nonreward, respectively, and θ_i would be replaced by the relevant rate parameter. Spence offered examples in terms of arbitrary scale units but specifically assumed that nonreward would produce no decrement unless V_i had some positive value, which would be the case if λ_j were positive during a sequence of rewarded trials, then at the onset of nonreward were set at zero.

The rules for performance in a selective learning situation according to Spence consisted of (a) a choice rule, which asserted that the animal will choose (approach) the alternative stimulus complex whose separable stimulus elements in combination yield the greatest aggregate excitatory value, and (b) a combination rule that prescribed how the excitatory strengths of the various components combined. The latter rule was simply that the aggregate excitatory strength of a choice alternative was equal to the algebraic sum of the excitatory strengths of its component features.

Consider a choice situation in which stimulus component A is arranged always to be followed by reward whereas component A', differing from A along some dimension such as brightness, is arranged always to be followed by nonreward. In addition to these "relevant" components, one can identify numerous dimensionalizable "irrelevant" components, such as position, that are relatively uncorrelated with the occasions of reward and nonreward. On a particular choice trial the subject thus may be faced with the alternatives

$$[A, B, C', \ldots, X] \quad \text{versus} \quad [A', B', C, \ldots, X']$$

and on another with the alternatives

$$[A, B', C, \ldots, X] \quad \text{versus} \quad [A', B, C', \ldots, X'],$$

etc., through all of the scheduled combinations of the relevant and irrelevant cues on different trials. When any complex including A is chosen and followed by reward, the excitatory strength of each component is assumed to be incremented. When any complex including A' is chosen and followed by nonreward, the excitatory strength of each component is assumed to be decremented. And the choice that will occur on each trial will depend upon the cumulative strength of the alternative aggregations, for example,

$$[V_A + V_B + V_{C'} + \cdots + V_X] \quad \text{versus} \quad [V_{A'} + V_{B'} + V_C + \cdots V_{X'}]$$

or

$$[V_A + V_{B'} + V_C + \cdots + V_X] \quad \text{versus} \quad [V_{A'} + V_B + V_{C'} + \cdots + V_{X'}].$$

Within Spence's theory then the stationarity of choice performance with respect to the relevant cues (A versus A') during a "presolution period" was explicable in terms of the overriding contribution of other cues (e.g., B versus B') to the excitatory value of the alternative compounds. That is, whereas V_A may be systematically increasing in relationship to $V_{A'}$, such will not be detected *in choice performance* until the difference between V_A and $V_{A'}$ is sufficiently large relative to the difference between V_B and $V_{B'}$, V_C and $V_{C'}$, etc., that it will influence the relative frequency that the associative value of the occurring compounds including V_A will be greater than the occurring alternative compounds that include $V_{A'}$. Until then the subject should perform at a "chance" level with respect to A versus A', and indeed may respond systematically in relationship to other cues that do have more substantial difference in excitatory strength, perhaps as a result of pretraining tendencies. The sudden shift in choice performance following the presolution period was interpreted by Spence as just that, that is, a sudden shift in *the particular performance measure of association*, as the difference between the relevant cues was eventually allowed to show through the obscuring tendencies of the remaining components.

To evaluate Spence's interpretation of the Lashley–Krechevsky problem it was necessary to employ alternative assessments of the differential excitatory tendencies of the relevant cues during the presolution period when such presumed tendencies were not detectable in the choice measure. Support came in the form of demonstrations that (*a*) presolution reversal of the significance of the discriminanda retarded eventual problem solution (e.g., Ehrenfreund, 1948; McCulloch & Pratt, 1934; Spence, 1945); (*b*) speed of approach to the rewarded discriminandum was faster than that to the nonrewarded discriminandum prior to the development of consistent choice of the former (e.g., Eninger, 1953; Mahut, 1954); and (*c*) when an animal *first* abandoned systematic responding in terms of an irrelevant stimulus dimension, it was more likely to do so by approaching a cue complex containing the relevant rewarded stimulus than approaching a cue complex containing the relevant nonrewarded stimulus (e.g., Sutherland & Mackintosh, 1971, p. 98).

Spence's formulation was eventually challenged by a variety of more pointed issues concerning stimulus selection that we will address in later sections. One further example will be considered here as it helps to elucidate the workings of Spence's approach and the difficulty in rejecting its adequacy in many situations. The Pavlovian "overshadowing" experiment which we chose to introduce the problem of stimulus selection can be arranged in a choice situation as well. The general case is referred to as a "redundant-relevant-cue" experiment, and may be exemplified in a choice situation by a recent study by Lovejoy and Russell (1967). In the latter study two groups of rats were given discrimination training on a Lashley jumping stand with vertical (V) versus horizontal (H) rectangles as relevant stimuli correlated with reward versus nonreward. For one group only this single cue dimension was relevant. For another group there were two (redundant) relevant cues, as the vertical stimulus was always black (B) and the horizontal stimulus always white (W). To equate overall experience with the two dimensions the single-cue group also received black and white figures on each trial, but, in this case, uncorrelated with reward, that is, the vertical stimulus was half of the time black and the horizontal stimulus white, whereas half of the time their brightnesses were reversed. The question in the experiment was whether the signal properties that accrued to the V versus H cues would be diminished in the two-cue group as opposed to the single-cue group, as a consequence of the presence of the redundant B versus W cues. Evidence was obtained following discrimination training by presenting both groups of subjects with a choice between the V and H stimuli without the usual difference in brightness, that is, with both stimuli gray. The results of the test clearly revealed that the two-cue group responded less discriminatively (showed less tendency to choose the rewarded vertical stimulus) than did the single-cue group. The presence of the redundant brightness cues during training interfered with the development of stimulus control exhibited by the orientation cues.

At first glance these results might appear to discredit Spence's assumption that the associative tendencies of the separate stimuli are modified by their pairings with reinforcement and nonreinforcement, without regard to the additional stimuli also experienced in relationship to the signaled events. One need then be reminded that Spence's account requires attention to the exact schedule of stimulus exposure and reinforcement actually received during training. Only to the extent that the one-cue and two-cue groups of the Lovejoy and Russell experiment received identical training with H followed by reward and V followed by nonreward, should one necessarily expect equivalent choice between the two.

In fact, the Lovejoy and Russell groups did not experience equivalent reinforcement histories with respect to the tested choice alternatives. Wagner (1969a) pointed out that during the initial discrimination learning phase, the subjects in the two-cue condition quickly reached essentially 100% choice of the correct, reinforced compound, whereas the one-cue animals only slowly approached a terminal asymptotic level of about 80% correct responses. Thus, the two-cue animals received a large number of reinforced trials with the to-be-tested, positive cue, V, but only a small number of nonreinforced trials with the negative cue, H. In contrast, animals in the single-cue condition experienced relatively fewer reinforced trials with the vertical stimulus and many more nonreinforced trials with the horizontal stimulus. Wagner (1969a) suggested that, "The subsequent finding that the single-cue group responded more discriminatively to the different orientation cues than did the two-cue group may consequently reveal no more than that nonreinforcing responses to H was overall more effective in producing discriminative behavior between V and H than was reinforcing responses to V [p. 108]."

It is important to recognize that, according to Spence's model, the presence of one set of potential signals for the reinforcement contingencies *may* interfere with the extent to which another set acquires differential control over behavior: to the degree that behavior is controlled by one set the animal's history of reinforcement with the second set may be altered. Such an alteration in the animal's reinforcement history may then deprive the animal of the experience necessary to provide the alternatives within the set with sufficiently different excitatory strengths to produce differential choice behavior. It is a tribute to Spence's formulation that the above analysis can be sensibly applied to a number of contemporary examples of stimulus selection (e.g., Mackintosh, 1965b; Sutherland, Mackintosh, & Mackintosh, 1965; vom Saal & Jenkins, 1970) obtained from more complicated experimental designs, which in some instances have been interpreted as providing evidence for more complicated theoretical schemes.

In summary, Spence's theory was developed in response to the problem of stimulus selection as posed by Lashley and Krechevsky in describing the course of selective discrimination learning. The analytic approach Spence brought to the problem, with its emphasis on identifying the stimulus elements of the task and their relationship to the animal's reinforcement history, served not only to clarify this issue but also to provide a conceptual framework that has remained useful in approaching contemporary experimental examples of stimulus selection. Perhaps more important is the fact that this same approach has provided a solid theoretical structure upon which to build more complicated theoretical arguments. Spence embellished the 1936 model with additional assumptions about the generalization of the incremental and decremental effects of reward and nonreward and was able to show how the phenomenon of "transposition" might be derived (Spence, 1937). The essential properties of this more elaborate model still prove fruitful in dealing with contemporary phenomena such as "peak shift" (e.g., Bloomfield, 1969; Hearst, 1969), which occurs in stimulus generalization curves following differential reinforcement of two stimuli belonging to a common dimension. Finally, the degree of success of Spence's approach, with its emphasis upon identifying certain elementary principles and combining them to derive phenomena not transparently evident from the principles themselves, has served as an encouragement to rigorous theory construction for later researchers.

B. Modified Continuity Theory

Although Spence's continuity theory may be adequate to account for certain redundant-relevant cue experiments in selective learning, such as that of Lovejoy and Russell (1967) described above, it is interesting to note that it offered no obvious explanation for the similar Pavlovian overshadowing observations. In Pavlovian conditioning the sequence of stimulation the animal receives is not dependent upon the subject's choice behavior but is under more prescribed experimenter control. Thus, barring more subtle arguments as to how the subject may yet dictate what learning experiences are provided, continuity theory would seem to be embarrassed by any finding from Pavlovian conditioning in which the presence of redundant-relevant cues diminishes the acquired responding to a given CS.

Perhaps because of doubts as to the exact experimental protocols observed in Pavlov's laboratory, the overshadowing phenomena he reported had little impact upon continuity theory until research (e.g., Kamin, 1968; Wagner, 1969a; Wagner, Logan, Haberlandt, & Price, 1968) confirmed and extended the observation. A brief discussion of two of these experiments illustrates the force of the data.

Kamin (1968, 1969) sought to determine whether or not the amount of conditioning that occurred to one member of a compound CS would be influenced by the animal's history of conditioning experiences with the other members of the compound. In Kamin's basic experiment, rats were given fear conditioning involving a compound CS, AX, and a shock US. The important comparison conditions differed in that one group was given a number of A–US presentations *prior* to conditioning with the AX compound, whereas the other group received no such pretraining. Following the compound conditioning trials both groups were tested on the X component of the compound. The results of this test revealed that animals that had been pretrained to the A element responded less to the X element than did those that had only experienced compound training. The presence of a preconditioned element in a compound CS thus appeared to reduce or "block" conditioning to the other element.

Wagner (1969a) asked a related question: Would the *extinction* of the conditioned properties of a cue be influenced by the animal's conditioning history with other concurrent stimuli. In his experiment, rabbits that had acquired a conditioned eyelid closure response to a CS, X, were extinguished to the X cue by presenting it in compound with another element, A, and nonreinforcing the AX compound. The groups differed in that for one the A element had previously been paired a large number of times with the US, whereas for another only a few A–US pairings were administered. In the subsequent test with X alone, the animals for whom the A element had been the *more often paired* with the US gave evidence of the most extinction to X. The presence of a highly trained A element thus in some way enhanced the demonstrable association between X and nonreinforcement that resulted from the AX extinction training.

The theoretical approach that was formulated to deal with this pattern of data was referred to by Wagner (1969a) as a "modified continuity theory." It follows Spence's approach in being elementistic and invoking no special selective mechanism, apart from the basic associative apparatus. Although the essence of the theory originated with Kamin's (1968) interpretation of his blocking experiments, the important features of this approach and the difference between it and previous continuity theory are most apparent in Rescorla and Wagner's (1972) relatively formal modal.

As noted in Section II.A, Spence's specification of the change in the associative value of a cue that results from a conditioning episode can be represented by Eq. (1), $\Delta V_i = \theta_i(\lambda_j - V_i)$. When applied to conditioning with compound CSs this approach asserts that the associative value of a component cue, i, will be changed in accordance with the difference between its current associative value, V_i, and λ_j, the asymptotic associative value the US can support. The corresponding equation offered by Rescorla and Wagner is

$$\Delta V_i = \theta_i(\lambda_j - \bar{V}), \tag{2}$$

which differs from Equation (1) only in the substitution of V for $\bar{V}_i$. Rescorla and Wagner define $\bar{V}$ as the algebraic sum of the associative values of *all* component stimuli present on a conditioning trial. When a compound of cues is followed by reinforcement, it should be expected that the signal value of each component will be changed according to the discrepancy between λ and $\bar{V}$. The signal value of all components should commonly be incremented without regard to their individual values, V_i, except as the latter contribute to $\bar{V}$.

Although the Rescorla–Wagner formulation may appear to involve a relatively minor change in the expression for associative change as compared to earlier continuity theory, the modified theory leads to quite different predictions in many situations. The earlier continuity theory, for example, wrongly predicts that the acquisition to one cue in a compound, as in Kamin's blocking experiment, Wagner's extinction experiment, or Pavlov's overshadowing experiment, would be indifferent to the associative strength of the remaining cues. In contrast, modified continuity theory nicely anticipates the findings.

As indicated, modified continuity theory asserts that changes in the associative value of a component of a compound CS will take place only as differences between $\bar{V}$ and λ_j exist. Thus, Kamin's "blocking" effect is anticipated as A–US pairings prior to AX–US training should increase $\bar{V}$ and reduce the discrepancy between $\bar{V}$ and λ_j on AX trials as compared with the case in which no such pretraining is given. Pavlov's overshadowing observation is anticipated by similar reasoning. When two cues are trained over a *series of trials*, the associative strength that develops to each on trial n contributes to $\bar{V}$ on trial $n + 1$ and thereby "blocks" what associative strength may be acquired by the remaining cue. In extinction λ_j is assumed to take the value of zero and decrements in associative strength are generated as $\lambda - \bar{V}$ yields a negative value. Wagner's finding that the extinction of the conditioned properties of a cue is enhanced the greater the signal value of the remaining cues in the compound follows as increasing $\bar{V}$ should make $\lambda - \bar{V}$ more negative.

In addition to accounting for these stimulus selection phenomena, the Rescorla and Wagner model has proved to have other deductive advantage over earlier continuity theory. One important benefit is that it provides natural framework for interpreting the Pavlovian phenomenon of conditioned inhibition. When an organism is given a training experience involving rein forced trials with A alone (A^+) and nonreinforced trials with an AX compound (AX^-), the X component can acquire the ability to suppress conditioned responding normally evoked by a cue paired with the reinforcer. This conditioned tioned inhibitory property of the X cue can be demonstrated by showing that its presence reduces the amount of conditioned responding otherwise seen to a third cue, B, which also had been paired with the reinforcer. The Rescorla Wagner model implies that the training schedule the organism experiences with X should result in the associative properties of X being opposed to those of a cue paired with the US. The A^+ trials should result in increments to V such that on nonreinforced AX trials $V_{AX} > \lambda$ and both V_A and V_X should be decremented. Without prior training it may be assumed that $V_X = 0$, so that as a consequence of AX^- trials, X will be decremented below zero and have a negative V^- value. If X is subsequently presented in compound with an excitatory B cue, the net associative strength of the compound, $\bar{V}$, should be less than that to B alone. An important testable assertion that this model makes is that *more* conditioned inhibition will accrue to a stimulus such a X in an A^+, AX^- paradigm, the greater is the associative strength of the cue with which it is nonreinforced in compound. The reasoning is exactly the same as in the Wagner (1969b) extinction study referred to above: The greater the value of $\bar{V}$ on AX^- trials, the greater the decrement in V_X that should be expected. Wagner (1971) has confirmed this prediction.

In addition to asserting that more conditioned inhibition should be established to a cue if it is nonreinforced in compound with cues that have been strongly associated with the US, the Rescorla and Wagner model makes the symmetrical assertion that increments in the associative value of a CS can be *enhanced* by reinforcing the CS in compound with a previously established conditioned inhibitor, that is, a cue with a negative V. This prediction follows because the presence of an inhibitory stimulus should serve to reduce $\bar{V}$ and thereby increase $\lambda - \bar{V}$ in comparison with the case where the CS is paired with the US in isolation. Evidence consistent with this implication also has been provided (Wagner, 1971).

The general observation that the amount of conditioning that occurs to a component CS is affected by the animal's past history with the aggregation of cues present at the time of the US can be expressed in a less formal way in terms of variations in the "expectedness" of the US (e.g. Kamin, 1968, 1969; Rescorla, 1969; Wagner, 1969b). To the extent that the US in unexpected, that is, not well signaled by the totality of cues present at the time, it will promote conditioning. To the extent that the

US is expected, that is, well signaled by the totality of cues present at the time, it will *fail* to promote conditioning. In the Rescorla–Wagner formulation the expectedness of a US can be identified with the extent of the difference between λ and $\bar{V}$; the more closely $\bar{V}$ approximates λ, the more expected in the US.

The view that variations in the expectedness of the US result in variations in the amount of conditioning the US will produce has resulted in some theorists (e.g., Kamin, 1969; Wagner, 1971) speculating about the associative processes that might be sensitive to differences between expected and unexpected USs. Kamin, for instance, proposed that unexpected USs instigate additional posttrial processing of the CS–US experience. Specifically, Kamin (1969) suggested that "for an increment in associative connection to occur, it is necessary that the US provoke the animal into a backward scanning of its memory store of recent stimulus inputs: only as a result of such a scanning can an association between a CS and US be formed [p. 293]." Wagner (1971) also suggested that expected and unexpected USs might have differential effects on the amount of posttrial processing of the CS–US episode. He conceptualized the process as a rehearsal-like activity which resulted both in the establishment of functional associative connections between the CS and US (in long-term memory) and in prolonging the functional persistence of information about the elements of the experience (in short-term memory). Recently, some experimental support for the view that a posttrial rehearsal-like mechanism might be responsive to the variations in conditioning associated with expected and unexpected USs has been presented (Terry & Wagner, 1975; Wagner, Rudy, & Whitlow, 1973). On the assumption that the rehearsal process engaged by an unexpected US is a limited capacity process, Wagner and his colleagues reasoned that it should be possible to interfere with the rehearsal of a CS–US experience, and hence the development of conditioned responding to the CS. This could be done by exposing the subject, shortly after the CS–US experience, to another Pavlovian episode which could also be expected to require "rehearsal." From this argument, it follows that if the second episode contains an "unexpected" as opposed to an expected US, there should be a slower rate of conditioning to the original CS because the unexpected US should require more rehearsal. The results of their experiment were consistent with this line of reasoning. Terry and Wagner (1975) have presented evidence that subjects "rehearse" unexpected USs by demonstrating that such USs have stimulus control properties that endure over a longer time interval than do expected USs.

In summary, modified continuity theory was developed in order to deal with a pattern of stimulus selection data that appeared to be out of reach of the existing continuity framework. Although the important change in continuity theory that was introduced (the change in associative value of component stimuli of a compound CS is determined by the difference between the combined associative values of components and the asympototic level of conditioning the US will support) appears to be only a minor departure from the existing approach, this assumption has proved to greatly increase the theoretical power of the continuity formulation. Stimulus selection phenomena such as blocking and overshadowing which are not expected on the basis of the early continuity model are easily derived from the modified approach. Moreover the modified continuity model provides a theoretical framework for interpreting conditioned inhibition and has led to the discovery of several new conditioning phenomena (e.g., Rescorla & Wagner, 1972; Wagner, 1971).

III. SELECTIVE ELEMENTISTIC THEORY

Although the continuity models of learning provide an adequate account of a variety of instances of stimulus selection, in the late 1940s, Lawrence (1949, 1950) reported a series of experiments demonstrating a stimulus selection phenomenon not anticipated by Spence's continuity theory nor easily approached by the modified continuity approach of Rescorla and Wagner. The phenomenon is well illustrated by the following study (Lawrence, 1950). In the first stage of the study, rats were required to master a *successive* discrimination problem in a T maze involving one relevant and one irrelevant stimulus dimension. For example, the arms of the maze could be black (B) or white (W), and chains (C) or no chains (NC) could be hung in the arms of the entrances. If the brightness cues were relevant, the animals might solve the problem by learning to go left if both arms were black and go right if both arms were white. On some occasions chains would be present. On other occasions chains would be absent. However, the presence or absence of chains in this case would be uncorrelated with the choice response requirements. In the second phase of the study, the subjects had to learn a *simultaneous* discrimination task in which both members of the brightness and chains dimensions were present on each trial as redundant, relevant cues. Thus, for example, entrance into a black arm with chains present might be consistently rewarded (BC+), whereas a response to a white arm containing no chains would not be rewarded (WNC-). Given this training arrangement, the subjects could learn to approach the B cue while avoiding the W cue and/or approach the C cue while avoiding the NC cue. To evaluate the relative control over choice behavior that accrued to the stimulus alternatives of the simultaneous problem, Lawrence gave his subjects an *opposition test* in which he formed new compounds, each of which contained one previously reinforced and one previously nonreinforced cue from the separate dimensions. Thus, if the subject had been trained to choose between BC+ and WNC-, it was tested with BNC versus WC. The important finding Lawrence reported was that the cues of the stimulus dimension which had been relevant in the earlier successive problem exerted more control over choice responding in the opposition test than those which had been irrelevant in the successive problem. Thus, for example, those animals whose discrimination performance in the successive task had been controlled by stimulus brightness chose the arm containing the reinforced brightness cue more often than the arm containing the reinforced chains cue although the two stimuli during the simultaneous task had been equally often associated with reward. When a compound of cues was correlated with reinforcement in Phase 2, subjects appeared to learn more or less about the separable components, depending upon the relevance of the cues in a prior discrimination task. Since the response requirements of the successive and simultaneous problems were different, it may be assumed that specific stimulus–response associations acquired during the successive problem did not determine this outcome. Lawrence argued that the result could be explained by assuming that, although they solved the initial successive problem, the animals, in addition to acquiring the correct stimulus–response associations, acquired a mediating response that altered their perceptual representation of the stimuli. Thus, the relevant cue of the successive problem could be assume to have become functionally more available for association with the correct response of the simultaneous problem than was the irrelevant cue of the first problem.

A.   Two-Stage Attention Theory

The implication that Lawrence drew from his data is that an adequate theory of discrimination learning must include a separate *stimulus selection process* in addition to the associative machinery. There is now a large number of specific theories (e.g., Atkinson, 1961; Lovejoy, 1966; Restle, 1955; Sutherland & Mackintosh, 1971; Trabasso & Bower, 1968; Zeaman & House, 1963) that, like Lawrence's (1950) proposal, can be categorized as *two-stage attentional* theories, each having a similar conception of what the stimulus selection process involves. In each case, the nominal stimulus is conceptualized as a complex of isolable dimensions or elements of which the learner is assumed to *selectively attend to* only a limited portion. That is, the stimulus selection process is assumed to fractionate the subject's environment into a set of functionally active elements (which control trol behavior and are modified in their signal value by the ensuing reinforcement events) and a set that are not functionally active. Members of the latter set are assumed neither to control behavior nor to have their signal value modified by reinforcement. A second common assumption of this class of theories is that the subject has a limited attentional capacity. Therefore, there should be an *inverse* relationship between the likelihood of attending to one set of stimuli and that of attending to another set.

In the typical discrimination learning problem, the stimulus elements or features that are relevant, that is, correlated with the reinforcement events, are presented among an array of irrelevant stimulus features. If the subject's attending behavior were only inconsistently captured by the relevant set of elements, the discrimination problem would never be solved. Likewise, if the elements, as attended to, were not associated with the consequent events (for example, the occasion for reward and nonreward), the discrimination problem would never be solved. Thus, for attentional theories, the solving of a discrimination problem is a two-stage process. The subject must acquire an appropriate attending response and must associate the cues to which it attends with the reinforcement consequences.

Spence (1937) pointed out in a footnote to his classic paper on discrimination learning that in many discrimination-learning problems, the task is not structured so as to insure that the animal will necessarily receive consistent differential stimulation from the relevant stimulus dimensions. He suggested that for an animal to solve such a problem, it must acquire *receptor orienting behaviors* that consistently bring it in contact with the relevant stimulus dimension. And he pointed out that one particular receptor orientation could be expected to be chosen over another for the same reason that one stimulus complex would be approached rather than another, that is, because it was, among the alternatives, maximally followed by reward. It is notable that subsequent two-stage theories of discrimination learning have taken a similar tack in specifying how the subject comes to fractionate the environmental stimuli into those which are functionally active versus those which are functionally inactive. Whether the selection process is viewed as a peripheral orienting response or a "central" stimulus processor, it is conceptualized as having properties of an instrumental response: if the fractionation that occurs is followed by reward, it is assumed to be made more likely in the future; if it is followed by nonreward, it is assumed to be made less likely. The subject is assumed to learn a particular "attending response" because it is more generally followed by reward than are alternative attending responses.

To see how this process works, we could consider any number of specific "attentional" theories (e.g., Atkinson, 1961; Lovejoy, 1966; Sutherland & Mackintosh, 1971; Trabasso & Bower, 1968; Zeaman & House, 1963). A brief discussion of a rather simple model presented by Lovejoy (1966), however, will serve to illustrate the general approach. Lovejoy assumes that for each stimulus dimension that is represented by different members in a discrimination-learning problem (brightness, shape, position, etc.) there is a orresponding attending response that has some probability of occurrence at he start of training. Lovejoy further assumes that the subject can attend to out a single dimension on any trial. In a two-choice problem the subject on any given trial can either attend to the relevant dimension or not (A or $\bar{A}$, espectively) and can make an eventual correct choice (R_C) or an incorrect choice (R_I). There are thus four possible chains of behavior that might occur on a given trial:

1. The subject might attend, A, to the relevant stimulus dimension and also make the correct choice response, R_C.

2. The subject might attend, A, to the relevant stimulus dimension but make the incorrect choice response, R_I.

3. The subject might *not* attend, $\bar{A}$, to the relevant dimension but make the correct choice response. R_C.

4. And, finally, the subject might not attend to the relevant stimulus dimension, $\bar{A}$, and make the incorrect choice response, R_I.

By definition a behavior chain which begins with the subject attending to irrelevant dimensions (that is, Chains 3 and 4) can only end in a correct response (and a reward) by chance. In contrast, although the initial probability of a subject making a correct response given that the relevant attending response is made might also be a chance occurrence, this tendency will be *increased* on each occasion that a trial begins by the subject making the relevant attending response. This is because trials that terminate in reward will increase the likelihood of the correct response (given an attending response) and those that end in nonreward will decrease the likelihood of the incorrect response (given an attending response). Note that, once this process begins to result in the probability of a correct response exceeding .5 (given an attending response), it will be the case that the relevant attending response will be experienced in relationship to a more favorable reinforcement schedule than will the irrelevant attending behavior. Such differential reinforcement of the relevant and irrelevant attending response then will ultimately result in the subject consistently beginning a trial by attending to the relevant dimension. Lovejoy represents this process formally by assuming that each of the component elements contained in the four behavior chains has some associated probability of occurrence. Components which occur on a given trial are assumed to have their probability values modified according to the general equation

$$\Delta P_i = \theta(\lambda - P_i), \tag{3}$$

where λ takes the value of 1 on rewarded trials and 0 on nonrewarded trials, and θ is also assumed to vary according to whether a rewarded or nonrewarded outcome occurs. Simulation of Lovejoy's model indeed shows that the probability of the correct response increases toward unity *and results in the subject acquiring the relevant attending response.*

B. Application of the Theory

Two-stage theories such as Lovejoy's have been fruitfully applied to a number of outcomes of discrimination learning experiments. Lovejoy (1966), for example, illustrated how the model we have just described can provide an explanation of the paradoxical overlearning reversal effect (e.g., Mackintosh, 1962; Reid, 1953). The basic experiment for demonstrating the overlearning reversal effect (ORE) is relatively simple. Subjects are either trained to some criterion of solution or are "overtrained" for some extended number of trials on a discrimination problem, and are then shifted to a new problem in which the significance of the discriminanda is reversed. The ORE occurs when the overtrained animals *more rapidly* solve the reversal problem than do those reversed immediately after criterion. This is a perplexing outcome. But the boundary conditions that dictate the occurrence of the ORE appear to encourage a two-stage interpretation. Lovejoy (1966), in his careful analysis of the conditions under which the ORE is or is not observed, arrived at the conclusion that the ORE is obtained when the relevant stimulus dimension is not likely to be readily attended to or received by the organism (e.g., Capaldi & Stevenson, 1957; Reid, 1953). In comparison when the relevant stimulus dimension is highly salient (e.g., D'Amato & Schiff, 1965; Erlebacher, 1963), the ORE may fail to emerge. The argument that has been proposed to integrate these data assumes that the two response tendencies of the behavior chain, the tendency to make the relevant attending response and the tendency to make correct response given a relevant attending behavior, are not equally affected by overtraining. Overtraining is assumed to add little to the tendency to respond to the attended to stimulus, whereas it may increase the strength of the relevant attending response. Overtrained animals thus master the reversal problem in fewer trials because they are less likely than criterion animals to abandon the still relevant attending response even though it initially leads consistently to nonreinforcement. However, if the relevant dimension is otherwise likely to be attended to, there should be little influence of overtraining upon performance of the reversal problem. From this standpoint, the failure to find the ORE when the relevant stimulus is highly salient or easily discriminable is sensible. Lovejoy (1966) has, in fact, shown in computer simulation how his model will generate an ORE or not, depending upon the choice of the initial probability of attending to the relevant dimension and the rate parameter for changing this probability.

Since it provides for the acquisition of a stimulus selection bias in addition to the specific stimulus–response associations, such a theory also is potentially in a position to deal with transfer phenomena such as that reported in the Lawrence (1950) study we have discussed. All one need assume is that at the completion of the initial successive discrimination problem, the animal has acquired a bias to selectively attend to the relevant stimulus dimension of that problem and not attend to the irrelevant dimension. This would mean that there would be a higher probability of the animal attending to that same stimulus dimension at the outset of the second problem. And, since both dimensions were relevant in the simultaneous problem, there should have been no basis for systematically changing this behavior. Thus, the previously relevant stimuli should have been more likely to be functionally present and enter into new associative control over behavior.

Our understanding of transfer studies involving comparisons of intradimensional and extradimensional shifts following the learning of an initial discrimination problem (e.g., Eimas, 1966; Shepp & Eimas, 1964) has benefited in a similar way from a two-stage analysis. In a dimensional-shift discrimination problem, the subjects are typically required to solve an initial problem in which two dimensions, for example, color, involving red versus green stimuli, and shape, involving a triangle versus square, are presented, but only one dimension is relevant. Following mastery of this problem, the subject is shifted to a new problem involving the same stimulus *dimensions* but new instances, that is, granted the above stimuli, the colors might then be yellow and blue and the forms might be a circle and a star. For subjects in the *intradimensional* shift problem, the stimulus dimension relevant in the first problem is arranged to be relevant in the new task, whereas for the subjects in the *extradimensional* shift problem, the dimension irrelevant in the first task is arranged to be relevant. In such experiments involving rats (e.g., Shepp & Eimas, 1964) and children (e.g., Eimas, 1966) the typical finding is that the subjects presented with the intradimensional shift master the new problem more quickly than those presented with the extradimensional shift. If this effect occurs regardless of which *member* of the dimension relevant in the second problem is paired with which consequence (that is, reinforcement or nonreinforcement), it would be difficult to attribute it to the positive transfer of any specific stimulus–response associations acquired in the first problem. A most reasonable conclusion then seems to be that an intradimensional shift is easier to accomplish than an extradimensional shift because the same attentional response is appropriate in both the preshift and postshift problem.

There are a variety of theories that share the assumption that discrimination learning is a two-stage affair, consisting of a stimulus-selection process that fractionates the available stimuli into those that are functional and those that are not, and an associative mechanism that relates the selected elements and their environmental consequences. Not all theories falling into this classification, however, share the same understanding of the stimulus selection process in the sense of how the stimulus set is fractionated. A number of different labels for the stimulus selection mechanism have been employed. Some of these can probably be used interchangeably, for example, "attends to a stimulus dimension" (Zeaman & House, 1963) versus "switching in a stimulus analyzer" (Sutherland & Mackintosh, 1971), or are purposefully meant to be indifferent to more particular characterization, for example, "adopting a coding response" (Lawrence, 1963). In other cases, however, the terminology suggests very different ways in which the nominal stimulus is assumed to be fractionated into functional and nonfunctional components. For example, appeal to an overt "observing response" or "reception orienting act" (Spence, 1937; Wyckoff, 1952) would allow a segregation of those stimuli that emanate from one place in the environment from those that emanate from another, or allow a segregation of those stimuli that require one receptor from those that require another. Alternatively, appeal to a "stimulus analyzer" would allow a segregation of those stimulus differences that fall along one dimension (brightness, pitch, shape, etc.) from those differences that do not fall on such dimensions. In still a different terminology, "adapting irrelevant cues" (Restle, 1955) might suggest a segregation on the basis of yet more specific characteristics, that is, those limited to a particular training set.

These distinctions have important consequences when we ask what transfer of training effects to expect. Yet, about all that appears to be certain is that a characterization based solely on overt observing behavior is inadequate in some situations and that some dimensional-like learning can occur (e.g., Shepp & Eimas, 1964). At this point the working assumption of two-stage theorists appears to be that *some* attending response is likely to be involved in any training situation, but the character of that response is likely to be dictated by the organism's perceptual system, and the contingencies of reinforcement in the same manner as is the ultimate discrimination performance.

IV. NONSELECTIVE CONFIGURAL THEORY

A. The Stimulus Overlap Problem

Among the several faces of the stimulus selection problem one of the most theoretically provocative has been the so-called "overlap problem" (e.g., Estes, 1959). This problem arises in any discrimination-learning situation in which the discriminanda have some similarity or "overlap," but can be especially appreciated where the "overlap" involves isolable components. Thus, in paired-associate learning one compound, AX, may be paired with one response term, R_1, whereas a second compound, BX, is paired with a different response term, R_2. Or, in Pavlovian conditioning a tone and a light, AX, might be reinforced, $+$, whereas a different tone and the same light, BX, mights be nonreinforced, $-$. In such cases the common X event is trained in relationship to two different consequences so that it would be expected to be reacted to alone as an ambiguous signal. And, to the degree that AX and BX are reacted to in a manner that reflects the training relationships in which their separable components have been involved, the common X event should interfere with the development of discriminative performance to the compounds. The problem is that on both kinds of evidence, that is, the responding to X alone and the responding to AX versus BX, X does not appear to be as effective as expected. The common cue, when tested alone, is not responded to in the same manner as if it had been trained in the absence of the unambiguous A and B stimuli (e.g., Wagner et al., 1968). And subjects may eventually reach essentially errorless levels of discriminative responding to AX versus BX (e.g., Robbins, 1970; Uhl, 1964).

How much X should be expected to interfere with discriminative performance on AX versus BX depends upon the specifics of one's theory. Errorless performance in the face of overlapping cues, however, is decidedly problematic for certain versions of stimulus-sampling theory in which the probability of response to an experimental stimulus is identified with the proportion of elementary stimuli generated by that event that are associated with the designated response. If, for example, the elementary stimuli are assumed to be initiated by components (e.g., Burke & Estes, 1957) and are treated as equally likely to be available for sampling on any trial in which the initiating component occurs, then in an AX versus BX discrimination the *maximum* probability of the correct response to AX, P_{AX}, and the *minimum* probability of the same (then incorrect) response to BX, P_{BX}, are related by the equality, $P_{AX} = W + P_{BX}$, where W is the proportion of the elements in each of the compounds that are nonoverlapping (assuming for simplicity that the proportion is the same on AX and BX occasions). As W is made less than 1 by the occurrence of overlapping X elements, P_{AX} and P_{BX} are restrained from concurrently taking the values of 1 and 0, respectively, and P_{AX} and P_{BX} become similar, that is, there must be nondifferential responding.

As seen in an AX versus BX discrimination the overlap problem is an instance of overshadowing, in which the common X cue has less effect upon behavior than would be expected. It would thus appear natural to address it with one of the elementistic approaches we have already discussed. Indeed, the problem of overlap as revealed in this instance has frequently been taken as encouraging a two-stage model such as that of

Atkinson (1958), Restle (1955), Zeaman and House (1963), or Lovejoy (1966). If cues that occupy the position of X in an AX versus BX discrimination come to be unattended to, then X alone would not be reacted to as a signal (e.g., Wagner et al., 1968), whereas AX and BX could support errorless discrimination (e.g., Robbins, 1970; Uhl, 1964). Alternatively, Rescorla and Wagner (1972) have shown how their modified continuity theory could also predict an "overshadowing" of X in an AX versus BX discrimination, without appeal to an attentional mechanism.

But the overlap problem occurs in other discrimination situations in which any simple elementistic account appear to be inadequate. Consider a pattern versus component discrimination in which a compound, AB, is trained with one consequent event, while each of the components is trained in isolation with another consequent event. For example, Woodbury (1943) in his classic research on this problem, rewarded dogs for responding in the presence of a light and tone compound but did not reward responses to the separate stimuli, and alternatively for other subjects, rewarded responses to the separate stimuli but did not reward response to the compound. That essentially errorless responding eventually resulted in both instances is problematic for stimulus sampling model such as that of Burke and Estes (1957), for reasons we have noted, but it is equally embarrassing to any model that treats the compound as the simple sum of the constitutent components. In this case there would be *no* elements in the discriminanda that are consistently nonoverlapping. Discriminative behavior could be expected to occur, if at all, only to the degree that the sum of two response tendencies is different from that of the separate components. Thus, for example, assuming that prior to training Woodbury's subjects were biased not to respond ot either A or B and that the partial reinforcement of these stimuli during training increased the tendency to respond to both, subjects could appear to acquire an AB^+ versus A^-, B^- discrimination (so-called "positive patterning"), as there would be a greater response tendency resulting from the sum of the tendencies to A and B than to either alone. But then the subjects trained with AB^- versus A^+, B^+ (so-called "negative patterning") would be expected to behave in a manner opposed to the prevailing contingencies.

B. Configural Cues

One consistent way to address the overlap problem, in this instance as well as in an AX versus BX discrimination, is to assume that the stimulus terms that may enter into association on each training trial are not elements that may occur equally in different compounds, but are instead stimulus *patterns* or *configurations*. If the patterns that are initiated by AX trials are assumed to be different from the patterns initiated by BX trials, there is no necessary assumption of effective overlapping stimuli and no problem of accounting for errorless discrimination between AX and BX when it occurs. Similarly, if the patterns initiated by AB trials are different from the patterns initiated by A trials and by B trials, there is no problem of accounting for pattern versus component discrimination learning. Estes (1959) has presented a version of stimulus-sampling theory that adopts this manner of dealing with the overlap problem. Hull (1943) saw the same kind of approach as necessary to deal with pattern versus component discrimination, and proposed that "afferent neural interaction" occurs such that each component of a compound stimulus can potentially modify the effective stimulation produced by the remaining components. In practice, Hull made little use of the configural notions involved; (for example, in a treatment of discrimination, he spoke of the "neutralization" of common cues in an AX versus BX type discrimination without offering any justification beyond the effects of partial reinforcement (Hull, 1952). Spiker (1970) has attempted to show the general utility of a conception of neural interaction in dealing with selective discrimination learning from the point of view of Hull–Spence theory. For an earlier rigorous development of configurational theory the reader should also consult Gulliksen and Wolfle (1938a, b).

Configurational theory allows for potent stimulus selection effects: an isolable cue will or will not appear to be learned about on a training trial, depending upon the presence or absence of additional cues, because it is always the configuration of occurring cues that enters into association. Yet, configurational theory has not been as well developed as elementistic theory. The basic reason for this is that at some point the theory must address the similarity or dissimilarity of different configurations. When it is necessary to do this, as, for example, in accounting for transfer of training effects during discrimination learning, one returns to the same problem of "overlap" as faced by elementistic theories (see, e.g., Estes & Hopkins, 1961). Furthermore, it becomes difficult to deny the utility of the simplifying assumptions that characterize elementistic theory.

Consider again Pavlov's (1927) observation of overshadowing. If a CS, A, is trained in relationship to reinforcement then the configuration of "A alone" (which would include, in addition to the nominal CS, various "background" or "situational" sources of stimulation, e.g., Dweck & Wagner, 1970) should be associated with reinforcement and should be responded to as a signal. If the compound CS, AB, is trained in relationship to reinforcement, then the AB configuration (again including "background" stimulation) should be associated with reinforcement and should be responded to as a signal. That A alone is not responded to after the latter training (that it is overshadowed) can be attributed to the fact that the configuration A alone is different from the configuration AB.

What is to be said then when B alone is responded to after the same AB training that produced overshadowing of A (e.g., Pavlov, 1927)? Clearly, it must be assumed that the configuration B alone is similar to the configuration AB in a degree that the configuration A alone is not. Pavlov (1927) observed that "strong" CSs (ones that readily developed substantial CRs when trained alone) were likely to overshadow "weak" CSs (ones that more slowly and less consistently evoked CRs when trained alone). According to configurational theory a compound of a strong and a weak CS would then have to be assumed to produce an effective configuration that is more similar to the configuration produced by a strong CS in the absence of the weak CS than to the configuration produced by the weak CS in the absence of the strong CS.

What should be apparent is that the necessary argument above, as expressed in configurational terms (that is, the stimulus consequences of AB are similar to the stimulus consequences of B but dissimilar from the stimulus consequences of A) could be as well conveyed in elementistic terms (that is, by the assumption that B is more likely to be attended to in an AB compound than is A). It is seldom the case that such translatability can be confidently denied, at least with the forms of stimulation usually employed in the literature under consideration.

We can make this observation in a more general way. A nonselective elementistic theory, such as that of Spence (1936) proceeds from the simplifying assumption that there are independent aspects of the stimulus complex that can be identified such that the discriminability, for example, of AC versus C can be assumed to be equal to the discriminability, of AD versus D (corresponding to the presence versus absence of A in either case). A selective elementistic theory such as that of Sutherland and Mackintosh (1971) denies the general utility of such invariance assumptions in proposing, for example, that the discriminability of AC versus C as opposed to AD versus D will depend upon the relative "attention" demanded by C and D. But then it introduces its own simplifying assumption that the relative attention demanded by C and D should be invariant over different combinations of cues. Thus, for example, if AC versus C is less discriminable than AD versus D, then BC versus C should be less discriminable than BD versus D. The uniqueness of configurational theory in dealing with the differential similarities of different stimulus complexes shows through only as it has the opportunity to deny both simplifying assumptions of these elementistic theories, for example, to assert that AC versus C may be less discriminable than AD versus D, whereas BC versus C is more discriminable than BD versus D. In the absence of the rules for such interaction, or independent scaling evidence, the language of the laboratory remains essentially elementistic.

The lasting bow that has been made to configurational theory however is the general acceptance of configural cues as realities that need to be reckoned with in associative learning, at least in certain situations. Thus, Spence (1952b) acknowledged that in order to account for some instances of discrimination learning, such as so-called "successive discrimination," one would need to assume that differential associative strengths could be acquired by the different patterns of the separable components apart from the components themselves. Spence, however, proceded to treat a pattern stimulus as simply another element of the compound, albeit a nonisolable element. Wagner (e.g., 1971) has made this gambit explicit within modified continuity theory by stating that the associative strength to a compound of cues AB, that is, V_{AB}, should be considered as the sum of V_A, V_B, and $V_{\overline{AB}}$, where the latter term represents the strength of those stimuli arising from the *combination* of A and B. According to Wagner and Rescorla (1972), elementistic accounts can often ignore the latter kind of pattern elements as they may not be very salient constituents of the compound. It could equally be proposed that in the case of some compounds the pattern elements are the most salient so that the remaining elements can be theoretically ignored. Within stimulus-sampling theory, Atkinson and Estes (1963; see also Friedman, 1966; Friedman & Gelfand, 1964; Friedman, Trabasso, & Mosberg, 1967) have presented a "mixed model" that makes component association subordinate to pattern association but allows for transfer of training via components when a pattern association is unavailable.

If the development of configural theory has not proceeded apace with elementistic theory, at least it has provoked us to catch up with some important phenomena of associative learning. Even in the eyelid conditioning of the rabbit it is possible to demonstrate a biconditional discrimination when four isolable components are trained in the pairs AC^+, AD^-, BC^-, BD^+ (Saavedra, 1975). Likewise, Asratyan (1961) reports that dogs may be trained to salivate to cue A and lift a limb to cue B in one experimental room, while lifting the limb to cue A and salivating to cue B in another experimental room, as a result of the reversed pairings of the two CSs with food and shock in the two situations. Such data clearly require the assumption that association can involve the specific pattern or configuration in the discriminanda. It remains to be seen how important is the contribution of such configural cues in situations in which their use is not demanded by the training contingencies. An interesting step in this direction is occurring in the analysis of the developmental changes at different age levels in so-called reversal versus nonreversal discrimination learning, often taken (e.g., Kendler & Kendler, 1962) to reflect a progression from nonselective associative learning, á la Spencian theory, to selective associative learning á la attentional theory. There is now reason (e.g., Sanders, 1971; Tighe, Glick, & Cole, 1971) to suspect that associative learning occurs with respect to the different patterns of stimuli involved and that the developmental changes reflect changing response strategies that may be seen when the significance of all of the patterns is changed (in reversal learning) as opposed to only some of the patterns (in nonreversal learning).

V. SELECTIVE CONFIGURAL THEORY

It should be obvious that one could construct a selective configural theory that would have the same relationship to nonselective configural theory as selective elementistic theory has to nonselective elementistis theory. By the addition of an attentional-like mechanism the effective configuration could be assumed to vary systematically not only with the nature of the stimulus compound but with the nature of the subject's prior experience with the same or related experimental stimuli. Gulliksen and Wolfle (1938b), for example, noted that their configural theory was not prepared to address the kind of problem posed by Lashley and Krechevsky that we have discussed as being in the background of Spence's continuity theory (see Section II.A). They proposed that to handle a sudden change from presolution to solution behavior within their theory would require some mechanism for sudden shifts in the perceptual distance separating the discriminanda: "An emphasis upon some aspect of the configurations might make two of them seem very close together; an emphasis upon some other aspect might make their apparent distance much greater. A sudden increase in the perceptual distance between two configurations would result in a sudden decrease in difficulty of the problem" (Gulliksen & Wolfle, 1938b, p. 247). In a somewhat different mixture of attentional and configural notions Atkinson (1959) proposed that subjects may shift between different "perceptual states" in accordance with their reinforcement histories so as to respond to a stimulus situation either as a pattern or as a combination of components. We trust that the general characteristics of such theory, incorporating a mechanism of shifting attention, can be appreciated from our earlier discussion of the similar selective elementistic models, without further elaboration. It is most instructive to see that the type of mechanism that has been proposed as a useful adjunct to the associative apparatus in order to account for stimulus selection effects can take other forms.

Again we can point to a particular observation of stimulus selection as providing the major impetus for the theoretical proposal that we will discuss. Suppose that a subject is trained with a compound, AB, of isolable cues paired with a consequent event. Suppose further that occasional test trials are arranged in which A, B, and AB are evaluated to determine the degree to which they are each reacted to as signals for the consequent event. Razran (1971) summarizes the results (e.g., Sergeyev, 1967) Voronin, 1957) from a presumably large number of Soviet investigations of Pavlovian conditioning which have this simple form. The finding of interest is that as training with the AB compound continues there is a differential change in the degree of responding to the compound versus the components; while responding to AB shows a simple monotonic increase with training, responding to the separate A and B components at first increases and then *decreases*. With extended training in which the isolable cues continue to be reinforced in compound, they appear to lose their tendency to be reacted to alone as signals, whereas their compound increases or maintains its signal characteristics.

Configural theory has, in principle, no difficulties in accounting for the relative responding to the compound and components at any single point in training. The terminal performance of responding to the compound but not the components is to be expected when the configurations produced by A alone and B alone are highly discriminable from the training AB configuration. The earlier performance of responding to the components as well as the compound is to be expected when the configurations produced by A alone and B alone are not so discriminable from the training configuration. However, in the absence of differential reinforcement, there is no basis for anticipating the observed shift in relative responding to the components versus the compound.

To account for such data Razran (e.g., 1971) has proposed that the effective stimulus systematically changes during training by a process termed "*configuring*." The product of configuring is for a stimulus complex to change from being processed as a set of separate components to being processed as a unitary pattern. The necessary and sufficient condition for configuring is assumed to be the simple repeated experience with the stimulus complex. This repetition may occur during the course of association training when the complex is paired with a consequent event, but could occur as well in the absence of the latter event, that is, during simple iterated stimulation with the complex. Configuring is *not* assumed to be an instance of associative learning, in which one component comes to signal another (as might be said to occur in "sensory preconditioning" for example). It is assumed to be a distinctly different learning process wherein the separate components lose any isolable identity to the perception of a unitary configuration.

Unfortunately, Razran left the mechanism for configuring largely unspecified. He proposed (1971) that it would eventually be understood along with the development of perceptual constancies, images, and Gestalten, perhaps as a recoding in terms of the organism's "effector reaction feedback." Otherwise, he simply enumerated the apparent implications of the Soviet literature, for example, that some stimuli configure more "naturally" than others (there is a "preparedness" for configuring?), that configuring is more likely to appear with simultaneous than with successive occurrence of the components, and that it may require the involvement of "higher cortical regions."

Without further elaboration of the thoery it is impossible to stipulate the configuring that is to be expected in any interesting range of experimental situations, and hazardous to speculate concerning its potential utility in accounting for the stimulus-selection effects that have concerned other theorists. Indeed, it should be pointed out that it is not even clear how useful this theory is in relationship to the data domain that we have been discussing. First, there is some doubt as to the reproduceability of the basic phenomenon, that is, a shift from component to compound responding during simple compound conditioning. Of the several investigations of the phenomenon in the United States (e.g., Baker, 1969; Booth & Hammond, 1971; Saavadra, 1975, in press; Thomas, Berman, Serednesky, & Lyons, 1968; Wickens, Nield, Tuber, & Wickens, 1970), none has reported a decrease in test responding to the components concommitant with an *increase* in responding to the compound. Thus, it has not been possible to discount the possibility that all test stimuli were experiencing similar fates, albeit more or less detectably. Second, the theory, in telling us that the effective stimulus in training progresses from a complex of components to a configuration does not tell us why a once-associated component should lose its signal value. Presumably some "forgetting" must occur when the component is no longer effectively present in training. It is probably safe to say that the usefulness of incorporating a configural process into our treatment of associative learning has yet to be determined.

VI.   CONCLUSION

We have reviewed only a small portion of the experimental investigations of stimulus selection. That which we have referenced, however, offers abundant testimony that the behavioral indices of association between particular experienced events may be influenced by other stimuli contemporaneously experienced during training. A relationship will or will not appear to be learned about depending upon the context of environmental events in which it is imbedded. Beyond making this point, the literature that we have emphasized has served as the principal basis for different theoretical departures. Stimulus selection is manifest in the change from presolution to solution performance in selective learning, in the Pavlovian phenomena of overshadowing and blocking, in the acquired distinctiveness of cues, in the overlap problem in discrimination learning, and in the shift in stimulus control that is sometimes referred to as "spontaneous configuring." What we have attempted to show is how each of these faces of the same general problem has served to provoke the development of conceptualizations that are now part and parcel of our theories of learning and that have utility considerably beyond the original problem. Many of our working assumptions concerning the processing of episodic information, much of our conceptual machinery for representing associative changes, and many of our rules for how association is mapped into performance originated in attempts to deal with stimulus selection.

In attempting to elucidate the different theoretical developments that have issued from concerns over stimulus selection, we have conscientiously attempted to avoid a confrontation strategy of pitting the various theories against one another. The several approaches do, in fact, have different abilities to deal with the complete range of stimulus selection phenomena. Furthermore, in some situations the different approaches may lead to conflicting expectations which are important to evaluate. However, emphasis on the relative power or situational appropriateness of the different approaches can obscure what is also the case; each of the theoretical responses we have reviewed contains some important conceptualizations that are likely to remain viable in the years to come and should be accepted as part of our theoretical armamentarium, to be exploited whenever possible in the further understanding of associative learning.

Granted the present development of our theories, stimulus selection appears to be an overdetermined phenomenon. It can occur for a variety of reasons, any number of which may be operating in a particular situation. Consider again the outcome of the Lovejoy and Russell (1967) experiment discussed in Section II.A. Their experiment revealed that the amount subjects learned about the alternatives of one stimulus dimension was reduced by the presence of relevant alternatives of another dimension. Such an outcome may result because subjects that were trained with redundant relevant cues experienced different histories of reinforcement with the test alternatives than did subjects in the comparison condition, as suggested by Spence's (1936) continuity theory. Alternatively such reduced learning might occur to cues that had been redundantly relevant because they had to share the limited associative strength provided by the reinforcement events, as suggested by modified continuity theory (Rescorla & Wagner, 1972). Or the subjects may have learned to attend more to the cues of the test dimension if they were the only cues relevant during training, as suggested by two-stage attentional theory (e.g., Lovejoy, 1966). Or, perhaps the consistent compounding of the component members of the two dimensions in the two-cue relevant condition resulted in stimulus control accruing to the configuration of cues present as opposed to the elements per se, as suggested by configural theory (e.g., Spiker, 1970). It must be allowed that some, or all, of these factors may have contributed to the results obtained by Lovejoy and Russell.

Although a particular stimulus selection observation could result from any of the reasons we have considered, the literature reflects the tendency of some theorists to consider only an attentional interpretation. For example, in the human paired-associate learning literature, there are dozens of reports of stimulus selection when compound stimuli are employed (e.g., Richardson, 1971). A study by Underwood Ham, and Ekstrand (1962) illustrates the nature of this observation. They required their subjects to learn a list of paired associates in which the stimulus members of the pairs were compounds consisting of trigrams surrounded by redundantly relevant distinct colors. Tests with the individual components following learning revealed that the subjects were unable to retrieve the correct response when cued with the trigrams but were quite capable of doing so when presented with the color components. Since it is likely that the trigram elements would have retrieved the correct responses if training had involved only these elements, the presence of the color components then apparently interfered with the acquisition of trigram-response associations.

Observations of the kind made by Underwood and his associates have invariably been interpreted within a two-stage attentional framework (e.g., Martin, 1968; Richardson, 1971; Trabasso & Bower, 1968), that is, by assuming that the subject failed to attend to the nonassociated components during training. Rudy (1974) recently noted, however, that it is just as reasonable to interpret such data within a modified continuity framework. Granted that the component stimuli in such cases are not equally salient, a stimulus selection effect could result if the more salient element of the compound more quickly becomes associated with the correct response. This is because once the more salient component retrieves the correct response, the associative processing or rehearsal necessary for functionally relating the less salient element to the response might fail to occur. An appreciation of this interpretation encouraged Rudy to compare a number of stimulus selection findings which emerge from paired-associate transfer of training experiments (e.g., Merryman & Merryman, 1971; Richardson & Stanton, 1972) against his version of modified continuity theory. He noted that this approach not only accounted for findings which had previously been interpreted as evidence for two-stage attentional theory (Martin, 1968) but also could interpret data (e.g., Williams & Underwood, 1970) considered to be evidence against attentional theory. It also should be pointed out that Atkinson and Wickens (1971) have incorporated notions similar to modified continuity theory into the general information processing memory model of Atkinson and Shiffrin (1968) and have shown the combination to be useful in interpreting a number of effects concerning distribution of trials observed in the paired-associate situation. Such examples should suffice to make this point. A stimulus might fail to become a signal for behavior for any one of several reasons and the ideas that have been developed to allow for such effects might be applied fruitfully to the understanding of a broad range of associative learning phenomena.

ACKNOWLEDGMENTS

The preparation of this manuscript was supported in part by National Sciences Foundation Grants GB-38322 and GB-30299X.

REFERENCES

Asratyan, E. A. The initiation and localization of cortical inhibition in the conditioned reflex arc. *Annals of the New York Academy of Sciences,* 1961, **92,** 1141–1159.

Atkinson, R. C. A Markov model for discrimination learning. *Psychometrika,* 1958, **23,** 309–322.

Atkinson, R. C. A theory of stimulus discrimination learning. In K. J. Arrow, S. Karlin, & P. Suppes (Eds.), *Mathematical methods in the social sciences.* Stanford, California: Stanford University Press, 1959. Pp. 221–241.

Atkinson, R. C. The observing response in discrimination learning. *Journal of Experimental Psychology,* 1961, **62,** 253–261.

Atkinson, R. C., & Estes, W. K. Stimulus sampling theory. In R. D. Luce, R. R. Bush, & E. Galanter (Eds.), *Handbook of mathematical psychology.* Vol. II. New York: Wiley, 1963, Pp. 121–268.

Atkinson, R. C., & Shiffrin, A. M. Human memory: A proposed system and its control processes. In K. W. Spence & J. T. Spence (Eds.), *The psychology of learning and motivation: Advances in research and theory.* Vol. 2. New York: Academic Press, 1968. Pp. 89–195.

Atkinson, R. C., & Wickens, T. D. Human memory and the concept of reinforcement. In G. Glaser (Ed.), *The nature of reinforcement.* New York: Academic Press, 1971. Pp. 66–120.

Baker, T. W. Component strength in a compound CS as a function of number of acquisition trials. *Journal of Experimental Psychology,* 1969, **79,** 347–352.

Bloomfield, T. M. Behavioral contrast and the peak shift. In R. M. Gilbert & N. S. Sutherland (Eds.), *Animal discrimination learning.* New York and London: Academis Press, 1969. Pp. 215–241.

Booth, J. H., & Hammond, L. J. Configural conditioning: Greater fear in rats to compound than component through overtraining to the compound. *Journal of Experimental Psychology,* 1971, **87,** 255–262.

Burke, C. J., & Estes, W. K. A component model for stimulus variables in discrimination learning. *Psychometrika,* 1957, **22,** 133–145.

Capaldi, E. J., & Stevenson, H. W. Response reversal following different amounts of training. *Journal of Comparative and Physiological Psychology,* 1957, **50,** 195–198.

D'Amato, M. R., & Schiff, D. Overlearning and brightness discrimination reversal. *Journal of Experimental Psychology,* 1965, **69,** 375–381.

Dweck, C. S., & Wagner, A. R. Situation cues and correlation between CS and US as determinants of the conditioned emotional response. *Psychonomic Science,* 1970, **18,** 145–147.

Ehrenfreund, D. An experimental test of the continuity theory of discrimination learning with pattern vision. *Journal of Comparative and Physiological Psychology,* 1948, **41,** 408–422.

Eimas, P. D. Effects of overtraining and age on intradimensional and extradimensional shifts in children. *Journal of Experimental Child Psychology,* 1966, **3,** 348–355.

Eninger, M. U. Habit summation in a selective learning problem. *Journal of Comparative & Physiological Psychology,* 1953, **46,** 398–402.

Erlebacher, A. Reversal learning in rats as a function of percentage of reinforcement and degree of learning. *Journal of Experimental Psychology,* 1963, **66,** 84–90.

Estes, W. K. Component and pattern models with Markovian interpretations. In R. R. Bush & W. K. Estes (Eds.), *Studies in mathematical learning theory.* Stanford, California: Stanford University Press, 1959. Pp. 9–52.

Estes, W. K., & Hopkins, B. L. Acquisition and transfer in pattern-vs.-component discrimination learning. *Journal of Experimental Psychology,* 1961, **61,** 322–328.

Friedman, M. P. Transfer effects and response strategies in pattern-versus-component discrimination learning. *Journal of Experimental Psychology,* 1966, **71,** 420–428.

Friedman, M. P., & Gelfand, H. Transfer effects in discrimination learning. *Journal of Mathematical Psychology,* 1964, **1,** 204–214.

Friedman, M. P., Trabasso, T., & Mosberg, L. Test of a mixed model for paired associates with overlapping stimuli. *Journal of Mathematical Psychology,* 1967, **4,** 316–334.

Gulliksen, H., & Wolfle, D. L. A theory of learning and transfer: I. *Psychometrika,* 1938, **3,** 127–149. (a).

Gulliksen, H., & Wolfle, D. L. A theory of learning and transfer: II. *Psychometrika,* 1938, **3,** 225–251. (b).

Hearst, E. Excitation, inhibition and discrimination learning. In N. J. Mackintosh & W. K. Honig (Eds.), *Fundamental issues in associative learning.* Halifax: Dalhousie University Press, 1969. Pp. 1–41.

Hull, C. L. *Principles of behavior.* New York: Appleton-Century, 1943.

Hull, C. L. *A behavior system.* New Haven, Connecticut: Yale University Press, 1952.

Kamin, L. J. 'Attention-like' processes in classical conditioning. In M. R. Jones (Ed.), *Miami symposium on the prediction of behavior: Aversive stimulation.* Miami, Florida: University of Miami Press, 1968. Pp. 9–33.

Kamin, L. J. Predictability, surprise, attention and conditioning. In B. Campbell & R. Church (Eds.), *Punishment and aversive behavior.* New York: Appleton-Century-Crofts, 1969. Pp. 279–296.

Kendler, H. H., & Kendler, T. S. Vertical and horizontal processes in problem solving. *Psychological Review,* 1962, **69,** 1–16.

Krechevsky, I. "Hypotheses" in rats. *Psychological Review,* 1932, **39,** 516–532.

Lashley, K. S. *Brain mechanisms and intelligence: A quantitative study of injuries to the brain.* Chicago: University of Chicago Press, 1929.

Lawrence, D. H. Acquired distinctiveness of cues: I. Transfer between discriminations on the basis of familiarity with the stimulus. *Journal of Experimental Psychology,* 1949, **39,** 770–784.

Lawrence, D. H. Acquired distinctiveness of cues: II. Selective association in a constant stimulus situation. *Journal of Experimental Psychology,* 1950, **40,** 175–188.

Lawrence, D. H. The nature of stimulus: Some relationships between learning and perception. In S. Koch (Ed.), *Psychology: A study of a science.* Vol. 5. New York: McGraw-Hill, 1963. Pp. 179–212.

Lovejoy, E. Analysis of the overlearning reversal effect. *Psychological Review,* 1966, **73,** 87–103.

Lovejoy, E., & Russell, D. G. Suppression of learning about a hard cue by the presence of an easy cue. *Psychonomic Science,* 1967, **8,** 365–366.

Mackintosh, N. J. The effect of overtraining on a reversal and nonreversal shift. *Journal of Comparative & Physiological Psychology,* 1962, **55,** 555–559.

Mackintosh, N. J. Selective attention in animal discrimination learning. *Psychological Bulletin,* 1965, **64,** 124–150. (a).

Mackintosh, N. J. Incidental cue learning in rats. *Quarterly Journal of Experimental Psychology,* 1965, **17,** 292–300. (b).

Mahut, H. The effect of stimulus position on visual discrimination by the rat. *Canadian Journal of Psychology,* 1954, **8,** 130–138.

Martin, E. Stimulus meaningfulness and paired associate transfer. *Psychological Review,* 1968, **75,** 421–441.

McCulloch, T. L., & Pratt, J. G. A study of pre-solution in weight discrimination by whie rats. *Journal of Comparative and Physiological Psychology,* 1934, **18,** 271–290.

Merryman, C. T., & Merryman, S. S. Stimulus encoding in the *A–B', AX–B* and the *A–Br', AX–B* paradigms. *Journal of Verbal Learning & Verbal Behavior,* 1971, **10,** 681–685.

Pavlov, I. P. *Conditioned reflexes.* London and New York: Oxford University Press, 1927.

Razran, G. *Mind in evolution.* Boston: Houghton Mifflin, 1971.

Reid, L. S. The development of noncontinuity behavior through continuity learning. *Journal of Experimental Psychology,* 1953, **46,** 107–112.

Rescorla, R. A. Conditioned inhibition of fear. In N. J. Mackintosh & W. K. Honig (Eds.), *Fundamental issues in associative learning.* Halifax: Dalhousie University Press, 1969. Pp. 65–89.

Rescorla, R. A., & Wagner, A. R. A theory of Pavlovian conditioning: Variations in the effectiveness of reinforcement and nonreinforcement. In A. H. Black & W. F. Prokasy (Eds.), *Classical conditioning II.* New York: Appleton-Century-Crofts, 1972. Pp. 64–99.

Restle, F. A theory of discrimination learning. *Psychological Review,* 1955, **62,** 11–19.

Richardson, J. Cue effectiveness and abstraction in paired associate learning. *Psychological Bulletin,* 1971, **75,** 73–91.

Richardson, J., & Stanton, K. S. Some effects of learning to a set of components on stimulus selection. *American Journal of Psychology,* 1972, **85,** 519–533.

Robbins, D. Stimulus selection in human discrimination learning and transfer. *Journal of Experimental Psychology,* 1970, **84,** 282–290.

Rudy, J. W. Stimulus selection in animal conditioning and paired-associate learning: Variation in associative processing. *Journal of Verbal Learning & Verbal Behavior,* 1974, **13,** 282–296.

Saavedra, M. A. Pavlovian compound conditioning in the rabbit. *Learning & Motivation,* 1975, in press.

Sanders, B. Factors affecting reversal and nonreversal shifts in rats and children. *Journal of Comparative and Physiological Psychology,* 1971, **74,** 292–297.

Sergeyev, B. F. *Evolution of associative temporary connections.* Moscow: Akademiya Nauk SSSR, 1967.

Shepp, B. E., & Eimas, P. D. Intradimensional and extradimensional shifts in the rat. *Journal of Comparative and Physiological Psychology,* 1964, **57,** 357–361.

Spence, K. W. The nature of discrimination learning in animals. *Psychological Review,* 1936, **43,** 427–449.

Spence, K. W. The differential response in animals to stimuli varying within a single dimension. *Psychological Review,* 1937, **44,** 430–444.

Spence, K. W. An experimental test of continuity and noncontinuity theories of discrimination learning. *Journal of Experimental Psychology,* 1945, **35,** 253–266.

Spence, K. W. Mathematical formulations of learning phenomena. *Psychological Review,* 1952, **59,** 89–93. (a)

Spence, K. W. The nature of response in discrimination learning. *Psychological Review,* 1952, **59,** 89–93. (b)

Spiker, L. L. An extension of Hull–Spence discrimination learning theory. *Psychological Review,* 1970, **77,** 496–515.

Sutherland, N. S. & Mackintosh, N. J. *Mechanisms of animal discrimination learning.* New York: Academic Press, 1971.

Sutherland, N. S., Mackintosh, N. J., & Mackintosh, J. Shape and size discrimination in octopus: The effects of pretraining along different dimensions. *Journal of Genetic Psychology,* 1965, **106,** 1–10.

Terry, W. S., & Wagner, A. R. Short-term-memory for "surprising" vs. "expected" USs in Pavlovian conditioning. *Journal of Experimental Psychology: Animal Behavior Processes,* 1975, **104,** 122–133.

Thomas, D. R., Berman, D. L., Serednesky, C. E., & Lyons, J. Information value and stimulus configuring as factors in conditioned reinforcement. *Journal of Experimental Psychology,* 1968, **76,** 181–189.

Tighe, T. J., Glick, J., & Cole, M. Subproblem analysis of discrimination-shift learning. *Psychonomic Science,* 1971, **24,** 159–160.

Trabasso, T., & Bower, G. H. *Attention in learning: Theory and research.* New York: Wiley, 1968.

Uhl, C. N. Effect of overlapping cues upon discrimination learning. *Journal of Experimental Psychology,* 1964, **67,** 91–97.

Underwood, B. J., Ham, M., & Ekstrand, B. Cue selection in paired associate learning. *Journal of Experimental Psychology,* 1962, **64,** 405–409.

vom Saal, W., & Jenkins, H. M. Blocking the development of stimulus control. *Learning and Motivation,* 1970, **1,** 52–64.

Voronin, L. G. *Comparative physiology of higher nervous activity.* Moscow: Moscow University Press, 1957.

Wagner, A. R. Stimulus validity and stimulus selection in associative learning. In N. J. Mackintosh & W. K. Honig (Eds.), *Fundamental issues in associative learning.* Halifax: Dalhousie University Press, 1969. (a)

Wagner, A. R. Stimulus selection and a "modified continuity theory." In G. H. Bower & J. T. Spence (Eds.), *The psychology of learning and motivation: Advances in research and theory.* Vol. 3. New York: Academic Press, 1969. Pp. 1–40. (b)

Wagner, A. R. Elementary Associations. In H. H. Kendler & J. T. Spence (Eds.), *Essays in neobehaviorism: A memorial volume to Kenneth W. Spence.* New York: Appleton-Century-Crofts, 1971. Pp. 187–213.

Wagner, A. R., Logan, F. A., Haberlandt, K., & Price, T. Stimulus selection in animal discrimination learning. *Journal of Experimental Psychology,* 1968, **76,** 171–180.

Wagner, A. R., & Rescorla, R. A. Inhibition in Pavlovian conditioning: Application of a theory. In R. A. Boakes & M. S. Halliday (Eds.), *Inhibition and learning.* New York: Academic Press, 1972. Pp. 301–336.

Wagner, A. R., Rudy, J. W., & Whitlow, J. W., Jr. Rehearsal in animal conditioning. *Journal of Experimental Psychology Monograph,* 1973, **97,** 407–426.

Wickens, D. D., Nield, A. F., Tuber, D. S., Wickens, C. Classical conditioned compound-element discrimination as a function of length of training, amount of testing, and CS–US interval. *Learning and Motivation,* 1970, **1,** 95–109.

Williams, R. F., & Underwood, B. J. Encoding variability: test of the Martin hypothesis. *Journal of Experimental Psychology,* 1970, **86,** 317–324.

Woodbury, C. B. The learning of stimulus patterns by dogs. *Journal of Comparative and Physiological Psychology,* 1943, **35,** 29–40.

Wyckoff, L. B., Jr. The role of observing responses in discriminative learning. *Psychological Review,* 1952, **59,** 431–442.

Zeaman, D., & House, B. J. The role of attention in retardate discrimination learning. In N. R. Ellis (Ed.), *Handbook of mental deficiency: Psychological theory and research.* New York: McGraw-Hill, 1963. Pp. 159–223.

8

Stimulus Generalization

Eric G. Heinemann

Brooklyn College
of The City University of New York

Sheila Chase

Hunter College
of The City University of New York

Most learning is the result of encounters with a limited number of environmental circumstances. In laboratory experiments the environment is usually held as constant as possible, or else just one or two selected features of the environment may be manipulated. For example, a pigeon may be fed if it pecks at a yellow spot on the wall of an experimental chamber but not fed if it pecks elsewhere. The pigeon may have been indifferent to the spot originally, that is, it may have been no more likely to peck at the spot than to peck on other parts of the wall, but as a result of the training procedure it becomes more likely to peck, and the pecks come to be predominantly on the yellow spot.

What has the pigeon learned? Obviously enough, it has learned to peck on the spot and not on the wall, but that is a very incomplete description of the results of the training procedure. If the color of the spot is changed from yellow to green, the pigeon may peck at the green spot also, though perhaps less often and less vigorously. More generally, it will be found that the probability of pecking is now an orderly function of the dominant wavelength of the light coming from the spot. However, the color of the spot is by no means the only property of the environment that now affects the pecking behavior of the pigeon. The intensity of the light coming from the spot, the size and shape of the spot, the texture of the spot, as well as the physical properties of the surrounding wall may all affect behavior in new ways. To get a full picture of the way the training procedure has affected the pigeon's propensity to peck at objects in its environment, it is necessary to vary a great many physical properties of the enviornment and to note how these variations affect the pecking behavior.

Even this procedure does not provide a complete picture of what was learned, for it may be that behaviors other than pecking were also affected by the training procedure. For example, rats trained to run through a maze may swim through the maze if it is filled with water. A comprehensive description of what was learned would have to deal also with the way the training procedure affects a great variety of behavior patterns, but that subject will not be treated here. This chapter deals with theories and experiments concerned with the question of how a particular behavior comes to be governed by environmental events other than those encountered during training.

The subject under discussion is usually called "stimulus generalization," and the procedure of varying the physical properties of the training environment in order to study their effects on the learned behavior is called a "generalization test." In a complete generalization test a great many physical properties or *stimulus dimensions* have to be varied. We shall not discuss the term "stimulus" in detail but note that the only physical properties of interest naturally are those capable of affecting the sensory systems of the organism under study. Thus electromagnetic radiation in the frequency range known to stimulate the visual system or other receptors is of interest, radiation at the frequencies used in radio communication generally is not. Even with respect to those properties that *can* affect an organism, there are some physical distinctions that are not relevant to the study of behavior. For example, there are an indefinite number of physically distinguishable lights, the so-called *metameres* of colorimetry, that are indistinguishable to human beings. When studying behavior we need concern ourselves only with the effects of varying lights that are colorimetrically distinct for the organism under study. In what follows it is to be understood that all references to stimulus variations are to variations of dimensions that are capable of producing differential effects on the organism.

I. SOME BASIC TERMS

The terms listed below occur in most discussions of stimulus generalization, but usages vary somewhat among authors. We shall adhere to the following definitions.

A. Discrimination

The word *discrimination* refers to variation in behavior with variation in stimulation. We say that an organism discriminates between two stimuli if the behaviors that occur in the presence of these stimuli differ in some measurable way. In most experiments on discrimination each of two stimuli is presented many times and the observed values of the response measure (number of responses per trial, latency, etc.) may be represented in two frequency distributions, conditional on the two stimulus values. If the two distributions do not overlap, the discrimination is perfect, in the sense that the two stimuli never evoke identical responses. At the other extreme, if the two distributions are identical, there is no discrimination. In general, a rational measure of the degree of discrimination would appear to be one that specifies the degree to which the distributions of the behavioral measure overlap. If the two distributions are normal and have the same variance, a convenient rational measure is

$$d_b' = (\bar{x}_2 - \bar{x}_1)/\sigma_x,$$

where $\bar{x}_2$ and $\bar{x}_1$ are the means of the two distributions and σ_x is their common standard deviation. The subscript b is used to distinguish this measure from the d' of signal detection theory, which refers to distributions of stimulus values or of internal states induced by stimuli.

B. Generalization

Historically, this term has been used in an empirical sense, in which it refers to behavior, and in several theoretical senses in which it refers to inferred physiological or psychological processes. Some of the theoretical usages of the term will be considered in subsequent sections. In its empirical sense *generalization* is simply the opposite or inverse of discrimination. If the degree of discrimination is given by d_b', then the degree of generalization is $1/d_b'$.

C. Discriminability

1. Discriminability of Stimuli

In discussing discriminability it is useful to speak of features of the environment to which an organism may respond as sources of signals received by its sensory systems. How well an organism discriminates among signal sources depends on many factors, such as the conditions of training or motivation. One important factor is how much the sources differ from each other in their physical properties. No matter what the nature of the sources, if the physical differences between them are sufficiently small, perfect discrimination is not possible under any conditions. The extent to which differences between two sources can be resolved (by any device) is determined by the statistical properties of the sources and will be called their *absolute discriminability*. For example, the ability of any device to distinguish between two sources that emit flashes of light differing only in intensity is limited by the fact that the energy content of each flash varies from presentation to presentation, owing to uncontrollable fluctuations in the number of quanta emitted by the sources. If the difference in the mean energy delivered by the two light sources is sufficiently small, the distributions of energy delivered by the two sources on repeated presentations will overlap, so that even a device that is capable of counting the number of quanta delivered in each flash without error cannot distinguish the sources perfectly. Detailed discussions of the principles governing absolute discriminability may be found in Peterson, Birdsall, and Fox (1954), and Green and Swets (1966).

2. Discriminability of Internal States

Numerous experimenters have compared the ability of human observers to distinguish between various simple stimuli with the limits set by absolute discriminability (see Green & Swets, 1966; Nachmias, 1972). Under most conditions man's performance falls short of what could be achieved by appropriate ideal detecting devices. Most theories of discrimination account for the limited resolving power demonstrated in these experiments at least in part by assuming that the organism adds variance to the signal distributions. Each presentation of a stimulus is assumed to give rise to an *internal state*. Repeated presentations of the identical signal source produce a distribution of internal states. The variance of this distribution of internal states reflects both the variance of the signal distributions and the variance that is added by the organism. When two stimulus sources are presented repeatedly, the distributions of the corresponding internal states may overlap and it is this overlap that limits the ability of the organism to distinguish the stimulus sources. Various measures related to the overlap of the distributions of internal states may be used to specify the discriminability of these internal states. In the discussion that follows the word "discriminability" invariably refers to the discriminability of internal states (also called "sensitivity" in psychophysics.) It is worth noting that discriminability in this sense is a quantity that can be evaluated only on the basis of a theory which specifies how the parameters of the distributions of internal states are related to behavior under various conditions. This matter is discussed further in the next section.

D. Similarity

Similarity is the obverse of discriminability. The greater the overlap of two distributions of internal states, the greater the similarity of these distributions.

II. THEORIES OF GENERALIZATION

In this section we consider a recently developed model for generalization that is based on the theory of signal recognition (Blough, 1969; Heinemann, Avin, Sullivan, & Chase, 1969) and discuss briefly the more widely known treatments of generalization that are part of the conditioning theories of Hull (1943, 1952) and Spence (1936, 1937) and of stimulus-sampling theory (Atkinson & Estes, 1963; Bush & Mosteller, 1951; LaBerge, 1962). More detailed discussions of the treatments based on conditioning concepts may be found in Mednick and Freedman (1960), Kimble (1961), Hilgard and Bower (1975), and Neimark and Estes (1967).

Each of the theories to be considered may be viewed as consisting of three component theories, more or less developed.[1] The first component is the *theory of internal states,* which specifies a formal scheme for representing the internal states induced by the presentation of a single stimulus and the possible states induced by repeated presentations of the same stimulus. The second component is the *response theory,* which specifies a rule for transforming internal states to responses. The third component is the *stimulus theory,* which specifies how the parameters of the stimulus are related to the parameters of the internal states.

The core of most theories of generalization consists of a theory of internal states combined with a response theory. A combination of a state and response theory can specify the relation between response variables and indices of discriminability. However, the application of a generalization theory to the results of experiments (which necessarily involve the presentation of at least two different stimuli) requires some specification of the relation between the parameters of the internal states induced by different stimuli. This requirement is usually met by introducing assumptions concerning the manner in which variations in particular stimulus dimensions,

[1] Our discussion of component theories is based on a recent discussion of psychophysical theories by Nachmias (1972).

such as variations in the intensity of light or the frequency of pure tones, affect the characteristics of the corresponding internal states. Some of the specific assumptions that have been put forward will be discussed in the sections that follow.

A. The Theory of Signal Recognition

1. Basic Principles

In the theory of signal recognition the internal states produced by stimuli are represented by a continuous random variable, called the *decision variable*. The decision variable is usually assumed to be normally distributed. In discrimination experiments the subject is presented with at least two stimuli that give rise to distributions which may differ in the value of the mean and the variance. In all applications considered in this chapter it will be assumed that distributions for all stimuli whose internal effects vary along the same undimensional axis have the same variance. For two distributions of equal variance the discriminability is specified by

$$d' = (\mu_2 - \mu_1)/\sigma,$$

where μ_2 and μ_1 are the means of the two distributions and σ is their common standard deviation.

The response component of the theory implies that behavior is always determined by the relation between at least two distributions of internal states. These distributions are transformed to responses by means of a decision rule which divides the continuum of internal states into two or more segments and relates each segment to a particular response. The simplest possible condition involves two stimuli, S_1 and S_2, that represent values on a continuum, such as intensity, for which it is plausible to assume that the mean value of the decision variable is a monotonic function of stimulus value. Further, it involves one response, R_1, which is reinforced in the presence of S_1, and an alternate response, R_2, which is reinforced in the presence of S_2. In this case, it is assumed that on each trial the subject compares the momentarily present internal effect x to a fixed criterion value, x_C, and responds R_1 if $x \leq x_C$, and otherwise R_2.

The subject is presumed to choose the criterion value in order to achieve a well-defined goal, such as making as few errors as possible or collecting the largest possible average reward (maximizing "expected value"). These goals and a number of others can be achieved by choosing a criterion, x_C, such that the likelihood that x_C was produced by S_1 relative to the likelihood that x_C was produced by S_2 (likelihood ratio) has some specified value. It has been shown that decision rules based on properly chosen likelihood ratio criteria are optimal, that is, that subjects can do no better by following any other rule (Green & Swets, 1966). If the goal is to maximize the percentage of correct responses, the value of the best criterion likelihood ratio is equal to the relative frequency of S_1 and S_2 trials. If the goal is to maximize expected value, then the optimal criterion likelihood ratio depends upon the costs and values of incorrect and correct responses (payoff matrix) as well.

In work with human subjects experimenters often try to manipulate the criterion value by instructions, which may include detailed descriptions of the payoff matrix. In work with animals prolonged training with constant presentation frequencies of S_1 and S_2 and a constant payoff matrix takes the place of verbal instructions. Boneau and Cole (1967) have shown that an animal that remembers the relative frequencies of the internal states that occur during training and the proportions of reinforcement associated with each can, in principle, establish a decision rule equivalent to the likelihood ratio rule of the ideal statistical decision maker.

In applying the theory to results of experiments with animals, we shall assume that the subject's decision rule always takes into account the internal states produced by *all* sources of stimulation present during an experiment. Effects arising from stimuli that are constant throughout an experiment or from stimulus variations that are not correlated with reinforcement have no effect on the decision rule and may be ignored, in practice.

To derive generalization gradients, we assume that, during a generalization test, the subject continues to follow the decision rule it learned during prior discrimination training. Consider a generalization test done after training in the simple two-choice situation described in the second paragraph of this section. The decision problem is illustrated in Figure 1a. Distributions 3 and 5 represent the effects of the two training stimuli and the remaining distributions the effects of various test stimuli. Point C represents the criterion. The proportion of R_2 responses expected to occur over a large series of presentations of any particular stimulus is given by the portion of the area under the curve for that stimulus which falls to the right of the criterion. If the proportions of R_2 responses for each of the distributions shown are plotted against the means of the distributions, the resulting curve (the generalization gradient) is a normal ogive identical with the ogive obtained by cumulating the area under the particular curve, the mean of which is equal to the criterion (Curve 4). If the y axis of Figure 1b is changed from proportions to normal deviates (z), the ogive becomes a straight line (Figure 1c) with slope equal to $1/\sigma$, where σ is the common standard deviation of the distributions shown in Figure 1a.

The axis of internal effects may be replaced by an appropriately scaled stimulus axis if it is assumed that the decision variable x is a monotonic function of the stimulus variable S. In that case the deviations of x from the mean value produced by any particular stimulus are represented as

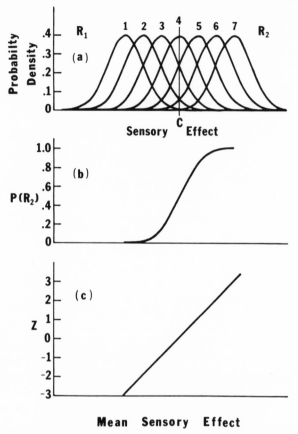

Mean   Sensory   Effect

FIGURE 1. (a) Assumed distributions of internal states produced by repeated presentations of each of seven different stimuli. (b) Proportion of R_2 responses when the criterion is at C. (c) A replot of (b) with the y axis scaled in normal deviate units (z). (From Heinemann & Avin, 1973. Copyright 1973 by the Society for the Experimental Analysis of Behavior, Inc.)

random fluctuations in the stimulus value, and the subjects may be regarded as basing their decisions directly on the stimulus quantities. When the independent variable is a stimulus quantity, the slope of the line in Figure 1c has the dimensions *d' per stimulus unit;* in other words, the slope is a measure of the discriminability of the stimuli (see Heinemann & Avin, 1973).

The effect of a change in criterion is to move the entire ogive parallel to the x axis, leaving the slope unchanged. Note that for the distribution with mean equal to the criterion, the proportion of R_2 responses has the value .5. Conversely, the stimulus value that yields $p(R_2) = .5$ has a distribution with mean equal to the criterion. This stimulus value then represents the criterion on the stimulus axis.

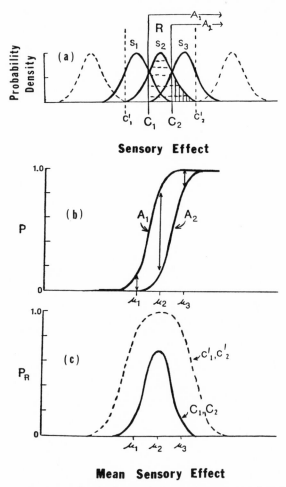

Sensory Effect

Mean Sensory Effect

FIGURE 2.   (a) Assumed distributions of internal states produced by repeated presentations of each of five different stimuli. (b) Proportion of R_2 responses expected on the basis of single-criterion decision rule based on C_1 or C_2 alone. (c) Plot of the difference between the two functions shown in (b).

Experimental situations other than the simple one considered thus far may present decision problems that require more complex decision rules. Gradients of the familiar bell-shaped form can result from a decision rule that involves two criteria. Such a decision rule would be reasonable, for example, if a subject were presented with three ordered values from a stimulus dimension, S_1, S_2, and S_3, and a response R were reinforced in the presence of S_2 but not in the presence of S_1 or S_3. The distributions produced by S_1, S_2, and S_3 as well as distributions for two test stimuli are shown in Figure 2a. Also shown are the criteria, C_1 and C_2, that would be appropriate if the cost of an unreinforced response were equal to the value of a reinforcement (assuming that the subject is attempting to maximize expected value). The decision rule is: respond if the internal effect falls between C_1 and C_2, otherwise do not respond.

For this situation the proportion of responses occurring over a large series of presentations of a given stimulus is equal to the proportion of the area under the corresponding density function that falls between C_1 and C_2. This area is equal to the difference between the total area falling to the right of C_1 (designated A_1) and the portion of A_1 that falls to the right of C_2 (designated A_2). A plot of A_1 and A_2 against the means of the internal effects induced by the various stimuli is shown in Figure 2b. The proportion of responses expected to occur in the presence of the various stimuli is given by the difference between the heights of the two normal ogives. The relation of this difference to the mean value of the decision variable (the expected generalization gradient) is shown in Figure 2c by the unbroken line.

As noted before, changes in the frequency with which the various stimuli are presented and changes in motivational conditions are assumed to affect the placement of the criteria. For example, if the value of a reinforced response were increased relative to the cost of an unreinforced one the separation between criteria C_1 and C_2 would be increased, leading to higher levels of responding for all stimuli, as illustrated by the broken-line curve in Figure 2c. It should be noted that the two curves shown are based on the same distributions of internal effects, and that the differences in the apparent steepness of these curves reflect changes in the position of the criteria, not changes in the discriminability of the stimuli. Changes in the variance of the internal-effect distributions also affect the form of the generalization gradients, of course. In order to interpret the effect of an experimental manipulation on the form of a bell-shaped gradient then it is necessary to estimate from the data both the criterion positions and the discriminability of the stimuli.

The theory of signal recognition can be applied to situations in which variation of a stimulus parameter causes internal effects to vary along several orthogonal dimensions, and to situations in which variations in several types of stimuli, for example, lights and sounds, are correlated with the consequences of a specific behavior. Some applications of this sort will be considered in subsequent sections.

2. Criterion Variability

The discussion so far has been based on the implicit assumption that subjects can maintain a perfectly constant criterion, but it is probably more realistic to assume that the criterion varies from trial to trial. The consequences of criterion variability have been considered by Wickelgren (1968) and others. One way to treat the matter is to regard the subject as basing its decision on a decision variable defined as the difference $(x - C)$, where x is the sensory effect experienced on any particular trial and C is the value of the criterion on that trial. For the simple two-choice situation considered in the previous section the appropriate decision rule would then be: respond R_1 if $(x - C) \leq 0$, otherwise respond R_2. If x is a normally distributed variable with mean μ_x and variance $\sigma_x{}^2$, and C a normally distributed variable with mean μ_C and variance $\sigma_C{}^2$, then $(x - C)$ will also be normally distributed with mean $\mu_x - \mu_C$ and variance $\sigma_x{}^2 + \sigma_C{}^2$. Thus adding criterion variance is equivalent to increasing the variance of x, the original decision variable.

The effects of criterion variability on the form of a generalization gradient are illustrated in Figure 3. The four parallel curves represent gradients expected for four different fixed criterion values. If the criterion were to assume these four values equally often over a series of trials the gradient based on the average results for that series would be the one labeled "Mean." The illustration shows that the effect of criterion variability is to flatten the gradient.

3. Correction for Inattention

Under conditions for which signal recognition theory predicts gradients of the form shown in Figure 1 the gradients actually obtained sometimes have lower and upper asymptotes that depart from the theoretical values of $p = 0$ and $p = 1.0$. One way to account for the failure of the asymptotes to lie at the required values is to assume that on some trials the subject's behavior is not governed by the stimuli manipulated by the experimenter but by factors that are independent of these stimuli (the subject "guesses" on some trials). In previous discussions (Heinemann & Avin, 1973; Heinemann et al., 1969) we have referred to this state of affairs

FIGURE 3. Normal ogives that differ from each other in the value of the criterion (thin lines). The thick line represents the arithmetic mean of the four thin-line curves. (From Heinemann & Avin, 1973. Copyright 1973 by the Society for the Experimental Analysis of Behavior, Inc.)

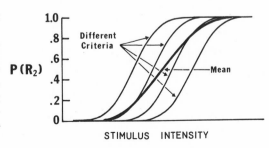

STIMULUS   INTENSITY

by saying that the subject does not "attend" to the experimentally manipulated stimuli on all trials.[2]

If it is assumed that the probability of attention to a set of stimuli is independent of the dimension in which they differ, then the observed probability of either response (in the two-choice situation) can be expressed as the sum of two joint probabilities as follows:

$$p(R) = p(A) p(R|A) + p(\bar{A}) p(R|\bar{A}), \qquad (1)$$

where $p(R|A)$ is the conditional probability of response given attention to the stimulus dimension in question, $p(R|\bar{A})$ the conditional probability of response given inattention, $p(A)$ the probability of attention, and $p(\bar{A}) = 1 - p(A)$.

It can be shown that the probability of attention $p(A)$ is the difference between the upper and lower asymptotes of the empirical gradient, and Eq. (1) can be used to correct each observed response proportion for the effects of inattention. A more detailed discussion of this matter may be found in Heinemann *et al.* (1969).

Gradients of the bell-shaped type sometimes have horizontal asymptotes that lie well above zero. If the peak of such a gradient represents a response proportion of 1.0, then the probability of attention is equal to the difference between this peak value and the value of the horizontal asymptote. If the greatest observed response proportion is smaller than 1.0, the probability of attention is difficult to estimate in practice, but in principle it can be estimated by using the relations shown in Figure 2, that is, by constructing the two ogives and determining their upper and lower asymptotes.

B. Conditioning Theories

1. The Theory of Hull

Hull postulates a theoretical generalization gradient that has the form (for all stimulus continua) of a decay function in which the independent variable is the number of just noticeable differences (JNDs) that separate the new stimuli presented during a generalization test from the stimulus that was directly conditioned. The values of the JNDs are treated as given by psychophysics, considered as a more or less independent science.

Hull's approach creates an awkward problem. As mentioned in Section I.C.2, psychophysicists can derive measures of discriminability only on

---

[2] In the sense in which "attend" is used here the statement that the subject attends to a stimulus dimension is equivalent to the statement that the subject bases its response on the value of the decision variable for that dimension, in accordance with a specified decision rule.

the basis of a theory that specifies a response rule and makes assumptions concerning the effects of motivational variables on behavior. The trouble is that the psychophysical theories on which available measures of discriminability are based make assumptions concerning response rules and the effects of motivation that appear to be incompatible with those made by Hull. It is difficult to see how this problem can be solved except by developing, within the framework of Hullian theory, an account of discriminability. These considerations apply also to the closely related theory by Spence (1936, 1937).

There are empirical results which indicate that the assumption that gradients for all stimulus continua have the same form, on a stimulus axis that is scaled in units of JNDs between adjacent stimuli, is probably wrong. For example, Blackwell and Schlosberg (1943), working with rats, found greater generalization between tones differing by an octave than between tones closer together in frequency, and several experimenters working with pigeons (Blough, 1961; Wright & Cumming, 1971) found greater generalization between monochromatic lights from the extreme ends of the visible spectrum than between lights that are less widely separated in terms of cumulated JND units.

2. Stimulus-Sampling Theory

Stimulus-sampling theory has led to the development of numerous special models, each based on somewhat different assumptions. The model on which the best-developed treatment of generalization is based is called the *component model*. In this model all stimuli (for example, optical, acoustical, response produced) that can affect an organism in a specific environment (stimulus situation) are represented as a finite set of stimulus elements, S, of which only a sample is effective at any given time. Two stimulus situations that differ from each other are represented by different sets, and their similarity is defined by the overlap of the two sets, that is, the fraction of elements that each set has in common with the other. This representation may be regarded as the counterpart of the "state" component of signal recognition theory.

Stimulus sets are related to behavior by the assumption that a conditional relation (connection) may obtain between any particular response, R, and any number of elements in S. The usual way to refer to this state of affairs is to say that R may be conditioned to any number of elements in S. The probability that a particular response R will occur in the presence of S is assumed to be equal to the proportion of elements in S that are conditioned to R. We shall not consider the learning rules of stimulus sampling theory except to note that a conditional relation between specific elements and a particular response, R, is assumed to result from reinforcement of R in the presence of the elements referred to.

To show how stimulus sampling theory deals with stimulus generalization we begin with two stimulus situations, represented by sets S_a and S_b. S_a represents a training stimulus in the presence of which a particular response R has been reinforced, and S_b represents a test stimulus that was not presented during the training procedure. On the assumption that S_b had none of its elements conditioned to R before the experiment it follows from the axioms of the model that the probability with which R occurs to S_b over a series of test trials, denoted p_b, is equal to the fraction of elements S_b has in common with S_a, and conversely, that p_b is a measure of the overlap of S_a and S_b.

More generally, Atkinson and Estes (1963) show that if the proportion of elements of S_b conditioned to R before the experiment is g, not necessarily equal to zero, the probability of R to stimulus S_b after conditioning of response R to S_a is given by

$$p_b = w_{ab}(p_a - g) + g, \qquad (2)$$

where p_a is the posttraining probability of R in the presence of S_a, and w_{ab} is the fraction of elements S_b has in common with S_a.

Equation (2) is the equation of a linear gradient of generalization in which p_b is the dependent variable and w_{ab} is the independent variable.

Predictions of the effects that stimulus variables have on responding during generalization tests depend on assumptions concerning the relation between the parameters of particular stimuli and the properties of the corresponding sets. Systematic differences in the form of generalization gradients along different stimulus continua can be dealt with by introducing different assumptions concerning the relation just referred to.

Atkinson and Estes (1963) have attempted to specify some of the properties that distinguish dimensions of the sort Stevens (1957) calls additive or *prothetic*, from those he calls substitutive or *metathetic*. The primary example of an additive dimension is stimulus intensity; an example of a substitutive dimension is the frequency of tones. Atkinson and Estes have not presented a fully developed treatment of intensity but they suggest that variations in stimulus intensity affect the size of the stimulus sets; more intense stimuli are represented by larger sets. To understand some of the consequences of such variations in set size it is important to note that, as defined in stimulus sampling theory, similarity is not a symmetric relation unless the sets referred to are of equal size. If two sets S_a and S_b differ in the number of elements they contain then the proportion of elements S_a has in common with S_b does not equal the proportion of elements S_b has in common with S_a. One result of this asymmetry is that generalization from the larger set to the smaller set, after training with the larger set, will not equal the generalization from the smaller to the larger set after training with the smaller.

The term "substitutive" refers to continua in which stimuli are ordered, often by spatial position at the receptor surface, without variation in intensity or magnitude. A particularly simple example of a substitutive continuum is the position of a point of light in the visual field. For continua of this sort Atkinson and Estes assume that the sequence of sets corresponding to constant changes in the stimulus variable is generated by deleting a constant number of elements from the preceding set and adding the same number of new elements to form the next set. Their treatment also assumes that once an element is deleted, it does not reappear in any set formed as the stimulus value is changed further (as it might, for example, if the stimulus continuum were circular). A further assumption is that the overlap between two stimulus sets is directly related to the distance between the corresponding stimuli, specified in physical units. According to this model, the response probability attains a value of zero at a point on the stimulus scale represented by a set that does not overlap the training stimulus set. However, if only a single property of the environment is varied during a generalization test, for example, the wavelength of a light, it is impossible for any pair of stimulus sets to be disjoint because the sets contain elements that represent components of the stimulus situation that are not varied during the generalization test. Thus, empirical generalization gradients are not expected to fall to zero at any stimulus value.

The model under discussion applies to simple conditioning, a term which refers, roughly speaking, to a procedure in which a subject is exposed to a single stimulus situation in which occurrences of a particular response are reinforced.[3] The results of experiments that come close to realizing the conditions specified for simple conditioning (e.g., Jenkins & Harrison, 1960) tend to confirm the prediction that generalization gradients obtained after simple conditioning do not fall to response probability levels near zero.

In many experiments generalization has been measured after discrimination training, for example, after training in which the subject is trained to make one response to one of a pair of stimuli and a different response to the other. In experiments of this sort it is often found that response probabilities vary, as a function of stimulus values, from values very close to one to values very close to zero; in other words, that there are essentially perfect discriminations between some of the stimuli presented during the generalization test.

[3] The distinction between simple learning and discrimination learning is arbitrary; strictly speaking all learning situations involve discrimination. According to Atkinson and Estes (1963): "The principal basis for differentiation between the two categories of learning seems to be that in the case of discrimination learning the similarity, or communality, between stimuli is a major independent variable; in the case of simple learning stimulus similarity is an extraneous factor to be minimized experimentally and neglected in theory as far as possible [p. 239]."

Component models for discrimination learning (e.g., Burke & Estes, 1957) do not account for perfect discriminations between two training stimuli, nor do they, if combined with the general treatment of generalization discussed above, account for perfect discriminations among test stimuli. The special problem presented by perfect discriminations is a result of the assumption, shared by all conditioning theories, that the responses that are reinforced in discrimination situations become conditioned to the elements that the various stimulus situations have in common as well as those that are unique to each situation.

Several theorists have dealt with this problem by introducing special assumptions, for example, that the common elements are "neutralized" (Hull, 1952), or "adapted" (Restle, 1955), or that the overlap between stimulus sets decreases as discrimination learning progresses (Bush & Mosteller, 1951). Another approach to the problem, explored by stimulus sampling theorists, is based on a reinterpretation of the stimulus units that are assumed to be sampled and conditioned. For example, in some models (Estes & Hopkins, 1961; Johns, 1965) the stimulus situation on a given trial is viewed as a unique pattern rather than a sample from a set of elements. Pattern models can predict perfect discriminations, but they do not provide a straightforward way to describe generalization to new stimuli, or even to scale stimulus similarity. Neimark and Estes (1967) suggest that a possible solution is the development of mixed models that incorporate some of the desirable features of the component and pattern models. Some possible mixed models are discussed by Atkinson (1959) and Atkinson and Estes (1963).

III. COMMENTS ON EXPERIMENTAL METHODS

A. Response Measures

The principal response measures that have been studied in experiments on generalization are response magnitude (Hovland, 1937; Pavlov, 1927) latency (e.g., Flagg, Medin, & Davis, 1974; Heinemann et al., 1969) and frequency of occurrence (e.g., Guttman & Kalish, 1956; Hanson, 1959). Measures of magnitude and latency present special problems because most theories relate their constructs directly to *probability of response* but require elaboration and additional assumptions to deal with magnitude and latency of response. Magnitude measures have received relatively little attention from theorists but there are many theories of latency. Estes (1950) and Bush and Mosteller (1955) have theories that relate latency to response probability, and the treatment developed by Estes has been adapted to his own theory by Spence (1954). Numerous theories of latency have also been developed within the framework of signal recongition theory (see Laming, 1968, for a review).

A consideration of theories of response magnitude and latency would take us too far afield, so in the sections that follow, we shall concern ourselves mainly with experiments in which the frequency of response occurrence was studied. These experiments fall into two classes: choice experiments and free operant experiments. Choice experiments involve at least two alternative responses, and in these experiments a trial is typically ended by the first response that occurs. In free-operant experiments (on generalization) only one class of responses is usually studied, for example, pecks on a single response disk. Trials are of fixed duration and typically quite long, so that many response occurrences may be recorded during a single trial. The primary dependent variable in these experiments is the number of responses per trial.

Choice experiments yield straightforward estimates of response probability. Each trial represents a single opportunity to respond; thus, if a particular response occurred N times given N_0 opportunities, the estimated probability of the response is

$$p = N/N_0. \tag{3}$$

In principle, the number of responses occurring on each trial of a free-operant experiment may be converted to an estimate of response probability also, but the trouble is that there is no good way to estimate the number of response opportunities, N_0. It seems reasonable to assume that N_0 is determined by the time required to make a single response and by physical and physiological factors that impose some minimum delay between successive responses. In any case, if it can be assumed that N_0 is constant in a given experiment, then N, the number of responses on any trial, is proportional to the probability of the response, as can be seen by multiplying both sides of Eq. (3) by N_0.

Generalization gradients obtained by the free-operant method are often presented with *relative* number of responses as the dependent variable, for example, the number of responses made in the presence of each particular stimulus divided by the number of responses made in the presence of the training stimulus. This measure represents a ratio of two probabilities and is difficult to relate to such theoretical quantities as discriminability, criterion value, etc.

There is one other matter we wish to consider. The simplest treatment derivable from each theory regards successive responses as statistically independent. In experiments in which a single response ends the trial, sequential dependencies among responses can be reduced to negligible levels by separating trials by long intervals of time. However, in free-operant experiments responses may follow each other quite quickly and as a result there are usually strong sequential dependencies among responses. For example, Blough (1963) has shown that the probability that a pigeon will peck at an object at any moment is strongly controlled by the occurrence of previous pecks. This means that in generalization experiments done with the free-operant method the effects of environmental stimuli are confounded with the effects of response-produced stimuli. Ray and Sidman (1970) have discussed this matter in detail.

B. Problems of Testing

The usual purpose of a generalization test is to assess the effects of a particular training procedure. Ideally one would want to make such an assessment by methods that do not themselves change the behavior under study, but that is impossible. In order to test, new stimuli have to be introduced, and the behavior that occurs in the presence of these new stimuli necessarily has consequences (for example, reinforcement or nonreinforcement) that affect the behavior. Every test situation is, in fact, a new learning situation, and as a test proceeds, the behavior observed invariably changes.

Experimenters usually try to minimize the problem by arranging conditions under which behavior will change relatively slowly. For example, with the free-operant method responding usually is not reinforced at all during testing. In the absence of reinforcement the frequency of responding gradually decreases, and eventually the subject may stop responding altogether. The rate at which the frequency of responding decreases in the absence of reinforcement depends strongly on the manner in which reinforcement was scheduled during training, and it is possible to ensure a relatively slow rate of decrease by reinforcing responses only intermittently during training. Even so, the test procedure usually produces some changes in the behavior under study, and the magnitude of these changes is often difficult to assess. It seems reasonable to regard the measurements taken near the beginning of a prolonged test procedure as providing the most accurate picture of the results of the training that preceded the test.

Interpretation of generalization curves is also complicated by the fact that the stimuli presented during a test may serve several different functions in the control of behavior. For example, the presentation of a stimulus may serve as a reinforcing event, or alternatively, may serve to suppress the behavior under study. Stimuli also serve as sources of information concerning the likely consequences of various behaviors. It is with the latter function (the discriminative function) that this chapter is primarily concerned. The distinctions mentioned are purely abstract; in most situations there are stimuli that serve several functions. Thus, stimuli that provide information concerning the likelihood of reinforcing events usually serve also as conditioned reinforcers (Wyckoff, 1952).

The changes in response probability that occur when stimulus parameters are varied during a generalization test done by the free-operant method may reflect changes in any of several stimulus functions. Thus, a change in response probability observed when a loud sound is introduced during a test might be related to the informational properties of the sound or it might indicate that the sound suppresses the response under study, perhaps by evoking emotional behavior that is incompatible with the performance of that response. It is necessary to assess the possible nondiscriminative effects of stimulus variations by appropriate control procedures (see Blough, 1959). Choice methods that involve two symmetrical responses, such as turning left or right, have an advantage here. Nondiscriminative effects of a stimulus, say, a tendency to suppress locomotion, would be expected to affect the time that elapses before a response occurs, but there is no obvious reason why the probability of occurrence of the two symmetrical responses should be affected differentially.

IV. RESULTS OF EXPERIMENTS

The theoretical problems encountered, the behavioral processes that must be taken into account, and the form of empirical generalization gradients obtained all vary with the nature of the stimuli that are presented during training and testing.

A. Variations in Stimulus Intensity

Gradients obtained after training to discriminate between two stimuli that differ only in intensity usually have a roughly S-shaped form. Figure 4 shows some gradients obtained by Heinemann et al. (1969) in an experiment that used a two-alternative choice method, pigeons as subjects, and intensity of white noise as the stimulus variable. During training the pigeons were presented on each trial with one of two levels of intensity, and were reinforced for pecking on one disk when presented with one intensity, and pecking on the alternate disk when presented with the second intensity. The three groups of subjects for which results are shown differed in the difficulty of the discrimination presented during training, that is, in the difference between the two levels of intensity.

Results obtained with rats under generally comparable conditions by Weinstock, Robbins, and Chen (in press) are shown in Figure 5. The

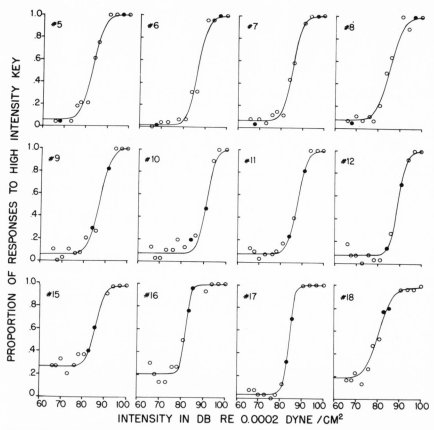

FIGURE 4. Choice curves obtained during generalization tests after training to discriminate between two levels of intensity of white noise. The differences in the two levels were: top row, 29 dB; middle row, 7 dB; bottom row, 2.3 dB. The filled circles indicate the stimuli used in training. (From Heinemann, Avin, Sullivan, & Chase, 1969. Copyright 1969 by the American Psychological Association. Reprinted by permission.)

experiment was done in a T maze in which the intensity of a spot of light, located at the choice point, signaled whether a right turn or a left turn would lead to reward.

To differentiate among theories it is important to know whether the upper and lower "tails" of these S-shaped gradients are horizontal, and, if so, whether they would still be found to be horizontal if the stimulus range were extended on either end. S-shaped gradients with horizontal tails are predicted by signal-recognition theory for conditions under which the optimal strategy is to divide the continuum of internal effects into two segments by a single criterion, etc. These conditions probably obtain for intensity continua since mean sensory effect is almost certainly a monotonic

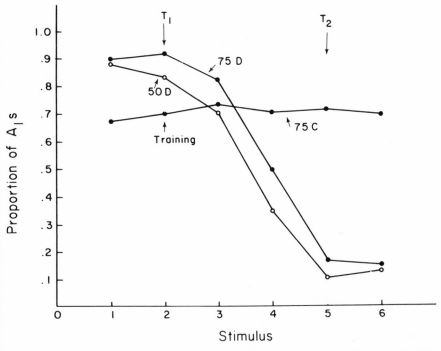

FIGURE 5. Choice curves obtained after training to discriminate between two levels of light intensity ((Groups 75D and 50D) and after single-stimulus training (Group 75C). The training stimuli T_1 and T_2 were presented with equal frequency for Group 50D and in the ratio 75:25 for Group 75D. Goup 75C received probability-learning training ($\pi = .75$) during which only T_1 was presented. The fact that the curve for Group 75C is virtually a horizontal line indicates that single-stimulus training did not result in the development of stimulus control. (From Weinstock, Robbins, & Chen, in press.)

function of stimulus intensity. A model based on stimulus-sampling theory, the "recruitment model" of LaBerge (1962), also predicts S-shaped gradients with horizontal tails for intensive continua (see Flagg *et al.,* 1974). On the other hand, according to the theories of Hull and Spence the upper and lower tails of the gradients under discussion should curve downward and upward, respectively.

The theoretical predictions described above do not take into account the effects that the (generalization) test procedure may have on the form of the gradient, and it is therefore difficult to make exact experimental tests of these predictions. The main problem is that the form of gradients based on average results of lengthy generalization tests is determined in part by what the subject learned during the test (see Section III.B). To minimize the effects that experience in the test situation may have upon the form of the gradient, generalization tests should be kept as short as possible. If

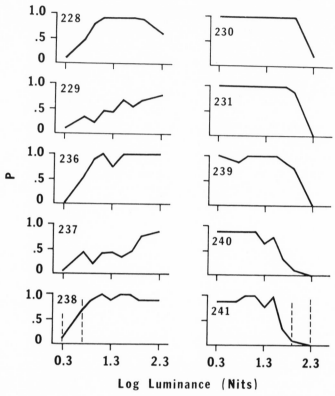

Log Luminance (Nits)

FIGURE 6. Choice curves obtained during generalization tests after training to discriminate between the two levels of luminance indicated by the dashed lines in the bottom row of panels. For the left-hand column of figures P represents the proportion of responses to the choice-disk designated as correct for the more intense of the training stimuli; for the right-hand column P represents the proportion of responses to the disk designated as correct for the less intense of the training stimuli. Each panel represents results for an individual pigeon. (From Chase & Heinemann, in press.)

the results obtained during lengthy generalization tests are to be compared to theoretical predictions, it seems best to consider only measurements made near the beginning of the test procedure.

Figure 6 shows results of an experiment by Chase and Heinemann (in press), in which the two training stimuli were placed near the very end of the stimulus range so that the tails of the gradients might be observed over a relatively large stimulus range. The results shown are based on the first nine choice responses made by each of ten pigeons in the presence of each of the light intensitities presented. The gradients of Birds 229 and 237 provide no information concerning the form of the tails, for these gradients do not attain an asymptotic level within the stimulus range that was used. All but one of the remaining gradients have tails that are either horizontal lines or show only unsystematic fluctuations about horizontal lines. The exception is the gradient of Bird 228 which shows a decrease in response probability at the highest stimulus value. Chase and Heinemann mention that this decrease in response probability at the highest stimulus value is not seen in the gradient based on only the first six choice responses made by Bird 228, suggesting that it may be the result of prolonged experience in the test situation.

As the tests were continued (beyond nine responses per stimulus) the form of all the gradients gradually changed. Specifically, the tails became curved, concave downward. These changes in the form of the gradients may well be attributable to the fact that, in the procedure used by Chase and Heinemann, correct responding in the presence of the training stimuli was reinforced intermittently during the test, but responding in the presence of the (new) test stimuli was never reinforced. Under these conditions the subjects may soon notice that responding in the presence of the test stimuli does not pay and may then simply respond at random, particularly in the presence of stimuli that are easy to discriminate from the training stimuli, such as those near the end of the range.

In similar experiments with rhesus monkeys, Flagg et al. (1974) found gradients with curved tails after only 12 presentations of each stimulus. Moreover, the statistical analyses made by these workers revealed no significant differences between gradients based on the first six and the second six stimulus presentations, indicating that the curvature of the tails was either present from the outset or developed very rapidly. The discrepancy between these results and those obtained with pigeons in our laboratory has an interesting parallel in the gradients of response latency. Flagg et al., found a W-shaped gradient of response latency, the shortest latencies occurring at the values of the training stimuli. In the experiments of Heinemann et al. (1969) the function relating stimulus intensity to latency was a horizontal line during the first few days of testing, but changed to a W-shaped curve similar to that found by Flagg et al., as the tests continued (the effects of continued testing were not described in detail by Heinemann et al.). Thus, with respect to latency as well as relative response frequency the monkeys of Flagg et al., behaved in a manner seen in our experiments only after the subjects had considerable experience in the test situation. Whether the discrepancies in the results of these experiments are attributable to differences in procedure or to differences in the species studied is not known.

All of the experiments considered thus far were done with choice methods. We consider next the form of gradients obtained in comparable experiments with the free operant method. Ernst, Engberg, and Thomas

(1971), working with pigeons and the luminance dimension, found gradients with strongly curved tails, and Thomas and Setzer (1972), working with intensity of white noise, found similar gradients for rats and guinea pigs. All of these gradients are based on the total number of responses made on numerous presentations of each stimulus. In a repetition of the experiment of Ernst *et al.*, we examined gradients based on only the first presentation of each stimulus (Chase & Heinemann, in press). The stimuli used during training and testing were the same as those used in the choice experiment by Chase and Heinemann described above. In each of the two conditions the stimulus at the very end of the range was the negative training stimulus (no reinforcement) and the second stimulus indicated in the bottom panels of Figure 6 was the positive training stimulus (reinforcement on a variable interval schedule). The tails of the gradients obtained for the condition in which the negative stimulus was the most intense value on the stimulus range were horizontal. However, the gradients obtained for the condition in which the negative stimulus was the least intense value had curved tails. As the tests continued the horizontal tails obtained in the one condition became curved, and the tails that were curved from the outset became more strongly curved. The initial curvature of the tails observed in one of the conditions appears to have been caused, at least in part, by nondiscriminative effects of light intensity, for a similar curvature is found in so-called "preference" experiments in which responding in the presence of all stimulus intensities is reinforced equally (Blough, 1959; Chase & Heinemann, in press).

We have yet to consider the effect of the difficulty of the discrimination presented during training. According to Heinemann *et al.* (1969), gradients obtained after training on difficult discriminations are steeper than those obtained after training on easy ones. All of the gradients obtained by Heinemann *et al.*, were well fitted by normal ogives when the data were first corrected for the effects of inattention (see Section II.A.3). When these ogives are transformed to straight lines by expressing the dependent variable in normal deviate units, their slope has the dimensions d'/dB. Thus, in the terminology of signal recognition theory, the difficulty of the discrimination affects discriminability as indexed by d'. One possible reason for the observed dependence of d' on the difficulty of the discrimination is that the latter affects the variability of the criterion. From a common sense point of view it is reasonable to expect that a subject will hold its criterion more steady when faced with a difficult discrimination than when faced with an easy one. If the subject's goal is to minimize errors or maximize expected value, then any deviation of the criterion from its optimal value entails losses, but these losses are much more severe if the distributions overlap greatly (as they do in a difficult discrimination) than they are if the distributions overlap only a little.

B. Spatial Properties of Visual Stimuli

Analysis of how changes in the position, orientation, size, and shape of visual stimuli affect behavior is very difficult. Part of the problem is that any selected part of the environment defined as a "visual stimulus" may differ from other parts of the environment in many ways at once, for example, in size, shape, luminance, texture, and it is necessary to know which features of the stimulus actually affect the behavior under study. The subject's viewing habits may also affect the results of an experiment. For example, it is important to know whether the subject stares rigidly at a relatively restricted part of the environment or whether it scans a large portion of the environment. To illustrate some of the factors involved we shall consider several simple experiments done with pigeons.

1. Position and Luminance of a Spot

In an experiment done in our laboratory by Karen Kadison (unpublished) pigeons were trained to peck on one disk when presented with a small circular spot of light that was projected on a larger evenly illuminated circular field, and to peck on an alternate disk when presented with the large illuminated field without the spot. The visual display was located between the two choice disks. During a subsequent generalization test Kadison varied the position of the spot within the larger circular field and also the luminance of the spot. Her results are shown in Figure 7. When the spot was in the center of the field, where it had been during training, the effects of varying its luminance were similar to those described for luminance variations in Section IV.A. The first point on the left of each curve represents the blank field. Presumably, as the luminance of the spot is raised from this level, the spot becomes more and more easy to distinguish from its background, and the proportion of correct choices increases. However, once the luminance of the spot exceeds that of the background by a few tenths of a log unit, further increases in luminance do not result in further improvements in performance. The discussion that follows concerns spots that are bright enough so that further increases in their luminance do not improve performance.

The proportion of trials on which the pigeons treat such spots as though they were not there at all is proportional to the difference between the height of the horizontal asymptote of each curve and the height of the point corresponding to the blank field. When the spot was located at the top of the large field, both birds responded on virtually all trials as though they had been presented with a field that does not contain a spot. In other locations

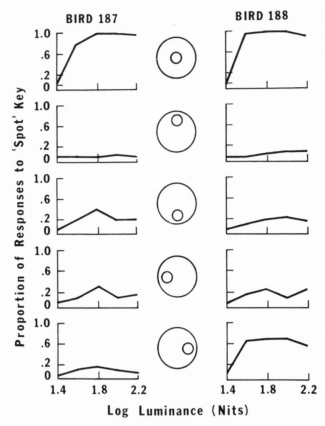

FIGURE 7. Choice curves obtained by Kadison when the spot was in the positions shown. The spot and the surrounding field are not drawn to scale; the diameter of the spot used was .5 cm; that of the surrounding field was 7.62 cm. The subjects were trained to discriminate between the large field when it contained a centrally located spot of luminance 1.8 log ft L and when it was presented without the spot. Luminance of the large field: 1.4 log ft L.

the birds sometimes noticed the spot and sometimes did not (Figure 7). These results may indicate that the birds look mainly at the center of the visual display, with occasional glances elsewhere, and that they base their choices on the presence or absence of a luminance difference in the area of the display that they inspect. According to this interpretation, moving the spot away from the position it occupied during training affects the choice behavior only indirectly, by removing the spot from the pigeon's field of view.

The sort of rigid staring at the center of the display that is implied by this interpretation should not be thought of as behavior typical of pigeons, but as behavior that results from the circumstance that the spot was always in the same position during training. Jenkins and Sainsbury (1969) have shown that when a spot is moved about from trial to trial during training, pigeons learn to search for it.

2. Orientation and Luminance of Lines

A great many experiments done with the free-operant method have used straight lines in various angular orientations as stimuli. Training is usually done by one of two methods. In the first of these (nominally "single stimulus training") a line in fixed orientation is presented on the response disk and the pigeon is reinforced for pecking on the disk. In the second (successive discrimination training) there are two types of trials, usually presented in random sequence. On one type of trial a line is presented in a particular orientation and on the other type either a line in a different orientation or an evenly illuminated disk may be presented. Responding is reinforced in the presence of one of the stimuli, S⁺, but not in the presence of the other, S⁻.

Gradients obtained after "single-stimulus training" and those obtained after successive discrimination training in which a line serves as S⁺ and an evenly illuminated disk as S⁻ (sometimes called "orthogonal-dimension training") have roughly similar forms. They show a relatively sharp maximum at S⁺ and fall off in symmetric fashion on either side of this maximum (Hearst, 1969; Hearst, Koresko, & Poppen, 1964). Gradients of similar form are also obtained after training to discriminate between two lines that differ in orientation, if the difference in orientation is quite large, for example, vertical versus horizontal. On the other hand, if the difference in the orientation of the two lines is quite small the peak of the generalization gradient often does not lie at S⁺ but above a point on the stimulus axis that is further removed from S⁻. This peak shift is in the direction predicted by the theory of Spence (1936) which holds that the observed gradient reflects the algebraic sum of two underlying theoretical gradients, a gradient of inhibitory potential centered on S⁻ and a gradient of excitatory potential centered on S⁺. A further prediction from Spence's theory, that the peak-shifted gradients will lie below control gradients obtained by the single-stimulus or orthogonal-dimension methods, has been found to be wrong. Peak-shifted gradients are usually much taller than the appropriate control gradients (see Hearst, 1969).

An important prerequisite for the application of theory to the results of experiments of the sort just discussed is a more precise specification of the features of the visual displays that govern the subjects behavior. We shall describe very briefly some experiments done in attempt to isolate some of the controlling features (Heinemann, in press). These experiments were done with methods identical to those of Kadison (Section IV.B.1) except that lines in different orientations were used instead of spots in different positions. The results obtained by Heinemann are highly similar to those Kadison obtained with spots and can be interpreted in the same way. When so interpreted, the results indicate that the pigeons inspected a small part of that region of the visual display in which one of the lines presented in training appeared (typically a region corresponding to an end of the line), and that they chose one response when that region was evenly illuminated and the alternate response when it was not. According to this analysis, changes in the angular orientation of a line affect behavior indirectly, by changing the likelihood that some portion of the line will appear in the portion of the display observed by the pigeon.

In some of Heinemann's experiments pigeons were trained to discriminate between a vertical line and one tilted 15° with respect to the vertical. With such a small angular separation it might well be true that, if the birds were to stare at a region of the display coinciding with the end of one of the lines, the other line would be seen also so that a discrimination based on the presence or absence of a nonuniformity in luminance would be impossible. The birds solved this problem by staring at a point outside of the angle that would be formed if the two lines were presented simultaneously, so that only one of the lines could appear in the field of view. This process results in phenomena analogous to the peak shift observed in comparable experiments that are done with the free-operant method.

C. Behavior Governed by Multidimensional Effects of Stimuli

We now consider experiments and theories that deal with what is learned in situations in which the stimuli encountered during training, as well as the internal effects produced by these stimuli, differ from each other in more than one dimension. The experiments with spots and lines that were considered in the previous section also dealt with effects of varying several dimensions of stimulation, but they represent very special cases in that it is possible to interpret the results on the assumption that the subjects base their choice on the internal effects of luminance contrast alone. The experiments considered below were done with stimuli whose effect upon the receptor organs does not depend critically on the orientation of the receptor, for example, sounds and extended sources of light.

1. The Redundant Case

In the experiments to be considered now subjects are trained to discriminate between two binary stimulus compounds, for example, a soft sound combined with a dim light versus a loud sound combined with a bright light. One of the earliest experiments of this sort was done by Pavlov (1927). Working with a stimulus whose components differed greatly in intensity or "strength," Pavlov found that the weaker element, when presented alone, failed to elicit a conditoned response after a series of trials that would have been sufficient to establish a conditioned response had the weaker element been presented alone during training. This is the phenomenon of "overshadowing." Subsequent investigators (e.g. Chase & Heinemann, 1972; Kamin, 1969; Miles & Jenkins, 1973) have found that both of the stimulus components may acquire some influence over behavior.

One of the factors that determines the relative influence acquired by the two components is the discriminability of the pairs of values from each of the two stimulus dimensions varied during training. Evidence for this statement comes from experiments by Miles and Jenkins (1973) and Chase and Heinemann (1972). Miles and Jenkins trained pigeons to discriminate between a compound consisting of a pure tone plus a light of intensity L_1 and one consisting of the absence of the tone plus a light of different intensity, L_2. L_2 was assigned different values in different experimental groups. Generalization tests done after training showed that the steepness of the gradients for light intensity increased with increasing difference between L_1 and L_2, and that the influence the tone had on behavior diminished with increasing difference between L_1 and L_2 (that is, the tone cue was overshadowed).

A second factor known to determine how strongly each of two stimulus dimensions comes to affect behavior is prior training with only one of the dimensions. A number of investigators have found that, if subjects are first trained with one component or dimension and a second component is added later, the degree of influence acquired by the second component is smaller than it is if subjects are trained with the compounds from the outset (Chase, 1968; Kamin, 1968, 1969; vom Saal & Jenkins, 1970). This phenomenon is often called "blocking."

Chase and Heinemann (1972) have analyzed situations of the sort we are discussing in terms of signal recognition theory. In their experiments pigeons were trained to choose one response, R_1, when presented with a soft sound combined with a dim light, and an alternate response, R_2, when presented with a loud sound combined with a bright light. The decision problem is illustrated in Figure 8. The decision variables for light and sound are assumed to be independent. The two three-dimensional bell-shaped surfaces shown in Figure 8 are the joint probability density functions for the internal states produced by the two light-sound compounds presented in training. The effects of additional stimuli presented during a generalization test can be represented by similar surfaces.

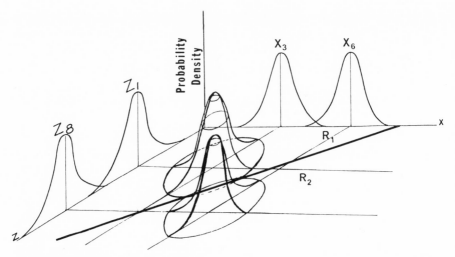

FIGURE 8. Joint probability density functions for the compound stimuli used in training, and the marginal functions of x and z. (The diagonal line located in the x–z plane is the decision line.)

If the two stimuli are presented equally often, the probability of error can be minimized by partitioning the x–z plane along a straight line, as shown, and following the decision rule: make response R_1 if the internal effect falls to one side of this line, and make response R_2 if it falls to the other side (or on the line). The probability with which each response is expected to occur in the presence of a particular light-sound compound then is given by the portion of the volume under the joint density function that lies on the appropriate side of the straight line (the "decision line").

The decision line is the locus of the internal states that are produced with equal probability by the two compound stimuli used in training. If the x and z axes are scaled in normal deviate units then the slope of the optimal (minimization of errors) decision line is equal to $-d_x'/d_z'$, where d_x' is the discriminability of the two lights used in training, and d_z' the discriminability of the two sounds. (A detailed mathematical treatment may be found in Chase & Heinemann, 1972.)

The results of a generalization test in which both sound and light intensity are varied can be represented by a set of gradients for which light intensity is the independent variable and sound intensity the parameter (to be called *light gradients*) or, alternatively, by a set of gradients for which sound intensity is the independent variable and light intensity the parameter (to be called *sound gradients*). According to the signal recognition model the sets of light and sound gradients just mentioned each form a family of normal ogives that differ from each other only by a displacement parallel to the stimulus axis. If the vertical axis is scaled in normal deviate units, each family of gradients becomes a set of parallel lines, and it can be shown that the slope of the light gradients is $-m/\sqrt{1 + m^2}$, and that of the sound gradients is $1/\sqrt{1 + m^2}$, where m is the slope of the decision line.

We shall now discuss briefly how the slopes of the light and sound gradients are affected by the relative discriminabilities of the pairs of lights and sounds used in training (that is, by the slope of the decision line). As the slope of the decision line approaches zero, as happens when the sounds are much more discriminable than the lights, the sound gradients approach their maximal steepness and the light gradients approach horizontal lines. In the limit, where $m = 0$, variations in light intensity have no influence on the choice behavior, and the sound gradients are all identical with the gradient expected after training to discriminate between the sound intensities alone. The reverse is true at the other extreme. As m becomes indefinitely large, the light gradients approach their maximal steepness and sound intensity becomes irrelevant to the choice of response. To summarize, changes in the slope of the decision line have opposite effects on the slopes of the light and sound gradients; an increase in m steepens the light gradients and flattens the sound gradients, and vice versa. This trading relation has often been noted by experimenters and has sometimes been attributed to the partitioning of a fixed amount of "attention."

We now consider how this model accounts for overshadowing and blocking. Overshadowing is evaluated by comparing how strongly two stimuli that vary in a single dimension come to influence behavior under two conditions of training. In one the stimuli are presented alone during training, and in the other the stimuli are embedded in a compound, that is, each is accompanied by a second stimulus that provides redundant information. If embedding the stimuli in a compound results in their developing less influence, then these stimuli are said to be overshadowed (at least partially) by the added components. As indicated in the previous paragraph, the generalization gradient obtained under conditions in which only a single dimension has an influence on behavior is always steeper than one obtained under conditions in which both dimensions affect the behavior. This means that overshadowing always occurs when behavior is controlled jointly by two stimulus dimensions, the amount of overshadowing depending on the slope of the decision line.

In discussing blocking we shall use the following notation: X and Z represent the two stimulus dimensions (for example, light intensity and sound intensity); X_1 and X_2 represent the particular values of X used in training, Z_1 and Z_2 the particular values of Z used in training, and X_1Z_1, X_2Z_2 the two compounds used in training.

The research of Chase and Heinemann (1972) included an investigation of blocking. The results of this investigation show that, if subjects are first trained to discriminate between X_1 and X_2, and trained later to discriminate between compounds X_1Z_1 and X_2Z_2, the generalization gradients along dimension X are steeper, and those along dimension Z are flatter than corresponding gradients for a control group that was trained only with compounds X_1Z_1 and X_2Z_2. The correlated changes in the slopes of the gradients along the X and Z dimensions are such as are produced by a change in the slope of the decision line; in other words, pretraining with X_1 and X_2 results in a change in the slope of the optimal decision line. According to Chase and Heinemann this effect occurs because training to discriminate between X_1 and X_2 causes these stimuli to become more discriminable, that is, increases the value of d_x', perhaps by reducing criterion variability (recall that the slope of the decision line is equal to $-d_x'/d_z'$).

The model discussed above assumes that the subject's choice on every trial is based on information provided by both of the stimulus sources. Chase and Heinemann have also proposed a more general model in which this assumption is relaxed. The assumptions made in the more general model are as follows: (a) the probabilities of attention to each of the stimulus dimensions are independent; (b) the statistical decision model just described applies to those trials on which the subject attends to both dimensions; (c) on those trials on which the subject attends to only one of the dimensions it follows the decision rule that would be appropriate if the dimension not attended to were irrelevant; and (d) on those trials on which the subject does not attend to either of the dimensions, its choice of response is independent of the stimulus values. The probability that one of the choices, say R_2, will occur in the presence of any particular combination of light and sound intensity can be expressed as the sum of four quantities representing the probabilities of the four attentional states (attention to both dimensions, attention to either alone, and attention to neither dimension), each multiplied by the probability of R_2 given that attentional state. In equational form,

$$p(R_2|X_iZ_j) = abp_C + a(1 - b)p_x + (1 - a)bp_z + (1 - a)(1 - b)k, \quad (4)$$

where a and b are the probabilities of attention to light and sound, respectively, p_C is the volume under the bivariate surface for stimulus X_i, Z_j that falls in the acceptance region for response R_2, p_x and p_z are the areas under the marginal distributions X_i and Z_j, respectively, that fall in the acceptance region for R_2, and k is the probability of R_2 given attention to neither of the stimulus dimensions.

Some of the results obtained by Chase and Heinemann, together with the best-fitting curves derived from the more general model, are shown in Figure 9. The curve fitting procedure that was used yields estimates of the slope of the decision line and the probabilities of attention to each

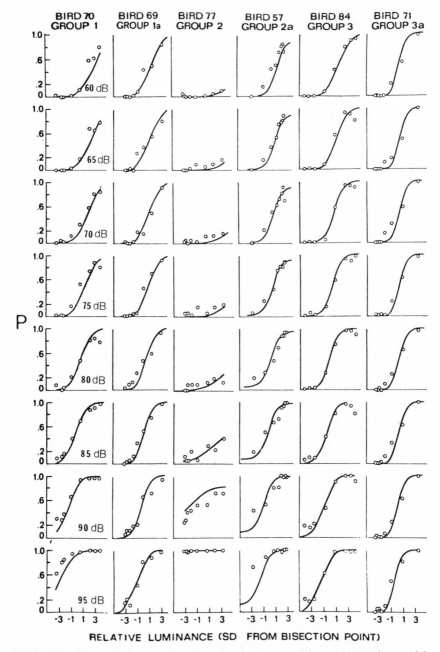

FIGURE 9. Theoretical curves based on the signal recognition and attention model. *P* represents the proportion of responses to the choice disk designated as correct for the more intense of the two light–sound compounds presented in training. (The various groups in this experiment differed either in the relative discriminabilities of the lights and sounds or in the pretraining they received. The "bisection point" is the point on the stimulus axis that falls midway between the training stimuli.) (From Chase & Heinemann, 1972. Copyright 1972 by the American Psychological Association. Reproduced by permission.)

of the stimulus dimensions. It was found that the relative discriminability of the pairs of training stimuli and the conditions of pretraining had very strong effects on the slope of the decision line but only minor effects on the probabilities of attention. This analysis lends no support to theories (e.g., Sutherland & Mackintosh, 1971) which hold that phenomena such as blocking and overshadowing indicate that one of the dimensions is less likely to be attended to than the other.

Finally, if it is assumed that the subject's decision goal is to maximize expected value then the placement of the optimal decision line (but not the slope of this line) should vary with the payoff matrix. The influence of motivational variables upon generalization gradients has not been investigated in the redundant cue situation. However, in an investigation of blocking that was confined to the effects of the training stimuli Kamin (1969) found that a pretraining procedure that would otherwise have caused virtually complete blocking did not do so when, at the beginning of the second phase of training, the intensity of the unconditioned stimulus (electric shock) was raised substantially above the level used during the first phase. Effects of this sort are predictable from the signal recognition model if it is assumed that the value of the unconditioned stimulus is reflected in the placement of the decision line.

2. The Conditional Case

The way an organism reacts to variations in a particular stimulus property usually does not depend on that property alone but also on the context provided by other stimuli. For example, a pigeon that discriminates perfectly between two levels of sound intensity by pecking on one illuminated disk or another may fail to respond at all if the disks are not illuminated. In this case the intensity of the illumination on the disks may not influence the choice the pigeon makes but determine only whether it responds at all. Under other conditions contextual cues may affect the nature of the choice also. Thus, Lashley (1938) was able to train rats to jump to an erect triangle and avoid an inverted one when these triangles were presented on a black background, but to jump to the inverted triangle and avoid the erect one when both triangles were on a striped background.

Discriminations of this sort are often called "conditional discriminations," and in some discussions one set of stimuli, for example, the backgrounds in Lashley's experiment, are called "superordinate" and the other set, for example, the triangles in Lashley's experiment, "subordinate." We shall examine the exact meaning of the term "conditional discrimination" in more detail at the end of this section. In one sense of the term all discriminations are probably conditional discriminations, for in all experimental situations some features of the environment that are not experimentally manipulated probably function as "superordinate" stimuli in the absence of which the behavior studied will be altered or will fail to appear. Stimuli that arise from within the organism, particularly those associated with motivational states, may also function as "superordinate" stimuli in this sense.

An important special case of conditional discrimination is that in which the subordinate stimuli are responded to differentially when they are accompanied by certain values of the superordinate stimuli, but are not responded to differentially (that is, are irrelevant to behavior) when accompanied by other values of the superordinate stimuli. Conditional discriminations of this sort may play an important part in the organization of behavior, for example, in selecting aspects of the environment to be responded to and in preventing the interruption of ongoing sequences of behavior by the intrusion of currently irrelevant stimuli.

Generalization following conditional discrimination training has been investigated by Blough (1972), Heinemann, Chase, and Mandell (1968), Heinemann and Chase (1970), and Zuckerman and Blough (1974). Heinemann and Chase (1970) have extended the signal recognition and attention model to this situation.

In the experimental situation analyzed by Heinemann and Chase pigeons were trained to choose between two responses when presented with each of the four compounds that can be produced by combining two levels of light intensity with two levels of sound intensity. The responses required in the presence of each of the four light–sound combinations are shown in Table 1. The decision problem the pigeons faced during training is illustrated in Figure 10. In that figure, X_1 and X_8 represent the probability density functions for the two lights presented in training, and Z_1 and Z_8 the corresponding functions for the two sounds. The concentric circles represent the joint density functions for the four light–sound compounds. As in the treatment of the redundant case, the decision variables for light and sound are assumed to be independent.

In this situation the proportion of correct responses can be maximized by partitioning the x–z plane along a contour that is the locus of those joint effects that are as likely to be produced by X_1Z_1 as by any of the

TABLE 1
Responses Required in the
Presence of Each of the
Light (X_1, X_8)–Sound (Z_1, Z_8) Combinations

	X_1	X_8
Z_1	R_1	R_2
Z_8	R_2	R_2

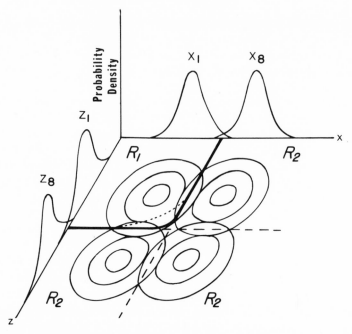

FIGURE 10.   Isodensity contours for the probability density functions of the compound training stimuli; and the marginal functions of x and z. (From Heinemann & Chase, 1970. Copyright 1970 by the American Psychological Association. Reproduced by permission.)

three remaining compounds, and following the rule: make response R_1 when the joint effect falls to one side of this contour (or on it), otherwise make response R_2. The exact form of this optimal decision contour depends on the relative discriminabilities of the pairs of light and sound intensities presented in training. For the distributions shown in Figure 10 the optimal decision contour is the thick, unbroken line. The dashed-curve shown in the figure is the decision contour that would be appropriate for marginal distributions that have twice the variance of those shown.

As the values of d' for both light and sound stimuli become large the optimal decision contour comes to be more and more similar to the two intersecting straight lines shown in Figure 10. In other words, when the stimuli are very easy to distinguish, a decision rule based on the division of the decision plane by straight lines, as shown, will be almost as good as the optimal decision rule.

The additional light–sound combinations presented during a generalization test can be represented in the same manner as those used in training, of course, and the proportion of trials on which each of the two responses is expected to occur in the presence of any particular stimulus can be obtained by computing the portion of the volume under the surface that falls in the acceptance region for the response in question. A detailed mathematical treatment of this model can be found in Heinemann and Chase (1970).

This statistical decision model can yield useful descriptions of behavior only if it is true that every response the subject makes reflects a decision based on the information provided by both stimulus sources. A more general model proposed by Heinemann and Chase allows for the possibility of inattention. The more general model is based on the following assumptions: (a) the probabilities of attention to the two dimensions are independent; (b) the statistical decision model described above applies to those trials on which the subject attends to both dimensions; (c) on those trials on which the subject attends to only one of the dimensions, it compares the value of the decision variable for that dimension with a criterion located at the point at which the optimal decision contour intersects the decision axis (Figure 10), and selects reponse R_2 with probability 1.0 when the criterion is exceeded and with probability k when the criterion is not exceeded; and (d) on those trials on which the subject attends to neither dimension, response R_2 occurs with probability k. The value of k is assumed to be independent of the stimulus values.

Figure 11 shows results obtained by Heinemann and Chase during generalization tests done after training under the conditions specified in Table 1, together with the best-fitting curves derived from the more general model. (The theoretical curves shown were computed on the assumption that the decision contour consisted of two intersecting straight lines. For the particular stimulus values used in this experiment such a decision contour is a close approximation to the optimal one.) The most significant feature to note is the decrease in the effect that variations in light intensity have on the choice proportions as the sound intensity is increased. When accompanied by the highest sound intensity used (95 dB), variations in light intensity had almost no effect on choice behavior.

The curve-fitting procedure yielded estimates for the probabilities of attention to light and to sound that were very close to 1.0. According to this analysis then, the fact that variations in light intensity have less and less effect on the choice proportions as the intensity of the accompanying sound increases does not indicate that the intensity of the sound governs the likelihood that the subjects will *attend* to variations in light intensity.

We shall now reconsider, briefly, the meaning of the term "conditional discrimination." As commonly used, the term implies that the two stimulus dimensions have different functions in the control of behavior. Something of this sort is clearly implied when one of the dimensions is called "superordinate" and the other "subordinate." Since the model discussed above treats the two dimensions in a completely symmetric way, it is, in a sense, not a model for conditional discrimination. The principal feature that distinguishes this model from one that describes "true" conditional discrimination

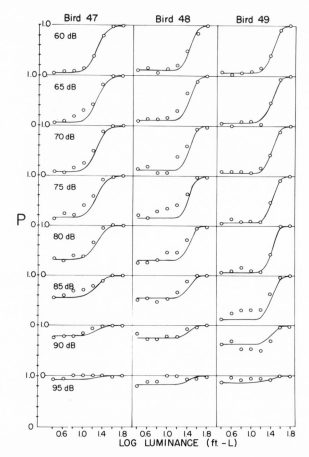

FIGURE 11.   Theoretical curves derived from the signal recognition and attention model fitted to the results obtained for three pigeons. P is the proportion of R_2 responses. (From Heinemann & Chase, 1970. Copyright 1970 by the American Psychological Association. Reproduced by permission.)

is the assumption that the probabilities of attention to the two stimulus dimensions are independent, a state of affairs that may also be described by saying that the two dimensions are processed "in parallel" (see Neisser, 1966). The concept of "conditional discrimination" seems to imply a sequential decision process in which attention to one dimension is contingent on attention to the other.

It is possible to account for the results obtained by Heinemann and Chase by assuming a sequential decision process. Assume that the subject has a separate criterion on each of the decision axes (Figure 10). Assume further that on any given trial the subject attends first to only one stimulus dimension and proceeds according to the following rule: if the value of the decision variable exceeds the criterion, (on the dimension attended to) make response R_2; if the value of the decision variable falls below the criterion, attend to the other dimension, and make response R_2 if the decision variable for that dimension exceeds the criterion, otherwise make response R_1. It can be shown (Heinemann & Chase, 1970) that this model is equivalent to the parallel processing model presented previously if the probabilities of attention to light and to sound are both equal to 1.0. Since the probabilities of attention estimated from the results of Heinemann and Chase were both very close to 1.0, these results are compatible with both models.

3. Color

A very large number of experiments with pigeons have used the wavelength of monochromatic light as the primary stimulus variable. We cannot review this work and the many theoretical problems related to it in the available space but we would like to indicate briefly how problems of wavelength generalization might be approached by combining signal recognition theory with some concepts drawn from theories of color vision.

a. *Sensory states and discriminability.* It is widely believed that the pigeon, like man, has trivariant color vision, that is, the pigeon's response to light depends on three physical parameters (see Blough, Riggs, & Schafer, 1972; Riggs, Blough, & Schafer, 1972). In some situations these parameter can be specified as luminance, dominant wavelength, and purity. If vision is trivariant in this sense, then it must be true that the sensory effects induced by lights vary along at least three orthogonal dimensions. To keep things simple, we shall consider only the situation in which all lights presented have the same luminance. At constant luminance, the effects of the remaining two variables can be represented in a two-dimensional space. Not enough is known to identify the coordinate axes of such a space with specific physiological process. One possible interpretation is to identify them with the opponent processes of the Hering theory (Hering, 1964). On this interpretation the origin represents a perfect balance of the opponent processes, resulting in an achromatic experience. Constant hues are represented by straight lines radiating from the origin, saturation increasing with increasing distance from the origin.

If it is assumed that repeated presentations of any specific light evoke a normal distribution of responses from both the red–green and yellow–blue systems, and that the distributions induced by all stimuli have the same variance, then the effects produced by any stimulus can be represented by a circular bivariate distribution in the space under consideration, and the decision problems that arise during training and during tests for generalization can be treated in the same way as those considered in the preceding sections.

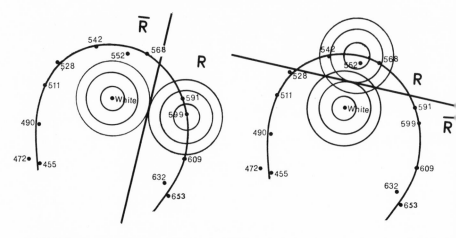

FIGURE 12. The roughly circular configurations that are labeled with numbers representing the wavelengths of monochromatic lights represent the color space for pigeons determined by Schneider (1972). The points shown represent means of values reported by Schneider for two experiments. The concentric circles represent distributions produced by stimuli used in the experiment of Guttman and Kalish (1956).

The situation we are now considering differs from that considered in the previous sections (combinations of light and sound intensities) in that now a change in a single stimulus parameter produces a change in both of the variables represented on the coordinate axes.

To make the theory workable it is necessary to have a geometrical representation of all possible lights which has the property that the discriminability of any two stimuli is invariantly related to the distance between them. A configuration that has the desired property has been constructed by Schneider (1972) and is shown in Figure 12. It is based on data from pigeons and was obtained by nonmetric scaling methods. The number written next to each point is the wavelength of the spectral light represented by that point. The point labeled "White" represents light that appears achromatic to human observers.

b. An application. To show how such a theory may be related to the results of experiments we consider its application to the results obtained in the well-known experiments of Guttman and Kalish (1956). In these experiments pigeons were trained to peck on a single disk that was illuminated by spectral light of fixed wavelength, and were subsequently tested for generalization by illuminating the disk with lights of other wavelengths. The training given is usually called "single stimulus training" but it may be regarded as a form of "simultaneous discrimination training" (discrimination between properties of the disk and the surrounding wall).

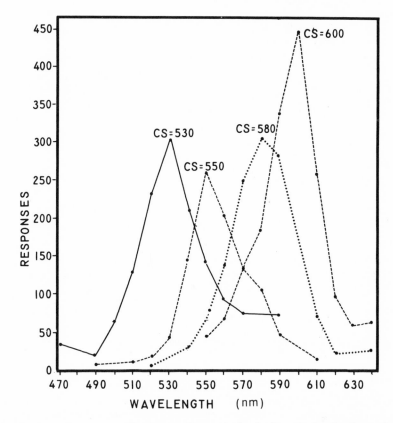

FIGURE 13. Mean generalization gradients obtained after single-stimulus training with lights of four different wavelengths. (From Guttman & Kalish, 1956. Copyright 1956 by the American Psychological Association. Reproduced by permission.)

The results obtained by Guttman and Kalish are shown in Figure 13. In the simplified theoretical treatment that follows differences in the luminance of the disk and the wall will be ignored. The distributions corresponding to a "white" wall and a disk illuminated by monochromatic light are represented by concentric circles in Figure 12. Two different training situations are illustrated, in one the wavelength of the monochromatic light is 600 nm; in the other it is 550 nm. In each situation the decision contour required to minimize the proportion of errors is a straight line that intersects Schneider's circle at two points. These points of intersection would be represented by two criteria if the decision variable corresponding to wavelength were treated as unidimensional.

This schema predicts gradients of approximately the form found by Guttman and Kalish and also provides a possible explanation for the differences in the heights of the gradients centered at 550 and 600 nm. Note that light of wavelength 600 nm is more discriminable from "White" than light of 550 nm, and that a relatively greater portion of the volume of the 600-nm distribution falls into the "Respond" region of the decision space.

V. CONCLUDING REMARKS

Because of space limitations we have chosen not to consider the many experiments on generalization done with human subjects. A review of such experiments may be found in Mednick and Freedman (1960). Many of these experiments have been modeled on those done with animals, but, whereas some have used conditioning procedures (e.g., Hovland, 1937), most have been concerned with "voluntary" behavior involving verbal instructions to the subjects. The results of such experiments have often been quite comparable to those obtained with animals.

The procedures used in experiments on generalization are essentially similar to those used in psychophysics for the measurement of thresholds and the like. The principal difference between these two classes of experiments seems to lie in the problems to which they are addressed and in the independent variables that are manipulated. It can be argued that much of the work concerned with detection and decision processes in psychophysics may also be looked upon as dealing with generalization. From this point of view, the adequacy of any theory of generalization may be judged in part by its ability to describe results obtained in psychophysics and perception.

ACKNOWLEDGMENTS

Preparation of this chapter was supported by United States Public Health Service grants MH 18246 to E. G. Heinemann and MH 25883 to S. Chase.

REFERENCES

Atkinson, R. C. A theory of stimulus discrimination learning. In K. J. Arrow, S. Karlin, & P. Suppes (Eds.), *Mathematical methods in the social sciences*. Stanford, California: Stanford University Press, 1959. Pp. 221–241.

Atkinson, R. C. & Estes, W. K. Stimulus sampling theory. In R. D. Luce, R. R. Bush, & E. Galanter (Eds.), *Handbook of mathematical psychology*. New York: Wiley, 1963. Pp. 121–268.

Blackwell, H. R., & Schlosberg, H. Octave generalization, pitch discrimination and loudness thresholds in the white rat. *Journal of Experimental Psychology,* 1943, **33,** 407–419.

Blough, D. S. Generalization and preference on a stimulus-intensity continuum. *Journal of the Experimental Analysis of Behavior*, 1959, **2**, 307–315.

Blough, D. S. The shape of some wavelength generalization gradients. *Journal of the Experimental Analysis of Behavior*, 1961, **4**, 31–40.

Blough, D. S. Interresponse time as a function of continuous variables: A new method and some data. *Journal of the Experimental Analysis of Behavior*, 1963, **6**, 237–246.

Blough, D. S. Generalization gradient shape and summation in steady-state tests. *Journal of the Experimental Analysis of Behavior*, 1969, **12**, 91–103.

Blough, D. S. Recognition by the pigeon of stimuli varying in two dimensions. *Journal of the Experimental Analysis of Behavior*, 1972, **18**, 345–367.

Blough, P. M., Riggs, L. A., & Schafer, K. L. Photopic spectral sensitivity determined electroretinographically for the pigeon eye. *Vision Research*, 1972, **12**, 477–486.

Boneau, C. A., & Cole, J. L. Decision theory, the pigeon, and the psychophysical function. *Psychological Review*, 1967, **74**, 123–135.

Burke, C. J., & Estes, W. K. A component model for stimulus variables in discrimination learning. *Psychometrika*, 1957, **22**, 133–145.

Bush, R. R., & Mosteller, F. A model for stimulus generalization and discrimination. *Psychological Review*, 1951, **58**, 413–423.

Bush, R. R., & Mosteller, F. *Stochastic models for learning.* New York: Wiley, 1955.

Chase, S. Selectivity in multidimensional stimulus control, *Journal of Comparative and Physiological Psychology*, 1968, **66**, 787–792.

Chase, S., & Heinemann, E. G. Choices based on redundant information: An analysis of two-dimensional stimulus control. *Journal of Experimental Psychology*, 1972, **92**, 161–175.

Chase, S., & Heinemann, E. G. On the form of generalization curves for luminance: Choice and rate measures. *Journal of the Experimental Analysis of Behavior* (in press).

Ernst, J., Engberg, L., & Thomas, D. R. On the form of stimulus generalization curves for visual intensity. *Journal of the Experimental Analysis of Behavior*, 1971, **16**, 177–180.

Estes, W. K. Toward a statistical theory of learning. *Psychological Review*, 1950, **57**, 94–107.

Estes, W. K., & Hopkins, B. L. Acquisition and transfer in pattern-vs.-component discrimination learning, *Journal of Experimental Psychology*, 1961, **61**, 322–328.

Flagg, S. F., Medin, D. L., & Davis, R. T. Stimulus generalization in monkeys following discrimination training with gray stimuli, *Animal Learning and Behavior*, 1974, **2**, 19–22.

Green, D. M., & Swets, J. A. *Signal detection theory and psychophysics.* New York: Wiley, 1966.

Guttman, N., & Kalish, H. I. Discriminability and stimulus generalization, *Journal of Experimental Psychology*, 1956, **51**, 79–88.

Hanson, H. M. Effects of discrimination training on stimulus generalization. *Journal of Experimental Psychology*, 1959, **58**, 321–334.

Hearst, E. Excitation, inhibition and discrimination learning. In N. J. Mackintosh & W. K. Honig (Eds.), *Fundamental issues in associative learning.* Halifax: Dalhousie University Press, 1969. Pp. 1–41.

Hearst, E., Koresko, M. B., & Poppen, R. Stimulus generalization and the response-reinforcement contingency. *Journal of the Experimental Analysis of Behavior*, 1964, **7**, 369–380.

Heinemann, E. G. Control of pigeons' choice behavior by line tilt and luminance contrast. *Journal of the Experimental Analysis of Behavior*, (in press).

Heinemann, E. G., & Avin, E. On the development of stimulus control, *Journal of the Experimental Analysis of Behavior,* 1973, **20,** 183–195.

Heinemann, E. G., Avin, E., Sullivan, M. A., & Chase, S. Analysis of stimulus generalization with a psychophysical method, *Journal of Experimental Psychology,* 1969, **80,** 215–224.

Heinemann, E. G., & Chase, S. Conditional stimulus control, *Journal of Experimental Psychology,* 1970, **84,** 187–197.

Heinemann, E. G., Chase, S., & Mandell, C. Discriminative control of "attention." *Science,* 1968, **160,** 553–554.

Hering, E. *Outlines of a theory of the light sense.* (Translated by L. M. Hurvich & D. Jameson.) Cambridge, Massachusetts: Harvard University Press, 1964.

Hilgard, E. R., & Bower, G. H. *Theories of learning.* (4th ed.) Englewood Cliffs, New Jersey: Prentice-Hall, 1975.

Hovland, C. I. The generalization of conditioned responses: I. The sensory generalization of conditioned responses with varying frequencies of tone, *Journal of General Psychology,* 1937, **17,** 125–148.

Hull, C. L. *Principles of behavior.* New York: Appleton-Century-Crofts, 1943.

Hull, C. L. *A behavior system.* New Haven, Connecticut: Yale University Press, 1952.

Jenkins, H. M., & Harrison, R. H. Effect of discrimination training on auditory generalization, *Journal of Experimental Psychology,* 1960, **59,** 246–253.

Jenkins, H. M., & Sainsbury, R. S. The development of stimulus control through differential reinforcement. In N. J. Mackintosh & W. K. Honig (Eds.), *Fundamental issues in associative learning.* Halifax: Dalhousie University Press, 1969. Pp. 123–161.

Johns, M. D. Supplementary report: Transfer of a pattern vs. component discrimination following training in a probabilistic situation. *Journal of Experimental Psychology,* 1965, **70,** 506–509.

Kamin, L. J. "Attention-like" processes in classical conditioning. In M. R. Jones (Ed.), *Miami symposium on the prediction of behavior: Aversive stimulation.* Miami: University of Miami Press, 1968. Pp. 9–33.

Kamin, L. J. Selective association and conditioning. In N. J. Mackintosh & W. K. Honig (Eds.), *Fundamental issues in associative learning.* Halifax: Dalhousie University Press, 1969. Pp. 42–64.

Kimble, G. A. *Hilgard and Marquis' conditioning and learning.* New York: Appleton-Century-Crofts, 1961.

LaBerge, D. A recruitment theory of simple behavior, *Psychometrika,* 1962, **27,** 375–396.

Laming, D. R. J. *Information theory of choice-reaction times.* New York and London: Academic Press, 1968.

Lashley, K. S. Conditional reactions in rats. *Journal of Psychology,* 1938, **6,** 311–324.

Mednick, S. A., & Freedman, J. L. Stimulus generalization. *Psychological Bulletin,* 1960, **57,** 169–199.

Miles, C. G., & Jenkins, H. M. Overshadowing in operant conditioning as a function of discriminability. *Learning & Motivation,* 1973, **4,** 11–27.

Nachmias, J. Signal detection theory and its application to problems in vision. In D. Jameson & L. M. Hurvich (Eds.), *Handbook of sensory physiology.* Vol VII/4, *Visual psychophysics.* Berlin: Springer-Verlag, 1972.

Neimark, E. D., & Estes, W. K. *Stimulus sampling theory.* San Francisco: Holden-Day, 1967.

Neisser, U. *Cognitive Psychology.* New York: Appleton-Century-Crofts, 1966.

Pavlov, I. P. *Conditioned reflexes.* London and New York: Oxford University Press, 1927.

Peterson, W. W., Birdsall, T. G., & Fox, W. C. The theory of signal detectability, *Transactions of the IRE Professional Group on Information Theory*, PGIT-4, 1954, 171–212.

Ray, B. A., & Sidman, M. Reinforcement schedules and stimulus control. In W. N. Schoenfeld (Ed.), *The theory of reinforcement schedules.* New York: Appleton-Century-Crofts, 1970. Pp. 187–214.

Restle, F. A theory of discrimination learning, *Psychological Review*, 1955, **62**, 11–19.

Riggs, L. A., Blough, P. M., & Schafer, K. L. Electrical responses of the pigeon eye to changes in wavelength of the stimulating light. *Vision Research*, 1972, **12**, 981–991.

Schneider, B. Multidimensional scaling of color difference in the pigeon. *Perception & Psychophysics*, 1972, **12**, 373–378.

Spence, K. W. The nature of discrimination learning in animals. *Psychological Review*, 1936, **43**, 427–449.

Spence, K. W. The differential response in animals to stimuli varying within a single dimension. *Psychological Review*, 1937, **44**, 430–444.

Spence, K. W. The relation of response latency and speed to the intervening variables and *N* in S–R theory. *Psychological Review*, 1954, **61**, 208–216.

Stevens, S. S. On the psychophysical law. *Psychological Review*, 1957, **64**, 153–181.

Sutherland, N. S., & Mackintosh, N. J. *Mechanisms of animal discrimination learning.* New York: Academic Press, 1971.

Thomas, D. R., & Setzer, J. Stimulus generalization gradients for auditory intensity in rats and guinea pigs. *Psychonomic Science*, 1972, **28**, 22–24.

vom Saal, W., & Jenkins, H. M. Blocking the development of stimulus control. *Learning & Motivation*, 1970, **1**, 52–64.

Weinstock, S., Robbins, D., & Chen, W. Y. Successive brightness discrimination learning and stimulus generalization in the *T*-maze. *Journal of Experimental Psychology*, (in press).

Wickelgren, W. A. Unidimensional strength theory and component analysis of noise in absolute and comparative judgments. *Journal of Mathematical Psychology*, 1968, **5**, 102–122.

Wright, A. A., & Cumming, W. W. Color naming functions for the pigeon. *Journal of the Experimental Analysis of Behavior*, 1971, **15**, 7–17.

Wyckoff, L. B., Jr. The role of observing responses in discrimination learning. Part I. *Psychological Review*, 1952, **59**, 431–442.

Zuckerman, D. C., & Blough, D. S. Conditional discrimination in the goldfish. *Animal Learning and Behavior*, 1974, **2**, 215–217.

Author Index

Numbers in *italics* refer to pages on which the complete references are listed.

Subject Index